THE SOCIALIST CASE

THE SOCIALIST CASE

by

DOUGLAS JAY

Rev - ed - 1947 also in stock

FABER AND FABER LIMITED
24 Russell Square
London

First published in September Mcmxxxvii
by Faber and Faber Limited
24 Russell Square London W.C.1.
Printed in Great Britain by
Latimer Trend & Co Ltd Plymouth

To
H.G.J.

PREFACE

The purpose of this book is to sum up the case for socialism on the basis of an examination of the fact of poverty as it exists in the contemporary world. It may be thought that such an examination is co-extensive with the whole of economics. But this is not so; for economics as a science quite rightly investigates economic phenomena in abstraction from their social, legal, and institutional context. This book seeks to consider the problem of poverty in relation not merely to ultimate economic causes but also to the social institutions of a modern industrial community. The argument that follows is consequently not planned on the basis of any particular traditional system of thought. It attempts to ascertain the facts—both of practice and of principle—and to draw on the traditional systems in so far as they throw light on these facts.

In general the circumstances discussed are those of a modern industrial country. For purposes of clarity, however, the existence of international exchange is ignored, except where it is for some special reason relevant to the argument. Normally it is simpler and clearer to pursue the inquiry on the assumption of an economically 'closed' system, such as the world as a whole.

The conclusion which the argument of this book suggests is the entirely unoriginal one that democratic socialism, properly understood, is the best cure for poverty and the best method of furthering the happiness of the human race. There are of course a great many other lines of argument of a political, scientific, aesthetic, religious, or personal kind which tend to the same conclusion. With these other arguments this book is not concerned. It is written in the belief that the fundamental case for socialism rests on the necessity to alleviate economic privation. The argument is therefore based on considerations which would normally be called economic. Such questions as whether socialism could or could not abolish war are consequently not discussed.

Nor is there any consideration of questions of political tactics or even political strategy: such as the proper measures to be taken by a socialist government faced with a politically inspired capitalists' strike of the kind which M. Blum has encountered. The object of this book is to discover what would be the right policy to pursue, supposing we were able to choose any one we liked, and not to inquire whether one or another policy is likely to be successful in given political circumstances. Both questions naturally have to be answered before a programme of action can be drawn up. But it is best to keep them distinct.

There is nothing in this book which will be new to the economic expert. It only seeks to sum up the case for socialism in the light of the practical experience and the scientific advances gained in the years of the Great Depression and the succeeding armaments boom, and to state it in a form intelligible to the interested non-expert public. Such an attempt is always bound to some extent to puzzle the layman while not enlightening the expert. But it may nevertheless be worth making.

The output of literature by even the most eminent economists in the last twenty years has been large; and to most of them, and above all to Mr. J. M. Keynes, the majority of us are deeply indebted. The argument of this book owes in particular a great deal to *Plan or No Plan* by Barbara Wootton, *An Introduction to Economic Analysis and Policy* by J. E. Meade, and to Mr. E. F. M. Durbin's two books, *Purchasing Power and Trade Depression* and *The Problem of Credit Policy*. I also have to thank Mr. Hugh Gaitskell for reading the typescript of this book and pointing out various errors in the argument.

CONTENTS

xi

CONTENTS

PART I
POVERTY AND INEQUALITY

CHAPTER I

POVERTY, INEQUALITY, INSECURITY

That poverty is a great evil, to be cured at almost any cost, seems hardly capable of denial. Yet it has been denied. Sheer destitution, with all the mental and physical suffering it involves, has presumably never been advocated as a good, except by those who deliberately choose it for some fanatical reason. But men, generally rich men, have been found to argue that poverty above the starvation level is not a really terrible evil. 'Material things', these persons tell us, are comparatively unimportant, and happiness is consequently by no means dependent on income.

The refutation of this argument is not very difficult. 'Material wants', when they are satisfied, are doubtless of minor importance; but when they are not satisfied their importance is clearly overwhelming. If there is anything about which everybody, plain men and philosophers, ancient and modern, have always agreed, it is that the mental and physical distress involved in acute economic privation is an immeasurable evil. Should anyone find difficulty in persuading himself of this, he need only open his eyes and use his imagination. It is perhaps true that in individual cases poverty is not the greatest of evils. Physical pain, and even some kinds of mental suffering unconnected with poverty, may in individual cases very possibly be worse. But, in general, if we consider the number of persons affected throughout the world and throughout history, we cannot doubt that poverty has been and still is the greatest of human evils. Judged by this criterion, nothing but war and disease can ever, perhaps, have been comparable with it.

Ever since the days of early Greek thought moralists have of course delighted to point out that some poor men are happy and some rich men unhappy. But the very constancy, and the paradoxical air with which this observation has been repeated, is itself the best proof how almost universal is the common-sense view that poverty and happiness are normally incompatible. The common-sense view is surely right. Some extremely poor men have, it is true, claimed to be perfectly happy. And discontent is not unknown among the idle rich; though in their case it is usually due not to their riches but to their idleness. But these two human freaks, the happy beggar and the discontented plutocrat, need not confuse us. For the vast majority of the human race poverty makes happiness impossible. Indeed, when the argument has been carried to its logical conclusion, it will appear that poverty in the end means nothing else than the absence of certain means to happiness.

As soon as all the 'material' wants of humanity have been satisfied, the economic problem will doubtless sink into insignificance, and non-'material' things of much greater value will begin to occupy men's minds. But this is precisely why the cure of poverty is of such supreme importance. It is important, first, because poverty in itself is a great evil, secondly because it is the cause of almost all other evils, and thirdly because it is an almost impassable barrier to the things that give value to human life. Poverty is the main cause of unhappiness, ignorance, superstition, disease, ugliness, war; and it cuts off the vast majority of the human race not only from happiness, but from knowledge, beauty, freedom, and all the activities of civilized man. The cure of poverty is not something which will distract attention from those activities. It is, for most of the human race, the only means to them.[1]

There are some who contrast the present age with medieval civilization, and infer that the troubles of the twentieth century are due not to its poverty but to its wealth. The peasant of the Middle Ages, it is said, was far poorer than the working man of to-day; yet he was contented with the beauty of the country, with religion, and with primitive art. Accordingly, the troubles of to-day must be due to a change of values which has induced men to expect happiness automatically to follow from wealth. In this argument there is perhaps some truth. The medieval pea-

[1] In Marshall's words (*Principles of Economics*, eighth edition, p. 3): 'The study of the causes of poverty is the study of the causes of the degradation of a large part of mankind.'

sant was certainly happier than the modern working man would be if he had to live at a medieval standard of living; and the opportunity of aesthetic and other non-economic means to happiness are perhaps less widely spread to-day than they were in the Middle Ages. But it does not follow that the cure of our contemporary discontents is to abandon the economic problem and attempt to improve the intellectual values of our fellow men. In the first place the average medieval peasant was probably very much poorer and less contented than the spectacle of a Gothic cathedral would lead us to suppose. Secondly, the working man is discontented to-day not because he is poorer than his ancestors five hundred years ago, but because he is poor in a world where he might be rich. The opportunity of happiness is greater to-day. But if we are to take it, we need to abolish poverty as well as to cure ourselves of the debased intellectual values which only too clearly exist. The cure of poverty is really the most indispensable condition of a genuine modern renaissance.

The second greatest of economic evils is inequality. Inequality is an evil both in itself and because it is a cause of poverty. One of the chief reasons why the poor are very poor is that the rich are very rich. Only when there is more than enough for all can unlimited inequality be possible without poverty—and then, of course, there could be no inequality. At present there is not more than enough for all. At present, therefore, poverty and inequality imply one another, and poverty cannot be removed without some mitigation of inequality. No doubt after a point greater equality will increase and not diminish the poverty even of the poorest. For after a point the reduction of the incomes of certain classes of the rich may, as is suggested later in the argument, diminish the income of the community as a whole to an extent which would actually impoverish those who were becoming, relatively, less poor. The perfect equality advocated by Mr. Bernard Shaw is consequently not desirable on economic grounds. There is a certain point beyond which greater equality will mean greater poverty for all, individually as well as collectively; and beyond that point it would clearly be foolish to go. But it would also be foolish to stop short of it.

Inequality is in itself an evil. To state this truism, however, is to invite the resurrection of a swarm of sophistical arguments. Universal equality, we are told, would be dull, monotonous, ugly, or even irreligious. These contentions[1] are in the first place irrelevant; since absolute universal equality is hardly advocated by anybody to-day. In the second place, they are untrue. For they are really reducible to the simple assertion that inequality is in itself good. This idea is part of the normal apparatus of the type of mind that likes ritualism, eccentricity, and perversity for their own sakes, which prefers the 'picturesque' to the beautiful and the antique to the artistically good. It is in fact a well-known type of sentimentality; and as such cannot be refuted. The philosophic fallacy on which it rests, however, is not difficult to dissect. Because there are many different kinds of good things, our sentimental inequalitarians argue, difference must itself be good. One might as well argue that because many works of art are large, size must itself be beautiful.

In fact inequality is in itself bad. It is bad because it propagates a false scale of values: a false servility and sycophancy on the one hand, and a false complacence on the other. The illustrated 'society' papers, with their rich clientèle and their poor readers, are symbolic of much that is not pleasant in modern capitalist society. Nor could there well be anything more unpleasant than the spectacle of one human being, idle and self-satisfied, giving orders to another human being, overworked and unwilling, because the one happens to have been left money and the other has not. It is impossible to deny that inequality destroys freedom, independence, self-respect, and integrity. To some extent, of course, these evils are inevitable, since to some extent inequality is inevitable; but they are evils to be reduced to a minimum, and not virtues to be glorified.

But besides all this, inequality is evil because it is unjust. It is an intolerable injustice that one man, and one man's children, should have five times as much of the blessings of life as another man and another man's children, when neither he nor they have done anything to earn or deserve them. The injustice of economic inequality is certainly the unkindest of all social evils, and therefore the one which is likely to cut deepest.

The evil of insecurity has seldom been adequately recognized —except by the insecure, who are only too often inarticulate. And the failure to recognize it lies at the root of a great many

[1] For a classical refutation of this kind of argument, see Professor Tawney's *Equality*.

of the fundamental contradictions between economic theory on the one hand and social and political aspiration and practice on the other. One of the most important simplifications made by the classical economists and almost all their successors has been the assumption that the objective of any economic system should be the attainment of what economists would call the highest possible 'average real income per head'. This means, broadly speaking, the highest possible aggregate consumption of goods and services. Now it is quite easy to show that the attainment of this objective requires the greatest possible freedom in the adjustment of economic resources to changing conditions of supply and demand. If demand for some commodity dwindles, unemployment, bankruptcy, and losses must be allowed to have their most brutal effect in order that labour and capital may be shifted away from that industry as quickly as possible. Nothing must be done, for instance, to mitigate the pressure of low wages, long hours, and unemployment in the British coal industry because the world's long-term demand for coal is shrinking, and labour and capital consequently ought to be transferred to other industries. Similarly if one country suddenly ceases to be able to produce some commodity as efficiently and cheaply as another, it should unhesitatingly permit a whole industry to fall into complete ruin. British agriculture, for instance, should be allowed to become entirely bankrupt at once, since almost all its products can now be imported more cheaply than they are likely to be produced at home.

If the attainment of the highest possible real income per head is really the one and only objective of an economic system, these arguments are undoubtedly correct. The sooner resources are moved away from a contracting industry, the better; and, therefore, the greater the distress caused in such an industry, the better also. The ultimate increase in the real income of the community will exceed the temporary losses sustained by one portion of it. Unfortunately, however, no community has ever been willing to accept this argument in practice. Obstinately and persistently nations and groups have protected themselves, at the cost of lowering their total incomes, against the agonies of rapid change. This, according to orthodox economic analysis, is merely an example of a selfish minority exploiting an impotent and deluded majority. But is there not really more in it than that?

May not insecurity and loss of income be two separate but real evils which have to be balanced one against the other?[1] It is clear that in innumerable cases in which the individual has a perfectly free choice, greater security is preferred at the cost of some sacrifice of income. For what other reason are insurance premiums paid? And, quite apart from insurance, a man will frequently accept a job at a very much lower wage or salary for the sake of greater security. This shows that freedom from fear of unemployment may often be worth a definite sacrifice of income.

This fact, which is plain enough in the case of individuals, should certainly be taken into account by those framing social policy. We have to decide how much increase in security is worth how much loss in average income per head. And surely this has in fact been taken into account, in a confused instinctive way, by many of the protectionist devices which are usually denounced as mere group selfishness. The great majority of such devices are admittedly indefensible; but a few may be justifiable if the increase in security achieved is worth the loss of income. In an exceptional case, for instance, where a country imports heavily for consumption and exports one or a few commodities liable to great fluctuations in price, it may actually pay it to produce some of its articles of consumption more expensively at home as an insurance against the day when the price of its exports may fall heavily in world markets. Similarly if an important industry like the British coal industry is contracting, it may be better to retard its contraction so that those workers who are too old to develop the aptitude for another occupation may at least have jobs for the rest of their working lives. This would be better both for them and for the community than that they should remain permanently unemployed.

To allow too much weight to such considerations would of course be fatal. It would retard the increase in the standard of living of whole communities together. The real task is to realize that the two evils of poverty and insecurity must be weighed against one another in order that a balance may be struck. And it must not be forgotten that economic insecurity, the fear of unemployment, weighs much more hardly on the poor than on the rich. Insecurity is at once an effect and an aggravation

1 Cf. Professor Allan G. B. Fisher's book, *The Clash of Progress and Security*, for an attempt to give a detailed and comprehensive answer to this question.

6

of poverty; and as such it is of the greatest importance. Undoubtedly the average working man would prefer some slight sacrifice of income for the sake of freedom from the fear of unemployment. It is for this reason that whole communities pursue policies designed to remove unemployment at almost any cost. The truth is that unemployment is so terrible a scourge that the old economic criterion of the highest possible real income per head has become, by itself, inadequate to the modern industrial world. In some particulars this explains the discrepancy between the teachings of economic theory and the behaviour of the human race. The classical economists undoubtedly underestimated the importance of insecurity.

No remedy for poverty which ignores inequality and insecurity can therefore fully succeed. This is what chiefly complicates the problem, even when means only and not ends are being considered. Poverty, inequality, and insecurity are partly interdependent, in the sense that the cure of one will necessarily cure the others. But they are also partly antithetical, in the sense that one can only be cured at the cost of intensifying the others. Each has consequently to be weighed against the others, as well as against the remaining social losses and gains involved, in seeking the appropriate remedy.

CHAPTER II

'UTILITIES' AND DESIRES

Before examining the practical organization of the present social system we must answer a more theoretical but quite fundamental question about the nature of poverty and inequality. To question whether poverty exists, or whether one man can be called richer than another, may strike the average man, and certainly the average socialist, as hypocritical and ridiculous. Indeed, the economists who hold this sceptical view are apt to be denounced by socialists as obviously disingenuous. It is much better, however, to recognize that a real difficulty exists, and to see whether a careful scrutiny of it leads to a vindication or otherwise of the plain man's view.

What is wealth? Or to put it another way, what is it that makes one man richer than another? It is clearly not the possession of money. For the value of money depends upon how much it will buy; and if there are no goods to consume, all the money in the world is worthless. Is it then fair to say that a man's income consists in the quantity of goods he is able to consume? This interpretation was adopted, in substance by many eighteenth- and nineteenth-century thinkers. It fitted the 'materialist' assumption of Victorian days; and it was still latent in English economics right up to the war. Its weaknesses, however, are not really far to seek. A man 'consumes' not merely physical commodities but the services of his fellow men. The services of a doctor, a dentist, an actor, a bus driver, or an errand boy are none the less valuable because they do not result in the creation of a physical commodity. They satisfy a want and consequently enrich the person whose want is satisfied.

This plain fact was, of course, recognized by the economists of the nineteenth century. It led them to define wealth or income in terms of satisfactions, or rather more obscurely, in 'utilities'.

8

Now this in itself was not necessarily fallacious. But there became attached to the doctrine two sets of assumptions which are surely contrary to the facts. First, it was apt to be assumed that any given commodity or service possessed a given 'utility' which remained the same whoever was consuming it, and whenever and wherever it was being consumed. Yet long before this fallacy had become enshrined in orthodox economic theory its untruth had been enshrined in more than one popular proverb: 'One man's meat is another man's poison', 'There is no accounting for tastes.' A holiday at Southend might be paradise for one man and the very reverse for another. It is clear that the satisfaction yielded by a given commodity or service varies from consumer to consumer. And in the case of a given consumer it varies with time and place. A man's desire for a swimming-pool depends on the temperature, for food on the time of day, for clothes on the time of year, for transport on where he is, for cigarettes on whether he has eaten something sweet, and so on and so on. Every one of his desires and needs in fact will depend on a thousand circumstances which are changing from minute to minute. We may take it, therefore, as quite demonstrably true that the satisfaction yielded by a given commodity or service is seldom exactly the same, even for a single consumer.

Secondly, the Victorian economists tended to assume in common with their philosophical colleagues, the utilitarians, that the 'utility' of a commodity was something measurable in units, like length or weight or time. How far is this true and how far is it not? This is an extremely important and extremely confusing question, and it is necessary to be very clear exactly what the question is. In the first place what is usually called the utility of the commodity is not really a quality of the commodity, but of the consumer. It is hardly even accurate to call it the satisfaction of the consumer; because the intensity of the satisfaction does not seem necessarily to vary with the intensity of the want satisfied. Nor is a satisfaction the object of our desires. A thirsty man wants water, not the satisfaction of drinking it; though the drinking of it, just because he wants water, will doubtless give him satisfaction. What was supposed to be measured therefore by the 'utility' of a commodity seems generally to have been the intensity of the want which a man satisfied by consuming it.[1]

[1] Cf. F. H. Knight, *The Ethics of Competition*, p. 85 note: 'the idea that

That one want can be, and indeed normally is, more or less intense than another want, nobody probably will dispute. The want or desire of a given individual in given circumstances for a given object may be, and indeed almost certainly must be, greater, or less than, or equal to, his desire for something else. We are most of us prepared to say, for instance, whether we want black coffee or white. Ordinary reflection shows that the various wants of a single individual vary in strength or intensity, and that their intensity, at any rate in some instances, can be compared. And this applies not merely to what are commonly called 'material' wants or desires but to desires and wants which depend on moral or aesthetic judgements. The desire to read a poem may be compared in strength with the desire to smoke a cigarette.

Agreement, however, that the desire or wants of a single individual may be greater or less than one another does not by any means imply agreement in what sense they may be greater or less. Here it is necessary to introduce an important distinction which some economists, in their desire to eschew metaphysics, have rather improvidently neglected. There are some things which are greater or less than one another in quantity, i.e. in definite units of some kind. And there are other things which are greater or less, but not in definite units. Of the first kind are space and time, which are indisputably measurable in miles and hours. Of the second kind are brightness, darkness, loneliness, tiredness, beauty, ugliness, cruelty, kindness, vice, virtue, and innumerable other things. One distance can be twice as great as another, and one time twice as long. But one poem, though it can indubitably be more beautiful than another, no less indubitably cannot be twice as beautiful. Nor can one act of a man be twice as virtuous as another. Moreover, whereas the difference between two distances is spatial, the difference between two cruelties is not cruel. There are certain things such as heat, loudness and speed which appear to be measurable in units but in reality are probably not. It is temperature, for instance, and miles per hour which we measure in units, not heat and speed. Whatever the

quantity of satisfaction corresponds to quantity of desire is one which seems quite too unreasonable for any thinking person to entertain.'

Professor Knight's whole discussion of the philosophical background of economics is unusually penetrating and illuminating.

truth in this case, however, we may safely assume that two general classes of things exist, both capable of being greater and less, but one in intensity or degree and the other in quantity.

Of which kind are human desires? Surely of the former. When the question is clearly put, there seems little doubt about it. Neither desires, needs, nor satisfactions are really measured in units. It is perfectly natural to talk about desires varying in intensity; it is nonsense to talk about them varying in quantity. To say that my desire for sleep is greater than my desire to read is certainly sense. To say that it is twice as great seems to be no more sense than to say one piece of sculpture is twice as good as another. Nor is it possible to say that the difference between a more and a less intense desire is itself a desire. The reason why so many nineteenth-century economists, perhaps including Marshall,[1] assumed 'utility' to be measurable in units seems to have been that they seldom clearly asked themselves whether it was so or not. They seldom, if ever, produced precise reasons for positively supposing that it was.

Undoubtedly, however, there is one reason which has disposed the ordinary man, if not the economist, to believe that desires must be measurable in units. It is plainly possible to establish some sort of relation between our desires and a scale of money prices, and it consequently seems that since money is measurable in units, desires must be measurable also. If I am willing to spend a shilling on one thing and sixpence on something else, surely my desire for one must be twice as great as my desire for the other. And must it not be true that I have an equal desire for all other things on which I am just willing to spend sixpence and neither more nor less?

This argument is very plausible, but it does not seem to be conclusive. It neglects entirely the 'marginal' principle which, though it has been pushed too far, is one of the greatest discoveries of theoretical economics, and which ironically enough

---

[1] Marshall (*Principles of Economics*, Book I, ch. ii) recognizes that 'mental states' are not quantitative, and takes note of the philosophical objections brought by T. H. Green and others against the measurement of pleasure and pain in units. But he contends that the 'incentives' to action in which the mental states eventuate are quantitatively measurable; and he seems to conceive of these incentives sometimes as desires and sometimes as satisfactions, e.g. 'The measurement of desire by the action to which it forms the incentive'.

has been the principal burden of the song of those very economists who have believed most strongly in 'units of utility'. As
ordinary unreflecting laymen we undoubtedly all believe, more
or less explicitly, that for every shilling or every £10 we
spend we satisfy a desire of the same intensity. Surely, we instinctively believe, it would be irrational to expend one sum of
£10 on the satisfaction of a greater want than we satisfy by
the expenditure of another £10. Yet, paradoxical as it may
seem, this is true. For there are some things, like bread and
milk, of which we want a little so much that we are prepared to
spend almost anything on it, but of which we want more so little
that we are not, after a point, willing to spend anything on it
at all. And there are other things, like, say, evening papers or
flowers, on a little of which we would not be willing to spend
much, but on successive additional amounts of which we may
be prepared to go on spending the same amount for quite a long
time. It may be that I spend £20 a year on flowers and £20 a
year on bread. Yet so great is my desire for bread that I should
be prepared to spend almost my whole income, if necessary, on
only a quarter as much as I normally get for £20; while so comparatively small is my demand for flowers that I would not spend
perhaps more than £5 on a quarter of my usual annual supply,
even if it meant going without it altogether. The plain and
obvious fact is that I want a little bread very much more than I
want a little flowers. But the corollary of this platitude is the
apparently remarkable paradox that I spend the same sum of
£20 on the satisfaction of a very great and a very small want.

How does this come about? It comes about as a result of the
concrete situation in which I necessarily find myself. The only
way I can in practice rectify the apparent paradox is to spend
more on one commodity and less on another. But it would only
be advantageous to do this if the new want thus satisfied was
greater than the one now left unsatisfied. I shall only spend a
shilling more on bread and a shilling less on flowers if the extra
bread bought satisfies a greater want than the flowers relin-
quished. But, *ex hypothesi*, this will not be so; because if it was I
should already have been spending more on bread and less on
flowers. What in fact I must do is to order my expenditure so
that I cannot achieve a net gain by spending a little more on
one thing and a little less on another. The last or 'mar-

ginal'[1] sixpence which I spend on bread does satisfy an equally important want as the marginal sixpence I spend on flowers: otherwise I would spend more on one and less on the other. And this must apply to the marginal sixpence I spend on everything, or rather to the marginal penny or farthing. For it is not till the amount approximates to being infinitely small that I can justifiably say that the wants satisfied by the expenditure of that amount are equal. In so far, however, as they are very small, the wants satisfied must be more nearly equal. It is accordingly perfectly rational after all to expend £20 on bread and £20 on flowers, though the total wants so satisfied are of completely different intensity, simply because there is no way open to me of altering the situation which enables me on balance to satisfy a greater want. Curious as it seems, we are inextricably involved in this insoluble practical difficulty; and no amount of piety nor wit can set us loose.

The conclusion is therefore that though we arrange our purchases so as to satisfy an equal want by the expenditure of the marginal unit of money on each commodity, we nevertheless do not satisfy an equal want by the expenditure of every pound or £20 or £100. This disposes of the strongest argument for believing that wants are measurable in units. For it shows that we cannot arrange our wants according to a unitary scale of money, and say that a want satisfied by the expenditure of £20 must be twice as great as a want satisfied by the expenditure of £10. All that the 'marginal' analysis—the contention that our expenditure on final small amounts is crucial—requires is that wants satisfied by these final amounts should be capable of being equal to or greater or less than one another. They need not be twice or half as great. And this is precisely what we have postulated in putting wants in the category of things which may be greater or less, but not measurable in units.

---

[1] It is unfortunately impossible to avoid using the at first highly confusing word 'marginal'; for any other word is misleading. The word 'marginal' need not be too puzzling if its implication is clearly realized. It assumes a situation in which a certain number of shillings every year are being spent on a number of units of various commodities. If I spend 400 shillings on 400 loaves of bread in the year, the satisfaction I get for the 'marginal loaf' means not the satisfaction obtained for any single loaf, but the added satisfaction of consuming 400 rather than 399 loaves a year. Similarly the 'marginal' shilling does not refer to any actual shilling but to the expenditure of 400 rather than 399 shillings.

How far the conclusion that wants vary in intensity but not in quantity affects the geometrical arguments connected with the drawing of 'demand and supply curves', and the whole introduction of the calculus into economics, does not concern us here. But the conclusion is one which most economists would now accept. Marshall and Wicksell were loath to abandon 'units of utility', and Professor Pigou[1] does not seem to have explicitly done so; but the reluctance of these economists seems mainly to have sprung from their conviction of the fundamental importance of the marginal analysis. And it is the merit of the Austrian school of economists to have shown that that analysis does not stand or fall by the assumption of units of utility. We can with good conscience abandon the units of utility, and still recognize that a man's expenditure of his income depends, at least in certain cases, on a comparison of the wants he satisfies by consuming a little more or a little less of different commodities. We need not assume that the expenditure of one more shilling on bread and one less on flowers would satisfy a want *half* as great but merely one *less* great. So far the development of modern economics away from utilitarianism has unquestionably brought it nearer to the facts.

But some contemporary economists have gone much further, and one or two of them seemingly too far—or at least in the wrong direction. They have abandoned the whole conception of 'economic welfare' on which English economics, and in particular, the work of Marshall and Professor Pigou, has been brought up. Professor Cassel has gone furthest of all. In his recent book, *Quantitative Thinking in Economics*, he still maintains that economists ought to abandon not merely units of utility but also both the assumption that any such things as desires exist at all, and even the marginal analysis itself. Professor Cassel would like to start from the assumption that certain people are willing in certain circumstances to buy or sell certain things at certain prices, and leave it at that. And the school represented by Professors Robbins, Hayek, and Mises, though anxious to preserve the marginal analysis, is at one with Professor Cassel in assuming that no desires, wants, or mental states whatever need be taken to exist.

Now it is certainly possible to assume that desires do not exist,

1 *The Economics of Stationary States*, pp. 2–3.

and to deduce a great many sound economic doctrines from the fact that people exhibit certain preferences in their action. But it is surely neither necessary nor desirable to do so. Wicksell,[1] in commenting on Professor Cassel's peculiarly fanatical iconoclasm, writes as follows: 'He [Professor Cassel] asserts that the psychological phenomena lying behind price do not belong to the economist's domain. The idea reminds us of the English stockbroker who earned his income year in year out by buying and selling railway stock, without knowing where the railway was.'

Similarly Professor Pigou writes: 'It is true that if we start from scales of preference we cannot draw inferences about the *absolute* intensities of desires and aversions; only about the ratio of these intensities at the margin. But if we start with desire attitudes and aversion attitudes we can infer, without any ambiguity, associated scales of preference. It is open to us therefore if we choose, to start there.'[2]

This is surely the most sensible attitude. For what reason is there, after all, for refusing to take account of the existence of 'desires and aversions'? Two not very clearly expressed motives seem to be discernible in the writings of Professors Robbins, Hayek, and Mises.[3] The first is a certain uneasy suspicion that if such things as desires are admitted to exist, the whole precarious structure of what these writers call 'equilibrium analysis' may begin to quake. Of this we shall have more to say later in the argument. The second seems to be the existence in their minds only half perceived of the old philosophical error, particularly rampant in the Victorian age, that nothing is real unless it is observable by the senses,[4] or even unless it is measurable in units.

[1] *Lectures on Political Economy*, vol. viii. Also F. H. Knight's *The Ethics of Competition*, p, 79: 'An explanation which stops at facts of consciousness is idle and useless.'

[2] *The Economics of Stationary States*, p. 3.

[3] Cf. especially *The Nature and Significance of Economic Science*, by Lionel Robbins, and *Collectivist Economic Planning*, edited by F. von Hayek.

[4] Professor Knight (*The Ethics of Competition*, p. 91 note) brings this fallacy clearly into the light of day, when, after discussing whether we have 'scientific' knowledge of desires, he says: 'It would of course be possible to quibble over the meanings of both the words "objective" and "science". They are used here in the sense in which natural scientists use them to refer to verifiable observation through the senses.'
But if we define science as observation through the senses, we naturally have no 'scientific' knowledge of desires, or for that matter of economics. But

Professor Robbins is very fond of asserting that though desires may or may not exist, for all he knows, they are no concern of the economist. It is doubtless important to delineate the subject matter of different sciences clearly; but it is at the same time perverse to allow these delineations to obscure our perception of reality. What we want to understand are the real facts of human life, not whether this or that writer can properly be called an economist. The fundamental assumption made by both Professor Robbins and Professor Hayek, as numerous passages[1] in their writings suggest, seems to be that nothing is really knowable unless it is observable by the senses and measurable in units, and that no other form of knowledge but such measurement is 'scientific'. What do these writers mean by 'scientific'? Presumably, if the word is not a mere piece of uncritical jargon, it means objective. If it means objective, then they are assuming that the only objective knowledge is either empirical observation or sense perception,[2] or measurement in units—it is not quite clear which. But this is itself a philosophical judgement, and it is one for which these writers give no good reason and for which no good reason could be given.[3]

For if we abandon the question-begging word 'scientific', what justification is there for the assumption that a man's direct awareness of his own 'desires and aversions' is a less objective form of knowledge than the complicated processes of observation, measurement, and 'verification' described by Professors Robbins and Hayek? There is none. Indeed the argument is all the other way. Of all the possible forms of knowledge there are none which

---

1 Cf. for instance, *Collectivist Economic Planning*, pp. 16 and 25; *The Nature and Significance of Economic Science*, pp. 120–5.

2 As Professor Knight seems to assume in the passage just quoted.

3 Professor Robbins would not presumably deny that ethics is a science. It is a body of objective knowledge; and this is presumably what we mean by a science. If, of course, he chooses to mean by science only a quantitative science, it is highly misleading to use the term 'unscientific' of judgements made by other sciences. For, to the ordinary man 'unscientific' means inaccurate or irrational.

---

that is not to say we have no knowledge at all. We may have complete knowledge. The whole passage only emphasizes Professor Knight's own remark: 'What is needed is nothing less than the basing of social science upon a groundwork of philosophy of knowledge and reality.' It is the more the pity that Professor Knight, after a brilliant beginning of this task, degenerates into a mere vague pragmatism (*The Ethics of Competition*, pp. 97–9).

are more certainly objective and infallible than a man's direct perception of his own feelings and desires. Compared with these, the processes of measurement and observation mentioned above are derivative, dubious, fallible, and capricious.[1] Does Professor Robbins really think that his direct awareness of his own desire for butter is less immediate and objective than his awareness of the foreign exchange market or the banking system of America? Of course he does not; or would not if he asked himself the question clearly. How comes it then that he has apparently performed such an astonishing intellectual somersault in formulating the philosophical assumptions underlying his method of economic argument? The reason would seem to be that he has been led astray by what he himself has called 'slavish behaviourism'. Professor Robbins complains that the belief of economists in the reality of desires is 'simply the accidental deposit of the historical association of English economics with utilitarianism'. One might reply in the same spirit that Professor Robbins's own doubt about their reality is nothing more than the withered ghost of naïve Victorian 'materialism' still pirouetting on the stage.

There is thus no good reason for contending or assuming that human desires do not exist or cannot be objectively known. We are philosophically justified in accepting the common-sense view that desires exist and are one of the immediate causes of men's economic actions. I buy bread because I want it. Moreover, these desires vary in intensity, though not, as we have seen, in quantity. And any individual can compare the intensity of one, at any rate, of his many desires with those of others. But there is another question entirely distinct and practically more important than any one yet considered: can the desires (or satisfactions) of *different people* be compared in intensity? Now the plain man certainly thinks that they can. He believes that it is sense to talk of 'rich' and 'poor' and to say that one man is richer or poorer than another. But if the desires of different people cannot be compared, this is not so. For though, as is argued later, a man's 'real' income consists in the possession of all the means to happi-

---

[1] Cf. F. H. Knight, *The Ethics of Competition*, p. 101: 'The higher values seem to have a claim to real existence as high as that of the data of observation, which are by no means immediately known, but are constructed by elaborate purposive inference and organization of 'immediate sense-data', whose own existence is in fact hypothetical.'

17

ness, and not merely in the satisfaction of desires: nevertheless if it cannot be said that the desires satisfied, or left unsatisfied, in one man's case are greater or less than those left satisfied or unsatisfied in another man's case, it can seldom if ever be said that any man is richer or poorer than any other.

Now this is so violently paradoxical a contention, and so completely opposed to common-sense belief, that we shall not be justified in accepting it unless there are strong positive reasons for doing so. The onus of proof is definitely on the man who contends that there are really no rich or poor. None of the classical economists ever had the hardihood to do so. It has been left to Professor Robbins and Professor Hayek to indulge in this exercise of intellectual audacity. Lest it be thought that no man can ever really have asserted such a thing, the following two passages may be quoted. Professor Hayek (*Collectivist Economic Planning*, p. 25) says: 'It is now generally recognised. . . that there is no scientific criterion which would enable us to compare or assess the relative importance of needs of different persons, although conclusions implying such illegitimate inter-personal comparisons of utilities can probably still be found in discussions of special problems.'

It will be noticed here that in Professor Hayek's opinion any judgement which is not 'scientific' is 'illegitimate'. It is 'illegitimate' to say that one man is richer than another.

A corresponding passage from Professor Robbins may be quoted at some length, since it is very characteristic of his whole position and method of argument: 'But it is one thing to assume that scales can be drawn up showing the *order* in which an individual will prefer a series of alternatives, and to compare the arrangements of one such individual scale with another. It is quite a different thing to assume that behind such arrangements lie magnitudes which themselves can be compared as between individual scales. This is not an assumption which need anywhere be made in modern economic analysis, and it is an assumption of an entirely different kind from the assumption of individual scales of relative valuation. The theory of exchange assumes that *I* can compare the importance *to me* of *bread* at sixpence per loaf and sixpence spent in other alternatives presented by the market, or—to empty out even the explanatory assumption of introspection—it assumes that confronted with such opportunities in certain circumstances my response will be of a determinate nature. And it assumes that the order of my preferences thus exhibited can be compared with the order of preferences of the baker. But it does *not* assume that at any point it is necessary to compare the satisfaction which *I* get from the spending of sixpence on bread with the satisfaction which the *baker* gets by receiving it. That comparison is a comparison of an entirely different nature. It is a comparison which is never intended in the theory of equilibrium and which is never implied by the assumption of that theory. It is a comparison which necessarily falls outside the scope of any positive science. To state that A's preference stands above B's in order of importance is entirely different from stating that A prefers *n* to *m* and B prefers *m* to *n* in a different order. It involves an element of conventional valuation. Hence it is purely normative. It has no place in positive science.

'If this is still obscure the following considerations should be decisive. Suppose that a difference of opinion were to arise about A's preferences. Suppose I thought that at certain prices he preferred *n* to *m*, and you thought that at the same prices he preferred *m* to *n*. It would be easy to settle our difference in a purely scientific manner. Either we could ask A to tell us. Or if we refused to believe that introspection on A's part was possible, we could expose him to the stimuli in question and observe his behaviour. Either test would be such as to provide a settlement of his difference of opinion.

'But suppose that we differed about the satisfaction derived by A from an income of £1000, and the satisfaction derived by B from one twice that amount in magnitude. Asking them would provide no solution. Supposing they differed. A might urge that he had more satisfaction than B at the margin. While B might urge that on the contrary, he had more satisfaction than A. We do not need to be slavish behaviourists to realize that here is no scientific evidence. *There is no means of testing the magnitude of A's satisfactions as compared with B's.* If we tested their blood streams that would be a test of blood, not satisfactions. Introspection does not enable A to discover what is going on in B's mind, nor B to discover what is going on in A's. There is no way of comparing the satisfactions of different people.'[1]

1 *The Nature and Significance of Economic Science,* pp. 122–4.

Throughout the whole passage Professor Robbins surely falls into a major confusion. He does not seem to know whether he is proving the 'satisfactions' of different people to be incomparable in practice or in principle. The distinction is vital. Supposing someone wished to compare the Aryan race with Waterloo Station, the task would be plainly impossible. The two have nothing in common and are consequently impossible to compare, in principle. But supposing someone wished to compare the population of Shanghai with that of Paris in circumstances in which nobody had counted or could count the population of either, the situation would be quite different. It is true that no comparison could be made in practice, because if one asked anybody how large the population of either city was, nobody would know. But this would not in the least alter the fact that one was actually larger than the other. Each of them has a population of a determinate magnitude which is greater or less than (or equal to) that of the other. They must consequently be comparable in principle, even if not in practice. In the same way every star must be, at a given moment, a determinate distance from every other star, even if nobody in fact knows what that distance is.

Now every one of Professor Robbins's arguments is devoted to proving that the desires of different people are not comparable in practice. He does not produce a single reason for thinking they are not comparable in principle. Yet this is the crucial question. Are the desires of different people incomparable in principle, like the Aryan race and Waterloo Station, or are they, like the populations of uncounted cities, or unknown stars, impossible to compare in practice? The average man certainly believes that different people's desires and needs are comparable in principle; he thinks that the starving man's desire for bread is greater than the millionaire's desire for a third wireless set. Now is there any reason for doubting this? There could only be one. If the desires of different men were different things, then they would not be comparable even in principle. But if they are similar things in the sense that different men's weights or shapes or limbs are similar things, then they are in principle comparable in intensity. If a desire is a desire and has a certain intensity, then its intensity must be greater or less or equal to (like the population of the cities) that of any other desires.

But is there any reason to doubt that all human desires are similar, i.e. instances of the same thing and so comparable? Again, it seems, there could only be one. If we do not believe, that is to say, that other people like ourselves exist, but suppose that the things which appear to be other human beings are really something else, then we may reasonably doubt the existence of any human desires other than our own. But if there are other human beings, there are other human desires. There are exactly as good reasons for believing in the one as in the other. For every human being appears to have desires just as he appears to exist. To believe that another human being exists, i.e. has a mind, body, arms, legs, emotions, and thoughts, but no desires or needs, would surely be quite illogical and irrational.

Professor Robbins may then, if he likes, deny in principle the comparability of different people's desires. But if so he must admit himself a 'solipsist'; he must deny the existence of all human beings but himself. That would be his real position. Yet at the same time he is eagerly assuming the existence of wages, profits, entrepreneurs, rentiers, central bankers, factories, ships, railways, business cycles, international trade, and heaven knows what else of what, on his own assumptions, should be unknowable and inconceivable things. Any consistent thinker must either give up talking about these things, or must admit that the desires of different people are in principle comparable.

Not only does the denial of their comparability lead, however, to a philosophical absurdity, it leads by itself with equal directness to a very odd definition of economics. All we know, Professor Robbins tells us, is that each individual can arrange his desires in a scale of intensity, and act according to this scale in expressing preferences on a market;[1] and it may be, he would perhaps admit, that the individual can compare his desires with his 'aversions'—to use Professor Pigou's word. But, we are asked to believe, the desires and aversions of one man neither are, nor conceivably can be, compared with those of another. That they are not, in fact, compared by the process of free exchange and free pricing, is an all-important truth to which we shall return later.[2] But that they cannot conceivably be com-

---

[1] *The Nature and Significance of Economic Science*, pp. 180–200.
[2] Cf. ch. ix.

pared at all is a doctrine that, left to itself, reduces economics to a very curious condition.

Hitherto economists have usually supposed that their science was in a sense 'autonomous'; that there was such a thing as purely 'economic progress'; that communities can grow richer or poorer; and that policies can be economically desirable or undesirable, quite apart from moral considerations. This appears to be the kind of argument used by Professor Pigou in which 'marginal net products' are conceived as being added to the 'social dividend'. Now whatever the merits of this assumption, which is discussed in the following chapter, it is clear that if we apply Professor Robbins's sceptical arguments to it, and then put nothing in its place, the whole science of economics is reduced to something very different from what economists have generally believed it to be.

Given the individual's 'scale of preference', Professor Robbins would say, and his consequent disposition to buy and sell, we can infer the whole sequence of economic phenomena. We can follow out all the infinitely ramifying consequences of one man's decision to buy this rather than that on the whole system of prices, wages, profits, production, and consumption. We can show that after these consequences have worked themselves out a certain 'equilibrium' will have been reached. But exactly how much, in fact, could we really prove in this way? We could say that the individual who initiated the change had satisfied one more of his desires than before. But we could not possibly say that the community as a whole was richer or poorer than before; for we could not compare one man's loss with another man's gain. Indeed, on these assumptions it would practically never be possible to say that any given measure was or was not economically beneficial to a community. For almost any practical measure affecting the economic system must benefit some individuals and injure others. Supposing it were proposed to impose an import duty on wheat and increase the money incomes of a small wheat-producing section of the community, and at the same time reduce by raising bread prices the 'real' income in commodities of the whole of the rest of the community. It may be that, as a result of the import duty, the community as a whole would consume the same amount of wheat and less of all other things. But this could not justify the inference that the community as a whole was poorer; for such an inference must involve a comparison of the loss and gain of different persons. Thus on Professor Robbins's assumption it would not be possible to say that those who lost by the duty in having less to spend on things other than bread lost more than what was gained by the wheat producers who received more money for their wheat. A new 'equilibrium' would be reached after the imposition of the duty: and for all Professor Robbins could say it would be as good or as bad as any other equilibrium whatever.

Now Professor Robbins is perfectly willing to admit this. Indeed he insists that economics gives no approval to one equilibrium other than another; that there are no economic ends; and that economics is 'neutral between ends'.[1] 'There is no penumbra of approbation', he says, 'around the theory of equilibrium.' But the meaning of the statement that economics is concerned with means and not ends is not at first sight clear. It does not mean, as might appear, that economics merely describes and explains what happens and never affirms what ought to happen. For it clearly affirms, even on Professor Robbins's assumptions, that given a certain desirable end there is a certain disposition of resources which ought to be adopted. But what are the kinds of ends that are to be conceived as given? They are not of course simple technical ends such as the building of a bridge in a given place, for which the right material, design, and so forth have to be discovered. For this, Professor Robbins would be the first to insist, is not an economic problem but a purely technical one. If the problem is genuinely economic, if it has to be decided how certain labour and capital is to be employed, there seem to be two general questions which economics, on Professor Robbins's definition, could answer. First it could say that, given as an end the production of definite physical amounts of the different commodities, a certain distribution of capital, labour, and land would be the best (most economical) way of achieving that end. If, for instance, with one arrangement of capital, labour, and land it were possible to produce 5,000,000 gallons of milk and 5,000,000 tons of coal, but with another arrangement 5,000,000 gallons of milk and 7,000,000 tons of coal, then economics could say that the latter arrangement was better. Secondly it could say that when it was possible to satisfy the desires of one consumer more

[1] *The Nature and Significance of Economic Science*, pp. 124–30.

23

completely without affecting the satisfactions of any other, it was justifiable to do so. If, for instance, one consumer wanted a little more milk and a little less coal at prices at which they could be produced without affecting the consumption of any other consumer, then the change would be economically justifiable. The 'end' in these two cases would be the production of a given set of quantities of various commodities or the satisfaction of more of a single consumer's wants in so far as it could be done without affecting other consumers.

But it would never be justifiable for economics, on Professor Robbins's definitions, to say absolutely that the most economical distribution of resources or the highest possible output had been achieved; nor even to say, except in the two above senses, that one distribution of resources was more economical than another. For these judgements could only be made by reference to some such criterion as 'the total real income of the community' or the 'net social product'. But if we are thinking purely in terms of desires, and if the comparability of different people's desires is denied, these terms are meaningless. There is on Professor Robbins's definition no rational answer to any practically economic question in a community until we have already decided to benefit one set of people rather than another. For almost any act of economic policy in practice must benefit some people and injure others; and economics, on these definitions, could only pronounce on policies which make some people richer without making others poorer. Professor Robbins would doubtless accept this, but it is doubtful whether most of those who adopt his view have seen it to be one of their main implications.

Nor is this the last unexpected conclusion to which any economist must be driven who thinks only in terms of satisfactions but denies the comparability of the satisfactions of different people. He would also be precluded from saying that any community ever (or almost ever) grew richer or poorer; or that the real national income ever increased or decreased. There could practically never be any economic progress or development, and no economic decline. For almost every large-scale economic change in a community involves the contraction of certain industries: and this means the loss of income for a considerable period to many of those engaged in those industries. We could only say, therefore, that the community as a whole was economically progressing, if we assumed that the new desires satisfied in the case of the community as a whole outweighed the desires no longer satisfied in the case of those whose incomes had shrunk. But if the desires of different people are not comparable, this could practically never be assumed. For economic changes very seldom occur which result either entirely in increases, or entirely in decreases, in individuals' real incomes. The doctrines of Professor Cassel and Professor Robbins thus lead to very remarkable conclusions, if they are not supplemented by any other kinds of economic or moral judgements. Hitherto, in fact, economists have tended to be divided into those who made assumptions about the human mind which have turned out on examination to be untenable, and those who, by denying the existence or at any rate the comparability, of such things as desires have seemed to make nonsense of most economic reasoning, or at least to reduce it to a very curious position. Is it possible so to describe the psychological basis of our economic actions as on the one hand to avoid philosophical errors and on the other to provide a rational foundation for economic reasoning as a whole? Can we accept the substance of the traditional insistence on 'utilities', 'satisfaction', and 'welfare' as the basis of economics without making fallacious assumptions about 'units of utility'? It is plain that very curious conclusions follow from the simultaneous acceptance of the two assumptions that economic action is simply concerned with the satisfaction of desires, and that different persons' desires are not comparable. It therefore remains, first, to abandon this latter assumption and see if rational conclusions can be reached from the mere supposition that desires are comparable; and then, if this fails, to consider how far it is really true that we are only concerned with desires.

CHAPTER III

NEEDS AND HAPPINESS

=====

There is good reason, it has been argued, for believing that though desires cannot be measured quantitatively, they can nevertheless be compared in intensity, even when the desires in question are experienced by different people. Now it may be entirely inadequate and fallacious to suppose that the only motive of human action, or even economic action, is the satisfaction of desires, or that happiness consists in nothing else but the absence of unsatisfied desires. But supposing we accept these assumptions for the moment, how much progress can we make in forming a rational conception of wealth, poverty, and economic progress? If desires vary in intensity, and if the intensity of different desires can be compared in principle, then it seems clear that in exceptional circumstances they can be compared in practice. Professor Robbins's argument implies a denial that the starving man's desires for bread can be said to be stronger than the millionaire's desires for a third wireless set. Why does he deny this? Simply because in his opinion it is impossible ever to compare different persons' desires at all. If, however, we admit that such comparisons are in principle possible, then there is no need to deny that in this case the given comparison can be made. We may conclude, with as much certainty as is possible in human affairs, that the starving man's desire is the greater.

We shall thus avoid the necessity of indulging in a ridiculous paradox. But can we construct a clear and positive meaning for the conceptions of economic action and economic progress? Suppose again that a high tax is to be imposed on imports of wheat in the interests of a comparatively small section of wheat-growers. Admittedly the total consumption of goods by the community as a whole will be lowered by the tax. But this is not a sufficient criterion in itself: for the wheat-growers will be better

26

off. The effect of the tax will be to raise the income of the wheat-growers and enable them to satisfy more desires, and to lower the income of the rest of the community and enable them to satisfy less desires. Now if all the relevant desires of the majority were stronger than all those of the minority, we might reasonably argue that the community would be worse and not better off for the change. But if by imposing the tax we satisfy less strong desires in the case of the majority, and sacrifice stronger desires in the case of the minority, how are we to say whether the change is economically beneficial or not? Supposing again that by devoting such and such resources to the production of one thing we shall satisfy the comparatively weak desires of one million people, and by devoting them to the production of another we shall satisfy the comparatively strong desires of one hundred people, how are we to choose? We can only rationally choose, on our present assumptions, if we can somehow multiply the number of people by the comparative intensity of their desires. But unfortunately only number can be multiplied by number; and it has already been agreed that the intensity of a desire cannot be measured in units. On the assumptions that desires and satisfactions are alone relevant to happiness, therefore, it is impossible not only in practice but in principle, to give a rational answer to such questions.

Moreover it is not certain that this new difficulty does not affect comparisons between the different desires of a single individual, as well as comparison between the desires of different individuals. If by spending the week-end at the seaside a man could satisfy many mild desires, and by staying at home he could satisfy a few strong ones, how could he make up his mind? The answer is that by a calculus of desires alone he could not make up his mind, because the number and strength of his desires could not in any way be assessed one against the other. One desire may be stronger than another. But one desire cannot be said to be stronger than two others, for the simple reason that it cannot be twice as strong as one of them.

The insolubility of this problem suggests very strongly that the set of crude psychological assumptions which we have so far taken over from traditional economic literature are untrue or at any rate incomplete. So far Professor Robbins may be right. We have assumed, hitherto, that the sole motive of human action, the sole objective of economic systems, and the sole content of happiness is the satisfaction of desires. We have not denied that men act for the sake of ethical or aesthetic ends, but we have assumed that they must first desire so to act. To suppose, however, that a man's actions are the result of a struggle between desires, in which the strongest wins, does not appear on reflection to be justifiable. The dipsomaniac's desire for drink is probably the strongest he has; but it may be in his power to decide not to satisfy it. And this is not merely because he also has a desire to avoid the consequences of drinking; for it does not seem to be true to say that only when that desire is the stronger can he successfully decide not to drink. On first thoughts, no doubt, most people would probably say that a mere conflict of desires is in question. The plausibility of this view (which may be called psychological hedonism), however, seems to derive mainly from false analogy with the case of physical bodies and forces. It is a view so difficult to defend against criticism that very few philosophers, not even the Victorian utilitarians, professed it; or if they did, it was usually inconsistent, as in Bentham's case, with their other beliefs.

In the first place if all action is merely determined by a conflict of desires, in which the strongest wins, there is no sense in saying that we ought, or ought not, to do anything, or in talking of praise, blame, or remorse, or indeed in regarding ourselves as agents at all. This in itself is enough to render psychological hedonism very suspect. But the most convincing argument against it is perhaps the argument from experience, which is as old as Plato. There must be something more than a conflict of desires, Plato maintains,[1] because in the cases when we resist a desire (as in the case of the reformed dipsomaniac), the element in us which opposes desire must be something other than desire. For though the same element in us (i.e. desire) might be attracted to two different things at once, it could not be both attracted and repelled from the same thing. Or, in other words, we may desire strawberries and raspberries at once, but if we desire strawberries, and yet decide not to eat them, the faculty that impels us not to eat them must be something other than desire.[2] These arguments, which

[1] Mainly in Book IV of *The Republic*. Plato did not, of course, deny that there *is* a conflict of desires.

[2] We of course say loosely that we feel desire and aversion for the same

everyone must consider and evaluate for himself in the light of reflection on his own experience, do seem to establish that there is a faculty of will, or choice, through which the self expresses itself in opposition to individual desires. It appears, in fact, that individuals consider different courses of action, involving the satisfaction of various desires of their own and others, and then *choose*, for whatever reason, to adopt one course rather than another.[1]

This even appears to be the case in many decisions which would normally be called purely economic. Doubtless when a man is considering whether to eat oranges or apples he weighs one desire against another, and even decides on the principle of the 'marginal' amount of satisfaction he gets from the one or the other. But even here there is something more than a conflict of desires. And in the case of a great many economic decisions it does not even seem to be conflicting desires which a man is choosing between. When the father of a family decides to spend ten shillings on buying boots for one of his children rather than cigarettes for himself, does he really decide that it pleases him more that the child should have boots than that he himself should have cigarettes? It seems much more accurate to say that he decides he *ought* to buy the boots. And although, having done so, he doubtless desires to buy them, it does not appear to be necessary for this desire to be the strongest he has in order that he may decide to do so. The sheer calculus of desires, in fact, seems only to be used in making a certain restricted group of decisions.

Nor is it possible to maintain that happiness consists in the satisfaction of the strongest desires. Quite apart from the impossibility noted above of a calculus of desires, it is really

---

[1] For a full discussion of this issue one may refer to a modern philosopher on the one hand and a modern economist on the other: (*a*) H. W. B. Joseph, *Essays in Ancient and Modern Philosophy*, ch. ii, 'The Nature of the Soul'; (*b*) F. H. Knight, *The Ethics of Competition*, ch. i, ii, and iii.
Both these writers, starting from different points of view, reach substantially the conclusion outlined above. Professor Knight says: 'A human being cannot really regard himself as an organism expressing its nature in response to situations. To live on the human plane is to choose.'

---

thing at once: but this only means that we desire one aspect of it and dislike another.

impossible to contend that the dipsomaniac will find happiness through satisfying his strongest desires or that the happiest people have been those who have had the least unsatisfied desires. It has often been argued, of course, that saints and philosophers merely followed their strongest desires like other people, and that the only difference was that they had a different set of desires. It is doubtless true that saints have spoken of righteousness with every mark of passion; and Kant invoked the moral law in the language of erotic ecstasy. But to interpret the life of a saint as a mere victory of strong over weak desires would surely be a gratuitous perversion of facts. Nevertheless, the saint may easily be perfectly happy. It seems possible, then, for a man to achieve happiness, although the sole end of his actions is not the satisfaction of desires.

Moreover, a man may be precluded from happiness by the frustration of a want of which he is not even conscious. Some of those who live in slums not merely do not desire to be moved but positively desire not to be. Yet it is a common experience that very soon after they have been moved they find themselves happier than before. Similarly it is possible for a man on receiving something of which he has never conceived the existence nor felt the want, to experience satisfaction none the less. Those desires of which a person is not conscious, but the frustration of which prevent his being happy, may perhaps reasonably be called 'wants'. To some extent, no doubt, anyone who has avoided inner conflicts, and satisfied as far as possible all the desires of which he is conscious, is happy; but if he became conscious of new desires and satisfied them he might be even more completely happy. It is presumably this fact which has led people to emphasize satisfactions rather than desires. If both conscious and unconscious desires yield satisfactions, it might seem reasonable to suppose that we choose to follow one desire rather than another on a calculus of satisfactions alone. But unfortunately, as has been observed, the intensity of a satisfaction does not always correspond to the intensity of the desire satisfied—particularly when the desire has not been consciously felt at all. And there is surely no calculus by which an unconscious want which yields a strong satisfaction can be weighed against a conscious and very strong desire which yields a comparatively weak satisfaction. Again, therefore, it seems that men cannot make their decisions on a calculus of satisfactions alone.[1]

Ultimately, then, the purpose of an economic system, and of economic decisions, must surely be defined not as the satisfaction of desires, but as the provision of those scarce goods which are necessary to happiness.[2] The attainment of happiness will, of course, include the satisfaction of desires and wants, but will not consist wholly of it. The rational economic decision of an individual will consist in distributing scarce resources to the end of happiness; and his economic progress in his approximation to that end. By scarce resources are meant those means to, or parts of, happiness which exist in insufficient quantities to enable every one to have all that will satisfy them.[3] Excluded from these are the so-called 'free goods' such as air and water; but also the whole class of psychological or moral states necessary to happiness which may be difficult to attain but whose possession by one person does not imply the impoverishment of someone else. Neither of these classes of things can be considered scarce in the economic sense of the word. The lack of them makes a man unhappy, but it does not make him poor. What makes him poor is being deprived of those things which he wants but cannot have because other people want them too. By poverty, in the last analysis, we mean the lack of this kind of scarce goods, by wealth the possession of them, and by inequality the possession of an unequal share of them.

It is perhaps more accurate to speak of scarce parts of, rather than means to, happiness. For the happiness of different people depends on different things; and in some cases not merely the

---

[1] Cf. F. H. Knight, *The Ethics of Competition*, p. 22: 'The chief thing which the common-sense individual actually wants is not satisfaction for the wants that he has, but more and better wants. The thing which he strives to get in the most immediate sense are far more what he thinks he ought to want than what his untutored preferences prompt.'

[2] This is not meant to imply that 'happiness' is the sole end of man, to the exclusion of other goods, such as knowledge, beauty, etc. The word happiness must here be taken to include such ends. It must also include the satisfaction of desires for food, drink, etc., since these in themselves may be a man's whole aim. (see page 32). The relation of such desires to happiness cannot be analysed here. But it may be recalled that many philosophers (*e.g.* Butler) have distinguished between particular desires which are exhusted in their particular satisfaction, and those desires whose satisfaction is the satisfaction of the whole man.

[3] They must also, as Professor Robbins points out, be capable of alternative uses.

means but the end itself may be scarce. The chief purpose of a man's life may be the possession of a certain picture or the achievement of a certain ambition: and these may be things which only one man can possess or enjoy at a time. In that case the end itself is scarce and is a part rather than a means to the man's happiness. On the other hand there are just a few people in the world whose happiness does not depend on the possession of any of the things which in fact happen to be scarce. Such are the happy beggars, discontented plutocrats, lunatics, and saints.

Though this is all true, however, it is of the greatest importance to realize that for the vast majority of individuals happiness depends on the possession of certain simple things which all men desire. For the vast majority of men food, clothes, and houses are necessary to happiness. In perhaps the majority of cases, happiness is largely a matter of satisfying desires; and the things desired are, only too often, scarce physical commodities. Is not this why economics has so often been thought to be concerned with nothing but the production of commodities and the satisfaction of desires? Is not this why the wealth of a community has been conceived as the annual flow of physical commodities, and why a given amount of money has even been conceived to represent a given amount of 'economic value' in some absolute sense? If we assume, as is broadly true, that for most individuals most of the means to happiness are the same, and even consist in most cases of producible commodities, then there is substantial though not absolute, truth in conceiving of economic advance as the supply of an increasing amount of those 'material' goods to the individuals who desire them. There is a similar important approximation to the truth in measuring the 'economic progress' of a community by the actual increase in the production of certain staple commodities, as economic historians have always been compelled to do in practice, though economic theorists have been inclined to condemn their procedure in principle. There is even some sense in measuring the opportunity which people have of happiness by the size of their money income.

Though, however, it is thus possible to understand why the satisfaction of desires and the production of commodities are normally taken to be equivalent to economic progress, no answer has yet been given to the question how there can be such progress when some persons are gaining, as they normally must, at the expense of others. By simply defining wealth as the possession of scarce means to or parts of happiness, we can attain a rational conception of the wealth or poverty of an individual. But can we do so for a community? It seems that we cannot; for the old difficulty remains. Almost all economic change will involve an increase in some peoples' happiness at the expense of someone else's. And unless we can multiply the various numbers of people by the different intensities of happiness, we cannot possibly say that the change is economically better or worse. Similarly, we could not say that one community was better off than another; or that any economic policy was justified. For if intensities of desire cannot be arithmetically measured, it is certain that intensities of happiness cannot.

Yet in fact we have no doubt that a community in which everyone is enabled to be reasonably prosperous is better than one in which the majority are destitute and a few are luxuriously affluent. We have no doubt that it is justifiable to increase the happiness of a large number of comparatively ill-provided people at the expense of a sacrifice by a few of the best-provided ones; for instance, everyone would agree that it is right to remove a tax which enriched a comfortable and idle minority at the cost of the most numerous and hard-working section of the community. To deny these propositions would be absurd. But since they can have no rational basis in any calculus of desires or happiness, what is their rational basis? Surely it is this. They are in fact direct judgements of value,[1] similar to any other such judgements. We simply look at one society or another, and pronounce it good or bad, better or worse.[2] The validity of such judgements of value cannot of course be demonstrated by inference to those who deny it. It is only possible to point out to such people that if they make this denial, they cannot, among other

[1] In the absolute sense, of course, of aesthetic and moral values.
[2] Cf. F. H. Knight, *The Ethics of Competition*, p. 41: 'The facts as emphasized, are altogether against accepting any balance-sheet view of life. They point rather to an evaluation of a far subtler sort than the addition and subtraction of homogeneous items, towards an ethic of aesthetic criticism ... We cannot accept want-satisfaction as a final criterion of value because we do not regard our wants as final.' Professor Knight evidently talks of an 'evaluation of a far subtler sort' and of an 'ethic along the lines of aesthetic criticism' because he is afraid that the less discerning sort of critic would be offended if he said outright a 'judgement of value'.

things, form any comprehensive conception of the poverty or wealth of a community, or of its economic progress, or of a rational distribution of the means to happiness. An economic change which benefits everybody whom it affects may, without difficulty, be described as economic progress, and may be approved on what would be called 'purely economic grounds'. But a change which makes some people richer and others poorer cannot be so approved or condemned simply because there is no conceivable process of reasoning by which intensities of desire or happiness can be calculated against numbers of desires or numbers of persons. And almost all economic changes in practice, and practically every decision to apply resources to this rather than that end, must be of this kind. The State choosing collectively between the welfare of different sets of people must employ some other criterion than a calculus of desires or happiness. And the only possible criterion available for the collective choice is the direct judgement that this or that state of society, as a whole, is the better.

The more the problem is analysed, the more clear this becomes. We may say that an individual's object is the attainment of happiness and not the mere satisfaction of desires, and that the object of an economic system must be conditioned by this. But the fact remains that most men will be seeking happiness in the satisfaction of simple physical desires, while a few will be pursuing aesthetic, ascetic, and intellectual ideals. The question may arise whether resources should be devoted to the one or the other. In answering this question, however, the fact that one sort of end is more valuable than another (whether it is desired or not) must be taken into account. The question whether it is 'economic progress' to satisfy one desire rather than another cannot, therefore, be answered in such a case without making judgements of value.

Fundamentally this conclusion is perhaps not far different from that of Professor Robbins,[1] if allowance is made for his

---

[1] The helpful part of Professor Robbins's contribution will then be his emphasis on scarcity as a fundamentally economic concept, and his demonstration how very few of the judgements currently regarded as 'economic' are in fact independent of value judgements. The less helpful parts are his use of the conception of ends and means to express the distinction between value judgements and purely factual ones, his question-begging use of the word 'scientific' and his argument that 'there is no way of comparing the satisfactions of different people'.

rigorous desire to delimit the scope of economics. He would admit that such conceptions as the wealth or poverty or 'economic progress' of a community are seldom,[1] if ever, intelligible except in terms of value judgements, or 'ultimate obligations' as he calls them; and this is the essential point. He would infer, however, that they are not economic conceptions, because he wishes to make economics completely independent of such judgements. The ordinary man, however, certainly regards poverty, wealth, 'material' progress, and decline, as economic conceptions; and if he is intent on doing this, he must be shown that such economic conceptions in fact involve value judgements.

In order to avoid purely verbal controversies, and to establish the greatest possible measure of agreement, we may perhaps express the facts in the following way. Economists have hitherto been inclined to regard the economic welfare and progress of communities as economic conceptions involving no value judgements and intelligible in terms of 'utilities' and 'satisfactions'. The truth is that they are hardly ever intelligible except in terms of value judgements; and Professor Robbins wishes it to be therefore laid down that they are not economic. The alternative is to infer that a large part of economics cannot be made independent of such judgements. Whichever definition, however, we like to give to economics, the crucial point is that the question how productive resources ought to be distributed between alternative uses ceases almost inevitably to be a mere question of finding appropriate means to ends, and begins to involve a judgement of value, as soon as it begins to affect a community and not merely an individual.[2]

It is accordingly possible to see how remarkably unreal the traditional controversies have been between those who sought to approve or condemn an economic system because of some principle inherent in it. Those who justified free capitalism because of some pre-established harmony between individual and social self-interest, and those who condemned it because of the emergence of 'surplus value', were really, however correct or incorrect their actual argument, asking and answering ques-

[1] Only when all are growing richer or poorer at once.
[2] Even in the case of the individual choosing between several desires the value judgement is really involved. It is only truly absent when an individual is singly concerned with finding ways of satisfying a particular desire and nothing else is involved.

tions of very dubious meaning or relevance. Both Marxism and Benthamism were, in this intellectual sense, a wild-goose chase. The fact is that you can only judge an economic or social system by its results. If nineteenth-century capitalism is to be justified or condemned, it will not be done by demonstrating that every individual possessed economic freedom, or that rent and interest were paid to private capitalists. It will only be justified or condemned by a direct comparison between society as a whole at the beginning and end of the century, or by an estimate of what society might have been like under a different system. Similarly the answer to specific questions of economic policy must be given by a comparison of the results likely to follow in each case. And this is of course the kind of comparison which almost all critics or defenders of economic systems have in fact really made. They contemplate the results and pronounce them good or bad. Their disagreements spring from the fact that they do not see the results accurately and do not see them whole.

The conclusion[1] therefore seems to be that the poverty or richness of an individual cannot be less widely defined than as the presence or absence of those things which are for him both scarce and necessary to happiness,[2] and that even the economic advance or decline of a community cannot be demonstrated except by a direct value judgement that one state of society is as a whole better or worse then another. Similarly the decision to devote the productive resources to the satisfaction of one set of persons' needs rather than others' must rest on the judgement that it is better that these should be satisfied. Some may regard such judgements as sweeping, summary, or 'unscientific'. But in fact they are the only logical basis for the economic and social judgements all of us make and must make every day. We must accept them or be complete sceptics. And it is far best to drag our real implied assumptions into the light of day and state them clearly, fairly, and squarely. Moreover, though this is the ultimate logical assumption of most economic and social judgements, in a great number of practical cases we may judge an economic measure by the extent to which it satisfies the staple

[1] Cf. F. H. Knight, *Ethics of Competition*, p.55: 'The system must be judged on the conformity to ethical standards of the facts of demand rather than by the conformity to demand of the actual production and distribution of goods.'

[2] Happiness must be taken in the wide sense already described.

wants and desires of the great mass of mankind. For there are cases in which the desire or satisfaction of one man can with reasonable certainty be compared with that of another, and the only moral judgement involved in this case is the judgement that the intenser want ought to be satisfied. For the remainder of this book, therefore, the terms wants, desires, or satisfactions will be used only of comparisons of intensity, and the word 'need' only where some value judgement would prove on analysis to be implied.[1]

The traditional insistence of such economists as Marshall, Pigou, and Wicksell on wants and satisfactions as the real subject-matter of economics seems therefore to be justifiable, even though the possibility of quantitatively measuring these 'mental states' has to be denied. Similarly there is substantial truth in these economists' arguments about 'social utility', the 'social dividend', the desirability of transfers from the rich to the poor, and the greater value of a given unit of money to the poor than to the rich, even if they have been vulnerably expressed. For, whether or not we call it economics, we are rationally justified in judging that it is better to satisfy one set of wants than another, and even in some cases that it is better to satisfy one man's particular want than another's. This, which has been the germ of truth in the traditional teaching about 'utility', is all we need to know in order to give intelligible meaning to the words 'poverty' and 'inequality'.

It may seem that so much theoretical argumentation is hardly necessary to establish the reality of poverty and inequality, and the possibility of economic reform. In a sense, perhaps, it is not. Nevertheless, before undertaking a criticism of existing society and of the methods proposed for its reform, it is best to ascertain with the greatest possible clearness what is the really unassailable rational ground for our criticisms and our proposals.

[1] It is impossible to consider here the reality and nature of 'efforts', 'sacrifices', and 'aversions'. It must be assumed that the sacrifice implied in the non-satisfaction of a want or desire, is also comparable in intensity with other sacrifices; but that normally the comparison of sacrifices made by different people implies a judgement of value. Similarly it must be assumed that the intensity of a sacrifice is in principle comparable with that of a satisfaction.

CHAPTER IV

THE FACTS OF INEQUALITY

If a society or economic system is properly to be judged by its
results, we must be clear, before judging capitalism, what its
results are. How in fact is the national income distributed under
capitalism? And what degree of poverty or inequality does it
produce? A very great deal turns on the answers to these questions. The comparative validity of different political creeds
depends, much more than their holders commonly realize, on
the actual statistics of the distribution of the national income.
Many conservatives honestly believe that though there is some
inequality, it is neither overwhelming nor much greater than is
inevitable; and that while there is some extreme poverty, its
existence and cause are exceptional. The communists believe
that practically the whole of the community lives in sheer destitution, except for a tiny minority who enjoy the extremity of
affluence. It is remarkable what different answers are given by
different persons to the question what percentage of the community lives at a working-class standard of living. And with the
variation of these answers the political views of the answerer
often vary directly. Most of us judge society by its results; but
few of us are aware what those results are.

1. *The Distribution of Incomes in Great Britain*
   The facts, however, are perfectly ascertainable. It is possible
to give a reasonably accurate outline of the distribution of
money incomes, and the absolute and relative movement in
recent years of real incomes, both in Great Britain and the
United States. How, first of all, is the annual national income
in this country divided into the three main categories of
wages; salaries; and rent, interest, and profit? Mr. Colin Clark
has made a very full estimate of this; and the following table

is taken from his book, *National Income and Outlay*, p. 94.

(In millions of pounds sterling)

	1911	1924	1929	1932	1933	1934	1935
Wages	728 39.5%	1399 42.1%	1486 41.8%	1333 42.5%	1362 42.0%	1442 41.5%	1520 40.5%
Salaries	288 15.6%	841 25.4%	944 26.6%	890 28.3%	907 28.0%	922 26.5%	937 25.0%
Profit and Interest	623 33.8%	834 25.1%	821 23.1%	590 18.8%	642 19.8%	781 22.4%	949 25.4%
Rent	203 11.1%	246 7.4%	302 8.5%	325 10.4%	329 10.2%	334 9.6%	339 9.1%

This table discloses the remarkable fact that the aggregate of rent, interest, and profit payments is practically as great as the aggregate of all wages; though the aggregate of wages is of course distributed among a vastly larger number of people. In recent years, out of a total annual national income of about £3,500,000,000, about £1,400,000,000 has gone to wage-earners, about £1,200,000,000 to property-owners, and about £900,000,000 to salary-earners. Rent, interest, and profit, that is, get about one-third of the whole national income; wages get a little more than this; and salaries take the remainder, amounting to about one-quarter.

Distribution of Personal Income (1929)

Incomes	Numbers (in thousands)	Total Income (in millions of pounds)
Over £10,000	10	228
£2,000 to £10,000	100	388
£1,000 to £2,000	195	235
£500 to £1,000	481	309
£250 to £500	1,249	402
£125 to £250	5,827	1,009
Under £125	11,800	1,170
Total	19,652	3,741

Much more important is the question how the national income is divided between actual individuals. The above table, taken from Mr. Colin Clark's book, *National Income and Outlay*, p. 109, shows for the year 1929 (since when no great changes in income distribution have occurred) the number of individuals in the different income classes and the amounts of the national income which they received.

It is reasonable to take the figure of £250 per year as the upper limit of working-class incomes. This roughly corresponds with the health and unemployment insurance maxima and with what is commonly taken to be the income of the best-paid working man. Now the number of persons receiving incomes of under £250 a year is shown above to be about 17,600,000 and the total number of persons receiving incomes to be just under 20,000,000. There were, in fact, in 1929, about 17,600,000 working-class incomes in this country, each of £250 a year or less; and about 2,300,000 middle-class and rentier families receiving over £250 a year. At any time, that is to say, about nine out of ten income-receivers or families have a working-class income.

These figures are perhaps the most eloquent and significant comment on modern industrial society that can possibly be made. It is quite erroneous to speak of the 'community' or the 'public' in this country; as if the population consisted of a large mass of persons with moderate incomes, and a few extremely rich and extremely poor above and below them. It is also erroneous to think of the working class as if they represented one-half or perhaps two-thirds of the community, and their interests had consequently to be balanced against those of the middle classes in determining political action. It is equally erroneous again to think of society as consisting of a vast majority of practically destitute persons and a small minority living in great luxury, with nobody in between. In fact, in Great Britain, 17,600,000 out of 20,000,000 persons, or about nine in every ten, are working class, though not necessarily of course all manual workers; and 12,000,000 of these receive an income scarcely above the subsistence level. Another small but substantial group, of somewhere about 2,000,000, receive a middle-class or professional-class income ranging from £250 to £1,000. And finally there is a tiny group of 300,000 very rich persons, whose aggregate income makes up a very considerable proportion of the total national income.

Our society is one, in fact, which displays considerable poverty and very great inequality. The poverty is best revealed by the figure of 12,000,000 persons living on an income of less than £125 a year. Many of these 'persons', it must also be remembered, though not all, are really families. The extent of inequality is summarized in the following way by Mr. Colin Clark (*National Income and Outlay*, p. 110): 'Speaking of the years 1929–35, we can say that one-tenth of the whole working population, with incomes over £250, took 42 per cent of the whole total of personal incomes, or just under half of it if we allow for the fact that the greater part of the non-personal incomes, in the form of undistributed company profits and such, accrued for the benefit of the rich. A small class, comprising 1½ per cent of the population, with "four-figure incomes" and upwards, took 23 per cent of the whole total of personal incomes.'

In our modern industrial society, in fact, 90 per cent of the population do virtually all the work for barely half the income. That is the fundamental, brute fact.

Mr. Colin Clark also shows[1] that while only 13.7 per cent of the population live in the poorest and worst-nourished section of all in the community, no less than 25.3 per cent of the children are brought up in that group.

Such is the distribution of incomes in this country. It is also vital to know, however, whether the distribution is changing, and if so in what direction. There is a general belief, apparently based on the evidence of personal observation, that the standard of living or, if we like so to call it, the 'average real income per head', has been steadily rising, at any rate since the middle of the last century. Mr. Lansbury has himself testified that the standard of living of the average worker in the East End of London is substantially higher than it was when he was a child. This impression is borne out by statistics, if we measure 'real income' by the aggregate 'physical' amounts of goods and services consumed, and take no account of changes either in individual valuations or in the distribution of incomes. In an *Introduction to the Study of Prices* Sir Walter Layton and Mr. Geoffrey Crowther have calculated[2] an index of 'real wages', i.e. of the

[1] *National Income and Outlay*, p. 114.   [2] Pp. 265–6.

average consumption per head of the wage-earning class as a whole. There are, of course, many theoretical and statistical objections to such an index; but it gives the best practical estimate of the changes in the workers' standard of living. Starting from 100 in 1859, the index, which allows for unemployment, rose to 132 in 1875; fell to 121 in 1879; rose to 179 in 1900; fell to 169 in 1914; rose to 202 in 1920; and after various post-war oscillations had recovered to 202 in 1933. These figures confirm the view derived from individual observation that there has been a substantial advance in the workers' real income in the last hundred years, and that a great part of that rise was achieved during the convulsions of the war period. Sir Walter Layton and Mr. Crowther express the view that between 1929 and 1932, despite the huge increase in unemployment, the workers' average real incomes actually rose slightly. If this is true, their real income in 1937, owing to the fall in unemployment, must be definitely higher than it has ever been before, though since 1933 the real income per head of *employed* workers has been falling owing to the rise in the cost of living.

The indisputable fact, however, of a rise in the workers' standard of living does not necessarily prove that the total national income is now more evenly distributed than it was a hundred years ago. The rise may be entirely due to a rise in the total to be distributed. Sir Walter Layton and Mr. Crowther print a comparative table[1] showing the total money incomes of all wage-earners and of all income-tax payers between 1860 and 1901. The total wage-income starts at £300,000,000 in 1860 and rises to £705,000,000 in 1901. The total income-tax payers' income, on the other hand, rises from £290,000,000 in 1860 to £800,000,000 in 1901. In so far, therefore, as these figures fairly represent the incomes of the working class and of the whole of the rest of the community respectively, it seems that the workers' share of the national income actually fell from over 50 per cent in 1860 to about 45 per cent in 1901. This in general is consistent with Mr. Colin Clark's calculation, shown on page 39, and with that of Professor Bowley and Sir Josiah Stamp. Mr. Colin Clark puts the wage-earners' share in 1911 at 39.5 per cent, and Professor Bowley and Sir Josiah Stamp at 38.7 per cent. According to Mr. Clark[2] it rose from

[1] Cf. *An Introduction to the Study of Prices*, p. 270.   [2] See table on p. 39.

39.5 per cent in 1911 to 42.1 per cent in 1924, and fell again slightly to 40.5 per cent in 1935. The wage-earners' share in the national income in fact is appreciably smaller to-day than it was seventy-five years ago. In 1860 the wage-earners' received 55 per cent of the national income; and to-day they receive only just over 40 per cent. It must be remembered, of course, that this is partly due to a movement of wage-earners into the salary-earning classes. The number of salary-earners increased, according to Mr. Clark (*National Income and Outlay*, p. 99) from 3,140,000 in 1911 to 4,342,000 in 1929. But this does not account for the whole increase in the incomes of salary-earners. Indeed a large part of that increase is undoubtedly due to the conversion of private into public businesses and the consequent payment of new salaries (instead of 'profits') to business managers. Comparing 1911 and 1919, Mr. Colin Clark says that '10.5 per cent of the national income has been lost to "profits", of which 7.7 per cent has been taken by "higher salaries". The rest has gone to "lower wages".' By no means all of the increase in total salary-incomes, therefore, represents a rise in the standard of living of the poor.

The inequality of distribution may be measured by the statistics of property as well as incomes. Messrs. G. W. Daniels and H. Campion[1] have calculated the distribution of capital in England and Wales in 1911–13 and 1924–30 to have been as shown in the table on page 44.

It is clear from this table, first, that only about 20 per cent even of persons over twenty-five have property worth more than £100. Four out of five people, that is to say, die without leaving more than a negligible amount of property. Secondly, it appears that about 6 per cent of the population hold 80 per cent of the property, and that less than 2 per cent of the population hold 40 per cent of the property. Here is inequality of distribution so grotesque as to be almost unbelievable. But there is no doubt that these figures are substantially correct. It may be thought that the inequality is exaggerated by the fact that normally only one member of a family holds all or most of the property from which a whole family benefits. But it is doubtful if this is so: for commonly in a family where one person holds property, others will hold it too. The inequality of distribution

[1] *The Distribution of the National Capital*, p. 54.

43

of capital may accordingly be taken to be fairly accurately measured by these figures.

(Figures relate to persons twenty-five and over)

1924–30	Number of Persons		Amount of Capital	
	Number	Cumulative percentage	Income	Cumulative percentage
Total	thousands 22,336	100	million pounds 13,680–15,150	100
More than £100	4,774–5,283	21.3–23.7	13,183–14,255	93.6–96.8
£1,000	1,306–1,421	5.8–6.4	11,712–12,623	83.2–85.7
£5,000	357–386	1.6–1.8	9,319–10,013	66.2–68.0
£10,000	180–194	0.8–0.9	7,914–8,494	56.2–57.7
£25,000	64–69	0.2–0.3	5,891–6,317	41.8–42.9
£100,000	10–11	0.04–0.05	3,266–3,504	23.2–23.9
1911–13 Total	18,745	100	6,008–7,005	100
More than £100	2,196–2,529	11.6–13.4	5,608–6,305	89.7–93.4
£1,000	558–635	2.9–3.3	4,987–5,584	79.7–83.0
£5,000	161–180	0.8–0.9	4,021–4,485	64.0–67.0
£10,000	84–94	0.4	3,423–3,808	54.3–57.0
£25,000	30–34	0.1	2,548–2,824	40.3–42.4
£100,000	5–6	0.03	1,378–1,516	21.6–22.9

It will also be noticed that despite the death duties, once thought to be so crippling, there has been very little mitigation of inequality since before the war. Before the war there were 5,000 to 6,000 fortunes of over £100,000, totalling about 22 per cent of the total national capital. In 1924–30 there were 10,000 to 11,000, taking about 23.5 per cent. It is true that a fortune of £100,000 to-day is proportionately smaller than one of that size before the war, because the value of money has fallen. But these figures nevertheless show that the number of very large fortunes is not diminishing. Contrary to the belief of the propertied classes, the death duties are only just holding their own against the forces of private accumulation. The number of fortunes over £25,000 increased from between 30,000 and 34,000 before the war to 65,000 in 1924–30.

There has been some slight mitigation of inequality in the lower ranges; i.e. many of those who had less than £100 before the war had risen to the £100–£1,000 class by 1914–20. Before the war 12 per cent of the population held about 90 per cent of the capital. After the war 20 per cent of the population held about 90 per cent of the capital. In the opinion of Messrs. Campion and Daniels: 'Such reduction as has been made in the inequality of the distribution of capital since before the war is due in part to the change in the age distribution of the adult population during the period.'[1] It must also be remembered that a great many of the persons with capital of less than £100 nevertheless possess, as the Post Office and Savings Certificates figures show, some reserve, averaging probably £30 or £40. More than half the 17,000,000 below the £100 category probably possess some such reserve. We have in fact a working-class with a small reserve of savings, a gradually increasing propertied middle-class, and a solidly entrenched plutocracy. The salient fact remains, however, that about 17,000,000 persons (about the same number as have working-class incomes) have property of less than £100, while 6 per cent of the population hold over 80 per cent of the total national property.

Some may argue that whatever the statistics of income and property show, a huge redistribution of incomes has been achieved in the last twenty-five years by means of national taxation and the social services. A very great number of people in this country, including many sincere socialists, implicitly believe that this is so. It is consequently rather startling to find, on an impartial examination of the facts, that there has been scarcely any redistribution at all.

Two separate questions have to be answered. First, how far is the national income redistributed by taxation and social services to-day; and secondly how far has the workers' position improved or deteriorated as a result of public finance since twenty-five years ago. The extent to which income is redistributed through the Budget to-day depends not merely on how the money is spent but on how it is raised. A belief appears to prevail, at least among the propertied classes, that almost the

[1] *The Distribution of the National Capital*, p. 54.

whole of the national revenues are raised by income-tax, sur-tax, and death duties. In fact, however, about three-sevenths of the total is raised by indirect taxation; and indirect taxation by its nature presses very much more hardly on the poor than on the rich. The consumption per year of such staple commodities as tea, beer, and sugar does not vary very greatly from one class to another. A tax, therefore, which is levied on the price of these commodities is paid in equal amounts by individuals in all classes alike; a rich man and a poor man pay say £1 a year to the Treasury for their consumption of sugar. This is very unfair, since £1 is worth more to the poor than to the rich.[1] And, re-membering that the working classes represent numerically nine-tenths of the nation, we might at first sight be inclined to conclude that they in fact pay nine-tenths of the sum raised in indirect taxation. But that would be an overestimate, since one or two of our indirect taxes fall more heavily on the rich than on the poor—though this is to some extent counter-balanced by the con-tributions now made by the better-paid workers to income-tax. On the whole we shall not overestimate the amount paid in taxation by the workers if we put it at four-fifths of the total raised in indirect taxation.[2] In the Budget year 1936-7 some £320,000,000 was raised from indirect taxation (Customs and Excise), and £430,000,000 from direct taxation (income-tax, sur-tax, estate duties, stamps, excess-profits duty, corporation tax, land tax). It is fair to say then that in that year about £250,000,000 was raised in national taxation on the working classes and £500,000,000 in taxation on the rich.

How was the money spent? Our national expenditure is really of three kinds. First there is expenditure which does not directly benefit any class in particular, such as the upkeep of the Army, Navy, Air Force, and police, and of the administrative machine in general. Secondly there is expenditure on the social services which directly benefit the working classes. And thirdly there is the interest on the national debt which, mainly but not entirely,[3] benefits the rentier direct. Expenditure out of the

[1] As is argued later; see pp. 112 and 113.
[2] See *British Public Expenditure*, by Joseph Sykes, pp. 127, 128. The pro-portion of four-fifths is suggested by Mr. Sykes.
    Cf. also J. A. Hobson, *Rationalization and Unemployment*, p. 97.
[3] Cf. *British Public Expenditure*, ch. viii. Also the Report of the Colwyn Committee.

Budget on social services in 1934-5 (the latest year available) was £223,000,000 (that is on education, health, pensions, housing, and unemployment), and about £240,000,000 if allowance is made for the maintenance of the full administrative machine necessary for such services. Expenditure on the national debt in that year was £224,000,000. The remainder spent on the defence forces and police and other 'neutral' items was £256,000,000.[1] In the year 1934-5, the workers' contribution to national taxation was about £230,000,000.

At the present time, therefore, the whole of the money spent for the benefit of the working classes is raised by indirect taxation on the working classes themselves. About £230,000,000 to £250,000,000 is raised by taxation on the workers, and about £230,000,000 is spent directly for their benefit. Moreover, the sum spent in national debt interest and management, mainly for the direct benefit of the rentier, at £224,000,000, is almost as large as the total sum spent on the social services. But the average sum which the individual rentier in fact receives from the Budget must be many times larger than the average sum received by the worker. The plain truth is that the working classes themselves pay for virtually the whole of the social services; and the rich in turn having supplied themselves with the national debt interest,[2] provide the workers with the blessings of an Army, Navy, Air Force, and police. There is scarcely any redistribution of income between classes under our present Budget system, except in so far as the working classes receive for nothing their share in these possibly dubious blessings.

Almost as important, and more inequitable, is our system of municipal finance. About £435,000,000 a year is spent by local authorities on revenue account, of which about £180,000,000 is absorbed by housing, education, and health. The rates, from which most of the money is raised, may be regarded as a sort of compromise between direct and indirect taxation. In practice, however, they are preponderantly indirect. Rates are levied at so much per pound on the 'rateable value' of a house. It is true that the absolute amount of the payment varies, since a richer

[1] Cf. *The Economist*, Budget Supplement, 10th April, 1937, p. 10.

[2] We are here simply considering who physically gets the money. Whether the rich deserve it in return for financing the war is another question, which opens up the whole dispute whether war should be financed by taxation or borrowing.

man may be presumed to live in a more valuable house, but the ratio, five shillings in the pound, or whatever it may be, does not rise, like the income-tax, with a rise in income. Indeed, to some extent the rate is higher where incomes are lower. For in working-class areas, particularly where unemployment is heavy, the rate is necessarily high; and the average working man probably pays a higher rate per pound than the average member of the propertied classes. In general it is fair to say that the working man pays 2s. or 2s. 6d. a week at least in rates. If his income is £2 a week, in fact, he is paying over 5 per cent of it in local taxation. The Colwyn Committee estimated that a man with an income of £100 a year in 1925–6 paid in total national taxation some 11.9 per cent of his income to the Exchequer. This percentage is certainly not lower to-day. A working man earning £2 a week, therefore, pays something like 17 per cent of his whole income to the State in national and municipal taxation, not including such invisible levies as the wheat levy; and he certainly does not receive more than this, and probably not as much, in return in the form of social benefits.[1] This is a fact which might well be burnt into the memory of everyone who discusses economic, social, or political questions in this country.

Such to-day is the 'redistribution' of incomes effected by our fiscal system. Has it altered in the interests of the working man at any time during the last twenty-five years? The Colwyn Committee made a complete estimate of the percentages of individual incomes paid in national taxation, direct and indirect. If the incidence of indirect taxation is averaged over all consumers, the percentages paid in taxation have changed, according to the Colwyn Committee, as follows:

Income	Income Wholly Earned		Income Half Earned, Half Unearned	
	1913–14	1925–6	1913–14	1925–6
£	per cent	per cent	per cent	per cent
100	5.4	11.9	6.6	13.0
200	4.0	10.2	5.3	11.3
500	4.4	6.2	7.1	8.4
1,000	5.2	11.0	8.3	14.4
2,000	4.9	15.2	8.4	19.3
5,000	6.7	23.2	9.6	29.5
10,000	8.0	31.2	11.8	40.1
50,000	8.4	44.4	13.6	57.7

[1] Cf. for confirmation of this conclusion Colin Clark, *National Income and Outlay*, ch. vi, particularly tables pp. 145 and 146, and Joseph Sykes, *British Public Expenditure*, ch. xiii.

It will be seen that the working man paid in 1925–6 rather more than 10 per cent of his income in national taxation, compared with rather over 5 per cent in 1913–14. It is true that taxation on the rich has, as a percentage, risen rather more steeply. But benefits as well as payments must be considered if a fair estimate of the change in the relative positions of rich and poor in the last twenty-five years is to be made. Mr. Joseph Sykes, in his book, *British Public Expenditure*, has attempted to make such an estimate. After a long and detailed analysis of the various items in the Budget, he expresses the shift of benefits and payments by the following table:

	Percentage allocation of Taxation and Benefits			
	Benefits		Taxation	
	1913 per cent	1921–1 per cent	1913 per cent	1921–31 per cent
Richer	49	51.5	63.2	70.4
Poorer	51	48.5	36.8	29.6
	100	100	100	100

Any such table must not, of course, be taken too literally. It implies some rather arbitrary assumptions about the identity of 'the richer' and the 'poorer', as well as of the incidence of taxation and the destination of benefits. If, however, a complete scepticism is to be adopted about calculations of this kind, it becomes completely illegitimate to maintain that any redistribution of income is achieved by our system of public finance at all. We may reasonably conclude that the redistributive tendencies of the Budget can be traced in broad outline; if this be so, Mr. Sykes's estimate may be taken as substantially correct. His table shows that the proportion of benefits accruing from the Budget to the richer and poorer sections of the community respectively has not appreciably altered since before the war. The incidence of taxation has altered appreciably in favour of the poorer. From this calculation, therefore, an appreciable, but very slight, redistribution of incomes may be inferred.

Since 1931, however, there has been a marked shift in the opposite direction, owing to the increased consumption taxes imposed by the National Government. The percentage of revenue raised in indirect taxation rose from 38.7 in 1931–2 to 46.6 in 1936–7: and the percentage raised in direct taxation fell from 61.3 to 53.4. Most of the net gain achieved by the poorer since 1914 would accordingly seem to have been wiped out in the last five years. This conclusion may be verified by a direct comparison between 1913–14 and 1933–4.[1] Expenditure on education, housing, health, labour, unemployment, and civil pensions, i.e. expenditure in the interests of the poorer, increased by £162,100,000 in this period. But the contribution made by the poorer to indirect taxation (even if we put the proportion as low as two-thirds) increased by £140,000,000. 'The poorer classes of the community have therefore (in the words of *The Economist*) 'received back from the Exchequer approximately as much as their increased contribution. But there is very little sign that the system of taxation has effected any net redistribution of incomes between rich and poor. The very heavy taxation which has been imposed on the rich has not been necessitated by social service expenditure, but by the enormous cost of the war. Similarly the rise in the standard of living of the working class has not been achieved by a net subsidy from the Exchequer.'

Mr. Colin Clark, after a thorough examination of the revenue and expenditure of the State and local authorities, reaches similar conclusions.[2] He shows that the share of national and local taxation borne by the working class was 34.3 per cent in 1913–14, 28.6 per cent in 1925–6, and 33.0 per cent in 1935–6. There is no net change, if the margin of error in the figures is allowed for. The changes in expenditure by both the State and local authorities is summarized by Mr. Colin Clark as follows:

(In £ millions)

	Beneficial to Working Class	Beneficial to Well-to-do
1913–14	75.5	36
1925–6	310	336
1935–6	429	263

'In 1913', Mr. Clark says, 'it appears that the working class contributed more than the cost of the services from which they were the direct beneficiaries, leaving a surplus contribution to general revenue. In 1925 working-class taxation contributed 85 per cent of the cost of these specified beneficial expenditures; in 1935 79 per cent. Between 1925 and 1935 working-class taxation increased by £73,000,000, but expenditure on services beneficial for the working classes increased by £119,000,000. . . .

1 Cf. *The Economist*, Budget Supplement, 13th April 1935, p. 12.
2 *National Income and Outlay*, ch. vi.

'The net effect of taxation and local rates in 1935 can be described as a redistribution of £91,000,000, from the rich to the poor, in the form of services other than those provided for from the proceeds of working-class taxation. The £685,000,000 paid by the rich in indirect and direct taxation provides £263,000,000 of services beneficial to themselves, £91,000,000 for transfer as above, and the whole cost of general administration and of public services not covered by miscellaneous services.'

Mr. Clark's calculations thus suggest that rather more redistribution in favour of the working class is effected by British public finances than the figures given by other authorities. All authorities are agreed, however, that the great bulk of the social services are paid for by the working classes themselves, and that there has been only a very slight shift in their favour even since before the war. The policy of borrowing for war instead of taxing has enriched the rentier and offset most of the gains that would otherwise have accrued from Mr. Lloyd George's Budget and the insurance schemes. The 1937 National Government's policy of borrowing for rearmament is having the same anti-social effect.

Inequality of property, like inequality of incomes, seems to have remained roughly stable during the last twenty-five years. The table given on page 44 shows that in 1911–13 some 12 per cent of all the estates liable to duty accounted for 90 per cent of the total value of the estates; while 88 per cent of the estates accounted for only 10 per cent of the total value. And in 1924–30 some 77 per cent of the estates accounted for 5 per cent of the total value, and some 23 per cent for 95 per cent. There is accordingly very little sign of any redistribution of property, despite the death duties, even among persons who have any.

The broad picture confronting us, therefore, in this country is of a community in which nine-tenths of the individuals receive only 40–50 per cent of the income, just as they did twenty-five years ago. Their average standard of living has risen, though not radically, during the interval. But it has risen mainly as a result of a rise in the total national income, and not of a redistribution achieved either by trade-union pressure or Budgetary changes.

2. *The Distribution of Incomes in the United States*
   This sketch of British industrial society may be supplemented

E   51

by a scrutiny of the distribution of incomes in the United States. Very full statistics are available, thanks to the researches of Messrs. Maurice Leven, Harold G. Moulton, and Clark Warburton, in the volume *America's Capacity to Consume*, published by the Brookings Institution. Here again a preliminary estimate may be given of the distribution of income into three classes of (*a*) wages, (*b*) salaries, (*c*) rent, interest, and profit. It must be remembered, however, that in America the farmers constitute a numerous class whose incomes are more or less on a working-class level, though economically they must be classified as profit rather than wage incomes.

In the years between 1909 and 1915 in America the average share of wages in the national incomes was 38.5 per cent, of salaries 16.5 per cent, and of property incomes, including those of farmers, 45 per cent.[1] About 11 per cent of the total actually went to farmers. The 38.5 per cent received by wage-earners bears a remarkably close resemblance to the 39.5 per cent calculated by Mr. Colin Clark,[2] and still more so to the 38.7 per cent calculated by Dr. Bowley and Sir Josiah Stamp, as the share accruing to the British wage-earners in 1911. By 1921 the share going to wages in the United States had risen to 44.3 per cent, and that going to salaries to 22.5 per cent. In 1929, on the other hand, wages got 42.1 per cent, salaries 21.7 per cent, farmers 6.8 per cent, and all property incomes 28 per cent. The general development of the income structure in the last twenty-five years in the United States may be summarized as follows:

Percentage of total national income accruing to:[3]

	Wages	Salaries	Farmers	Rent, Interest, Profit, etc.
1911	39	18.8	10.9	32.3
1921	44.3	22.5	7.6	32.7
1929	42.1	21.7	6.8	28.1

Just as in Great Britain, the share of wages has not risen

1 *America's Capacity to Consume*, pp. 27–8.
2 *National Income and Outlay*, p. 96.
3 *America's Capacity to Consume*, p. 158. (This table does not include every single income.)

appreciably in the last twenty-five years, though salaries have gained somewhat at the expense of rent, interest, and profit. But this gain is probably as much due to a conversion of entrepreneurs into salaried managers as to a rise of the workers into the salaried class. If the total of farmers' incomes is added to that of rent, interest, and profit, the proportions going to wages, salaries, and property respectively are shown to have been almost the same in the United States and Great Britain in 1929.

The distribution of personal incomes in America in 1929 seems also to have been only slightly less unequal than in Great Britain. All incomes of $2,500 or under in America must be considered working-class incomes. An income of $2,000 a year is described by Messrs. Leven, Moulton, and Warburton as being only 'sufficient to supply basic necessities'. Out of a total of 49,041,000 incomes in 1929 in America, some 43,363,000, according to Messrs. Leven, Moulton, and Warburton, were below the $2,500 level. Rather over six out of seven persons in America, therefore, have working-class incomes, compared with nine out of ten in England. If the income distribution is expressed in terms of families instead of individuals, the following inferences can be made: 'About 21 per cent of the families received (in 1929) only 4.5 per cent of the income. The 11,653,000 families with incomes of less than $1,500 received a total of about $10,000,000,000. At the other extreme, the 36,000 families having incomes in excess of $75,000 possessed an aggregate income of $9,800,000,000. Thus it appears that 0.1 per cent of the families at the top received practically as much as 42 per cent of the families at the bottom of the scale.'[1] In the United States in fact, as in Great Britain, the inequality of incomes is enormous; and there is no tendency for it to diminish.

Such is the society which our modern capitalism with its freedom to buy and sell, its freedom to acquire property, and its freedom to bequeath it, has created before our eyes. It is one in which nine-tenths of the individuals, and perhaps six-sevenths of the families receive an income little more than 'sufficient to supply the basic necessities of life'. It is one in which some nine-tenths do all the manual work in the community for less than half of the available income; in which all but a fraction of the remaining tenth do all the brain work for 25 per cent of the

[1] *America's Capacity to Consume*, p. 56.

income; and in which less than one-fiftieth of the community receive the remaining 30 per cent of the income for doing, in most cases, no work at all. In Great Britain to-day about eighty-nine out of every hundred persons are members of the working classes earning less than £5 a week. Ten more earn middle-class and professional incomes of from £250 to £1,000 a year. And one person in every hundred receives, but in many cases does not earn, an income of over £1,000 a year. Nor is the distribution becoming more even with the progress of time; the gradual rise in the income of the workers is almost entirely due to a rise in the national total.

These are the facts. They are not consistent either with the communist view that society consists of almost universal destitution, tempered by occasional affluence; nor with the conservative view that it consists of general contentment tempered by occasional poverty. The truth is that there is in this country and the United States some, but not much, destitution, a great deal of poverty, and a wholly overwhelming inequality. These are the two countries in which modern capitalism has had its greatest and most glorious success, and in which democratic institutions have begun to mitigate the inequality of wealth. In many other countries of the world, in Germany, Italy, Spain, Central Europe, and Japan, both the poverty and the inequality are unquestionably greater.

The poverty existing to-day, we may admit, is mild compared with what it has been in most ages of the past. But it is nevertheless poverty for all that. And the inequality to-day is glaring, extreme, and, to all with a sense of humanity, intolerable. It is not tolerable that nine-tenths of a civilized community should be forced to do virtually all the work for only half the income.

PART II
THE CAPITALIST SYSTEM

CHAPTER V

SOME CONFUSIONS

To call the poverty and inequality that exist extreme is one thing; to call them intolerable is another. For they may be inevitable. Presumably this is what apologists for the existing system would contend. They would admit the poverty and inequality before their eyes, but contend that they were necessary evils. If this is true, we must of course accept it; but we must only do so if its truth is absolutely demonstrable. The onus of proof is plainly on those who maintain that evils are necessary.

Only a critical examination of the present social and economic system can decide whether the evils of poverty and inequality are in fact necessary or not. It has to be discovered how they arose and how, if at all, they can be abolished or mitigated. Certain immediate difficulties, however, confront anyone who tries to make such an examination. For the modern economic system is not a simple mechanism which one can inspect, as one would inspect a factory, by seeing each department in turn until there is none left to see. Unfortunately it is a thing of many aspects, and each is, as it were, an aspect of the whole; so that one can only begin to understand the whole when one has inspected each aspect separately and finally examined how each interacts with the other.

In the first place it is important to be clear about what one means by 'capitalism'. In this book it is taken to mean a system of free exchange in which the accumulation, ownership, and inheritance of property are included as a necessary part of such free exchange. Freedom of prices and freedom of ownership and inheritance are really implications of the central idea of free exchange. Logically it would be possible to retain free prices for commodities and services and abolish private ownership of property. Indeed, to some extent this is the desirable line of advance. Historically, however, free exchange has been associated with private ownership; and those who advocate one are apt to advocate the other. In criticizing the capitalist system, therefore, we shall take it to imply not merely free exchange but private ownership and inheritance of property.

There are three major confusions into which the unwary critic of capitalism tends to fall if he looks at the whole in only one of its several aspects. There is first the confusion between the system in the concrete and the system in the abstract; secondly, the confusion between the system when it is working properly, and when it is not working properly; and thirdly the confusion between the system as an economic and as a monetary mechanism. The central difficulty arises from the fact that every single unit in the whole—the factory or farm or worker—has at once a concrete, an abstract, and a monetary aspect; and each at any given moment is either functioning, or not functioning, as, according to the laws of the system, it should.

Perhaps the distinction between the concrete and abstract aspects of the economic system is the most confusing. In the concrete it consists of the objects we see before our eyes; the mills, mines, railways, ships, offices, coins, company directors, and so forth. But to observe and count all these is not to understand the system. We may watch a train-load of coal being hauled along the line from South Wales to London; but that does not tell us why the colliery manager decided to dispatch that amount of coal in that direction, nor why the railway decided to carry it rather than something else. The position of someone studying the economic system is, from this point of view, rather like that of someone watching a war from the air. Such an observer would mark every movement of troops, munitions, and supplies. But if he knew nothing of the mind of the generals, he could not tell why at any moment one body of troops was advancing or retiring. Similarly the mere spectacle and enumeration of the movements of commodities and men tells us little about the working of the economic system. Nevertheless it is essential to have a clear picture of all these concrete movements. The trouble is that economists usually assume their readers to have such a concrete picture, and proceed at once to analyse underlying principles; while economic historians merely describe changes in the concrete mechanism without ever describing that mechanism as a general whole. As a result the plain man seldom gets a comprehensive picture of the concrete mechanism whose principles or history he is supposed to be investigating. The best and most logical way out of this difficulty seems to be first to describe the economic system in the concrete, and secondly to analyse the principles of its working.

The second distinction between the system as it is when it is working, and as it is when it is not working, seems a simple one. But it is constantly ignored. Some may argue that, since the system plainly works very imperfectly most of the time, it is not worth arguing what would happen if for once it worked perfectly. This, however, is a great mistake. For it is essential to realize that some of the evils apparent before our eyes might still exist even if the system was made to work perfectly; while others might disappear. We have to distinguish very carefully between these two sorts of evils. And the best way to do so is first to show how the mechanism would work if it worked properly, and then to see which of the evils would nevertheless remain. It would be both unfair and unwise to discard one car in favour of another simply because it had run out of petrol.

The economic and monetary aspects of the system can only be clearly differentiated as the nature of the whole becomes apparent. But the distinction between them is, perhaps for practical purposes, the most important of the three. Each single incident in the system—the buying of a bar of chocolate by a child—has an economic and monetary aspect, and the concrete incident is only explicable as the effect of two causes working as it were on different planes: rather as every human act is perhaps the consequence of a mechanical and a rational set of causes. It follows that any given concrete fault in the system may have had a monetary or an economic cause, or both. And it is the attribution of monetary evils to economic causes, and economic evils to monetary causes, that has perhaps caused more confusion than anything else in contemporary economic discussion. Yet it is plainly foolish to tamper with the engine of a car when it has merely run out of petrol; or alternatively to flood the carburetter when the engine has broken down. What we have to do, therefore, is to see how the economic mechanism would work when the monetary mechanism was working perfectly, and then to discover how it is that the monetary system goes wrong.

SOME CONFUSIONS

In the pages that follow an attempt is accordingly made first of all to describe the economic system in the concrete; then to analyse the abstract principles of its working: then to see what evils would still remain if both it and the monetary mechanism worked perfectly: and lastly to trace the causes and effects of purely monetary failures.

CHAPTER VI

WORKER, CAPITALIST, AND ENTREPRENEUR

Any description of the existing economic system must take for granted the context of institutions, laws, and customs which constitute it. That context can and does change, and this should be remembered throughout every stage in the description of the system. But on the whole it seems best to describe the system first and then consider how far its essential features are inevitable and how far merely accidental. Similarly we must for the moment take the existence of money for granted. But we need only take it for granted as being what it is popularly supposed to be: something which facilitates and does not interfere with the working of the economic system as a whole. The real nature and significance of money can be investigated later.

The existing or capitalist economic system in the concrete consists of a large number of producing units and consuming units. Each producing or consuming unit is complete and distinct in itself; but it is related directly or indirectly to a number of other units. Moreover, though as producer or consumer each unit is complete, it may be producer and consumer at once; or alternatively the unit as producer may contain as a part of it, or be part of, consuming units. Normally, in fact, the various individuals who form part of the producing units are in themselves consuming units.

The consuming unit may be an individual; but it is more usually the family. In comparatively exceptional cases there may of course be larger consuming units; such as a royal household, or an army. But in all non-communist communities the family normally predominates. Everybody knows how the economics of the family work in practice. One or two members of the family earn money by virtue of the services they perform as members of a productive unit. Except in return for services no money will be received; though the 'services' performed, as we shall see, are not always work. The total income is then spent in the supposed interests of the family as a whole. The earning, or some other, single member of the family normally decides how much shall be spent on which needs of each individual member; and the making of this decision is by derivation the original meaning of the words 'economy' and 'economics'. It is not easy, however, to say on what principle such decisions are made. They are certainly not normally made on the principle of an individual taking as much as possible for himself and leaving the rest for other people. In what way, in fact, is it decided how much of the loaf of bread on the table each member of the family may have? Partly, presumably, by habit, and partly by what is the criterion of fairness. For it is not usually decided by the only other alternative—force. At any rate, when such decisions have been made, the money is spent in due proportion on the various goods and services which are offered for sale in the shops and elsewhere. The spenders of family income naturally find these goods and services already offered at certain prices independently of anything they themselves can do; yet it is ultimately the decisions of such people that determine almost entirely the demand for goods and services as a whole.

The consuming unit is thus linked in two ways with the producing units. First it receives a money income for the services one or more of its members perform to a producing unit; and secondly it spends its money income on the goods which those units offer for sale. The manner in which the money passes from income to expenditure within the consuming unit is simple and known to everyone. Much less simple is the link within the producing unit between the money received for the sale of goods and the money paid out to the individual producers. But it is this link which completes the whole circuit.

1. Work and Wages

The most obvious member of a producing unit (such as a mine or factory) is the worker earning a wage. He performs a service, manual or otherwise, and receives, normally at the end of a week, a payment supposed to be proportionate to the service he has performed. The principle is the same whether the payment is called a wage, salary, or fee, and whether the work done is manual, intellectual, administrative, or otherwise.

In the average medium-sized firm there are an enormous number of separate jobs to be done; and an almost equally enormous number of different salaries paid for them. No hard and fast distinction exists in principle or practice between a wage and a salary; though for convenience we may call anything which is paid weekly a wage. The general manager and even the director of the firm, whether or not we consider them under-worked or over-remunerated, must be considered in the essential sense wage-earners or salary-earners if they do a specific job for a definite wage or salary. In general the terms wage-earner and worker must be taken to have this wider meaning.

It is important to realize exactly what is meant by work. For what is a wage paid under conditions of free exchange? Not for so much effort, or for so much time, or so much moral desert. A wage is not a 'reward' in the same sense as the marks which a schoolboy receives for good behaviour. It is paid to induce someone to perform a certain function. A man receives a wage for driving a bus from Eastbourne to London, or for hewing so much coal; not for exerting so much effort, or giving so much time. For if he can drive the bus with less effort, or hew the coal in less time, he will receive the same wage as before. It is consequently neither 'labour-time' nor foot-pounds of energy which wages buy. It is true that a very great number of workers are paid by the shift or week or year. But this is merely because in many cases the unit of time is the most convenient way of measuring the real service performed. A postman or agricultural labourer or engine driver must, to all intents and purposes, perform a day's work in a day. In cases where this is not so, such as a coal-hewer, piece-rates, which are a direct method of paying according to the service performed, tend to spring up and supplement ordinary time rates. Throughout the whole system a persistent attempt is always being made to substitute for the clumsy calculus of hours and weeks some more exact criterion of the actual service performed. The essential thing is always the service or work, or perhaps more accurately 'job', that is done; for what matters to those in the bus is that it should be driven to Eastbourne. The 'job' involved in any piece of work is the performance of some function necessary to the productive system.

2. *Capital and Interest*

Are there any such functions which do not involve work? It is plain that the workers and managers are not the only component parts of the factory. There are the buildings themselves and the machines; and there are also the stockholders, with whose assistance the buildings and machinery were originally bought. To these stockholders periodical payments are made just as they are to the wage-earners. Why are the stockholders thus paid, and for what service, if any? They do not, in any sense of the word, work or perform any job. They stay at home, and, so far as the factory in question is concerned, do nothing; though they may of course work at something else. They are simply paid because they once lent the money with which the machinery was bought and have not yet been paid back.

The questions why they are paid as much as they are, and whether they ought to be paid at all, are quite different from the question what exactly the service is, if any, for which they are in fact paid. And it is this latter question which is at the moment being considered. There is at any rate no doubt about what actually happens. When a man or group of men wish to build a factory, or produce something, and cannot afford to buy the machinery themselves, they borrow money from other people and promise to pay them so much a year out of the proceeds of the sale of the factory's products. Why do they have to borrow? Because money accruing from the sale of these products will only be realized over a period of years. Machinery and buildings last a long time: and throughout that time they enable goods to be produced. And why are some people ready to lend the money and others not? Those who decline to lend do so because they wish, or are compelled, to spend such money as they have immediately. Those who agree to lend do so because they prefer to wait a little, whether in order to have a little more to spend later on, or for some other reason. For they are, of course, at any moment still owed the sum originally lent, although for many years they have received annual payments because of it. They lend the money, in fact, because they are willing to defer spending it in return for these annual payments. Inspired by a desire partly for a perpetual income and partly for the security implied in the existence of savings, their essential motive is a wish to wait before consuming, just as the essential feature of the

64

machinery which is bought with their money is that it goes on performing its function over a period of years.

This gives us a hint of what the service is that the lenders or stockholders perform. But it needs to be analysed further in a simple case if its real nature is to be fully and clearly grasped. Suppose an agricultural labourer, with no other source of income than his weekly wage, has a small piece of waste land attached to his cottage which he wishes to equip as a chicken-run in order to produce eggs. He cannot pay anyone else to do the necessary work, and he cannot do it all at once himself, since he would then lose his whole income. He might, however, agree with his employer to take, say, one day off each week for a year, at the cost of a certain deduction from his wages. He would then work on this one day a week at equipping his piece of land; but since he would be working one day less for his employer, he would actually be working altogether as much as before. He would be earning and consuming less, however, by the amount of the wages sacrificed, that is to say, the payment for one day's work a week. If one supposes that he had to buy wire-netting, wood, etc., for his chicken-run, he would have to sacrifice a further small part of his income. In the second year, i.e. the year in which he constructs the chicken-run, he would be working as much, but consuming less, than in the first year, i.e. the year before, when he was merely working for his employer and earning a normal wage.

At the end of the second year the chicken-run is completed and the eggs begin to be sold. Since the price for which they can be sold is slightly greater than the cost of chicken food, etc., the labourer obtains a money income from the sale of them. Since, however, he no longer has to work at equipping the chicken-run—we may suppose that feeding the chickens and collecting the eggs takes only a negligible amount of time—he can now work a full week for his employer once again. In the third year, therefore, he earns not merely more than in the second year, but actually more than in the first. This, of course, was the object of undertaking the whole operation. What has happened is this. Throughout all three years he has done the same amount of work; but the volume of his consumption has changed twice. In the second year he has deliberately refrained from consuming as much as in the first year, in order that in the third year he may consume more. He has 'waited' a year, in fact, to consume

65

a part of his income in order that his consumption may be permanently increased. And the product of his year's labour on the chicken-run has become embodied, as it were, in the wire-netting, sheds, etc., which enable eggs to be produced at a price greater than the mere cost of the chicken food. The income that accrues to him from this margin is the result both of his hitherto unrewarded day's work a week during the second year, *and* of his waiting to consume.

It is not merely the product of his work; for he is now the owner of the chicken-run as well. Supposing during the second year he had not constructed the chicken-run but had gone on working for his employer. He would have done just as much work as in fact he did during the second year, and he would afterwards, in the third year, have received the same income for his work. But he would not have received the additional income from selling eggs. It was therefore as a result, not merely of working, but of waiting to consume, that he has obtained the extra income. Suppose again that he had not decided himself to equip the chicken-run, but that a third person had induced him to do so by offering to supply the money necessary to make up for the loss of one day's wages a week. The third person would naturally only thus lend the money if he was himself to receive the money subsequently received by the sale of the eggs. In this case the labourer would both work and earn the same amount in the first, second, and third years. He would not wait to consume in the second year, and he would not find his income increased in the third year over and above what it had been in the first year. The lender, however, would have himself sacrificed what he could have bought with the money; and he would also obtain in the third year new income accruing from the sale of the eggs.

This new income is the result of the postponement of consumption; and it goes on just as long as the consumption is postponed. If the equipment of the chicken-run is pulled down and sold, or used for firewood, i.e. consumed, the extra income will cease at once.

These conclusions are important. For if they are correct, the Marxist theories of value, capital, and profits must be rejected as in principle untrue. Quite apart from work and wages, there are, it appears, at least four distinct, but closely related, realities involved in the full process of the construction of the chicken-run.

66

There is the act of waiting for consumption, which we may in general call 'waiting'. There is secondly the fund of time or labour or money, whichever it may be, which is made available by this waiting. In the case where the labourer cut down his consumption, this fund took the form of the one day a week made available for building the chicken-run. In the case where the money was lent by a third person, it took the form of this money, or, more accurately, of the commodities which might have been consumed by the lender if he had not lent the money, but in fact were consumed by the labourer. This fund we may call 'savings'. Savings are thus fundamentally the consumable goods or services made available by an act of waiting; though ordinarily we think of them as the money by means of which those goods and services are transferred from one person to another. In the normal case, of course, fewer consumable goods are produced; for the saver consumes less and the worker as much as before; so that the worker can produce capital goods instead of consumable goods. Thirdly there are the wire-netting, sheds, equipment, etc., which were built as a result of the act of waiting, and which subsequently produce the extra income that constitutes its 'reward'. Goods of this kind, the nature of which must presently be further analysed, may properly be called 'capital'. Fourthly there is the extra income resulting from the act of waiting and the creation of capital; and this may be called 'interest'. And finally there is of course the lender or 'capitalist', who performs the act of waiting, supplies the savings, owns the capital, and receives the interest.

Waiting, saving, capital, and interest are fundamental; in the sense that they must exist in some form or another in every economic system. For it is an immutable fact that certain things take a long period of time to be 'consumed'—or to yield their service, whatever it may be. In all communities—capitalist, communist, or feudal—houses, furniture, motor-cars, locomotives, ships, bridges, machinery, and a host of other things are durable goods. They last for years and are not fully consumed for a very long time after they are produced. Since a long time elapses between the performance of the work necessary to produce them and the full yield of the resulting income, somebody has to postpone a part of his consumption in order that they may be produced. If a hundred men build a house instead of growing potatoes, somebody has to go without the potatoes while the house is being built. And when the house has been built, somebody must refrain from the act of consumption which would take place if it were pulled down and used for firewood. The existence of durable goods, and the possibility of postponing consumption, are thus at once fundamental and complementary in any economic system whatever.

All 'durable' goods, i.e. those which take a long time to consume, are not, it should be observed, 'producers' goods'. Houses, motor-cars, and furniture are 'consumers' goods'. They are consumed, and are not used for the production of something else. Most 'producers' goods', on the other hand, are durable goods: factories, machinery, rolling stock, etc. And it is for this reason that we come to think of 'capital' and producers' goods as being the same thing. Actually, however, it is best to use the word 'capital' as synonymous with 'durable goods'; though it is not, of course, even true to say that all producers' goods are durable. Raw materials, wool, cotton, grain, are producers' goods, but are not in the full sense durable. In reality the distinction between durable and non-durable goods is more fundamental than that between producers' and consumers' goods. For durable consumers' goods, just like durable producers' goods, yield a service over a period of years. Only the 'service' happens to be consumed direct; whereas in the case of a durable producers' good, the service is normally to produce other goods. The distinction between producers' and consumers' goods may often become very thin. A house, a durable consumers' goods, performs the service of sheltering its inmates: and for this a rent is paid. A train, which would normally be thought of as a durable producers' goods, performs the service of carrying passengers; and for this a fare is paid. The distinction here is merely that a railway company is usually conceived as 'producing transport', while a landlord is not conceived as 'producing shelter'.

Nevertheless, for the practical purposes of the argument that follows, durable producers' goods are of the greatest importance. It so happens that most of the things which the human race now consumes require machinery and plant of some kind for their production; and this machinery and plant are in practically all cases durable. In order, therefore, that there may be any general increase in the world's production and consumption, the whole process—usually called investment—of waiting, saving, and the creation of capital has to occur. This is as true of the Soviet Five-Year Plan, which involved the postponement of consumption on an enormous scale, as of the more familiar process of investment in a capitalist country.

The existence of the next most important element in the factory after the workers, is thus explained. Corresponding to the worker and his wage there is the plant and the interest payments. The plant is necessary for the production of goods; and since the plant is durable, interest has to be paid to the capitalist to induce him to spread his consumption of the income over a long period of years. Interest is thus a payment for an indispensable 'service', if we mean by a service a definite economic function without which the production of goods cannot continue. This is not, of course, to justify the payment of interest; it is merely to establish the fact that interest is not a 'surplus' or free gift, but a payment necessary to evoke an indispensable economic activity entirely distinct from work. May it not still be true, however, that if there were no interest, there would still be saving? It is certain that some people would save if there were no interest; and it is possible—though improbable—that their savings might exceed the 'dissavings' of those who would consume their capital. This does not in itself, however, make the relations between interest and saving in principle different from those between wages and work. For even if there were no wages, *some* people would unquestionably work. They would work because they disliked doing nothing, and not for wages; just as some savers will save for the sake of security, and not for the interest.[1] It is reasonable, therefore, to describe capital or 'waiting' as a 'factor of production' additional to work, and interest as a 'cost' additional to wages.

The factory contains other factors of production, however, besides capital and labour; and these others are more difficult to distinguish. They may perhaps most easily be identified by examining the various other payments made by the factory and inquiring why these are made. There are certain payments which appear at first sight to be similar to, or closely connected with, capital and interest. Certain sums are paid annually by the factory under the heading of 'depreciation' and 'obsolescence'.

[1] See pages 71 and 190–192.

These are held in reserve for a period of years, and subsequently spent in one lump sum on buying new plant. They are not, however, of the nature of interest. For interest must be paid to induce the lender simply to refrain from consuming the resources he lends. It is implied that the resources themselves remain: their 'capital' value does not substantially change. If the plant, however, were not prevented from becoming rusty or obsolete, the resources lent would themselves disappear. The payments made for depreciation and obsolescence are consequently not really different in principle from these made for buying oil for the machinery, or raw materials in general. They differ only in so far as there is an element of waiting involved, both because the depreciation reserves may be accumulated over a period of years, and because the new machinery also yields its income over a period of time. In general, however, we may think of payments for depreciation and obsolescence as simple and straightforward, like payments for raw materials.[1]

3. *Land and Rent*

The factory also pays a rent for the land on which it is built; and if it is a coal-mining company it pays a 'royalty' for the right to mine a certain area of coal. It has long been debated whether there is any fundamental distinction between land and capital and rent and interest; and a variety of conflicting opinions have been held. There is at least one distinction which, whether or not fundamental, certainly seems clear. 'Land'—which to the economist means all natural resources, etc.—cannot normally be consumed or produced in the same sense as capital. This is not entirely true, as has often been pointed out. The draining of the Zuider Zee has 'produced land' in a very literal sense; and it is possible for drought and dust-storms equally literally to destroy land. One may reply to this that the element in the land due to irrigation schemes or any other human agency is really capital and that destruction of land by natural forces is merely an alteration of the absolute amount actually existing, and not of the fact that that amount is absolute. Moreover, capital such as railway cuttings, tunnels, etc., can no more be 'consumed' or used for other purposes than the land itself.

[1] Though from the monetary point of view there is an important distinction. See part III, ch. xvii.

This distinction, it then appears, begins to wear thin on analysis. Nevertheless there appear to be two fundamental questions which can be asked about producers' durable goods: (*a*) Are they producible? (*b*) Are they destructible? Land is usually neither the one nor the other. Minerals are destructible, but not producible. Ordinary plant and machinery are both producible and destructible. And tunnels, cuttings, etc., are producible but not destructible (i.e. do not wear out). In so far as land is not produced, it does not require saving or the diversion of goods from consumption for its creation. There is no rate of interest, therefore, to be paid in order to bridge over the period in which it is brought into existence. It is there already. And, in so far as it is not consumable, no rate of interest has to be paid to induce people not to consume it. The fencing round a field can be pulled down and used for firewood; the plough can be sold for scrap iron;[1] and the horses can be eaten. But the land cannot be carted away and consumed once and for all. It is no doubt true of some kinds of capital (such as cuttings and tunnels) that when they are once in existence they cannot be consumed. In this respect they certainly resemble land. The true distinction, therefore, seems to be not between 'land' and 'capital', but between those durable producers' goods which can be dismantled and consumed and those which cannot. And since a very large amount of the world's capital consists of either wood or iron, both of which can be consumed, it is not surprising that capital has come to be equated with what might be called consumable producers' durable goods.

What light does this distinction throw on the relation of rent and interest? Interest on capital is paid to induce the owner to continue waiting for the income yielded by the capital over a period of years rather than to dismantle it and consume it on the spot. It may be that every single saver would not cease to 'wait' if the rate of interest vanished; but taking the community as a whole, we must admit that interest is necessary to keep at any rate the major part of the existing capital in being.[2] But in

---

[1] It is true that there would not be much demand for iron if all the capital in the country was being dismantled and consumed. Nevertheless it might still be scarce. Motor-cars, it should be remembered are consumers' goods and not very durable ones.

[2] Mr. Keynes has lately denied this: it is further discussed on pages 190-2.

the case of land, or that part of the capital which cannot be consumed, interest cannot have to be paid for exactly this reason. For since it is physically impossible to consume the land, it is not necessary to pay interest to prevent it being consumed.

Yet rent is paid for the use of land; and it bears a superficial resemblance to interest on capital. It is reckoned annually and as a ratio to the market value of the land. This is of course because the owner of the land (or non-consumable capital) has to receive the income from it over a period of years. It is clear then why the individual receives a rent for land, but less clear why it is necessary to the existence of the community as a whole that it should be paid. If interest ceased to be paid, and nobody was willing to postpone consumption, in a community in which there was capital but no land, the capital would be consumed. But if nobody was willing to wait in a community in which there was land, but no capital, the land would not be consumed, because it could not be. On the face of it, therefore, it may appear that rent does not represent a distinct economic service in the same way as interest; that rent is consequently in a sense a 'surplus'; and that there is some truth in the contention of Henry George and his followers that interest is a socially necessary payment, while rent is not.

But there is obviously something wrong with this view. For in any capitalist community it is possible for anyone with savings to hold property in the form of capital or land, or both, or to change alternatively from one to the other. Now it is surely absurd to argue that a man who invests £100,000 in securities for one year and receives interest is performing some necessary economic service, while when he invests it in land next year and receives rent he is for some reason performing no necessary economic service. What is the solution to this difficulty? Perhaps it can best be answered by asking the following two questions: first, what would happen in a community in which everyone suddenly became unwilling to postpone consumption; and secondly what would happen if they merely became unwilling to hold land? In the first case, of course, capital would be consumed and land would go out of cultivation. For nobody would be willing either to hold land or advance the working capital—the labourers' wages, seed, etc.—necessary to cultivate it. The seed potatoes would be consumed and six months later there would be no potatoes. It would only be possible to gather the fruit which grew of its own accord.

It is more difficult to see what would happen if people continued to save but became unwilling to hold land. Indeed, it appears on reflection that no such thing could possibly happen. Supposing no private person would any longer hold any land, the landowners would find its value had fallen to zero. If it fell to zero, however, and no rent had to be paid for it, but it was still profitable to farm it, it would have to be decided by force who should farm it. It is clear, then, that for practical reasons some method of rationing land, whether rent or not, has to be discovered. In the case which we are considering, however, either there would have to be a law against holding land—in which case the State would have to decide arbitrarily who should have the right to farm how much—or else people would in fact be willing to hold it. For since it still remained profitable to farm it, farmers would be willing to pay a rent; and when the capital value of the land fell to a certain level the holders of securities would decide to buy it from the landowners. In effect, the landowners, that is to say, would have decided to cease postponing consumption, and the function of doing so would have been shifted to the security-holders. Supposing the security-holders had sold their securities to buy the land, and no net increase in saving had occurred elsewhere, the willingness to 'wait' of the community as a whole would have decreased, the rate of interest would have risen, and some capital not profitable at the new rate of interest would be consumed.

It appears clear, therefore, that if all the landowners refused to postpone consumption any longer, some capital in the community would immediately be consumed, although the consumption of the land itself is physically impossible. The fact is that in a community in which land and capital exist there is a certain amount of income which has to be waited for if capital is not to be consumed. This income, however, includes both the income from the land and the income from the capital. Of course, if the community as a whole owned both the land and capital, the waiting would be performed by the community as a whole. Under the system of private ownership and contract, however, the task of waiting may be assumed by a particular group of individuals. Because they are willing to wait there is more total capital, and the income and consumption of the community is therefore greater, than otherwise would be the case. It is for this function that interest and rent are paid; though here again it must not be assumed that there would be no waiting if there were no rent or interest, or even that any fall in rent and interest must reduce the amount of waiting.

In general, therefore, at any given moment, in a fully developed capitalist community, there seems little sense in distinguishing between the functions for which rent and interest are paid. Nevertheless, in origin, so to speak, there does seem to be a distinction. How have men come to own land? If they inherit it, the process is of course the same, *mutatis mutandis*, as any other form of inheritance. If, on the other hand, a man saves out of his income and buys land, he is taking over from the community as a whole the burden of waiting and enabling the rest of the community to consume more. Rent, in fact, if it does not prevent the destruction of land, at least decides *who* shall wait for its proceeds. In the first place, however, the decision who shall own land must necessarily be an arbitrary one and not dependent on the performance of any economic service. To bring capital into existence, saving is necessary, as we saw in the instance of the chicken-run; and interest is accordingly paid to the owner of the capital whose saving brought it into existence. To bring land into existence, however, no saving is necessary;[1] and it only has to be owned for the simple practical reason that if nobody owns it there will be chaos. When the conquering feudal lord or king confers the ownership of the newly won land on a group of favoured individuals, those individuals do not receive it as a reward for postponing the consumption of their income. For they may have no income to consume. They cannot sell the land, because there is as yet no one with savings to buy it. They get the land, therefore, because, fundamentally, somebody must own it in order that violence may be prevented. The rent they receive is simply a reward for their services in preserving law and order; and the feudal contract thus appears as deeply rooted in the nature of things. But of course in so far as the service of preserving order is inherent in the mere owner-

[1] As Mrs. Joan Robinson says (*Economics of Imperfect Competition*, p. 102); 'It follows from the definition of free gifts of nature that they are there in any case, and do not require to be paid in order to exist.'

ship of land, the receipt of it is merely the result of the original arbitrary free gift. If the State were strong enough, in the first instance, to preserve law and order, there would be no reason why it should not own all the land from the start. Nevertheless, after the first free gift has been made, and land has come to be bought and sold and exchanged for capital, its ownership ceases to be a function economically distinguishable from the ownership of capital, and rent ceases to be significantly distinguishable from interest.

There is thus a germ of truth in the distinction between land and capital and rent and interest, and even in the confused contentions of Henry George's followers. This germ of truth, however, is dependent on the 'powers of the soil', as Ricardo called them, being 'original' rather than on their being 'indestructible'. When land has been inherited and bought and sold it is not in any significant sense, although 'indestructible', distinguishable from capital; and rent and interest must then be regarded as payments for waiting in an indistinguishable sense.

There are, however, three different kinds of waiting or saving, or rather three ways in which saving can be used, which cut across the above distinction between rent and interest. First it is necessary, in order that existing capital may be maintained in being, that the community refrain from dismantling and consuming it. This activity of refraining from consuming one's capital is more naturally described as waiting than saving, since it does not involve any diminution of consumption or the expenditure of less than one's income. It merely involves the decision not to increase consumption. In a sense, however, it may be described as 'old saving'. Secondly there is the amount of actual new saving, i.e. actual expenditure by the community of less than its current income, which is necessary to keep the productive system working. This new saving is of two kinds. One is necessary for 'depreciation', i.e. to replace the existing fixed capital as it wears out; and the other to supply the 'working capital'[1] necessary to bridge over the gap between the beginning and end

[1] It may be thought that the inclusion of this as saving involves an odd definition of income. But it is nevertheless true that if goods are to spend some time in the productive process someone must refrain from consuming what could have been consumed if other goods had been produced for immediate consumption.

of the production period,[1] i.e. to pay wages and buy raw materials before the sale of the product. It is important to realize that both these functions require a large volume of saving out of current income. Thirdly there is new saving in the ordinary familiar sense; that is, saving over and above what is necessary to preserve the existing capital and keep it working. It is with this third kind of saving, which must of course be made out of income, that new capital is bought and the productive equipment of the community actually increased.

This brief and necessarily superficial account of capital and land and interest and rent may, it is hoped, make clear the general nature of the next two kinds of 'factors of production', after the wage-earners, to whom payments are made in the typical factory. We accordingly have two broad classes of productive service, work and saving, to which the payment of wages on the one hand, and rent or interest on the other, correspond. There is not much difficulty in distinguishing the rent of land in actual fact, though it is of course the payment made for the use of land and not payment made for the use of the factory (supposing it to be rented). Rent, in its popular sense, means not pure economic rent as defined above, but any payment made for the use of something, e.g. a house, over a period of time. This of course covers not merely rent of land, but the cost of the house, interest, depreciation, etc. Normally, however, the owners of a factory would only pay rent for land. Pure interest is represented, in the case of the factory, by the payments made to holders of debentures and all securities yielding a fixed return.

4. Enterprise and Profit

These payments in wages, salaries, depreciation, rent, and interest, exhaust the main categories of what would ordinarily be called 'cost' payments. Over and above this, however, there is something usually called 'profit' which goes in the case of a personal business to the owner, or in the case of a joint-stock company to the ordinary shareholders. What is profit? How is it paid? And how is it related to costs? The simplest answer to

[1] The phrase is used in its ordinary popular sense of the period of production of a consumable commodity between acquisition of the raw material and its final sale, not in the peculiar sense used by the followers of Böhm-Bawerk.

the question what is profit is to say that it is what remains over after all costs have been paid. It is the surplus of selling price over costs. Now this does not necessarily mean that there is no essential economic service to which it corresponds. This is clear enough in the case of a small one-man business. The hawker who buys fruit in Covent Garden, wheels it in a barrow to a pitch which he rents in the Strand, and sells the fruit, receives the surplus of sales over costs obviously as a payment for his very arduous services. In the most elementary case, therefore, profit clearly includes the wage of the organizer of the business. In the fully developed joint-stock company, however, the general manager, and even the directors and chairman, are paid a fixed salary as a remuneration for their services. Yet the business may show a profit after these fixed payments have been made. It is clear then that the wages of management and organization are not profit in the proper sense. Indeed, they are not distinguishable in any fundamental economic sense from ordinary wages and salaries. The president of the London, Midland & Scottish Railway, in earning a fixed salary, is receiving remuneration for work done in exactly the same way as any employee of the company. It is true that the president gets more than the engine driver. But so does the engine driver get more than the porter. The distinction is one of degree and not of kind.

If the wages of management are thus in principle comparable with any other wage, and are, in ordinary language, a 'cost', profit must clearly be something different. It follows from the definition of profit as the excess of selling price over costs that profit is something that varies from one period to another. In any community which is subject to the vagaries of nature, or to the working of free consumers' choice, or to both, the total proceeds of selling a commodity are bound to vary. But since costs are to a more or less degree fixed, the remainder is bound to vary also. The recipients of profit, therefore, unlike the recipients of wages, rent, and interest, do not know what their income is going to be from one year to the next. Indeed, they do not know if they will receive any income at all. This affords a clue to the real nature of pure profit. Since most men would prefer a secure fixed income to a slightly larger fluctuating one, and since in the nature of things the payment to somebody has to vary, it follows that a special premium has to be paid to those people who contract to receive an income which is unfixed and is calculated as a remainder after all the fixed incomes have been paid. Somebody, that is to say, must bear the inevitable risk or uncertainty in order that the other incomes may be reasonably secure. Profit, accurately defined, therefore, is the payment necessary to induce people to bear risk or uncertainty.

If greater accuracy is desired, one may distinguish that particular kind of risk which can, in the large, be predicted. The total number of fires which will occur in a whole country in a year is known with fair exactness, although nobody knows precisely where they will occur. In this case, if everybody makes a small payment to a central fund, it is possible for all the people who actually lose their property through fire to be fully indemnified and for the fund to remain solvent. If this is done, since everyone individually knows that they will receive the indemnity payment, nobody bears any risk; for the insurance company, by 'pooling' the risks, has in fact destroyed them. The premium paid to the insurance company is not therefore a payment to somebody for bearing uncertainty or risk but a payment to somebody for destroying them. Risk which can thus be pooled and so destroyed may perhaps be best called 'insurable risk'.

'Insurable risk' in this sense cannot give rise to profit. For since risk is destroyed, it cannot be borne; instead it is insured against and the insurance premium is a fixed-cost payment, not a profit. There is another sort of risk, however, which cannot be pooled. Nobody can predict how the tastes of the public will change, how much exactly it will cost to produce a commodity, what the price of other commodities will be, and so forth. This non-insurable risk may be called risk proper, as opposed to insurable risk. It is risk in this sense, and its inherence in the nature of things, which makes the exact total proceeds of a firm impossible to predict. It is consequently risk which gives rise to profit proper;[1] and the bearing of risk is the economic service to which profit corresponds. In particular, since the starting of a new business, or the starting of a new venture by an old, involves much risk of this kind, risk-bearing has come to be known as 'enterprise' and the risk-bearer as an 'entrepreneur'.

In any given case profit is difficult to distinguish from interest.

[1] If we leave aside for the moment monopoly profits.

For it is normally impossible to bear the risk involved in carrying on a business unless one has in fact lent some money to the business. When money has been thus lent, however, in return for the prospect of a variable dividend, profit may be regarded as the amount by which the average dividend exceeds the interest paid on a fixed-interest stock. If the yield on fixed-interest securities is 3 per cent, and 5 per cent is paid on an ordinary or preference stock, 3 per cent of that yield may be regarded as interest and 2 per cent as profit. The average rate of profit over the whole economic system must, of course, include the losses that are being made—the extent to which some ordinary dividends fall below fixed-interest payments. Indeed, there is no theoretical reason why the rate of profit should not at times be negative.

The various forms of intermediate dividend evolved by large-scale capitalism—preference and preferred stocks and so forth—must be regarded as devices for combining the two elements of interest and profit in varying degrees. A stock may carry interest fixed up to a given percentage and thereafter varying; or the total payable may be limited absolutely, or dependent on the rate paid on other stocks. There is clearly no end to the arithmetical variations which can be conceived. At root, however, in so far as a payment is absolutely fixed and secure, it may be regarded as interest; and in so far as it differs from the interest rate as profit.

In the case of the private business of the traditional type the distinction between interest and profit is much harder to make. Supposing a man borrowed all the money necessary to start a business, and contracted to pay a fixed rate of interest on the whole of it; and entrusted the whole conduct of the business to managers paid a fixed salary; and merely undertook himself to receive the surplus, or finance the deficit, which remained when all wage and interest payments had been deducted from total proceeds; that man might be said to be earning a pure profit. He would do no work and lend no money; he would merely contract to receive the profits or finance the losses of the business. If we mean by 'entrepreneur' the man who receives pure profit and nothing else, he would be of such a kind as this.

In fact, however, there are two clear reasons why such a man is almost never encountered in the world of practical business. First nobody, however 'enterprising', would be likely to face the colossal risk of meeting enormous losses hypothetically interspersed with enormous profits. The normal man, even the very rich man, prefers to have a slight element of interest mixed up with his profit, as some safeguard against the possibility of having to stand huge losses. In real life, therefore, we find a class who contract to receive variable dividends in return for the lending of money, and not a class who merely receive profits and finance losses.

Secondly it is psychologically very difficult, though economically possible, to separate risk-bearing from responsibility. In the days at any rate of the private business nobody was likely to incur the risk of profits and losses unless they had some share in the responsibility for major decisions of policy. It was not merely the elements of interest and profit, therefore, which became mixed up in practice, but the element of managerial wages as well. The traditional entrepreneur supplied at least some money of his own, and was therefore a capitalist; he also undertook to receive a varying return, and was therefore a profit-earner, or entrepreneur proper; he personally assisted in the management of the business, and was therefore a wage-earner. If the business was managed by a single entrepreneur who paid all his employees a fixed salary, and no dividends, and received the remainder or lack of remainder himself, it would of course be impossible to say how much of the actual money payment he received in any given year was interest, profit, or wages. No doubt very few large businesses are run in this way nowadays; though the private company with a handful of shareholders and directors is not very far from it. But there are innumerable small one-man businesses which are fundamentally of this precise kind. The small shopkeeper, the farmer, the garage proprietor, and taxi-owner-driver, are all running their own businesses, and receiving simultaneously interest, profit, and wages.

Indeed, it is only with the later developments of modern large-scale capitalism that the theoretically distinct elements of interest, profit, and managerial wages have come to be distinct in practice. In the giant public joint-stock company of to-day profit and interest are very largely, and profit and wages almost wholly, separate. The debenture-holder receives pure interest: though there is a slight element of profit in so far as the yield on his debentures exceeds the yield on Government stock, whose security is regarded as slightly greater. The ordinary shareholder receives both interest and profit. And the general manager, directors, and chairman receive a fixed salary. In this case responsibility is completely divorced from risk-bearing. The salaried chairman, directors, and general manager take vital decisions on policy, and the consequences are borne by the ordinary shareholders. In these circumstances there is no very obvious reason why the directors and managers should act in the interests of the ordinary shareholders; and, as is notorious, they do not always do so. There is a constant tendency, therefore, for the ordinary shareholders to shift an element of risk-bearing on to the directors and managers. Directors are forced to hold so many ordinary shares; and managers are paid partly a fixed salary and partly a percentage of the 'profits'. In these circumstances responsibility and risk-bearing are again united; the directors and managers receive interest and profit as well as wages; and the traditional conception of the entrepreneur becomes rather more alive.

Nevertheless, to whatever extent wages, rent, interest, and profit are mixed up in practice, they remain the fundamentals of the situation. To each, if the foregoing analysis is correct, a fundamental and necessary economic service corresponds. Wages are the payment for work, of whatever kind; interest for awaiting the income from consumable capital, and rent from non-consumable capital; and profit for bearing risk. If this is true, it will be seen that there is a very serious confusion involved in speaking of 'profit' as a 'surplus' and all other incomes as 'costs'. For these words imply that 'costs' are the payments necessary to get the commodity produced, while 'profits' are somehow a payment for nothing. In fact, however, profit is a payment for risk-bearing in just as real a sense as wages are for work: and risk-bearing is just as necessary as work to the actual production of goods and services. The distinction between costs and profits is really relevant, not to the nature or reality of the service involved, but to the *method of calculation of the reward*. It is after all inevitable that the payment for the service of receiving an uncertain remainder should be the reception of an uncertain remainder. In this sense only is it a 'profit': and for this very reason it is not a payment for nothing. From the point of view of all but the profit-earner himself, profits are in the full sense a cost. For they are a payment without which the production of goods and services could not possibly continue. In a socialist system, and indeed in any system which retains an element, however small, of free consumers' choice, there is bound to be non-insurable risk;[1] and someone, whether the State or private persons, must undertake the task of receiving the fluctuating income which inevitably results from this fact. The whole mistake of conceiving profits as in some fundamental sense not a cost arises from the habit, incurable in a capitalist world, of looking at everything from the point of view of the entrepreneur.

The point becomes clear if we ask 'by' whom and 'for' whom industry is run under the system of free capitalism.[2] It would normally be replied that industry is run by company directors 'for' shareholders. Sometimes, as has been observed, however, directors do not act in the interests of the ordinary shareholders; and cases are alleged to have occurred in the British coal and cotton industries in which the directors have conspired with local bank managers to run the business at a 'loss' contracted after directors' fees and bank interest, both counted as 'costs', had been duly paid. And certain large-scale public utilities, like railway companies, are probably run by their salaried managers and directors more with an eye to public opinion than to the sentiments of the ordinary shareholders.

In general, however, it may be agreed that directors primarily act in order to further the interests of the shareholders, whether because shareholders have the right to dismiss them or because they are shareholders themselves. Their object is to make as large a 'profit' as possible. But because this is the main motive of their actions it does not follow that it is their only effect. For in so far as perfect competition[3] prevails, the principal way to maximize profits is to organize the business as efficiently as possible, to attempt to maintain selling-prices, and to hold down costs to the level dictated by the process of free exchange. To say that industry is run 'for profit' therefore does not necessarily mean that the only effect of running it in that way is to make as large profits as possible. If the manager were simply receiving a

1 It may be argued that the State could pool even this risk. Cf. pp. 237, 238.
2 This argument has been very clearly brought out in Professor MacGregor's book, *Enterprise, Purpose, and Profit*, ch. i.
3 This is defined later. See p. 87.

fixed salary, and he carried out his task of organizing the business as efficiently as possible, he would, in competitive conditions, achieve exactly the same results as if he had acted 'for profit'. He would, that is to say, have made the organization of the business as technically efficient as possible, and he would have produced the greatest possible surplus of receipts over costs. This is clear enough in the case of the taxi-driver or farmer. The whole device, in fact, of putting industry under the control of a man who acts 'for profit' is in competitive conditions simply a way of seeing that the bearer of risk gets the reward which will induce him to continue performing that service. For since all the other partners are getting a more or less fixed reward already, it is clear that the profit-earner will get none at all unless the motive of the manager of the organization is to pay all the fixed costs and yet to make that reward as large as he can. And since control cannot in fact be divorced from responsibility, the organizer has to be made to some extent a profit-earner also. This is what is really meant by saying that capitalist industry is run 'for profit'.

Though, therefore, it is true that industry is run for profit, it does not necessarily follow that the relation of profit to risk-bearing is really different from that of wages to work or interest to saving. Supposing, as Professor MacGregor imagines,[1] that a group of workers chose to hire capital at fixed interest, hire a manager at a fixed salary, pay themselves fixed wages, and contract with a 'profit-earner' to receive the profit or finance the loss, the receipts of all concerned would be the same as if the business was in the normal sense run 'for profit'. Yet in this case it would be just as plausible to say that the business was run 'for wages' as 'for profit'. The running of industry 'for profit', in fact, is essentially a device for enabling the bearer of risk to continue performing that service; and the necessity and reality of that service are indicated by the fact that if there was nobody to finance possible losses, the business could not pay fixed interest and fixed wages, or indeed be carried on at all.

It must be concluded, therefore, that pure profit, in so far as its real nature and place in the economic system are concerned, and as long as perfect competition prevails, is normally a payment for an indispensable service, like wages, rent, and interest.

---

[1] *Enterprise, Purpose, and Profit*, ch. i.

It is a payment for risk-bearing; and the distinction between 'costs' and 'surplus' is only relevant, from this point of view, to the manner in which each is calculated.

5. *The Economic Community*

The different types of economic service, work, waiting, and risk-bearing, are of course fundamental and must be performed by some person, or some group of persons, in any economic system whatever. Whether, however, they are performed in return for a specific reward, and to whom that reward is paid, naturally depends on social and legal convention. In a system like the modern capitalism which we are at the moment studying, where all individuals are entitled to indulge in almost any economic activity they can and will, including the inheritance and ownership of property, these functions are naturally performed by individuals, and individual rewards are paid for their performance. All the incomes, therefore, paid by the typical factory are payments of one or another of these kinds to individuals. Some of the payments made by the factory are not, of course, incomes in the first instance; they are payments to other firms for raw materials and so forth. But all the current payments made to individuals are incomes, and they are all in the form of rent, wages, salaries, interest, and profit. Each individual may of course derive income in more than one form, and from more than one firm; but ultimately[1] it must be derived from the performance of one or the other of these productive services.

The economic community consists, therefore, of a number of productive units selling goods to consumers for money, on the one hand, and paying incomes to the various 'factors of production' on the other. The productive units naturally consist not merely of factories and joint-stock companies, but of farmers, shopkeepers, one-man businesses, doctors, dentists, etc. There are also, of course, various charitable institutions, and above all the State itself, which dispense income but appear at first sight to stand completely outside the productive system. Though these complicate the picture of producing and consuming units, however, they do not really falsify it. For we may either regard the

---

[1] A pension should presumably be regarded as a sort of deferred wage. Free gifts, on the other hand, as the income-tax authorities recognize, must not be classed as income.

State as a productive unit which happens to raise its income by taxation rather than the sale of goods—and the distinction is, for instance, rather a thin one in the case of the British Broadcasting Corporation—or else we may remember that the income of the State is derived from taxing the incomes of individuals, and is consequently indirectly derived from the wages, rent, interest, and profit paid out by private producing units. In general, therefore, the economic community may be said to consist on the one hand of a number of producing units manufacturing producers' and consumers' goods, and paying out incomes for the various productive services, and on the other hand of a number of consuming units receiving their incomes, saving a part of them, and spending the rest on the consumable goods produced.

To complete the outline picture however, one must apply to the community in the concrete the distinction already made in the nature of capital. There are really, from this point of view, four positions in which the community may find itself. First it may not even be willing to wait for the income from the land or fixed capital that exists, and consequently may be dismantling and consuming it. Secondly, though just enough waiting may be going on to prevent the existing capital being actually dismantled, there may be none left to provide for 'depreciation' —to prevent the capital decaying with the process of time. The distinction between these two positions is really secondary; and a community in either condition may be described as a 'retrogressive state'. Thirdly, there may be just enough waiting going on both to maintain the existing capital in existence and to prevent it depreciating. A community in this position will be neither increasing nor decreasing its stock of capital; and we may call it a 'stationary State'. Fourthly, the community may be saving enough not merely to maintain its existing capital but actually to increase it, and may accordingly be called a 'progressive State'. The normal condition of modern industrial communities is that of the progressive State; though it has not necessarily or always been so.

CHAPTER VII

PRICES AND COSTS

S uch is a brief outline of the economic system *in the concrete*, as it tends to develop on the basis of the economic freedom of individuals. The types of service, income, and institutions above described are those which would actually meet the eye of anyone casting a superficial glance over the economic system.

But such a glance would not in the least disclose how the system worked. It would show that there were various factories producing and various persons consuming. But it would not show why individual factories were producing so much of this and so much of that, nor why the individual consumers were receiving such and such an income, nor why they were spending it on this rather than that. These, however, are the really crucial questions which the student and critic of the economic system has to answer. It is of the first importance to realize that the purpose of an economic system is not merely to produce as many goods as possible, but to decide which shall be produced in what quantities, and how much each individual shall consume. Much confused criticism and confused defence of capitalism and socialism would be avoided if this were clearly understood. How often, for instance, do we hear the specious catchword repeated: 'The problem of production has been solved; only the problem of distribution remains'? Those who reiterate this cliché forget that the economic as opposed to the technical problem of production is the problem not of producing as much as possible of everything, but of determining how much of each individual service and commodity is to be produced. For it is impossible to produce 'as much as possible of everything'; in the long run the more of one thing is produced, the less labour and capital are available to produce something else. The essentially economic 'problem of production' is the problem of how much of the available resources are to be devoted to the production of one thing rather than another.

A similar confusion arises from the attempt, laudable in itself, to escape from the apparently unreal world of money and prices and concentrate on the 'real facts' of production and consumption. Up to a point this attempt may be valuable; but it ceases to be valuable and becomes intensely misleading as soon as it begins to imply that only *physical* processes are real.[1] In fact the act of saving or 'waiting', the relation of saving to spending, the ratio of all the various economic quantities to one another, are every bit as real as the physical and visible acts of production and consumption. The fundamental questions to be determined, therefore, are why the given amounts of actual goods and services are produced and why individual consumers consume as much of each product as they individually do.

1. *Demand and Prices*

In any economic system the decisions of individuals to produce, consume, and save will be determined partly by their own needs and desires and partly by the brute facts of the external world. In a system of free exchange these brute facts will tend to become concentrated in the one fact of price. For since in most cases there will be many producers and many consumers of each commodity, free exchange will tend to create conditions of competition and a market. It does not necessarily follow, however, that the competition and the market will be what is technically called 'perfect'; and in the whole analysis of the implications of free exchange a very careful distinction has to be made between conditions of perfect and imperfect competition. We may say that competition is perfect when (*a*) there are no artificial restrictions on the movement of capital and labour from one form of employment to another in search of the highest return; and (*b*) when no single buyer or seller can by his own action affect the price of the commodity he buys or sells. It is implied in the first condition that there are no restrictions either on the movement of resources into existing undertakings or on the starting of new undertakings; and it is implied in the second condition that there are a large number of buyers and sellers handling

[1] For an example of this confusion see Fred Henderson, *Capitalism and the Consumer*, ch. i–vi.

identical articles and reasonably fully aware of the prices obtainable in other parts of the same market. Competition will not, therefore, be perfect if a buyer or seller controls so large a part of the supply of or demand for a commodity that he can raise or lower the price by varying his part of the supply or demand; or if a buyer or seller has some reason of convention, habit, or sentiment for preferring the custom of an individual seller or buyer; or if a buyer or seller is so ignorant of the prices being paid elsewhere that he sells for less or buys for more than he need. There is a crucial difference between the consequences of free exchange in perfect and imperfect competition. It seems best, therefore, to consider the advantages and disadvantages of perfect competition; secondly the advantages and disadvantages of imperfect competition; and thirdly to inquire how far the one or the other prevails in the actual conditions of the modern world.

On the assumption first, of perfect competition, it is clear that a single price will tend to be established for each commodity. For no producer will sell at a much lower price than any of his competitors are selling; and no consumer will buy from one producer at a much higher price if he might buy from another at a lower. A certain definite price will therefore tend to be established for each commodity by free exchange. But what price?

Before attempting to answer this question it is perhaps worth pointing out that free exchange is necessarily beneficial to each party; otherwise it would not take place. This is no doubt obvious. Yet quite a number of recent criticisms of capitalism have been founded on the assumption that free exchange between private individuals must necessarily be 'exploitation' of one by the other because one 'makes a profit out of it'.[1] In fact, of course, free exchange benefits both parties (in the sense that each is better off than he would have been if the exchange had not taken place) because the desires of each for the commodities in question are of different intensities. A man exchanges sixpence for a packet of cigarettes because he wants the cigarettes more than the sixpence, and the tobacconist wants the sixpence more than the cigarettes.

The formation of a price in a market, however, is a complex

[1] There exists a whole pamphlet based on this remarkable error, *The Fallacy of Economics*, by John Middleton Murry.

process in which each consumer is confronted with the possibility of spending his money on any number of different amounts of different things. The first and worst complication arises from the fact that, while price is determined by the combined influence of the demand of all consumers and the supply from all producers, both that demand and that supply are themselves partly determined by the already existing prices. The whole process can most easily be made clear, therefore, if we first assume the prices to be given—as to individual producer and consumer they are—and see how each consumer and producer behaves, and then observe how their combined behaviour in fact determines prices.

Each consumer has a certain money income,[1] derived from his services as a producer, and he has to decide how much of this to spend on what amounts of what commodity. As has already been pointed out, the consumer is as often as not buying for a family rather than himself: and it may consequently be best to call him (perhaps usually her) the 'spender'. Similarly the decisions of the spender will be determined not merely by desire or self-interest but by habit, altruism, a sense of obligation, and every other human motive whatever.

Taking all this into account on the one hand, and the prices of all the commodities offered for sale on the other, the spender will so order his purchases that when all have been made he cannot obtain a more preferable arrangement by spending sixpence a week more on this and sixpence less on that. In so far as the things he buys are divisible into units, like bread or packets of cigarettes, or newspapers, he will go on buying more of each until the point is reached where to spend an additional sixpence on one seems less worth while than to spend it on another. For normally the more units of a commodity he buys, the less will each extra unit be worth to him. Something like satiety begins to be reached after a point. After spending a certain amount on bread, for instance, it may appear worth while to spend sixpence on cigarettes rather than more bread. After spending a certain amount on cigarettes it may appear more worth while to spend sixpence on newspapers rather than cigarettes. In the end, therefore, and over the long period, the whole

[1] The remuneration of his services as a 'producer', which is here taken to include the capitalist and rentier, is discussed later in this chapter.

income will be spent so that the amount of each separate commodity in which the 'marginal' sixpence is spent seems to the spender equally worth while. Supposing, that is to say, that a loaf of bread, a packet of cigarettes, and a day's newspapers each cost sixpence, and that in the course of a year the spender buys 500 loaves of bread, 400 packets of cigarettes, and 300 days' newspapers, and is satisfied that he would not have preferred to buy amounts different from these; we are justified in inferring that it was equally worth his while to buy 500 rather than 499 loaves of bread, 400 rather than 399 packets of cigarettes and 300 rather than 299 days' newspapers.[1]

We are only justified in inferring this, however, if we make a number of careful qualifications. First, its validity naturally depends on the extent to which the spender is behaving rationally and not just throwing his money away. Secondly, it is not true that all commodities can be bought and consumed in greater or less degrees. It is possible to buy more or less loaves of bread, or more or less packages of cigarettes, at any rate over a period of time. But in the case of buying, say, a car or a work of art, the choice may be simply between buying it and not buying it, however long a period is considered. And there does not seem very much sense in saying that, if one buys a car, it must have been just as much worth one's while to spend what one did on it rather than sixpence less as to have spent sixpence on a little more of something else; for one would not in fact have got any car or any part of a car for sixpence less than what one did actually spend on it. And a great many commodities are of this kind. One normally only has one of them. And, even in the case of those commodities of which one can buy more or less, it is not always true that one attaches less and less importance to every bit the more bits are consumed. The gain, for instance, of having two shoes instead of one is much greater than the gain of having one shoe instead of none.

For these reasons it has often been argued that the conception of the relative importance attached to successive bits or units of a commodity bought and consumed is quite unreal; and that

[1] It may sound simpler to say that the 'utility' of buying a five-hundredth loaf, and a four-hundredth packet of cigarettes, and a three-hundredth newspaper must have been equal to him. But this might be taken to imply the fallacy of 'units of utility' discussed in chapter ii.

all we can say is that people spend their money on whatever appears to them most worth while to spend it. On the whole however, it seems that we can say a little more than this. For even when a man buys an 'indivisible' commodity—say a fountain-pen—he tends more or less instinctively to look forward over a period of years, and not simply to ask himself how much it is worth spending on a fountain-pen as opposed to other things. The majority of commodities seem to be such that at any rate in the long run we can buy less or more of them. In general, then, it seems true, and if true an important truth, to say that in the long run we tend to buy more or less of different commodities in such a way that the extra unit of each obtained by the expenditure of the 'marginal' sixpence we spend on it is worth as much to us as the corresponding unit of another commodity.

Now what exactly does or does not this establish? In the first place there is really nothing sacred about the sum of sixpence. This must not be taken to mean any sum of money so small that the spender does not mind whether he spends it on this or that. An expenditure of sixpence a year more on cigarettes and sixpence a year less on bread would not result in a noticeable gain or loss. Secondly, when it is said that the marginal unit of this or that, or the expenditure of the marginal sixpence, is worth so much to the spender, it is not implied that the actual loaf of bread or packet of cigarettes bought or consumed last in time is worth more or less to him than any other unit. It merely means that the value of every packet is less when one hundred packets are bought than it would have been if ninety-nine packets had been bought. For, given the time and circumstances, any unit is worth as much to the spender as any other. Nevertheless, as we have seen,[1] the expenditure of *every* sixpence or pound or one hundred pounds, does not necessarily satisfy wants of equal intensity nor obtain results equally worth while to the spender. For a man might spend £25 a year on bread and £25 a year on cigarettes, although the want satisfied by the one is incalculably greater than that satisfied by the other. It is the benefits obtained from the four-hundredth packet of cigarettes and the five-hundredth loaf of bread which are equal, not those obtained from the four hundred packets and five hundred loaves.

[1] Cf. pp. 11–13.

Since, however, the five-hundredth loaf and the four-hundredth packet both cost sixpence, it is also true to say that the price of one commodity bought stands in the same relation to the price of another as the benefits obtained from the two marginal units stand to one another. For the price of one is equal to the price of the other, and the benefit of the one is equal to the benefit of the other. The ratio, that is to say, of sixpence to sixpence is the same as the ratio of the benefit obtained from the four-hundredth packet and five-hundredth loaf.[1]

Nevertheless it is quite untrue to say that the benefit or satisfaction obtained from the marginal unit of either commodity is *equal* to the price. For this in the nature of things is impossible. A price is the ratio in which a unit of one commodity exchanges for a unit of another—except in so far as we think of the price of something as representing what is given in exchange for it. To say that the price of a pint of milk is fourpence means that a pint of milk will exchange for (among other things) four boxes of matches. A pint of milk and a box of matches exchange in the ratio of 4 to 1. Now a ration of 4 to 1 cannot possibly be equal to the satisfaction obtained from a pint of milk, though the satisfaction obtained from four boxes of matches might conceivably be. For the satisfaction obtained from a pint of milk (or anything else), though dependent on any number of things, is itself of an absolute magnitude. It is not therefore true to say that the benefit obtained from the marginal unit of a commodity is equal to the price, but merely that the prices of two commodities must stand in the same relation as the benefits obtained by the marginal unit consumed.

2. *Supply and Prices*

Such, in outline, is the behaviour of the consumer or spender; and such may be taken to be the normal way in which demand affects price in the conditions of perfect competition. But prices are also influenced by supply; and the behaviour of the producers is not merely affected by, but itself affects, the behaviour of the consumer. How then does the producer behave? We may take

[1] The ratio is only the same because it happens to be equality. For since the benefits obtained or wants satisfied by different commodities have been agreed (ch. ii) to be capable of being equal to or greater than or less than, but not twice as great as, other commodities, the only possible numerical ratio between them is that of equality.

the typical producer to be the entrepreneur already described, since it is he who determines how much of each commodity shall be produced. On the assumption of perfect competition he must be conceived as operating in a world where the price of finished goods on the one hand and of land, labour, and capital on the other are fixed independently of his own actions. His problem is to produce so much of some particular commodity, and so to combine land, labour, and capital in its production as to secure the maximum 'profit' for himself. He will be confronted with the fact that every given amount of each commodity he might produce will require the expenditure of a certain total of land, labour, and capital: it will 'cost' a certain definite amount. To produce 100 motor-cars will cost so much, 1,000 gramophones so much, and so forth. It may be that the cost per unit produced will rise as more units are produced: or it may be that it will fall. The cost per car of producing 1,000 cars will almost certainly be less than that of producing ten; though it may be that the cost per unit of producing 1,000,000 cars would be greater than that of producing 1,000. It used to be thought that cost per unit always fell with increased output in industry and rose in agriculture. But this is not always or necessarily true. Up to a point in both cases costs will normally fall, and after a point rise; though there is no reason why they should not rise and fall again, or behave in almost any way whatever according to circumstances. It will almost always be true, of course, that if unused productive capacity is actually in existence,[1] an increase in production towards the point of existing capacity will mean a fall in cost per unit. The entrepreneur, however, who is considering *ab initio*, as it were, what to produce, as well as how much of it, naturally has to consider what the cost per unit will be *if* a certain amount of productive capacity is completely used. And this itself will vary with the amount of capacity.

Whether costs per unit will increase, decrease, or remain the same in a given case cannot be predicted *a priori*. Normally, as has been said, it will fall with increasing output up to a certain point, and then rise; and there will consequently be a certain volume of output at which cost per unit is lowest. The crucial

[1] And this has become almost the normal case in modern industry, except during armament booms.

93

fact is, however, that it will cost a certain definite sum to produce each possible given amount of each commodity. This sum will, of course, include payments to all the 'factors of production' (land, labour, and capital) employed; and those factors will have been arranged in a certain optimum way. For each given possible output of a commodity, that is to say, there will not merely be a certain total cost but a certain ideal arrangement of land, labour, and capital in relation to one another. For each output both the total cost of land, labour, and capital may vary, and the proportion which each represents of the total cost may vary also. The proportion of cost payments made in wages to that made in interest may be greater or less when 1,000 cars are produced than when 100 cars are produced. And the proportions will vary not merely for different amounts of the same product but for different products. The figure established therefore as the minimum total cost of producing a certain output of a certain commodity is itself the result of an ideal adjustment to one another of the amounts of land, labour, and capital.

Since for every possible output there is a certain cost, it must be true that for any given price (within limits) a certain output will be forthcoming. For if the price covers the cost per unit, including the entrepreneur's wage and the risk-bearer's normal profit, the commodity will be produced. By 'normal' profit and entrepreneur's wage is meant the average rate to which the various different rates of remuneration will tend to conform as a result of the competition of the different entrepreneurs. For if the rate of profit is abnormally high in a certain branch of production, entrepreneurs will tend to divert productive resources into that branch, and the competition of these resources will lower it. And if it is abnormally low, productive resources will be diverted away from it.

There consequently exist certain prices at which a given amount of a commodity will be bought, and certain prices at which a given amount of it will be produced. Now these prices may not coincide. It may be, for instance, that nobody will buy an aeroplane for more than £1,000, and nobody will produce it for less than £2,000. In this case aeroplanes will not be produced. But supposing they do coincide; supposing, that is to say, that there are certain prices at which a certain amount of a commodity will be both produced and consumed; then competition between producers, in so far as it exists, will force the price down to the lowest among these prices. The supply appropriate to this price will then be produced and consumed: and this will be the price that will prevail. Normally, as the supply increases the demand will diminish, owing to the fact of 'satiety' already discussed, and the price will consequently tend to fall. The supply will consequently be increased up to the point at which the price falls below the cost of producing it: it will be increased, in fact, up to the point where the extra cost of producing one more unit is greater than the extra return obtained by selling it. In competitive conditions, therefore, the price, i.e. the extra return obtainable from selling one more unit, must be equal to the 'marginal cost', i.e. the extra cost incurred by producing one more unit.

It is easy to see that if the cost per unit rises, or even remains the same with increases in output, the point will soon be reached at which the price, which is falling as a result of diminishing demand, drops below cost. And at this point or just below it, the increase in production will stop. If, however, cost per unit is falling with increasing output and falling faster than price, it is difficult at first to answer the question why production should ever stop: for it seems that the extra cost of producing one more unit may indefinitely be less than the return from selling it. The true answer seems to be that under perfect competition no equilibrium could be reached in these circumstances; for if an increase in output by a given firm reduced costs but did not reduce prices, it would clearly increase output continuously.[1] In fact, therefore, sooner or later one firm would drive out the others and become a monopoly; and it would then (for reasons discussed below) be restrained from increasing output indefinitely by the prospect of falling prices.[2]

In so far as costs do not fall faster than prices with increasing output, it is clear that output will not be expanded beyond the

[1] Cf. F. H. Knight, *The Ethics of Competition*, ch. vii. It is at any rate clear that under perfect competition equilibrium must be reached at the point at which average costs, i.e. costs per unit, cease to fall. This follows from the fact that competitive equilibrium can only be reached where average costs and 'marginal costs', i.e. the extra cost of producing the last unit, are equal.

[2] Cf. Joan Robinson, *Economics of Imperfect Competition*, ch. vii. If there is no point at which average costs cease to fall, competitive equilibrium is impossible and monopoly or imperfect competition is likely to supervene.

point at which prices have fallen so low as to leave no margin over and above costs. This does not mean that 'costs', in the limited sense, i.e. excluding profits, will be the same for every single producer, or that every single producer will be producing the same output. Certain entrepreneurs will earn a superior entrepreneur's profit or wage owing to their superior ability; but it will not be much greater than other entrepreneurs of similar ability are earning, nor much less than could be earned by the same ability in another situation. Certain risk-bearers will also be earning less or more than others owing to better or worse luck. But over the whole field, both of each industry and of all production, these will tend to be normal return both for bearing risk of a similar intensity and for providing services of a similar ability.

Given free exchange and perfect competition, therefore, the production of each commodity will tend to be pushed to the point at which, in all the circumstances of technique, demand, supply, and price, no more can be produced without a lower remuneration having to be offered to one or another of the factors of production than they are prepared to accept. Since profit is the immediately variable factor, this will mean in practice that production will stop where the rate of profit begins to be too low to induce the entrepreneur and risk-bearer to perform their services. The fact, however, that at this point the price of the commodity is equal to the minimum cost, including profit, for which that amount can be produced, does not mean that it is cost alone which determines the price. The price of the relevant amount of the commodity also equals the total of money which consumers are prepared to offer for it. It is determined by neither exclusively but by both simultaneously, rather as the heat of a room is determined simultaneously by the heat of a radiator on the one hand and the cold air entering the window on the other. If the radiator is turned off and the window remains open, there will be a certain change in the temperature: and if the window is shut and the radiator remains on, there will be an equally definite but different change. So if demand or supply alters—i.e. if the demand or supply forthcoming at a given price alters—while the other remains the same, there will be a certain change in prices. Moreover, demand and supply influence not merely prices but each other through the medium of prices, just as the cold air and the radiator influence each other through the temperature of the room. The cold air as it enters the room becomes warmer than it would have been if there had been no radiator, and the radiator is colder than it would have been if there had been no cold air. Despite this, however, the temperature of the room is always at a determinate, though possibly changing, level at any given moment. So the price tends to be at any given moment 'in equilibrium', though not necessarily in stability.

Price in these conditions of free exchange and competition consequently performs two functions: first that of adjusting supply to demand as a whole, and secondly of rationing the supply among the various individual consumers. It adjusts supply to demand as a whole by simple 'equilibrating' movements. If at a certain price supply exceeds demand,[1] the price will fall until demand is sufficiently stimulated and supply discouraged to bring them once again into equilibrium. And if at a certain price demand exceeds supply, the opposite will happen. Secondly, price rations supply among individual consumers by virtue of its relation to output and incomes as a whole. If the total demand and supply of any commodity are in equilibrium, the total money stream being spent on the commodity must equal the price per physical unit of the commodity multiplied by the number of units for sale. The supply will consequently be rationed among consumers in such a way that each will obtain the number of units his particular portion of the money stream can buy at the existing price. If 100,000 cars are for sale, and consumers are willing to spend £10,000,000 on them at a price of £100 each, then the price of each will be £100, and a consumer with £100 to spend will secure one car.

Such is indeed obvious. It is a little less obvious, however, that both these rationing functions of price are frustrated if attempts are made to fix prices without controlling production. Supposing some authority were to decree that the price of a car must not be less than £110; some of the consumers would decide that they 'could not afford' a car, less money would be spent as a whole, and in the short period some cars would almost cer-

---

[1] That is to say, a portion of the supply remains unsold. Supply can only 'exceed demand' *at a certain price*. To say simply that 'supply exceeds demand' is nonsense.

tainly remain unsold. For the time, supply would no longer be adjusted to demand. Supposing on the other hand that the authority decreed that cars should cost only £90: then more consumers would decide to buy cars, more than £10,000,000 would be offered, and if the producers did not refuse to sell, all the cars would be sold before all the willing consumers had obtained one and before all the money had been spent. Again for the time the rationing of the supply among consumers would have broken down. This is what happens when governments which have embarked on inflationary policies try to avoid the consequences by decreeing maximum prices. The result is a queue, and those at the wrong end of the queue necessarily go home unsatisfied. In the end, of course, supply and demand may settle down to a new equilibrium at the fixed price; but the periodic imposition of fixed prices, in the absence of any control of production, is bound to result in prolonged dislocation.

It is also worth noticing that the price established by free exchange is not in any sense a 'fair' or 'just' price. It is simply the price which happens under these conditions, and which has certain effects. The fact that a price has become customary or traditional under free exchange consequently endows it with no moral validity; nor does the fact that a certain total cost has been incurred in producing a commodity establish any presumption, moral or otherwise, that the commodity should be sold at a corresponding price. For the demand may not be sufficient. The 'equilibrium' price of free competition is nothing other than the price which tends to be reached in fact by a process of free bargaining between a large number of producers and consumers.[1]

If this is a true outline of the way in which supply and demand are controlled by price under perfect competition, we may ask here again exactly what are the implications and advantages of the existence of perfect competition. In the first place perfect competition ensures that every firm is of the optimum, i.e. most efficient, size, and that every consumer can buy any commodity at the lowest price (given of course existing legal conditions,

[1] When a man contemplates the sale of a commodity to a friend, he naturally inquires what is the 'normal' or 'fair' price. This presumably means that he is attempting to discover what the competitive price is: so that neither may lose or gain by making a personal exchange rather than buying or selling on the market.

structure of incomes, etc.) at which the relevant amount of that commodity can be produced. For under perfect competition the price of each commodity will be equal to the average cost, i.e. the cost per unit, and the marginal cost, i.e. the cost of producing one more unit. It must be equal to average cost, because if it were above it, abnormal profits would be made and new firms would come into the industry and decrease profits by increasing output; and if it were below it, existing firms would decrease output and so raise profits to the normal level. Secondly price must be equal to marginal cost because each firm will push production to the point at which the price, i.e. the return for producing one more unit, still just exceeds marginal cost, i.e. the cost of producing one more unit. But it can be shown that when marginal costs are equal to average costs, the individual firms will be of the optimum size. For when average costs are falling, marginal cost must be below average cost. If it costs £100 per car to produce 1,000 cars, but less than £100 to produce 1,001 cars, then the additional cost of producing 1,001 cars rather than 1,000 must be less than £100. Similarly, if average costs are rising marginal cost must be above average cost. If it costs £80 per car to produce 1,000 cars, but more than £80 to produce 1,001, the additional cost of producing 1,001 rather than 1,000 must be more than £80. Since, therefore, marginal cost must be below average cost when the latter is falling, and above it when it is rising, marginal cost must be equal to average cost when average cost is at the minimum. This point, however—the point of lowest average cost—is the point of optimum size or efficiency. But since, as we have seen, marginal cost must under perfect competition be equal to average cost, it follows that under perfect competition individual firms must tend to be of the optimum size.

This is a complex *a priori* argument which may not seem convincing at first sight. How does it come about in fact that perfect competition forces firms to assume the optimum size? Supposing the price at which the relevant amounts of goods could be sold was below the average costs of a firm of the optimum size, no firm at all would be able to cover its costs. Firms would therefore go out of production until the reduction in output had raised the price to the point at which the average costs of the most efficient firms were covered. If, on the contrary, the price were above the average costs of a firm producing the optimum output firms could make an abnormal profit by producing the optimum output and selling it at a price above their average costs. New firms would then be attracted into the industry, and output would increase until price had fallen to equality with the average costs of firms producing the optimum output. It is clear then that, on the assumption of perfect competition, individual firms will tend to be of the most efficient size.

3. Costs and 'Productivity'

In order to examine the further implications of perfect competition it is necessary to inquire how wages, rent, interest, and profit are determined under it. It used to be supposed that there was one great army of homogeneous 'labourers'—entirely distinct from salary-earners, capitalists, and entrepreneurs—who all received a similar wage determined by their 'cost of production'. The cost of production was, roughly speaking, the subsistence payment necessary to keep the 'labourer' alive; and if wages rose above this level, the supply of labourers would increase and competition would force down wages to the subsistence level once more. It was never satisfactorily explained by this theory, however, why the salary-earner or entrepreneur should be able to earn more than their 'cost of production': nor was the alleged tendency for wages to fall found to be in accordance with the facts. For these and other reasons—though this is not necessarily any contradiction between the two theories—a man's wage or salary is now generally conceived as being determined by his 'productivity'. And his 'productivity' is conceived as being measured by the extra money returns which his employment adds to the revenue of the business in question. No man, it is argued, will work for a wage or salary smaller than he could earn by working in any other way; and no entrepreneur will pay a man more than the contribution his services make to the total revenue of the undertaking. He will therefore tend to be employed where his services give the greatest possible money reward; and he will tend to receive neither more nor less than that particular money reward. Moreover, since the entrepreneur will employ additional labour of the kind in question up to the point at which the employment of another man brings a smaller return than the wage paid, and since all workers doing similar work must be paid a similar wage, it follows that any individual worker must receive a wage equal to his 'marginal product', i.e. the extra revenue resulting from the employment of the last extra man of that kind. If it is profitable for a transport company to employ a hundred bus-drivers, each driver will receive a wage equal to the additional revenue accruing to the company as a result of the decision to employ a hundred rather than ninety-nine men.

The same explanation, on the assumption of perfect competition, is applicable to interest, rent, and profit. The capitalist lends his money wherever it will receive the highest reward, and the entrepreneur employs capital up to the point at which an additional unit would increase total revenue by less than the reward paid to that marginal unit. The unit of capital corresponding to the 'physical' unit of land or labour may be conceived as a unit of land and labour 'waited for' over such and such a period of time; and the employment of more and more capital means either a lengthening of this period of time or an increase in the amount of land and labour thus 'invested'. In this sense we may say that increasing amounts of capital are used until the extra revenue attributable to the marginal unit is only just worth its cost, and that all units will then receive an amount equal to that revenue. So with land. More land will be employed until the marginal unit is just worth its cost; and all units will receive the corresponding amount as their reward. At first sight it appears that this is not true of land, since different acres of land receive different rewards. But this is merely because the acre is no more the relevant unit, economically, than is the 'labourer', though wages and rent are calculated according to these units for the sake of practical convenience. It is really the productive capacity of each that matters. Finally the entrepreneur, or risk-bearer, incurs more or greater risks until the extra risk incurred ceases to appear worth the extra 'profit' earned.

Such, in brief outline, is supposed to be the way in which the rewards of the worker, capitalist, and entrepreneur are determined under perfect competition. And this analysis is supposed to show, that there is a tendency for every factor of production to be paid a sum equal to the money value of its 'marginal product'. Is there any reason, however, to believe that all the separate marginal products of the separate factors will add up to the total product of the firm? There is no reason at all, except on the assumption that perfect competition prevails, that each firm is of the optimum size, and that there are a large number of homogeneous units of land, labour, and capital. On those assumptions competition will compel the payment to each individual factor of a sum equal to its marginal money product.[1] If perfect competition does not prevail, however, the whole argument falls to the ground.

And even if the general assumption of perfect competition is made, there are certain specific conditions in which the principle of marginal products can hardly be said to apply. In particular, as has often been observed, where a single unit of capital cannot be displaced without destroying the whole process, as in the traditional case of one man with one spade, it is clear that the 'products' are not separate amounts which add up to the total product. The man without the spade will not earn anything at all. To this it may be replied that when working with the spade the man will not earn less than he could in some other job, while he will not earn more than the maximum which leaves a return to the makers and owners of the spade just sufficient to induce them to make and maintain it. Here again, therefore, it is only in so far as there is competition for the job of digger and there are alternative jobs open to the digger, and also competition to supply spades and alternative uses for the capital concerned, that there seems to be meaning in the idea of the digger's and spade's 'productivity'.

In general, however, in conditions of perfect competition the receipts of any unit of land, labour, or capital will tend to equal the money value of its marginal product. Moreover the value of the marginal product of any factor of production will tend to be the same in all industries. For if in one industry the marginal product of labour is higher than in another, labour will tend to move into that industry and so to lower it; and if it is lower, labour will tend to move out and so to raise it. Land, labour, and capital, in fact, will tend to move into those industries where the product is high, and away from those where it is low; and so to equalize it over the whole economy.

[1] For a mathematical demonstration of this point see Wicksell's *Lectures on Political Economy*, pp. 127–30.

CHAPTER VIII

THE SIGNIFICANCE OF THE PRICE SYSTEM

It is a consequence of perfect competition, therefore, that the marginal utilities of different commodities to the same consumer are the same; that units of land, labour, and capital receive the value of their marginal product; that the price of a commodity is equal to its marginal costs; that firms are of the optimum size; and that the marginal product is the same in all industries. From these conclusions[1] two further important inferences may be drawn: that under perfect competition it is impossible by producing more of one thing and less of another to make one consumer better off without making another worse off, and that it is impossible with the given factors of production to produce more of one commodity without producing less of another.

The first inference follows from the two facts: (1) that consumers spend their money so as to make the marginal utility of different commodities the same; and (2) that factors of production move into that employment in which the value of their marginal product is highest. Since each consumer so spends his money that the marginal sixpence brings him a commodity of equal value, it follows that each consumer would be willing to sacrifice an amount of bread selling for sixpence in exchange for an amount of cigarettes selling for more than sixpence. A single consumer would therefore gain if he received that amount of cigarettes in exchange for that amount of bread. He would accordingly be better off without anybody being worse off if the system as a whole could, by a mere transfer of resources, and without any other change, produce the amount of cigarettes now selling for more than sixpence instead of the bread now selling for sixpence. But if such a change were possible, it would

[1] Cf. J. E. Meade, *An Introduction to Economic Analysis and Policy*, part II, ch. ii.

103

be effected by perfect competition. For if it were possible by shifting factors of production from the bread industry to the cigarette industry to produce cigarettes worth more than sixpence instead of bread worth only sixpence, the value of the marginal product of those factors of production must be higher in the cigarette industry than in the bread industry. They would consequently be shifted under the influence of perfect competition; and the single consumer would gain without any other consumer losing.

The remaining inference from the existence of perfect competition is that factors of production will be so employed that it is impossible to produce more of one commodity without producing less of another. This follows from the fact that only if the ratio between the marginal products of, say, labour and capital is different in different industries can it be possible so to increase output by shifting them about. If, for instance, the marginal product of capital was twice as great as that of labour in the bread industry and equal in the cigarette industry, it would be possible by moving labour from the bread industry (where its marginal product is relatively low) to the cigarette industry (where it is relatively high), and capital in the opposite direction, to increase the output of cigarettes without there being any restriction on the output of bread.[1] By causing a larger proportion of capital to labour in the production of cigarettes, and a smaller proportion in the production of bread, it becomes possible to produce more of the one without producing less of the other. This, however, is what would happen automatically under perfect competition. For in the circumstances supposed above a unit of labour and capital would receive an equal reward in the cigarette industries, while in the bread industries a unit of capital would receive twice as much as a unit of labour. Capital would therefore move into the bread industry and labour into the cigarette industry. This shift would continue until the ratio of the marginal products of each of the two factors had become the same in the two industries. And in this situation it is not possible to increase the production of one commodity by shifting productive factors without reducing the production of another commodity.

It is essential to state these theoretical arguments, not because

1 Cf. J. E. Meade, *An Introduction to Economic Analysis and Policy,* pp. 114–15.

perfect competition necessarily exists in the real world, but because the case for free exchange has been largely based on these arguments. Before dropping the unreal assumption of perfect competition, therefore, it is necessary to show that even if an economic system could be established on this impossible basis, there would be fundamental and overwhelming objections to it. With some justice perfect competition may be described as a dream and not a pleasant one. To be fair, however, in an estimate of it, let us set out as attractively as possible the hypothetical benefits which perfect competition would bestow. We have seen that under perfect competition consumers would obtain the same marginal utility from different commodities; the marginal cost of all commodities would be equal to their price; the factors of production would move into the employment where the value of their marginal product was highest, and would receive a reward equal to that product; firms would be of the optimum size; and it would never be possible to make one consumer better off without making another worse off. If, in order to do full justice to perfect competition, we translate these conclusions into rather more realistic language, we can construct the following superficially attractive picture of the competitive system.

The competitive system is one in which every consumer spends his money on all the objects of his choice in such a way that he can gain no additional satisfaction by spending a little more on one thing and a little less on something else. If his tastes change a little in any way, he will in fact slightly readjust his scheme of expenditure; and the aggregate effect of all the changing demands of all the changing consumers will be a varying stream of money directed towards all the different commodities and services offered for sale in the market. When consumers as a whole decide to spend more on a certain commodity, the stream of money directed to that commodity will expand, its price will rise, the profits made by its producers will also rise, and more producers will gradually be attracted into the industry which produces it until the rate of profit has fallen there to what is normal in the rest of industry. Meanwhile the money stream directed to some other commodity or commodities will have fallen by a corresponding amount, prices and profits in that industry will fall, and producers will be attracted away from it.

The result, in fact, of the change in demand will be a change in supply and a transfer of productive resources from one industry to another, and the transfer will continue until the rate of profit in both industries is again 'normal'. At this point the system will be in equilibrium once more. Similarly if some commodity becomes more scarce, or more difficult to produce than before, its price will rise; and some consumers will prefer to buy less of it and more of something else. If on the other hand it becomes easier to produce, owing to an improvement in technique or some other cause, its price will fall, the demand will increase, and more of it will be produced. Throughout the whole system, therefore, there is a self-regulating mechanism which adjusts supply to demand.

This applies not merely to consumers' demand for finished commodities but to the 'derived' demand for productive resources. Every worker, capitalist, and entrepreneur tends to seek the employment for his labour, savings, or enterprise that will bring the highest reward. As the general demand for commodities ebbs and flows, therefore, the supply of land, labour, and capital will tend to move hither and thither not merely between one industry and another, but also within a single industry. They will move away from the less efficient towards the more efficient firms, because the latter will be expanding under the influence of higher profits; and they will compete among themselves, capital with labour, capital with land, labour with land, and individual units of each factor with other factors. The rate of interest will have its function as a price in ensuring that the community's preference for saving or spending is translated into an increased diversion of resources into the production of producers' or consumers' goods. An increase in saving will lower the rate of interest and make the installation of real capital more profitable, and so more general. And a decrease in saving will have the opposite effect. Even rent will have its significance and function as a price index within the mechanism. Supposing it has to be decided at what point a tube railway is to come to the surface on reaching the outskirts of a city, its managers will compute the comparative costs of constructing a tube tunnel and of buying the necessary amount of land on the surface. As the railway proceeds farther into the suburbs, the value of the land will fall; and where it falls below the cost of making a tunnel, it will pay to bring the railway to the surface. For at that point the 'demand' of society as a whole for land on which to build houses and shops will have fallen below its demand for land on which to run a railway. The price mechanism will have solved automatically for us the otherwise apparently unanswerable problem whether the community as a whole would prefer to use a given piece of land for building a house or a railway.

Not merely, therefore, does the automatic price system perform the necessary practical function of adjusting supply to demand all round; but it does it in such a way as to take account of the two ultimate factors of demand and cost. Every consumer so adjusts his purchases as to allow on the one hand for the cost of production of the various commodities as reflected in their market prices, and on the other for his own comparative desires; and with each of these in mind he distributes his expenditure in such a way that no net gain can be secured by any further change. Similarly, each worker, capitalist, and entrepreneur takes into account both the effort or sacrifice of working and saving on the one hand and the rewards to be earned on the other; and he so chooses his job or investment as to gain the highest reward possible for that expenditure of effort. Moreover, he will tend to receive a reward just equal to the contribution he makes to the product; so that he must inevitably tend towards that employment where his contribution to the satisfaction of society's needs is the greatest possible. Every changing desire of every consumer, therefore, and every changing effort of every producer, is taken into account by the price system in its regulation of the process as a whole.

May we not conclude, therefore, that the competitive system not merely adjusts supply to demand smoothly and automatically, but also does it in such a way as to give due weight to all the desires and all the efforts and sacrifices of the community as a whole? Is it, in fact, not merely supremely practical, but benevolent and infallible as well? These are questions which seem to demand a little further consideration.

CHAPTER IX

NEEDS AND THE PRICE SYSTEM

The survey of the price system contained in the preceding section ends on the verge of an idyllic picture. Here is a system, it seems, in which all problems are automatically solved, in which every man receives his desert, and in which all resources are devoted to production for the greatest needs. Now this latter inference is one which economists themselves[1] have been very careful not to draw. They have usually explained that their task is confined to describing how the price system works; and that it is not for them to affirm or deny that its workings are beautiful or beneficent. But unfortunately their disciples have been quick to draw this inference, and the economists themselves, who to do them justice, usually knew the truth, have not been noticeably quick to refute it. A superficial knowledge of economic theory certainly seems to suggest the existence of an inhumanly perfect system inscrutably directed by some hidden power in such a way that all are rewarded according to their deserts and all enabled to satisfy their needs. No wonder that this has been the conclusion drawn by those whom the system happens to have favoured. No wonder that, in the eyes of nineteenth-century publicists, it came to be conceived as not merely humanly perfect but even divinely ordained.

Here then is a baffling paradox. The old economic analysis, which appears on examination to be in substance, and on its own assumptions, correct, suggests to the mind a just and orderly world. Yet before our eyes we see a world disfigured by gross inequality, extreme poverty, glaring injustice, and colossal waste; a world in which 90 per cent of the population receive less than half of the income, and in which nearly a third of all the productive resources available are periodically unemployed. There

1 With some notable exceptions such as Bastiat and Mises.

must have been few inquiring minds in the present generation which have not been acutely perplexed by this flagrant paradox. Indeed, anybody who refuses to be either blind to the facts, or superficial in his analysis of them, is bound to be troubled by the contrast. The easy methods of escape are of course either, with the complacent reactionary, to deny the existence of avoidable poverty and inequality at all; or else, with the complacent Marxist, to deride all the teachings of all orthodox economists as too obviously at variance with the facts to be worthy of serious examination. Yet, in fact, these attempts to escape the problem are neither successful nor necessary. They are not successful, because the existence of poverty is a reality, and because the economists' analysis is on the whole objective and impartial. And they are not necessary because there is really nothing in the economic analysis—even on the assumption of perfect competition—to suggest a world very different from that which we see before us.[1]

What exactly does that analysis show? It shows[2] in the first place that each consumer so adjusts his expenditure that the satisfaction he obtains from consuming a very little more of one commodity would be the same as that obtained from consuming a very little more of another. If a packet of cigarettes and a loaf of bread each cost sixpence, and if 400 packets and 500 loaves are consumed in a year by a given consumer, the extra satisfaction obtained by consuming 400 rather than 399 packets is the same as that obtained from consuming 500 rather than 499 loaves of bread. And the ratio of the price of one to that of the other is the same as the ratio of the satisfaction gained from consuming an extra unit of the other.

But although this is true, and although the prices of the various commodities are the same for all, it does not follow that the benefit obtained—or need satisfied—by the purchaser of even the marginal amount of the same commodity is the same for different consumers. This fact, which is surely the most impor-

---

[1] Cf. F. H. Knight, *The Ethics of Competition*, p. 48.

[2] The reality and meaning of a comparison between the needs and desires of different people is considered in part I, chs. ii and iii. As is suggested there, the statement that one person's need is greater than another's must rest in the end on an objective judgement of value about the state of society as a whole. The statement that one person's desire or real demand is greater than another's may also be significant and true, but it is not always relevant.

tant in the whole situation, has been curiously often overlooked.[1] For it may be that the price of a packet of cigarettes is sixpence and of a loaf of bread also sixpence, and that the benefit obtained by consumer A from the expenditure of an extra sixpence on cigarettes or on bread would be the same, and that the benefit obtained by consumer B from the expenditure of an extra sixpence on each would be the same. But it still does not follow for one moment that the benefit obtained by A from expending an extra sixpence on bread would be the same as that obtained by B from spending an extra sixpence on bread. It is perfectly possible that A's need for another loaf of bread may be enormously greater than B's, although the prices of bread and cigarettes are the same for each, and although the importance of the loaf on which an extra sixpence might be spent by A and of the cigarettes on which an extra sixpence might be spent by him were for him the same, and although the corresponding equivalence existed for B. The existence of free exchange in fact does not provide that the wants satisfied by the consumption of an extra unit of the same commodity by different people should be the same. It does not compare the wants of different people at all, but merely the different wants of the same person. This is all that is inherent in the fact that free exchange benefits both parties.

The practical significance of this is overwhelming. Indeed it is probably greater than that of the whole analysis of the price system. For it means that in deciding, as that system does, on a certain distribution of productive resources, the price system never attempts to estimate at all the absolute difference between different persons' needs. It takes account of change in the same person's comparative valuation of different commodities. If, for instance, the poor man decides to spend more on cigarettes and less on bread, the price mechanism reflects the change; and it is for this reason that so many people are deluded into thinking that prices do take account of comparative needs. For they dimly recognize that differences between people's comparative valuation of different commodities find some reflections in the

[1] The great English economists, at least, cannot be accused of overlooking it. Marshall points out (*Principles of Economics*, seventh edition, p. 471) that free exchange and perfect competition bring about an equilibrium in which no person can further improve his position by free exchange; but 'not of maximum aggregate satisfaction in the full sense of the term'.

price system. The fact that the poor man spends a greater proportion of his income on bread than the rich man has some effect. What the price system ignores entirely is the absolute difference in different consumers' needs. It ignores entirely the difference between the need for bread of a man who has got enough and the need for bread of a man who has not got enough. It takes account most accurately—in theory—of each single man's comparative valuations, and then adds them all up, without ever having established any common denominator between different persons' needs at all, into what is in effect a largely meaningless calculus. It may be, for instance, that the poor man's need for a better house is much greater than the rich man's need for such things as cigars and racing motor-cars, which the poor man does not buy at all. If productive resources were diverted from producing the former to producing the latter, there would consequently be a net social gain. But a price system which cannot compare these two needs cannot produce this diversion.

A general control of the distribution of social resources which thus ignores the difference between different persons' needs is surely vitiated at the root. The way in which the price system fundamentally works may perhaps be further illustrated by an extreme example. Suppose a man lost in a desert and dying for lack of water met another man supplied with a surplus of water and all the other necessaries of life. The possessor of the water, acting on the principles of free exchange and free prices, would refuse to give the thirsty man even a pint of water except in return for the highest price the latter was willing to pay. Although, therefore, the possessor's need for a pint of water would be almost nothing, he would be able to extort in return for it the whole of the worldly goods, present and prospective, of the thirsty man. The exchange would be perfectly free, and both parties would benefit from it. This is literally what would happen in this extreme situation, if free exchange prevailed and if such external authorities as existed merely exerted their influence to prevent 'force and fraud'—i.e. to prevent the dying man taking the water he needed.

It may be replied that this is a caricature of the price system, since it is an obvious case of isolated exchange. The possessor of the water is in a position, so to speak, of perfect monopoly. But even if we assume competition on both sides, the result is still grotesque. Suppose a hundred thirsty men meet a hundred caravans of water, and suppose the owners of the water are prevented by a higher power from agreeing among themselves to demand an extortionate price; the water-owners will offer a pint of water competitively at a lower and lower price until the one who values water lowest decides that it is not worth his while going lower. At that price the thirsty men will be able to buy water. But this price may still be equal to a considerable proportion of all their actual and potential wealth. In the extreme case, therefore, where the thirsty men have not enough present or potential wealth to offer, no exchange will take place. The water-owners, strictly observing the highest principles of free exchange, perfect competition, and private ownership, will take their surplus water away with them, and the thirsty men will die.

It is worth observing that in this parable all the theoretical implications of perfect competition may be realized. The price of water may be equal to its marginal cost—only the thirsty man cannot pay the price. Each thirsty man may have his purchases so ordered that he cannot increase his satisfaction by spending a little more on this and a little less on that—because he cannot afford to buy anything of what alone he needs. And it may be impossible by shifting productive resources to increase the satisfaction of one consumer without diminishing that of another—for if more productive resources had been devoted to the production and transport of water, less would have to be devoted to the production of some of the things on which the water-owners, and others, spend their incomes. All these things may be true; yet the thirsty men will die.

This is an extreme case. The essential point which it serves to illustrate is that the price system implied in free exchange, even in conditions of free and perfect competition, must ignore the difference in intensity between the needs of different people. And in doing so, the price system is not merely arbitrary and haphazard; it is powerfully weighted against those who start poorest. For though the system has no means of comparing different people's needs, it has a very easy way of comparing their 'demands'. It simply assumes that every sixpence or shilling or pound should count equally. This is necessarily implied in its method of comparing the different needs of the same person. For if a sixpence spent by a poor man on cigarettes is to count equally with a sixpence spent by the same poor man on bread, it is inevitable, in an uncontrolled money economy, that any sixpence spent by anybody must count equally with any sixpence spent by anybody else. The rich man's pound exerts exactly the same influence in determining the distribution of productive resources as the poor man's pound. Yet the need represented by the one overwhelmingly exceeds the need represented by the other. Those who deny the existence or comparability of such things as real needs or desires will of course dispute this. But, as has already been argued,[1] there is no good reason for doing so. The fact that in many cases it is impracticable to compare one man's desire with another's does not mean that each desire is not of an absolute determinate intensity, knowable in principle; or that in certain plain instances the comparison cannot be made in practice. Nor again does it mean that we cannot make objective moral judgements which justify the inference that one man's need for a given commodity is greater than another's. In the case of the water in the desert, for instance, the thirsty man's desire and need are plainly greater than that of the water-owners. To deny this is to voyage into a region of high philosophical scepticism which would make all economics and most other 'sciences' impossible. With all the certainty possible in human affairs, therefore, we may safely affirm that the poor man's need for necessities is greater than the rich man's need for luxuries. Yet the price system gives exactly the same weight to the pound spent by the rich man on luxuries as to the pound spent by the poor man on necessities. There is thus a far-reaching distortion of values pervading the whole working of the price system from the bottom upwards; and it is a distortion which works persistently and cumulatively to undervalue the poor man's needs in comparison with those of the rich.

But this is not nearly the end of the story. Not only does the price system fail to compare the intensity of one consumer's needs with those of another; it also fails to compare the intensity of one producer's efforts or sacrifices with those of another. The fact that every man is able freely to offer his services or his savings to whomsoever will pay the most for them ensures that

1 Cf. again chs. ii and iii.

nobody will make a greater effort or sacrifice than he considers worth the reward offered; and it ensures that all services and savings will tend to be employed where they will bring the greatest money reward. No man will sell an hour of labour, or lend a pound of savings for one purpose, if he could gain a greater reward for it elsewhere. Nor will he work an hour longer if he would prefer the extra leisure to the extra reward, nor save if he would rather consume. In his own mind, that is to say, he compares the intensity of the varying degrees of efforts he may make, as well as the varying degrees of satisfaction he may obtain, and also compares one against the other, and acts on the basis of the comparison. This comparison in the individual's own mind, therefore, has an effect on the price system through the medium of his expenditure and earnings.

But differences in effort or sacrifice between different people are not compared. One man may receive thirty shillings for working ten hours a day for a week. Another receives thirty shillings for working for five minutes, or merely for refraining from consuming a certain sum which he may perhaps have inherited from his ancestors. A productive enterprise will reckon as equal among its 'costs' £20,000 paid to a landowner to induce him to 'wait' a year for the product of his land and £20,000 paid to two hundred men to do a year's work each. That the effort or sacrifice involved in the one case is greater than in the other may be affirmed with as much certainty as the poor man's need for necessities may be said to be greater than the rich man's need for luxuries. Yet they are accounted equal by the price system in determining whether one thing or another should be produced. It might happen that some commodity would be produced if its production necessitated paying £20,000 a year to 200 men to work, but that, if it necessitated paying £40,000 to one man to refrain from consuming a part of his income, it would not be produced on the ground that the 'cost' was in the second case too great.

Even the statement that under the free price system a man tends to receive what he adds to the productive process is only true, in so far as it is true at all, in the sense that he tends to receive in money what his 'product' fetches in money. It does not mean that his effort is necessarily worth the satisfaction of the consumer who consumes his product. For if the price system thus fails to assess the comparative needs or the efforts of different persons, it follows *a fortiori* that it makes no attempt at all to weigh needs against efforts except where the needs and efforts are those of the same person.[1] It falls back here, as in all cases where a comparison between different persons is involved, on a purely money calculus. If the money 'demand' for a certain commodity exceeds the money 'cost', it will be produced. Otherwise it will not. It is perfectly possible, on this system, that a mass of semi-destitute workers may labour all the year round to produce luxuries for an affluent and idle minority. The price system provides that the efforts of the labourers do not exceed their rewards; and that the efforts of the few do not exceed their rewards either. It does not stop to ask whether the rewards of the few exceed the rewards of the many—or whether the efforts of the many exceed the efforts of the few. (These latter questions, are, in Professor Hayek's words, 'illegitimate'.)

Such is the fundamental nature of the free price system, even on the Utopian assumption of perfect competition. And little else, it would seem, is needed to explain the grim spectacle of poverty and inequality that we see in the real world. What indeed else could be expected of a system that never compared the intensity of any man's needs, or any man's efforts, with anybody else's, and never compared one man's efforts with another man's needs? Should one not expect exactly that paradox of destitution permanently existing by the side of luxury which humanitarians have lamented and economists have been thought to ignore or justify? The valuations of such a system are false and largely meaningless[2] throughout. The examples taken above are extreme; and the distortions caused by the free price system are not in all cases as grotesque as these. But the tendency to distortion is everywhere. The only sense, in fact, in which the price system either ensures the most 'economic' distribution of

1 It is here assumed that efforts and satisfaction can be compared, though not quantitatively, in the same sense as different satisfactions. If it is admitted that a single individual can compare an effort against a satisfaction, there is no further philosophical difficulty (beyond those considered in chs. ii and iii) involved in making this assumption. If, of course, efforts and sacrifices are regarded as simply the lack of certain alternative satisfactions, then the argument for efforts and sacrifices is the same and not complementary to that for satisfactions.

2 This does not imply that they may not have some practical usefulness, where there is no better alternative, as is suggested later.

productive resources, or the adjustment of supply to demand, is that it ensures the investment of resources where they will earn the most money, and it adjusts supply to demand in the sense that it ensures the production of those commodities whose money cost of production does not exceed the amount of money obtained by their sale. This implies that no consumer's satisfaction can be increased without diminishing that of another; it does not imply that one consumer's satisfaction might not be increased to an extent that enormously outweighs the resulting loss to another.

All this economists have really known well enough. At the time when 'units of utility' were thought an adequate way of describing the facts of human psychology economists used to point out that the utility represented by a given sum of money was greater for a poor man than a rich man. From this they inferred quite rightly that all mitigations of the inequality of wealth—as the man in the street could have told them—would result in a social gain. Though recognizing this, however, the classical economists were slow to draw the inference that the price system was grossly inequitable. The truth is that they were so predominantly—and in the nineteenth century perhaps rightly —concerned with the problem of increasing the national income as a whole that they gave little thought to the possibility of mitigating poverty by redistribution. As a result they underrated (and their disciples still underrate) the need for redistribution. And this lack of balance in their analysis has probably been one of the reasons why late Victorian reformers, who were largely under their influence, constructed a world in which the rise in the standard of living of the working classes sprang entirely from an increase in the total national income and not from an increase in their share in it.

There is much less excuse for those contemporary economists who, having quite correctly abandoned the errors involved in units of utility, have surrendered to the temptation to deny or ignore the reality of desires and needs altogether. For this is not to remove but to neglect the philosophical difficulty. So far from being an advance on earlier economists, it is a sad retrogression from the honourable tradition of Mill, Marshall, and Professor Pigou. What is needed to-day is not a complete neglect of everything except price, but a more accurate description than the utilitarians gave of the realities of desires and needs.

CHAPTER X

IMPERFECT COMPETITION AND MONOPOLY

The case we have so far made against capitalism has not taken into account the existence either of imperfect competition or of the social institutions that distort the working of the price system. It is consequently valid against private capitalism even in the ideal State imagined by its theoretical advocates.[1] We may assume, that is to say, perfect competition, an equitable social system, and the full utilization of all resources; and the whole of the above case is valid. But this ideal capitalism, as everybody knows, is one that never was on land or sea. The case that can be made against capitalism as it actually exists is very much more strong.

Economists are usually careful to explain that the ideal world of perfect competition and perfect knowledge is not the real world around us. It is rather one, they tell us, to which the real world 'tends'. But how far does it so tend? The economists are of course perfectly justified, like any other scientists, in studying an abstract world in which certain principles work themselves out unimpeded and then considering afterwards how far their working is in fact affected by the intervention of other factors. An economist can no more be expected to assume the existence

[1] Quite fairly the most intelligent defenders of the unregulated price system complain that the divergences of existing society from the ideal are no part of the case against it as an ideal. Professor Hayek (*Collectivist Economic Planning*, pp. 23-4) remarks: 'The system under which we live, choked up with attempts at partial planning, is almost as far from any system of capitalism which could be rationally advocated as it is different from any consistent system of planning. It is just interventionist chaos.' All the criticisms already made here, however, apply to the pure capitalism Professor Hayek would advocate. The criticisms that follow are also relevant because other less intelligent apologists defend capitalism *as it is*. Professor Mises, for instance (*Socialism*) argues that capitalist monopolies are beneficial because they restrict production of exhaustible ores which might otherwise be lost to posterity!

of violence, corruption, and war than a geometer can be expected to study an apple instead of a perfect sphere. But when we come to make judgements of value about the system, and about other possible systems, we must of course examine it as it actually exists and not as it hypothetically might.[1]

When we do this, the first assumption that must be removed is that of perfect competition. Admittedly there is some 'tendency' towards competition in the capitalist world: for the legal and social system is on the whole in most countries (at least in the capitalist democracies as opposed to the Fascist 'corporative States') such that it is possible for anyone with the necessary resources to enter any kind of business if he thinks he can do so profitably. But the limitations on this are enormous. In the first place there is a very forceful 'tendency' in a great many most important trades for the producers to combine. For 'freedom', as Professor Knight points out, is a very different thing from free competition. Freedom means freedom to combine; and 'under freedom all that would stand in the way of a widespread drift towards monopoly is the fortunate limitation of human nature which prevents the necessary organization from being feasible or makes its costs larger than the monopoly gains which it might secure.'[2] Normally, in fact, wherever there are monopoly gains to be secured, nothing but anti-trust laws will preserve competition; and the would-be monopolists will protest loudly against this 'Government interference' by which free competition can alone be preserved. *Laisser-faire*, or the absence of Government interference, it should be observed, is a very different thing from the presence of perfect competition.

Moreover, in many instances not even anti-trust laws[3] can prevent the development of monopoly. In industries, where average costs continue to fall more or less indefinitely with increasing output, the tendency to monopoly must be practically irresistible. If the demand for a commodity is such that it can be completely satisfied by a single firm of the optimum size, a monopoly is almost bound to be formed sooner or later. Anti-trust laws cannot compel competition in railway traffic between

[1] Mrs. Wootton, in her admirable book *Plan or No Plan*, is a little inclined to compare the capitalism of ideal imagination with the socialism of stark reality.
[2] Cf. *The Ethics of Competition*, p. 52.
[3] In the 'corporative State' there are of course pro-trust laws.

two towns if there is only enough traffic for one line. The second line will not be built; or if it is, one or the other will finally become bankrupt. In the majority of industries the demand will doubtless be too large to be satisfied by a *single* firm of the optimum size. But owing to technological progress, mass production, and so forth, there is a growing tendency for manufacturing industries to become concentrated in a *few* large firms. And an industry consisting of a few large firms is in a condition not of perfect, but of imperfect competition. Competition is only perfect if no individual firm is able to influence the price of the product by any action of its own, such as varying the quantity it produces. If there are 1,000,000 producers each producing a small fraction of the total output, there is true competition; for variations of output by a single producer will not affect total output appreciably. If, however, there are only three or four genuinely separate producers—as is commonly the case in modern manufacturing industry—it is probably possible for any one of them to influence the price by varying his own output.

Nor is this growth in the size of productive units the only reason for the development of imperfect competition. Fashion, convention, ignorance, distance, and advertisement are also powerful reasons. In conditions of genuinely perfect competition no single seller can vary his price to any extent from that of the market: for if he does, consumers in a body will buy from his competitors at a lower price. Supposing, however, that a substantial number of consumers either have formed the habit of buying from that particular firm, or are ignorant of the prices charged by other firms, or are too far away to get into touch with other firms, or have been persuaded by advertisement that the products of the firm in question are different from those of others, while really they are not; then that firm may be able to raise its prices a certain degree above those of its competitors without driving its customers away. It may not be able to raise them very far; for at a certain point its customers may take notice and begin to inquire about other sources of supply. But if it can raise them at all, it is not operating under conditions of perfect competition.

Now it is clear that in the real world a vast number of firms, particularly in retail distribution, hold quasi-monopolies of this kind. It may be that costs of distribution prevent outside firms from competing in a particular locality, or simply that personal connections, ignorance, or inertia prevent customers from worrying much about differences in price. But in all these cases there exists a margin within which output and price can be varied by the single firm in its own interest. And when these local and personal quasi-monopolies are added to those made inevitable by large-scale production, on the one hand, and the whole brood of cartels, trusts, and price-fixing schemes, which are no more than deliberate anti-social conspiracies, on the other, it becomes apparent that imperfect competition is the rule in the real business world and perfect competition the exception. What is more, the exception is a rare one. It is probably only in the world markets for farm products and raw materials—such as the wheat, cotton, and wool markets—that genuine perfect competition exists. Here there is a really perfect market, and no producer by his own efforts can control even fractionally the price of his own product. But over the overwhelmingly larger part of the economic system, he certainly can do so.

Since, therefore, imperfect competition is the rule in the real economic world, and perfect competition is the exception, it is necessary to analyse the nature and implications of free exchange in conditions of imperfect competition. If competition is imperfect among sellers, a single seller can influence the price of the product by varying the amount sold. Now this at once invalidates the fundamental argument, based on the assumption of perfect competition, that the price of a commodity must be equal to its marginal cost. In perfect competition the producer will increase production until the extra return due to selling one more unit just covers the cost of producing one more unit, i.e. marginal cost. Since the extra return due to selling one more unit must be equal to the price, marginal cost must be equal to price. But if competition is imperfect, the seller will reduce the price by the very fact of selling more. The extra return due to producing and selling one more unit will not therefore be equal to the price; and marginal cost (which the producer will equate with the extra return) will not be equal to price either.

Suppose in perfect competition cars are selling for £1,000 each, and a producer just finds it profitable to produce 101 cars. The extra receipts he gets by selling 101 rather than 100 cars is £1,000 (£101,000 minus £100,000). Since he finds it just profitable to produce 101 cars, and not more or less, his marginal receipts must be equated to his marginal costs. His marginal cost must therefore be equal to £1,000; which is the price. Marginal costs must therefore equal price, as we have already seen.

Suppose on the other hand that imperfect competition prevails, and that the result of increasing the firm's production from 100 to 101 cars is to reduce the price from £1,000 to £999. The extra receipts resulting from this increase in production will then be £899, i.e. (£999 × 101) minus £100,000. If therefore the firm finds that at this level of production its marginal costs are equal to its marginal receipts (i.e. the receipts due to producing one more unit), its marginal costs must also be £899. But the price is £999. In imperfect competition any firm will accordingly tend to equate marginal costs and marginal receipts at a level of output at which price is above marginal costs. This means that output will not be increased up to the point at which price falls to the level of marginal costs. Output, in fact, will be restricted below the competitive level; and prices and profits will be pushed above it.

It also follows that firms will not necessarily be of the optimum size under imperfect competition. Under perfect competition, it has already been agreed, they must be of the optimum size; for marginal costs must be equal to average costs; and that means that average costs must be at their lowest. Marginal costs must be equal to average costs because competition forces both of them to be equal to price. If marginal cost is less than price, production will be increased until they are equal; and if it is greater, production will be decreased. Similarly, if average cost is less than price, more firms come into the industry; and if it is greater some will move out. But under imperfect competition these things—within limits—will not happen. There is consequently no reason why price should be equal to average costs or to marginal costs, and therefore no reason why average costs should be at their lowest. There is no reason, in fact, why under imperfect competition firms should be at their optimum size.

The normal situation in imperfect competition, therefore, will be one in which firms of other than the most efficient size are producing less than the competitive output, charging more than the competitive price, and earning more than the competitive receipts. Yet the case for *laisser-faire* has usually been founded on the fact that under *laisser-faire* consumers will obtain the highest possible output at the lowest possible price that is *compatible with free exchange*, i.e. the competitive output and price. But under the normal condition of *laisser-faire*, i.e. imperfect competition, they will not do this. The producer will restrict production and earn a monopoly revenue represented by the difference between his average cost and the price at which he sells.

Moreover, the monopoly revenue will normally accrue to the profit-earners only, and will not be shared out between the salary-earners and wage-earners. For normally imperfect competition between buyers will exist in the labour market. (This is in itself one of the strongest arguments for the establishment of strong independent trade unions.) Normally, at least in any given place, a few firms will be competing for a large number of workers; and in this case, the purchasers, i.e. the management of the firm, will be able to affect the price of labour by varying their demand. In these circumstances the firm will not employ labour up to the point at which the wage paid is equal to the value of its marginal product. For in all cases the firm will take on more labour as long as what it adds to its costs is less than what it adds to its receipts by selling the resulting extra output. But if by employing more labour the firm raises the wage-rates that have to be paid, then by taking on one more labourer it will add to its costs more than the wage of that labourer; for it will increase the wages of all other labourers as well as having to pay the wage of the new one. The firm will therefore stop employing labour when the wage is still below the value of the labourers' marginal product; and the labourers will therefore all receive less than their marginal product. This will be true even if there is perfect competition in markets in which the firm sells its products. But if the firm is selling in an imperfect market also, there will be another factor tending to lower the labourer's wage below his marginal product; for in these circumstances the producer will add to his receipts, by employing one other labourer, less than the price at which the additional output is sold. In the normal case, therefore, in which there is imperfect competition both in the market for commodities and the market for labour, there will be two powerful factors tending to depress wages below the value of the marginal product of labour.

There are two remaining advantages of perfect competition, however, which turn out to be non-existent in the conditions of the real world. These two advantages are (a) that no single consumer's satisfaction could be increased without a modification in some other consumer's satisfaction; and (b) that no commodity could be produced in greater amounts without some other being produced in lesser amounts. The first advantage is only real if the various factors of production earn a reward equal to their marginal product; for the value of their marginal product represents the amount that consumers are willing to pay for that product. But since in imperfect competition factors of production will be paid less than their marginal product, they will not move into those industries where consumer's demand is greatest. The more sharply the conditions of the labour market in an industry diverge from those of perfect competition, the more sharply will the reward of the factors of production diverge from their marginal product. The adjustment of resources to consumers' money demands will thus be hopelessly distorted.

Secondly, under imperfect competition it cannot be shown that factors of production will be so combined in the different industries that more cannot be produced of one commodity unless less is produced of another. For this will only be so if the ratios of the marginal products of the factors are the same in different industries; and this, in return, requires, as has already been argued, that all the factors in all industries should be paid a reward equal to their marginal products. But under imperfect competition this will not be so, and there will consequently be no guarantee of this physically ideal arrangement of resources.[1]

Finally, the existence of surplus capacity in many industries will tend to be perpetuated under imperfect competition. If competition is perfect, excess capacity will result in an output too large to be sold at remunerative prices; and the redundant labour and capital will be diverted out of the industry. If competition is imperfect, however, output may be restricted and a sufficient monopoly revenue earned to distribute remunera-

[1] Cf. for a full and clear analysis of the implications of imperfect competition, J. E. Meade, *An Introduction to Economic Analysis and Policy*, part II, ch. 4–6.

tive incomes to the unnecessary labour and capital. This must produce very serious distortions in the structure of contemporary capitalism; and the existence of permanent excess capacity is a very familiar phenomenon in fact.

Here again it has been necessary to appeal to some apparently very theoretical arguments in order to analyse some of the main implications of the prevalence of imperfect competition. In fact, however, the conclusion is precisely what we should expect from a casual glance at the visible economic world. It is, in substance this: that the semi-monopolistic position held by the majority of producers, and particularly the larger ones, enables them to earn monopoly profits at the expense of both consumers on the one hand and wage-earners on the other. For imperfect competition prevents production and wages being increased to the highest point, and prices and profits reduced to the lowest point, consistent with free exchange. We have already seen that the best possible output and arrangement of resources attainable by free exchange and perfect competition is not in any true sense the ideal output and arrangement of resources, because it is dependent on a money calculus which ignores real needs and sacrifices. But even this very inferior ideal of an economy responding perfectly to the price and money calculus is not attained or even approached by the real world of quasi-monopolistic capitalism. Even if consumers' money demands were always faithfully reflected in the price system, and even if workers always received the value of their marginal product, it would not be saying very much. But in fact these things do not happen.

Moreover, the distortion of the money calculus is also not purely haphazard, but is biased against the poor. For imperfect competition enables the recipients of profits earned by the big firms to exploit both the consumers on the one hand and the wage-earners on the other. It is not, of course, always or only they who are exploited; but in the large and most of the time it is. And since the profit-earners are in general rich, and the wage-earners and consumers generally poor, the bias is once more against the poor. The prevalence of imperfect competition and monopoly thus enormously strengthens the case against a free price system unregulated by the State.

CHAPTER XI

EARNED AND UNEARNED INCOMES

By capitalism, as has been pointed out, we commonly mean a system of more or less free exchange and prices, supplemented by the grant to private persons of the right to own and inherit property. So far, in analysing the working of capitalism, we have only considered the price system. It remains, however, to consider the interrelation of the price system with the social institutions of private property and inheritance that have historically been associated with it. Great as are the injustices caused by the actual working of the price system, they are certainly not greater than those bequeathed by the social and historical context in which it works. The whole structure of incomes and opportunities in the capitalist world is very largely determined by the 'institutional' structure out of which it springs. It is not merely that the rich man's pound exerts the same pull in the price system as the poor man's pound, but that one man may be born poor and another rich.

The existence of private property and inheritance, however, inevitably raises the question—which any critique of capitalism must answer—whether there is any justification, economic or moral, for the payment of the incomes to which these institutions give rise. For since the moral justification has usually been thought to rest mainly on economic grounds, the economic and moral questions have to be considered together. At this point therefore the moral justifiability of the capitalist income structure has to be more directly scrutinized.

For to prove that the price system took accurate account of real needs and sacrifices, and that existing capitalism was an example of the ideal price system, would be one thing; but to prove that there was some ethical superiority about the scheme of distribution worked out by capitalism would be something else. Yet the two are often confused. It is supposed that if the price system pays everybody 'what they are worth', then it must be a good system. But even this does not follow. It has just been argued that the price system does not pay people what they contribute or what they are worth, even in money terms. But even if it did this, it would not necessarily be a just or ideal system of distribution.

As Professor Knight expresses it, the statement that the 'competitive organization of society . . . tends to reward every participant in production by giving it the increase in the social dividend which its co-operation makes possible may be true . . . but it is not a statement of a sound ethical social ideal'.[1] The price system, given the historical and social context, simply brings about a certain distribution of incomes. This is just a fact: and as such it has no moral pretensions. If a moral case has to be made out for the price system, it must be made on the ground that the social and moral goods implied in economic freedom exceed the evils. The goods involved in allowing a man to work and consume as, within limits, he chooses, exceed, it would have to be argued, the evils due to the narrowing of those limits by poverty.

If, however, the price system as such can claim no moral validity for its scheme of distribution, on what moral criterion should the distributive organization be based? All would agree that the artist ought not to starve while the speculator thrives, and that the miner ought not to be paid less than the rentier. But here there are two separate criteria. The artist ought to be paid because of the value of his work and the miner because of the effort it costs him. And unfortunately these two criteria do not coincide. It would be a very fortunate coincidence if, as Marxists have tried to persuade themselves, the value of a commodity, economic or aesthetic, corresponded in some measure with the effort necessary to produce it. In fact, however, the artist may produce a masterpiece with almost no effort at all, and the miner may labour all day to produce a pile of coal whose value, economic or aesthetic, is unfortunately very small indeed. It is inevitable, therefore, that if people are rewarded either entirely by the demand for their product, or entirely by the effort they put into it, the resulting distribution will be grotesque.

1 *The Ethics of Competition*, p. 48.

EARNED AND UNEARNED INCOMES

The question how these two criteria of effort and value can be fully reconciled must be considered later;[1] but it may be agreed at once that neither should be left wholly out of account. Nobody ought to be paid for services, however necessary, which involve no effort or sacrifice; just as nobody ought to be paid for services, however arduous, which have no value. The price system, however, entirely fails to satisfy the first of these two conditions.

For the differences of earned income which the price system engenders some case at least can be made. The higher salaries paid to administrative workers and entrepreneurs are paid to people who work and who possess abilities of a comparatively rare kind. These abilities, in most cases, are of great value to the community, and it is probable that their possessors would not use them to the full if they were not rewarded more highly than those of lesser ability. To some extent, no doubt, the level of rewards is conventional, and the exceptionally talented person is content if he is receiving a reward at least as great as those of similar talents. But this implies that some inequality of earned incomes is inevitable in a world where men do not predominantly act from altruistic motives.

There is indeed comparatively little that is unjustifiable and anti-social in the higher earned incomes. In the first place they are few. As Mrs. Wootton[2] has remarked, only barristers at the end of their career and film stars at the beginning can secure really enormous earned incomes. And even when the third kind of high earned income, that of successful business men, is included, the total of high earned incomes must be a very small proportion of the national income as a whole.

In the second place most of these incomes are well worth paying. The entrepreneur of genius, of the type of Sir Josiah Stamp on the one hand or Lord Nuffield on the other, is worth an incalculable amount to the community. Without a certain number of men of this degree of enterprise and organizing power a modern economic system could not be maintained at all. It has been the Soviet authorities' great problem to find them. Great entrepreneurs of this kind are of a value so great that it would be almost impossible to overpay them. For their services must be obtained if the community is to live; and nobody else can give them.

[1] Cf. pp. 313–14. [2] *Plan or No Plan.*

In the third place, though the entrepreneur or barrister is paid very highly, he cannot consume a very large share of the real national income; for he has not time. He may receive £50,000 a year; but if he is engaged in organizing a large business, he will not have time to consume the goods and services represented by that £50,000. He will in fact save; and if he does so he will be benefiting the community both by giving his services and by refraining from consuming his reward. He may, of course, spend it on his family, and they may be performing no services. But even so it is not usually in the lifetime of the original earner of a huge fortune that the abuse becomes really dangerous.

Finally the inevitable perversions of the price system caused by inequalities of wealth are perhaps less serious in the case of high earned incomes than in most other earned incomes. It may be that some men exist with a special talent for organizing the production of champagne and cigars; and if so their services would clearly be grossly overvalued in a society where incomes were very unequal. But business ability is normally more general. Clearly the abilities of Sir Josiah Stamp—or for that matter Charlie Chaplin—would be valued very highly in any society whatever. Sir Josiah Stamp would be of incalculable value in Soviet Russia, though it might be contrary to Soviet principles to pay him sufficiently highly to induce him to go there. Nevertheless it must be remembered that the unjustifiable inequalities resulting from social monopolies and quasi-monopolies undoubtedly distort even earned incomes.[1] There are privileged groups with a hold on certain jobs; and, though their incomes are earned, there is plainly a considerable monopoly element in them. In general, however, if certain freakish kinds of practical skill, such as gambling ability, are neglected, it cannot be contended on any of these counts that the payment of high earned incomes is seriously anti-social.

Equally on all counts, however, the payment of high unearned incomes must be condemned. Earned incomes may be defined as all those paid for work, i.e. wages and salaries, including the business man's managerial salary. Unearned are all those paid for waiting or risk-bearing, i.e. rent, interest, and profit. The economic distinction between earned incomes on the one hand and property incomes on the other thus coincides fairly closely

[1] Cf. ch. xiii.

with the legal one between earned and unearned incomes on which British income-tax is based.

It was argued at length in chapter vi that interest and profit, and even in some degree rent, are payments for a specific economic service. Interest and rent are payments for waiting and profit in the proper sense for risk-bearing. These are all services without which the process of production cannot go on. But this does not mean that property incomes ought therefore to be paid to private persons; still less that they ought to be paid on the scale customary in an automatic price system. The service of waiting or saving may involve an effort and sacrifice, if the saving out of income is performed by someone with a small earned income. But saving out of a large income, earned or unearned, may involve a merely negligible sacrifice. And the waiting which involves, not saving out of income, but merely the decision not to consume capital, only involves sacrifice in a purely academic sense. It is here that Lassalle's famous jibe about the 'abstinence' of the Rothschilds has its keenest point. For it is this which is the normal case in the modern capitalist world. The property-owner who merely consumes a huge unearned income, and refrains from consuming his capital at the same time, is rewarded by the price system on a collossal scale. Yet no effort or sacrifice whatever is in fact involved in the operation; and this in itself gives the property-owner, unlike the active business man, the time and opportunity to consume the whole of his income.

And not merely is the property-owner receiving a reward in return for no effort. He is also, again unlike the business man, performing a service that could easily be performed by society as a whole. It is true that if the community's capital is to be preserved somebody must refrain from consuming it. But if the property-title in question were transferred from the private owner to the State, and the State held it thereafter, the community's capital would be preserved in exactly the same way and the reward would accrue not to one undeserving individual but to society as a whole. Indeed, there would be a net gain. For the property-owner would be forced to work and so to increase the national income.

The service of waiting can certainly be socially performed, but it is not so clear that the service of bearing risk can. To some extent society can bear the losses arising from the fact that some existing industries must lose in any given year; for these losses will be balanced by other profits. It is less easy for it, however, to undertake the enterprise involved in starting more ventures. The significance of this must be discussed later.[1]

The demonstration, in fact, that rent and interest are payments for economic services does not in the least imply that they ought to be paid to private individuals. It does not imply that the recipients earn or deserve them. To suppose that it did would be to misconceive the nature of an economic service. Waiting and risk-bearing are only economic services in the sense that they are functions, like work, though different from work, without which the process of production cannot go on. Marxists have been wrong to deny this, and their mistake has involved them in a succession of sophistries that has done great harm to their cause. But the fact that waiting and risk-bearing are specific economic functions, to which the specific rewards of interest and profit are paid, does not mean that the recipient of these rewards 'earns' them or 'deserves' to receive them. It is probably the use of the ambiguous words 'earn' and 'deserve' that has so badly confused the issue here. Because the capitalist performs an economic function, it seems to be argued, he clearly 'earns' his rewards. For only if he was doing nothing for it would he not earn it; and he has been shown to be doing something. Therefore, since he 'earns' it he 'deserves' to receive it. In the second part of the argument, it will be observed, a moral sense is attached to the words 'earn' and 'deserve' which does not really follow from the premise. The mere performance of an economic function which costs no effort, and could be as easily performed by society as a whole, does not give a man a moral right to any reward. In no moral sense, therefore, does the capitalist earn or deserve his rent, interest, and profit, except when he has saved himself at real sacrifice out of his own earned income or performed an act of enterprise that could not have been performed by society. If he has not done these things, there has been no sacrifice, the reward is not deserved, and it may be properly and fairly described as unearned. Using the word 'earn' explicitly in its moral sense, therefore, we might define as 'unearned' all rent, interest, or savings not made out of the

[1] Cf. pp. 237-38.

wage or salary of the recipient. In general, however, throughout this book the phrase 'unearned income' is used in its popular sense of all income other than that earned by work. Unearned income not even derived from the recipient's own savings is called 'inherited income'. The conclusion, therefore, in broad outline, and for practical purposes, is not far different from the Marxist one. If to describe all property-incomes as 'profit', and define them as 'surplus value', simply means that they are not earned and ought not to be paid, it is not far wrong. It is wrong to some extent, because it identifies interest on the small savings of the wage-earner with the huge unearned income of the big capitalist. This is false analytically, since saving by the wage-earner does involve real sacrifice, and it is consequently resented in practice. In its broad practical implications, however, the Marxist position may be regarded as in general correct.

In principle, however, it is incorrect. Marxists have imagined, wrongly, that in order to prove property-incomes unearned they must show theoretically that no economic service corresponds to them. They have therefore become involved in asserting the theoretical existence of 'surplus value' and denying the existence of waiting and risk-bearing. And in this controversy they have been constantly refuted by the orthodox economists. Whereupon the ordinary man has either, if he is favoured by the capitalist system, inferred that property incomes are earned after all, or else, if he is not, inferred that the orthodox economists are merely inventing sophistries to delude him into accepting an unjustifiable system. In fact, however, the case against unearned incomes does not rest on any untenable theoretical analysis such as that of Marxism at all. It rests on the indisputable fact that the great majority of these incomes are rewards for services which cost no effort and can equally well be performed by society as a whole.

CHAPTER XII

INHERITANCE

Of all the social or institutional factors which distort the system of free exchange, inheritance, as the source of all inherited and most unearned incomes, is at once the most important and the least justifiable. Inheritance means that one man may be given for nothing the legal right to command for a lifetime (and even after) the services of a group of his fellow men. An inherited income, in effect, gives a man the right to invoke the whole legal and armed forces of the State in order to compel a certain number of his fellow citizens to work in perpetuity to satisfy his needs and desires. It means neither more nor less than this. For when a man of property dies a certain proportion of the national income is, so to speak, going begging. Somebody has to get it, and it must be decided who. The possibilities are either to devote it to the service of the needs of the community as a whole, or to a particularly necessitous or deserving section of it, or to a certain favoured individual or individuals. The choice of the third method in preference to the other two is what we call inheritance.

The fact of inheritance reinforces and clinches the case against unearned income. Inheritance gives a man an unearned income that is not even a reward for his own savings. He is not paid for saving out of income at all, but merely for not consuming his capital. And he never accumulated that capital, but received it as a free gift. That he should therefore receive a large income merely in return for not consuming his capital, when another man who received none has to work hard for a small income, is a plain injustice and absurdity. Suppose a man on a desert island had five sons, and left all the land to one of them. That one might live in idleness on a 'rentier' income for the rest of his life; and the rentier income would consist of the commodities produced by his four labouring brothers. The landowner would recline in his armchair and receive from his four brothers as 'rent' a piece of paper certifying that he had refrained from consuming the land; and he would hand this piece of paper back to his brothers in return for a substantial share of the annual produce of their labour. Such, when stripped of verbiage, is the institution of inherited property.

An institution like this, it may be argued, could not continue; the four labouring brothers would plainly rise up and compel their idle colleague to work or starve. Doubtless on a desert island they would. What is the social institution that prevents it happening in the modern capitalist world? In reply one feels inclined to quote the words of Marx, 'not liberty, equality, fraternity, but infantry, cavalry, artillery'. If there were only one property-owner and four workers, it would be easy enough for the four workers to impose their rights by force. But where there are 50,000 property-owners and 50,000,000 workers, it is equally easy for the 50,000, who in any case have all the advantages of wealth, education, and power already in their hands, to defend by force what cannot be defended by reason.

Now this in itself would be a crude and exaggerated picture of modern capitalist society. For that society does not consist simply of a few millionaire rentiers and a host of destitute workers. There are all sorts of intervening graduations and cross-divisions, as was shown statistically in chapter iii. But the statistics there given also show that the whole income structure in modern England and America is enormously distorted by the existence of a huge fund of rent, interest, and profit income which largely accrues to a very few individuals. Although all property-income does not go to the rich, and although all the income of the rich is not unearned, nevertheless almost 70 per cent of the incomes of those above the sur-tax level are unearned.[1] About three-quarters of this unearned income is probably inherited.[2] It is therefore inherited income which is the main factor in perpetuating the inequality of wealth. The total of inherited fortunes subject to death duties in Great Britain every year is about £450,000,000, which represents a command over about £20,000,000 of income; and Messrs. Daniels and Cam-

---

[1] Cf. Josiah Wedgwood, *The Economics of Inheritance*, p. 44.
[2] Cf. p. 234.

pion[1] have shown that even despite British death duties, the total of large fortunes is not tending to fall. Nobody in any case would deny that the bulk of the large incomes of to-day are derived from some form of property.[2]

The survival of inheritance from feudal times into the modern world is a remarkable social phenomenon. In a primitive or feudal society there is a fairly strong case for 100 per cent inheritance. In the first place the inequality of income is not very great, since standards of living cannot vary enormously in a primitive society; though even here the gap between destitution and sufficiency is hardly to be ignored. Secondly, when virtually all property is in land there are various non-economic, or quasi-economic, arguments in favour of inheritance. The identification of a certain person and his family with a certain piece of land, and the expectation that the connection will last indefinitely, probably stimulates the individual to cultivate and preserve the land more assiduously. Such a system may no doubt promote social values connected with the fondness of particular persons for particular places; and such emotions may perhaps be as stabilizing in a primitive society as they are disintegrating in the world of modern nationalism. The simple desire of a man to 'provide for' his wife and family after his death must also be allowed to offer some justification for inheritance, at least as long as no other provision is available. Thirdly, and perhaps most important, inheritance is necessary in a primitive society simply because there is no machinery by which at a man's death his property and income may be taken over by the State and thenceforward used in the interests of the community as a whole. Just as land must be given to someone after the initial feudal conquest in order to avoid chaos, so, if the State still cannot look after it, it must resort to some private individual after the original possessor's death.

The institution of inheritance, thus born of necessity in primitive society, continued to be at least partially justifiable on all these counts right up to the spread of modern industrialism. Even, say, in eighteenth-century England most property was in land; inequalities of income were comparatively mild; personal contact with property still survived; and machinery for collec-

1 *The Distribution of the National Capital.*
2 Cf. ch. xx.

tive consumption of unearned income hardly yet existed. But the continued survival of inheritance, only very partially mitigated, into the days of the modern industrial community, with its enormous productivity, its huge accumulations of wealth in the form of industrial securities, and its colossal inequalities of income, is one of the most glaring anachronisms of history. For to-day the typical man of property is the holder of a huge block of securities which have probably been inherited from his father, which are perhaps varied from month to month and day to day, but which nevertheless confer upon him the right to compel a certain share of the world's lands, labour, and capital to be exclusively devoted to the satisfaction of his needs and desires. It is perfectly possible for him—and in the circumstances who will blame him?—to deposit his paper claims to income in a bank, and to travel pleasantly round and round the world, enjoying the uninterrupted services, directly and indirectly, of perhaps 1,000 of his fellow creatures. Yet at the same time a State machinery exists perfectly capable of receiving this income, and distributing it to those who need it most.

Such an institution could never have been adopted on its own merits. It could only have survived from an age where it had utility and justification into one where it is a grotesque anomaly and injustice only preserved by the self-interest of those who happen to be favoured by it. And the survival of a feudal system of inheritance into a world of huge productivity and huge industrial fortunes is certainly responsible for a further substantial part of the chaos and misery that has so surprisingly accompanied the development of human knowledge and inventiveness and their application to production. Looking round the world, one sees enormous fortunes accruing to royalty-owners in the north of England because their distant ancestors conquered country under which coal was found centuries later; or to landowners on whose inherited fields London and New York chanced to be built; or to British and French aristocrats whose forefathers happened, in the seventeenth century, to discover the secret of moneylending; or to Japanese feudal lords, who to-day can sell their land to the builders of cities and buy securities in London, Paris, and New York with the highly valuable proceeds.

The succession of conquest, possession, and dispossession is of course one of the most familiar chapters in history. And naturally in any given age the possessors invent specious reasons to justify the retention of the spoils. In some of these reasons there is substance, and they must be examined on their merits when we come to consider how far the right of inheritance should be mitigated and how far maintained. For the moment it is enough to observe that the fact of inheritance is one of the most important of all the elements which determine, and distort, the structure of incomes and prices in a modern capitalist community.[1] Inheritance, in fact, is the chief of the institutional factors which weaken still further the claim of existing society to have discovered a valid criterion for the distribution of incomes.

[1] Cf. pp. 234 and 237–9.

CHAPTER XIII

OTHER SOCIAL MONOPOLIES

There is a second class of institutional factors, however, which push the distortion of the price system even further. Not only is the ideal world of free competition and perfect knowledge belied in fact by the existence of ignorance, convention, and other kinds of 'frictions' inseparable from human life in any conditions, it is also belied by the existence of social institutions which create and maintain monopolistic privileges in the interest of certain groups. In the first place the concentration of wealth in a few hands means the concession to a few of enormous advantages of education and influence. All men do not start equal in looking for a job. It is, of course, true that a working man of extraordinary force and ability can rise in modern England or America to almost any position; and dukes have been found unable to secure admission to universities. But the fact remains that a man of anything but superlative ability cannot, if he starts as a miner, rise to be the chairman of an industrial combine; while the expensively educated public-school boy, though also of only normal ability, is quite capable of *holding* the company directorship which he has obtained by influence. The man of average ability in any walk of life, bus conductor or bank chairman, can *hold* his position when it is once gained. Brief familiarity with the average bus conductor will show that he would be quite capable of holding a banking directorship if his father had given it him; and the perusal of some of our company chairman's speeches will also show that if they had started as bus conductors they would certainly be there still. It would be absurd to suggest that there are no men of superior ability among company directors or doctors or lawyers. But it remains true nevertheless that it requires a man of exceptional ability to rise from the place where he started, and one of exceptional stupidity to fall below it.

And the existence of this sort of social monopoly is more wide-spread than might appear at first sight. The general bias in favour of the propertied class is naturally its root; but it ramifies widely, much more widely, than this. There are whole fields of activity, such as the Bar, the Civil Service, the medical profession, the Stock Exchange, and a host of others, which are practically closed to all who do not possess advantages of education and wealth. The development of State education has greatly mitigated this evil; but it is still largely true that only those who can buy their way into these professions can get into them at all. In Great Britain, in particular, the ludicrous excessiveness of the incomes earned by those connected with the Stock Exchange and its attendant finance, banking and issuing houses, is unquestionably due to the close link between the City of London and our system of class education. The number of old Etonian ties in Throgmorton Street has to be seen to be believed.

The significance of this important social fact for economic theory, and its effect on the price system, has been carefully analysed by Mr. H. D. Dickinson in his interesting book *Institutional Revenue*.[1] Mr. Dickinson points out that the existence of privileged 'non-competing' groups creates a special kind of monopoly revenue. 'Supposing', he remarks, 'entry into the legal profession were restricted to red-headed men, we should have to pay our lawyers higher fees than we do now, because their services would be scarcer.' The red-headed men, that is to say, would be drawing a monopoly revenue which Mr. Dickinson calls their 'institutional revenue' on top of their proper competitive income; all the potentially able, but non-red-headed, lawyers would be earning less than they might; and the total national income would be lower because of the misdirection and partial waste of the services of these potential lawyers. This in a less flagrant degree is the effect which the highly exclusive class structure of private capitalism is actively producing every day. Who can doubt that there are among miners and agricultural labourers to-day, if not mute inglorious Miltons or poor unennobled Nuffields, at least potential lawyers, doctors, civil

[1] The idea has often been emphasized previously by Mr. Maurice Dobb, and of course by Professor Pigou.

servants, and business men of more than ordinary ability? But their social environment prevents their earning the income which even the price system at its best would concede; and the community is the poorer for the misdirection of their services.

CHAPTER XIV

THE CASE AGAINST CAPITALISM

Such in outline are the main counts in the case against what we call capitalism; that is to say, the combination of a more or less free price mechanism with private property and inheritance. It is a system which does not even in theory take account of the difference between different people's needs or efforts; which is grossly distorted by the existence of unequal and unearned incomes; and which is even further distorted by the prevalence of monopoly and imperfect competition in all their forms, and by social privileges of which the worst is inheritance. Indeed the existence of unequal and unearned incomes and of inheritance are enough in themselves to impair the belief in the virtue of the price system which the average individualist holds. Is the case for the price system, however, as well as the case for inheritance, completely destroyed by these facts? Or does it merely follow that that system ought to be drastically reformed? It is most important at this stage in the argument not to prove too much.

The existence of unequal and unearned incomes and of inheritance and other social monopolies certainly makes nonsense of what might be called naïve individualism, i.e. the belief that under *laisser-faire* every man is paid what he is 'worth'; that resources are necessarily directed into the 'most economic channels'; that they are necessarily put to the 'most profitable uses'; that 'demand' is the ultimate arbiter of production; that every man has a right to the income he gets and no more; and that receipts from the State or payments to the State are either 'charity' or 'confiscation'. All these words and arguments involve gross confusions of thought. The price system does not pay a man what he is 'worth' according to some criterion of natural justice, but what he would appear to be worth if all difference

140

of real needs, all irregularities of income, and all social privileges were ignored. Resources are not diverted into the most 'profitable' channels in any other sense than those which are most profitable if all these things are ignored; and the 'demand' which controls production is similarly 'demand' only in this emasculated sense. The popular view, therefore—popular, curiously enough, among the working classes as well as the privileged—that a man gets what he is worth or deserves, that further payments from the State are charity, and that taxation is a sort of confiscation—are in reality extremely superficial. There is nothing sacred about the scheme of incomes which the price system of contemporary capitalism happens to turn out. When carefully scrutinized, it at once appears to have a vast element of the haphazard about it. If one individual inherits a huge unearned income accruing from the rents of large numbers of propertyless workers, it is really that individual who is living on 'charity' at the expense of the rest of the community; and if his income is taken away by the State and distributed among the workers the State is merely returning to them what they themselves have earned.

It is curious how deeply the false attribution of sacrosanctity to the haphazard working of the price system runs through both popular and academic thought. Its popular manifestation may be seen in the working-class mother's refusal—still known, though happily rarer—to allow her children to receive free meals on the ground that such meals are 'charity', and its highbrow manifestation in such a book as that edited by Professor Hayek on *Collectivist Economic Planning*. In this work the idea of socialism is denounced on the ground that a 'rational' distribution of resources according to 'demand' is impossible except under free competition. The whole argument of the book rests on little else but the assumption that the free price system is a fair criterion of comparative needs and efforts.

We must consequently reject the whole social philosophy, economic vocabulary, and practical programme based on the assumption of the sacrosanctity of the capitalist price system. But we must emphatically not run to the opposite extreme and assume that the price system as such is worthless and ought to be abolished. We have merely shown that there are serious blemishes in its sacrosanctity; and that inferences based on the assumption of that sacrosanctity are meaningless or false. But it may be that in an imperfect world it is the only, or perhaps the least undesirable, system which is in fact available. We must above all remember the remark of that very balanced student of the price system, Professor F. H. Knight, that critics of the system 'generally underrate the possibility of doing vastly worse'. How far the price system and its social environment can and ought to be mitigated, are entirely different questions which must be considered at a later stage of the argument. Here it may be provisionally concluded that there are very serious and fundamental flaws in the price system, and that those flaws are practically all connected with the inequality of incomes.

PART III
MONEY AND THE TRADE CYCLE

CHAPTER XV

TOTAL EFFECTIVE DEMAND

So far in this book it has been assumed that capitalism works, if not according to its own theory, at least according to its own rules. It has been assumed that, though the distribution of incomes resulting from capitalism is unequitable and indefensible, full use is nevertheless made by capitalism of all the productive resources available. But it is now notorious that capitalism does not always work. It not only misdirects the resources of production, but it frequently leaves a large part of them unemployed. This introduces a wholly new element into the problem. Up till recently the main criticism of capitalism had always been, not that it failed to work, but that it worked only too well in the interests of the favoured few. Socialists in general concentrated on the existing maldistribution of wealth, and usually felt themselves to be on the defensive when arguing that socialism would actually work better than capitalism. Only the followers of Marx, who originally based his theories on the conditions of the 1840's, predicted that capitalism would 'break down' as a result of its own inherent 'contradictions'. Lately, however, as the existence of unemployed labour and capital began to dominate the economic scene, these theories have again become prominent. They have had one obvious and powerful attraction for socialists: the contention that the morally indefensible element in capitalism, the maldistribution of incomes, was also the source of the economic collapse. This naturally gave rise to a great deal of wishful thinking. How simple the world would be if all things which were unjust would not work! Such thinking, however, has greatly confused the issue; and made it all the more necessary to bring the socialist case up to date. For it may be that capitalism is unjust for one reason and unworkable for

145

another. At any rate we should not assume the reason to be the same without some dispassionate consideration.

The existence of unemployed labour and capital and the ability of the world to produce more than it can consume have been the dominant features of economic, if not of political, history in the last ten years. What has been the admitted immediate cause of this strange situation? Each individual producer has been compelled to reduce his production and allow plant and labour to remain idle because if he used them fully he would not be able to sell his product at a price which would cover his costs of production and ensure him a 'normal' profit.[1] Now it is, of course, part of the normal working of any free price system that when consumers' demand is transferred from one product to another, losses should be made and production contracted in the industry producing the product for which demand is falling. These losses, however, and this contraction of production will be balanced by abnormal profits and an expansion of production in the industry to which demand has been transferred. The less money spent, in fact, on the product of some industry, the more will normally be spent on that of another; and labour and capital will be transferred from one to another. General unemployment will not therefore appear.

It seems, accordingly, that if general unemployment appears something different must have happened. For in this situation producers all over the system are making losses; or at least the losses of some are no longer being balanced by the abnormal profits of others. And this must be due not to any transfer of demand or movement of relative prices within the system, but to a fall in the total amount of money spent by all consumers on all products. Or, more exactly, the total consumers' expenditure must have fallen, not necessarily below what it was before, but below the total of all costs (including a normal profit) that have to be paid to the various producers. The position may perhaps be most simply expressed in this way. Each producer has a certain sum to be paid in fixed costs, i.e. rent, debenture interest, wages, etc. It is of the greatest importance to realize that almost all of the producers' costs are fixed, in the short run, either by

1 This must be taken henceforth, in the light of the discussion in ch. vi, to mean such a return as, in all the economic and social circumstances, will induce him to carry on his business on the relevant scale.

law or by fact. Rent, interest, and any other legally contracted payments are fixed probably for a period of years; and wage rates are in effect fixed within the short period by trade-union pressure and the threat of strikes. For although the producer can reduce his total wage bill by contracting his production, he cannot reduce it in any other way in a short time. If full production is to be maintained, therefore, his wage costs must be regarded as virtually fixed. His raw material costs, though they may change from time to time, are also fixed in the sense that he cannot alter them at will in any other way than by reducing the scale of production (unless there are only a few buyers). The same is true of depreciation costs. For though, as Mr. Keynes has recently pointed out in his analysis of 'user costs',[1] depreciation may be reduced if output is reduced, it is bound to be virtually fixed in relation to a given output. There may perhaps be a small range of costs which are compressible in the sense that they can be reduced by the introduction of 'economies'. But such costs must be regarded as negligible in amount; for we could only suppose them to exist on a large scale, ready to be reduced at any moment, if we supposed all firms to be permanently organized in a highly inefficient manner. In effect, then, and in the short period, it seems that all the entrepreneurs' costs must be regarded as virtually fixed in the sense that the total of each kind of cost can only be reduced by a reduction in the scale of output. Costs, that is to say, per unit of each factor of production are virtually fixed.

Traditionally costs have been distinguished into prime costs and supplementary costs, i.e. those which could and those which could not be reduced by a decrease in production. This distinction is mainly designed to elucidate changes in average costs, i.e. costs per unit of the commodity produced, and the problem of the individual entrepreneur's equilibrium. It is consequently not immediately relevant to the relation of costs and demand over the whole system; though it is important to remember that the first sort of costs (rent, interest, etc.) are also normally fixed independently of the scale of production, while the latter (wages, salaries, etc.) are only fixed in relation to a given scale of production.

We may then regard each entrepreneur as having a certain

[1] *The General Theory of Employment, Interest, and Money*, ch. vi.

total of fixed costs to be paid, if full production is to be maintained, and a certain normal profit to be earned. This aggregate of costs and profit must be conceived as a money stream, a certain total of payments that has to be maintained *per year*. Suppose that a given entrepreneur, when his factory is working at full capacity, pays £95,000 a year in fixed costs, and receives £5,000 a year in 'profit'. It is clear that unless at least £100,000 a year is spent on the factory's product—enough, that is to say, to cover fixed costs and profit—the scale of production will be reduced and men will be thrown out of work. To the extent to which total receipts fall below £100,000 the entrepreneur will be making an inadequate profit or a loss. If, on the other hand, more than £100,000 is spent on his products, the entrepreneur will find himself making abnormal profits, and will consequently start expanding production and taking on extra men.

Suppose further that the total of the fixed costs of all producers of finished[1] goods all over the system are £95,000,000, and that the total of their normal profits is £5,000,000; it is again clear (if we assume for a moment that no new saving or investment is going on) that the total spending of the whole community on finished goods must reach at least £100,000,000 if the whole system is not to start running down. If less than this is spent, all entrepreneurs will not necessarily be making losses; but the losses of those who are losing will not be balanced by the abnormal profits earned by those who are not. For this would only happen if at least £100,000,000 were being spent over the whole system. Suppose there are 1,000 producers of finished goods, each with the cost structure described above, and that the total spending of the community falls to £90,000,000; then either the receipts of each will fall to £90,000, or the aggregate losses of those whose receipts fall below £100,000 must exceed the aggregate abnormal profits of those whose profits rise above it. In either case there is bound to be a net dismissal of labour, i.e. a fall in employment throughout the system.[2]

[1] The significance of this word will appear in the next chapter.
[2] It is perfectly true, as Mr. R. F. Harrod has recently pointed out, that what determines the level of output is not total profits but marginal profits. Each entrepreneur increases output until the extra revenue earned by producing another unit is less than the cost of producing it. In effect, however, since his costs (including profit) are virtually fixed in relation to any given level of output, there will be a certain total of demand which will induce

Moreover, the effects of this decrease in employment will be quite different from the effects of a dismissal of men by an individual entrepreneur in the case where demand had been transferred away from his products to some other product. For in this latter case, where the total demand does not fall, his losses will be balanced by another entrepreneur's abnormal profits, and the labour dismissed from one firm will be taken on by another. And the first entrepreneur will probably find that at the lower level of production and plant now accepted by his industry prices rise once more. In the case of a fall in total demand, however, there will be no abnormal profits to balance the losses, and the extra labour will not be taken on. The loss of wages of the men unemployed will therefore lead to a further fall in total demand; and an alarming cumulative process, never contemplated by the theory of the price system, will emerge over the horizon. For when the original fall in total demand occurs, the entrepreneurs making losses behave in the way which they ought to behave under the normal working of the price system; they contract production in the hope that when the supply falls prices will rise again. If it was a case of a transfer of demand from one industry to another, this would of course happen; and a new 'equilibrium' would be reached. But if there is a fall in total demand the very behaviour of entrepreneurs which is appropriate under the price system is itself bound to lead to a cumulative increase in unemployment.

Such a general and cumulative increase in unemployment can only therefore be due to a fall of the stream of total money demand below the level of the stream of total money costs. The question how such a deficiency arises is the Monetary Problem. The ordinary analysis of the price system, as Professor Hayek has lucidly pointed out,[1] suggests that all movements out of equilibrium are self-correcting; the greater they become, the more certainly they produce the necessary adjustment. But here is a movement away from equilibrium which is not self-

[1] *Monetary Theory and the Trade Cycle*, ch. ii.

him to produce his greatest possible output; there will be a certain price (which may be called the 'supply price') at which he will produce that output. We are, therefore, justified in thinking, for this purpose, in terms of total costs and total profits.

adjusting but cumulative. We are therefore now concerned not with the relation of various prices and costs, but with the relation of the total stream of money demand and the total stream of money costs. These two conceptions had consequently better be clearly defined. The first may perhaps be called 'Total Effective Demand'[1] and defined as the aggregate of expenditure of the community on all finished consumers'[2] goods. Effective demand in relation to any particular entrepreneur or industry will mean consumers' expenditure on the products of that entrepreneur or industry. Secondly, Total Costs will mean the aggregate per year of all the costs (including normal profits) of consumers' goods, i.e. the total payment which producers of these goods as a whole must receive if full production and employment is to be maintained.[3]

It must be always remembered that Total Costs not only have to be equalled by Total Effective Demand, if full output and employment are to be maintained; but that the proper ratio between the different elements within Total Costs has to be preserved. For instance, if Total Effective Demand has so fallen that there are no profits, it is no good increasing Total Effective Demand even by the requisite amount if it is added not to profits but wages. The condition of full output is that both the ratios within Total Costs and the equality between Total Costs and Total Effective Demand should be preserved. In the traditional discussions of the problem the ratios have been over-emphasized in relation to the totals. In what follows, therefore, though the ratios must not be forgotten, the emphasis is on the totals.

The main problem to be solved is accordingly in essence one of the relation between Total Effective Demand and Total Costs. We have to discover why it is that the two tend to diverge, and how they can be prevented from diverging.

That they do diverge, is clear from empirical observation. Large and rapid increases and decreases in unemployment, accompanied by ebbs and flows in the total of goods produced

1 This corresponds to Mr. Keynes's 'effective demand' and Mr. R. G. Hawtrey's 'consumers' outlay'.

2 The reason for the definition of Total Effective Demand or expenditure as *finished* consumers' goods is explained later. Cf. pp. 169–73.

3 This Mr. Keynes, using the orthodox terminology, calls the 'aggregate supply price of output as a whole' (*The General Theory of Employment, Interest, and Money*, p. 24).

and consumed, have long been observable in the great industrialized countries. Not only have there been such divergences,
however; they have been of a definite kind. They have developed
a recognizable rhythm and periodicity, and they have gradually
permeated every trading community in the world. What has
come to be known as the 'trade cycle' began to show recognizable symptoms (though they were naturally not then recognized)
in about the middle of the nineteenth century; and from about
1870 onwards its regular ebb and flow, interacting with shorter
trends, can be traced with fair statistical accuracy.[1] Since that
time every eight to ten years a peak of production and employment has been reached, followed by a sudden relapse, a period
of stagnation, and an upward movement accelerating to another
peak. Such peaks occurred in almost every important trading
country about the years 1872, 1880, 1891, 1900, 1907, and
1913–14. After this the cyclical fluctuations became submerged
in the tidal wave of the war. The post-war peak of economic
activity in 1920, however, was followed by a relapse till 1922–3;
a recovery up till 1929; a relapse thereafter which lasted in the
British Empire, Japan, and Scandinavia until the abandonment
of the gold standard by these countries at the end of 1931, in the
United States until the depreciation of the dollar in 1933, in
Germany until the beginning of the huge State expenditure on
rearmament in 1933, and in France until the beginning of similar expenditure in the autumn of 1935. The Great Depression,
as it has come to be called, of 1929–33, affected all countries in
the world except Russia; and before it ended it had provoked a
change of government in almost every country, including a
violent revolution in Germany, Spain, Austria, and about six
other countries, and peaceful revolutions in the United States,
France, and elsewhere.

An attempt has been made by some economists, including
Professor Cassel,[2] to maintain that the trade cycle is not a cycle
at all but merely a series of oscillations. The total volume of
economic activity, it is argued, is bound to change from time
to time: and since it can only move up or down, it is natural

[1] See in particular *Industrial Fluctuations* by A. C. Pigou, and *An Introduction to the Study of Prices* by Sir Walter Layton and Geoffrey Crowther, in
both of which books the history of the cycle is illustrated by full statistical
charts.

[2] *The Breakdown in the World's Monetary System* by Gustav Cassel.

that it should move up and down alternatively. Professor MacGregor[1] has shown statistically, however, that this argument is not valid. The trade cycle has a statistically ascertainable rhythm and periodicity which a genuinely random oscillation, such as the annual number of shipwrecks, has not.

Its rhythm, however, is not its only recognizable symptom. It also displays certain regular phenomena both in its downward and its upward phases. The most prominent features of the downswing, or depression, are falling production, consumption, and employment: and of the upswing, or recovery, rising production, consumption, and employment. Only slightly less prominent are the fall of prices, money wages, profits, and interest rates during the depression, and the rise of all these during the recovery. Slightly less prominent again is the fact that the intensity of both upward and downward movements is much greater in the trades producing durable goods than in those producing non-durable goods.

Now all or most of these phenomena are evidently what we should expect to be associated with an alternative excess of Total Costs over Total Effective Demand and of Total Effective Demand over Total Costs. An excess of Total Effective Demand must lead to rising profits, rising production, and rising consumption; and an excess of Total Costs to the reverse process. An excess of Total Effective Demand is also likely to lead to rising prices, an excess of Total Costs to falling prices; for though the price level is the ratio of Total Effective Demand, not to Total Costs, but to the physical total of all finished goods produced (which we may call Total Output),[2] the two are likely to be associated in the short run. There are consequently good *prima facie* grounds for believing that the problem of the trade cycle, as well as that of unemployed resources, is the problem of divergences between Total Costs and Total Effective Demand.

Since both these are quantities, or rather flows, of money, the problem may fairly be called a monetary one. This does not necessarily imply that it is mainly a problem of the monetary

---

[1] Cf. *Enterprise, Purpose, and Profit*, by D. H. MacGregor, ch. iii.

[2] It will be observed, however, that this is a vague concept, since tons of coal cannot be added to pints of milk, or 'train miles per engine hour' of transport, etc.

system. For there may be, and indeed clearly are, other factors than the monetary system which effect both these money flows. But it is only by affecting these two streams that other factors can produce the conditions of general unemployment and depression. We are thus brought to the point in the argument, anticipated at the beginning of chapter v, at which the practical significance of money must be considered. On the subject of money and the trade cycle as a whole libraries have already been written: and it is clearly impossible to analyse it thoroughly in the course of an examination of the case for socialism. It is possible, however, to survey the present state of the debate and to see what light our existing knowledge and understanding of monetary phenomena can throw on the socialist case. Moreover, monetary phenomena cannot be ignored; for partly owing to the theories of Marx, and partly owing to the confusions of thought engendered by the Great Depression, the analysis of the trade cycle and the case for socialism have become inextricably entangled. And there is at least a little truth in the view that the case for socialism rests partly on the existence of the trade cycle.

CHAPTER XVI

MONEY AND CREDIT

Before discussing the origin of changes in Total Effective Demand and Total Costs it is unfortunately necessary briefly to discover the nature of the medium of which these two flows consist. Discussions of the nature of money are apt to be extremely tedious: but such important misconceptions about the nature of bank credit have arisen, and so puzzling is the whole business to the plain man, that it is essential to elucidate the few broad factors in the nature of money which are relevant to an understanding of the trade cycle. Broadly speaking, anything must be conceived as 'money' which is generally accepted as a means of payment. The main difficulties seem to arise from the fact that the total of money in existence is at once a flow circulating, regularly or irregularly, round a certain channel in a certain time, and a stock existing in a given form at any given moment. It is probably best to consider these two aspects separately, and then consider how they interact.

1. *The Flow of Money*

There is no very great difficulty about the flow of money. It consists of a stream of coins, notes, and cheques which pass from consuming units to producing units and back again. The consumer pays the shopkeeper; who pays the wholesaler; who pays the producer; who pays partly the consumer again in his capacity as worker or capitalist, and partly other producers who in their turn pay consumers. This is the main stream; and it is divided into coins, notes, and cheques according to the size of the payment that has to be made. There are also certain subsidiary streams such as the Exchequer into which a considerable trickle flows in the form of taxes and emerges in the form of Government expenditure of one kind or another. Another more

154

complicated subsidiary stream arises from the fact that lending and borrowing, saving and investing, are going on throughout the whole system. In essence the process of saving and investment, in its monetary aspect, consists of the lending of money by A to B and the expenditure by B of that money on some sort of durable goods. In some cases, of course, individuals or companies invest their own earnings, but they still—though less predominantly—borrow them from other people. The chief machinery for this borrowing and lending is the banking system, the Stock Exchange, and the money market. Indeed almost all the mysterious operations that go on in the City of London, apart from insurance and dealings in commodities, are designed, in theory at any rate, to facilitate the process of lending and borrowing.

This subsidiary stream, it should be observed, is also normally a diversion, and not a stoppage, of part of the main flow. For the money that has been saved is usually lent to producers of one kind or another, who spend it on durable goods and so pay it out in wages, rent, interest, and profit to the persons who produce those durable goods. When an individual or institution saves money it is either deposited in a bank or 'invested' in the Stock Exchange. If it is deposited in a bank it will normally be lent by the bank to someone else as an overdraft, advance, or some other form of loan. If it is invested on the Stock Exchange, a security will be bought from its former holder. That holder will either spend the proceeds of the sale; in which case no net saving has taken place, since one man's 'dissaving', i.e. spending beyond his income, has offset another man's saving. Or else he will buy another security, in which case the process is merely pushed a stage further on. Or, finally, he will subscribe to a new issue. In so far as dissaving is not taking place, therefore, the new savings invested on the Stock Exchange will find their way into new issues,[1] and so into the hands of the purchasers of durable goods: for the great bulk of the money subscribed to new issues comes from the sale of other securities. If savings are put in the Post Office Savings Bank they will be used to purchase securities; and if they are deposited with a building society they will be lent to house purchasers or builders. In the end, there-

[1] Many new issues are of course mere conversions: in this case the transaction is a mere 'swapping' of securities.

fore, the stream of money diverging into savings should tend[1] to reappear as the incomes of the producers of durable goods.

2. Coins, Notes, and Bank Deposits

Such in very brief outline is the flow of money in a modern industrial State. It is much less easy to devise a clear picture of the stock as it exists at a particular moment. By 'money' the plain man ordinarily means coins, notes, and bank deposits (cheques being perhaps generally conceived as bank deposits on the move). About coins and notes there is no very great difficulty. They are familiar physical objects, expressed in the unit in which prices are calculated (the 'money of account'), and useful as a 'medium of exchange' and to some extent as a store of value. Originally coins were simply pieces of gold, silver, copper, or whatever metal there was, with their weight stamped clearly on them by some reliable authority. Their quantity then simply depended on the quantity of the metal which anyone chose to bring to the authority to have stamped. Now, however, coins are normally issued of greater value than the value of metal contained in them. Their acceptance at their 'face value', i.e. as equivalent to that unit of the 'money of account' stamped on their face, depends on their being legal tender; and their quantity is determined by the discretion of the issuing authority. In fact the issuing authority tries to accommodate the quantity to the public's demand for small change, and that demand depends partly on the level of business activity and partly on the volume of other money in circulation.[2]

Notes are not quite so simple. For whereas coins are merely physical objects, involving no complicated relationship between different persons or institutions, notes do involve such a relationship. The clearest way to conceive of notes, and of all 'money' other than coins, is as 'promises to pay' (ultimately promises to pay coin or bullion, though this does not matter). A promise to pay, or IOU, may assume two general forms, with varying intermediate degrees. It may either be simply a promise, i.e. an agreement between two persons who trust one another,

[1] Whether or not it _all_ reappears, must be discussed later. Cf. ch. xvii.
[2] For a full discussion of the nature of coins and notes see _What Everybody Wants to Know about Money_ (edited by G. D. H. Cole), ch. i.

existing nowhere except in those persons' minds. Or the promise may be written down on a piece of paper, though the piece of paper is of no great significance. In the next stage the promise is not to pay anyone in particular, but to pay the bearer of the piece of paper. In the next stage again, the piece of paper comes to be handed round from one person to another because everyone knows that the author of the promise would pay if necessary. And finally everyone is so sure that the piece of paper will be accepted in payment by everybody else that the promise is forgotten altogether, and the piece of paper becomes as truly 'money' as a coin.

State-issued notes are normally promises to pay that have assumed this final form. Normally nobody thinks of them as anything but 'money'. Similarly the central banks' notes that have succeeded Treasury notes in many countries to-day, including England, are regarded as money rather than as promises to pay. Indeed doubts have been expressed how exactly the Bank of England would fulfil, if requested, the promise to pay inscribed on its notes. In granting to central banks the right to issue notes governments have stipulated that the amount should be limited and that the profit on the issue should accrue to the Exchequer. The amount is usually limited by prescribing that the gold reserve of the Bank must be a certain percentage of the note issue, or, as in England, by prescribing that it shall equal the gold reserve *plus* a certain fixed figure (the 'Fiduciary Issue' of £200,000,000). The 'profit' accrues to the Treasury because the right to issue any money worth more than its commodity value, i.e. the value of the paper, confers on the issuer the power of getting rich quick. Banks do not give notes away. They pay them out in discharge of their liabilities, or buy assets with them. There is nothing to prevent a central bank buying gilt-edged securities with the notes it has printed. It can print £1,000,000 in notes (which would cost perhaps £10) and buy £1,000,000 worth of securities with them. It can then hold these securities and pay the interest on them to its shareholders. For the notes of the bank, it should be remembered, are, from its point of view, as soon as they have been issued, *liabilities*. They are promises to pay, an acknowledgement of debt due by the bank to the holders. This was the point overlooked by the legendary Irish crowd which, becoming infuriated with a certain bank, is said to have collected the outstanding notes of that bank and burnt them outside its doors.

Bank deposits are also promises to pay made by the bank, and are in essence the same as banknotes. The difference arises partly from the fact that the promise is not inscribed quite so obviously on a visible piece of paper. Actually, of course, it is inscribed on a piece of paper in the banker's ledger and in the pass-book of the depositor. But the piece of paper in this case is less important (except for reference) than the knowledge in the mind of the banker and depositor that the promise to pay exists. The other difference, not one of principle, is that a bank deposit is a promise to pay a definite person, the depositor, and not anyone who may happen to get hold of the ledger. Merely by writing a cheque, however, which should properly be conceived as an instruction to the banker to pay rather than a promise by the depositor, the depositor can convert the bank's promise to pay him into a payment to someone else. The someone else thereby receives the right to draw coins and notes out of the bank or to keep a deposit, i.e. a promise of the banker to pay him. In those cases—which predominate in the modern world—where any well-known bank's promise to pay is as universally acceptable a payment as actual coins, the bank deposit as well as the bank-note becomes in effect 'money'. Indeed, the bank deposit has now become the rule, and the note or coin the exception. In England in 1937, for instance, the total of bank deposits in existence was rather over £2,250,000,000, and the total of bank-notes, about £500,000,000.

The complete stock of money in existence at any moment in a modern community, therefore, consists of the coins and notes in the hands of the public, the coins and notes in commercial banks and the central bank, and the total of bank deposits. The situation of any commercial bank, or of all such banks together, may be conceived in the following simplified form. The bank or banks have a certain volume of promises to pay in existence. These are what it owes, its liabilities. Neglecting certain unimportant items, and assuming that the bank in question issues no notes, we may take its liabilities to consist entirely of its customers' deposits, say £100,000,000. Of these some will be current deposits, payable on demand, on which no interest is paid, and some 'time deposits' (known as 'deposit accounts' in England) for the payment of which the bank requires notice, and on which it accordingly pays interest. Both, however, are promises to pay and therefore liabilities of the bank.

On the other side of its balance-sheet it will have £100,000,000 of assets. These assets will consist to some slight extent of coins but preponderantly of other people's promises to pay. Some of these will be promises to pay of the central bank: the central bank's notes on the one hand, and the commercial bank's deposit at the central bank on the other. These promises to pay of the central bank will be considered so safe by the commercial bank that it will class them with its coins and call the total of all these items (coins, notes, and deposits at the central bank) its 'cash' reserve. This reserve will (if the ratios usual in England are observed) amount to about £10,000,000, of which perhaps £4,000,000 will be deposits at the central bank and £6,000,000 coins and notes. The remaining £90,000,000 of the commercial bank's assets consist of other and less reliable persons' promises to pay. Of these the biggest item is simply 'advances', i.e. loans made and overdrafts granted to the public in general. These are owed back to the bank by the persons concerned, and are consequently assets of the bank. The next biggest item is investments, i.e. gilt-edged, or mostly gilt-edged securities[1] purchased by the bank, and themselves promises to pay made by companies and governments national or local. Lastly, the bank holds a certain number of bills of exchange, which are in effect promises to pay the bearer a certain sum at a certain date.

The situation of the central bank will be in essence the same. In detail the structure of central banks varies a good deal; and the Bank of England is particularly complicated because it is somewhat archaically divided into a 'banking department' and an 'issue department'. Broadly speaking, however, one may say that central banks have liabilities, on the one hand, consisting of their own promises to pay, i.e. their own notes and the government's and bankers' deposits with them; and assets on the other, consisting of gold and silver coin and bullion, and securi-

---

[1] Securities are promises to pay in a rather special sense. They are promises to pay a certain sum (or an uncertain sum) annually, and in the case of a redeemable security, to repay the principal at a certain date. In the case of an irredeemable security they are simply a promise to pay an annual sum.

159

ties of one kind or another, mostly government bonds and treasury bills. A central bank's liabilities, for instance, might consist of £60,000,000 in notes in circulation, £30,000,000 in commercial banks' deposits at the central bank, and £10,000,000 in government deposits at the central bank. Its assets might then consist of £30,000,000 in coin and bullion, £50,000,000 in government bonds, £10,000,000 in treasury bills, and £10,000,000 in commercial bills.

A bank, therefore, central or otherwise, is at any moment in the apparently precarious position of having on the one hand a large volume of its own promises to pay, which it calls its 'liabilities', and on the other hand a small volume of coins *plus* a large volume of other people's promises to pay which it calls its 'assets'. It manages meanwhile to pay its staff and earn a profit by dint of charging on the average a higher rate of interest on other people's promises to pay than it pays on its own. Its position is not really quite so precarious as it looks. It is true that if everybody suddenly took the various promises to pay at their face value and demanded gold or silver for them they could not be satisfied, since there would not be enough in existence. There would then be what is known as a 'financial crisis', i.e. everybody would default on their promises to pay everybody else; and the government would have to step in, print limitless new promises to pay of its own in the form of notes, and allow the central bank to issue these in discharge of its promises to pay until the public began to behave more normally. All this happened in the United States in March 1933. Usually, however, and in particular in countries where the possibility of such crises has been forgotten, individuals only seek to 'cash' the banks' promises to pay when they really want the cash. The banks consequently find that all is well if they keep their 'cash' from falling below a certain minimum percentage of the total of their outstanding promises to pay.

3. *How Banks create Credit*

This brings us to the really crucial question: what determines the total volume of bank deposits? In the first instance it is determined by the volume of the banks' 'cash'. For since by convention the banks maintain their reserve at a certain minimum percentage of their total deposits—for the reason just explained—variations in their reserve must produce variations in the total of deposits. In England the minimum percentage is about 10, and the clearing banks (in 1937) consequently have a total cash reserve of about £225,000,000 against total deposits of £2,250,000,000. It is possible, of course, for the banks to let their 'cash ratio' rise above 10 per cent, but if they do this their earning assets are smaller than they might be, and they are consequently sacrificing profits. In general, therefore, they do not do so. Some part of the banks' cash consists of coins and notes, and the quantity of the notes is determined by the quantity of notes in circulation and therefore ultimately by the quantity of gold in the Bank of England. But in fact the quantity of coins and notes is generally regulated by the monetary authorities so as to conform to the total quantity of money.

The really important item is consequently the other part of the banks' cash, i.e. their deposits at the Bank of England. These in 1937 in Great Britain varied between £80,000,000 and £100,000,000. They are, as was pointed out, liabilities of the Bank of England; and it is, within certain legal and practical limits, within a central bank's power to vary the total of its assets and liabilities together. This is a critically important point which used once to be hotly disputed. Suppose somebody deposits with the Bank of England £100 worth of gold: he receives in return a promise to pay of the bank to that amount—either a note or a deposit. The bank's assets have then grown by £100 worth of gold, and its liabilities by £100 in deposits. Suppose, however, that the bank's new assets take the form of £100 in securities. It buys £100 worth of securities on the Stock Exchange and gives the seller a promise to pay of that amount, i.e. a deposit at the bank. Again the bank increases its assets and liabilities by £100. The same thing happens if it grants a new loan or 'discounts' a new bill (which is in effect the same thing). What happens, however, to the new deposits which the operation has created in each case? Normally the owner of the deposit will be a customer of one of the commercial banks, say Barclays, and he will consequently draw a cheque on his deposits at the Bank of England and pay it into his account at the commercial bank. He will convert, that is to say, the Bank of England's promise to pay him into a promise by the Bank to pay

Barclays,[1] and in return he will receive from Barclays a promise to pay him (an ordinary deposit) of £100. Now since the new Bank of England deposit which has come into the hands of Barclays is counted by Barclays as part of its cash, and since it can allow its deposits to be at least ten times as great as its cash, Barclays can now expand its deposits not merely by £100, but by a further £900, i.e. by £1,000 altogether. The purchase of £100 worth of War Loan on the Stock Exchange by the Bank of England from Mr. A has resulted in an increase of £1,000 in the total stock of money in the community!

Can the Bank of England, or any central bank, in practice so expand its assets and liabilities, and can the commercial banks really follow suit? The Bank of England is, of course, prevented by various laws and conventions from reducing the ratio of gold to total liabilities beyond certain limits, but these limits are wide and they can always be suspended or altered if it seems desirable in the national interest. In some cases the Bank is also limited by the fact that it takes two to make the bargain which increases its assets and liabilities. The traditional method of expanding its liabilities, i.e. 'expanding credit', was to reduce the rate at which it would discount bills; which meant in effect to lower the rate of interest at which it was willing to lend money. But if nobody was willing to borrow money, even at the lower rate, this would naturally have no effect. Similarly no bank can make advances to people who will not accept them. Nor can it be sure that people will wish to sell gold to it at the price it is willing to pay. There is nothing, however, in practically any circumstances to prevent a central bank from buying gilt-edged securities on the Stock Exchange. In all but the most exceptional circumstances there will always be persons willing to sell securities at the market price, and to sell them in large quantities if the price is forced a little upward. A central bank is always in a position to expand its deposits by giving them in return for securities, i.e. buying securities, and so to expand the commercial banks' cash; or to contract its deposits by giving securities in return for deposits, i.e. selling securities, and so to contract the commercial banks' cash.

But can the commercial banks, when their cash has been

[1] This process is very clearly explained in the Report of the Macmillan Committee, pp. 32–3.

expanded, proceed to expand deposits at will? Within almost the same limitations as the central bank, they can. It is again true that they cannot always find what they call 'credit-worthy borrowers' to whom to make loans; though it may be observed that a banker's estimate of a given customer's 'credit-worthiness' will probably vary slightly with the state of his cash ratio. Moreover, the willingness of the unexceptionally credit-worthy person to accept loans will also vary considerably with the rate of interest charged. And even supposing that the banker simply cannot induce any credit-worthy person to accept a loan or overdraft of any kind, it still remains possible for the bank to buy gilt-edged securities. It has only to pay the market price, and to grant the seller a newly created promise to pay. Now this is not a merely theoretical possibility. It is one of the most substantial and important factors in the whole of our monetary and economic system. It happened on a gigantic scale in Great Britain between 1931 and 1935; and its happening was probably the main single cause of the great economic recovery that took place. Between November 1931 and November 1935 the Bank of England increased its holding of securities from £57,000,000 to £85,000,000. The clearing-banks' cash rose from £173,000,000 to £214,000,000, the total of their 'investments', i.e. securities, rose from £300,000,000 to £621,000,000, and the total of clearing-bank deposits rose from £1,706,000,000 to £2,039,000,000. The huge purchase of gilt-edged securities involved in this increase of investments was the admitted origin of that rise in gilt-edged prices, and consequent fall in long-term interest rates,[1] which is now by common consent regarded as the main cause of the building boom which stimulated Great Britain's recovery of 1932-7.

Despite all this empirical and theoretical reasoning, however, there are still persons who deny that banks can 'create credit'. If by creating credit is meant an expansion of the total bank deposits within the limits set by cash ratios, and on condition that somebody can be found willing to sell securities at the market price, there is no doubt that banks can create credit. This is now admitted by economists of all schools of thought. The Macmillan Committee majority report (which was signed

[1] The full significance of this sequence of causation will be discussed in ch. xviii.

among others by Lord Macmillan, Mr. R. H. Brand, Professor
T. E. Gregory, Mr. J. M. Keynes, Mr. Cecil Lubbock (a director
of the Bank of England), and Mr. R. McKenna) summed the
matter up as follows: 'It is not unnatural to think of the deposits
of a bank as being created by the public through the deposit of
cash representing either savings or amounts which are not for
the time being required to meet expenditure. But the bulk of
the deposits arise out of the action of the banks themselves; for
by granting loans, allowing money to be drawn on overdraft,
or purchasing securities, a bank creates a credit in its books
which is the equivalent of a deposit.'[1]

Nobody now denies the fact that banks create credit, except
some bankers on the one hand—and bankers have always by
tradition attempted to justify their rather mysterious operations
not by defending but by denying them—and by those financial
journalists who conceive it to be their mission to state the bankers' case. It is not perhaps uncharitable to suppose that the
origin of the bankers' attitude is an uneasy desire to disclaim
any responsibility for the control of the nation's monetary
system.

There is, however, one disinterested motive which leads
people to doubt the banks' power of credit-creation: and that
is what may be called the 'cloakroom fallacy'.[2] The bankers, it
is argued do not create money: they merely lend to some people
the money that has been deposited with them by others. They
can no more create money than a cloakroom attendant can issue
more tickets than there are suitcases. Now it is of course true
that banks do lend on the money lent to them: but this is not
the whole story. The central misconception, which ramifies
widely through both financial and popular literature, springs
from a failure to analyse exactly what is the 'money' which is
deposited in a bank. If 'money' is deposited in a savings or building society, the money consists of either coins, notes, or bank
deposits; and naturally no man can lend on what he has not
received. But if money is deposited in a bank, that 'money' may

---

[1] Macmillan Report, p. 34. The same point will be found expressed by
Mr. Hawtrey, *The Art of Central Banking*, pages 150-66; Professor Hayek,
Monetary Theory and the Trade Cycle; and Mr. R. F. Harrod, *What Everybody
Wants to Know about Money*, ch. iii.

[2] To adopt the metaphor of an economist, now dead, who, it is to be
feared, himself fell into the fallacy in question.

be itself a bank deposit: and this makes all the difference. Supposing a bank grants a new loan, and the recipient of the loan leaves it as a deposit in that bank, a new deposit has plainly come into existence. The bank has increased its assets and liabilities: but the only money deposited with it is the loan—its own promise to pay. If the recipient of the loan pays it into another bank, he has a deposit there; and against that new deposit the second bank has a claim on the first.[1]

Perhaps the simplest and most convincing way to put it is this. A banker's promise to pay is money, because everyone else is willing to accept it; while other people's promises to pay are not. A bank's promise to pay is for this reason money: and it can create a promise to pay by the simple act of promising to pay. Therefore, beyond doubt, it can and does create money. Supposing a bank grants a new loan to Mr. A on the security of £100 of War Loan; or suppose it buys £100 worth of War Loan. Now, though Mr. A cannot buy a motor-car with £100 worth of War Loan, he can very easily buy a motor-car with a £100 deposit at the Midland Bank. Money has come into existence as a result of the transaction, simply because the bank's promise to pay is accepted by everybody as money while Mr. A's promise to pay, or even a share certificate, is not. Indeed, if money could not come into existence in this way, the volume of bank deposits could never have come to exceed the volume of notes and coin and bullion.[2]

Beyond question, therefore, a bank, or a banking system as a whole, can expand, i.e. create new credit[3] by purchasing one or another asset with its own promises to pay. That this has in fact happened on an enormous scale, is shown by the actual increase in bank deposits in all modern industrial countries. The total deposits in joint-stock banks in England and Wales increased from £809,000,000 in 1913 to £1,961,527,000 in 1920: and by 1937 they had risen to £2,225,000,000. It would be foolish to argue that the banks had in any way injured the national interest by issuing more promises to pay than they had cash, or in steadily increasing the volume of credit created. If any criticism

[1] See Macmillan Report, p. 34, and *What Everybody Wants to Know about Money*, pp. 129-40.
[2] As Mr. Harrod points out. *What Everybody Wants to Know about Money*, pp. 132-3.
[3] 'Credit' simply means, in effect, bank deposits.

is to be made of banking policy in general, it is that too little credit is apt to be issued rather than too much. Bank credit is the indispensible means of payment without which the complex modern economic system would not work: and in supplying credit to industry and providing a machinery for bringing short lenders and short borrowers together the banks are clearly performing a function of national importance. If they did not create credit, the economic system would come to a standstill.

But there is an aspect of the matter which is apt to escape notice. The right of issuing notes and coins of greater than their commodity value has always been a prerogative of the State, for the simple reason, already noticed, that the issue of such money is a method of getting rich quick at the expense of the community. When coins or notes are 'issued', they are not thrown out of the window of the mint or banking authority for passers-by to collect. They are used to purchase assets or to discharge liabilities; and the issuing authority is consequently the richer by the value of the notes less the cost of printing them. This is the 'profit' of issue. The profit is made ultimately out of the community as a whole, because an increase in the supply of money tends to raise prices and so to lower the value of the already existing money in the public's hands. It is in fact a kind of tax; and for this reason it has always been held to be a prerogative of the State. For the same reason, when the right of note-issue has been granted to a private bank, some concession has been exacted in return. The profit on the Bank of England's Fiduciary Issue, for instance, accrues automatically to the Treasury.

This has long been a recognized principle of money. What has not been so well recognized is that an expansion of credit by a bank is in all essentials the same as a new issue of notes. The credit, i.e. deposits, like the notes, is a promise to pay of the bank; like the notes, it is new money which exerts an influence on the price level; and like the notes it can be used by the bank to buy an asset. If a central or commercial bank buys £1,000 of securities with newly created deposits, the position is exactly and precisely the same as when it buys securities with newly created notes. Yet under existing British law the profit from the Fiduciary Issue accrues to the State while the profit from an expansion of credit does not.

It really cannot be doubted that, in so far as the total volume of bank deposits grows over a period of years, there is a certain element of 'coiner's profit' in the profits of the banking system as a whole.[1] It may not even be fantastic to suggest that this is one reason why banking profits are so consistently high in good years and bad. The moral, however, is not that the banks should cease to expand credit, but rather that their profits should be subjected to a special tax and that the banking system as a whole should be put under national ownership and control. There are, of course, other even better reasons than this for nationalizing the banks, as we shall see; but the possession by them of the power to create money, and the consequent special character of a part of their profit, establishes in itself an irrefutable moral case for their subjugation to State ownership and control.[2] There is really no reason why so many bankers should take refuge in a guilty denial of the patent fact that banks create credit. The creation of credit is a necessary, honourable, and expert business: but it is one that should be under the control of the State. Is it too much to hope that bankers will cease to deny what they are doing, and will come to recognize it instead as a task of national importance requiring and deserving the dignity of national regulation?

Such in essence is the modern system of money and credit, regarded from a static point of view. Money and credit also appear, as has been remarked, as a flow: and this flow, or at least part of it, is almost the same thing as what we have called Total Effective Demand. The question, therefore, how the stock of money is related to the flow, brings us back to the central problem of the origin of divergences between Total Effective Demand and Total Costs.

1 Much credit is due, and should be given, to Professor Frederick Soddy for pointing this out, though his arguments have been confused and he has not drawn the right moral. The right moral—that the banks ought to be nationalized—is drawn by Mr. Hugh Gaitskell in his essay 'Four Monetary Heretics', in *What Everybody Wants to Know about Money*, ch. viii. The evil is not quantitatively a great one. The annual profits of the clearing-banks range round about £12,000,000—not much, though enough to finance the abolition of the Means Test, or the building of one battleship.

2 The authors of the non-party manifesto, *The Next Five Years*, seem to recognize this when they write (p. 109): 'The greater part of the money of the country is deposited with the joint-stock banks and this alone would be sufficient grounds for subjecting them to public control, for regulation of the currency has always been among the prerogatives of the State.'

CHAPTER XVII

MAJOR DOUGLAS'S EXPLANATION

It remains to consider how the flow of Total Effective Demand comes to diverge from the flow of Total Costs. The plain man's first response to this question will perhaps be to inquire why the two should ever be the same. And this, it must be admitted, is a question that economists have often omitted even to ask, let alone answer. The early nineteenth-century classical economists, in particular Say and Ricardo, looking at the matter from the point of view of goods rather than money, propounded the thesis that total supply could not exceed total demand; for every commodity produced must constitute demand as well as supply. Commodities, that is to say, are produced either to consume or to exchange for other commodities: and in so far as they are offered in exchange for other commodities they may be said to constitute 'demand'. It is indeed almost a platitude that, since the whole process is one of exchange, the total supply of goods cannot exceed the total demand in goods.

But though this is true of the goods produced, it is not by any means obviously true of the money streams representing the goods in supply and demand, i.e. Total Effective Demand and Total Costs.[1] So well satisfied, however, were the classical economists with their proposition identifying total 'real' supply and demand, that (apart from Malthus) they forgot the problem of Effective Demand, and the very idea almost vanished from economics for nearly a century, as Mr. Keynes points out.[2]

[1] As Mr. Keynes insists in *The General Theory of Employment, Interest, and Money*, pp. 23–34. The point has also been made in this form by Professor Hayek, *Monetary Theory and the Trade Cycle*; also very clearly by Mr. P. W. Martin in his book, *The Problem of Maintaining Purchasing Power*.
[2] *The General Theory of Employment, Interest, and Money*, p. 32. He goes so far as to say: 'You will not find it mentioned even once in the whole works of Marshall, Edgworth, and Professor Pigou.'

What reason is there then for believing that Total Effective Demand and Total Costs should coincide?

Total Costs were defined above as the total of all cost payments, including profits, made in the firms producing *finished* consumable goods, and Total Effective Demand was defined as the total expenditure of the community on all *finished* consumable goods. The qualification, 'finished goods', is crucial; for it was through ignoring this qualification that Major C. H. Douglas came to believe that he had discovered a short cut to the solution of the question how Total Costs and Total Effective Demand came to diverge.

There are in general two main contentions associated with the name of Major Douglas. The first may be called the 'A+B thesis' and the second the 'technocrat thesis'. The A+B thesis is as follows: there are cost payments which every firm makes direct to consumers, e.g. wages, salaries, rent, interest, and dividends; which may be called A payments. And there are certain other payments which it makes to other producers, e.g. payments for raw materials, etc., which may be called B payments. Now since both these payments must be covered by the prices received for the goods sold, the total proceeds of the sale of all goods sold must be the total of all A+B payments. But since the total of consumers' incomes is only the total of A payments, it follows that consumers' incomes must fall short by the amount of all B payments of what the total proceeds of all goods must be if the system is to work.

Now this is only plausible so long as we fail to distinguish between all producers' costs and the costs of producers of finished goods. In order that all the bread produced may be sold at a remunerative price, it is necessary that there should be enough consumers' expenditure to cover all the costs (including profit) of all the bakers. But it is not necessary that there should be enough to cover all the costs of the bakers, plus all the costs of the millers, plus all the costs of the farmers. For those costs are already covered by the payments made by the baker to the miller. Supposing the bakers have for sale bread which has cost them £95,000 to produce, and after the baking of which they expect a profit of £5,000. This can be sold if £100,000 is distributed to consumers. And £100,000 will be distributed. The bakers themselves receive £5,000 in profit, and pay out say

£20,000 to other consumers in wages, salaries, and rent; £75,000 is therefore paid to the millers. They, in their turn, take, say, £10,000 in profit, and pay out £30,000 to consumers in wages, etc., £35,000 is therefore paid on to farmers for wheat (neglecting transport charges, etc., which in turn appear as someone's income), and the farmers naturally distribute this in the form of wages, rent, and their own profit, etc. It is clear, therefore, that £100,000 must normally in the end be distributed. And what is true of bread is naturally true over the whole system. Major Douglas forgets that the B payments become essentially somebody's income; otherwise, indeed, why should they be paid? If enough money were really distributed to consumers to cover all producers' costs, i.e. the bakers' £100,000 + the millers' £75,000 + the farmers' £35,000: total £210,000, Total Effective Demand would far exceed Total Costs. In this instance Total Effective Demand would be £210,000 and Total Costs £100,000. It has been calculated that in fact in modern industrial systems the B payments, i.e. payments between producers, are so large that if consumers' incomes were increased by a free grant equal to all the B payments, as Major Douglas proposes, Total Effective Demand would be nine times too large.[1]

It will be apparent why Total Effective Demand and Total Costs have been defined as expenditure on *finished* goods, and costs of producing finished goods. It is the public's expenditure on bread, and the bakers' total costs, that matter: not the millers' or farmers'. For they have already been taken into account in calculating the bakers' costs. The further reason why only *consumable* finished goods should be included in the definition must be left to emerge later[2] when the whole problem of saving and investment has been discussed.

Not only, however, is Major Douglas's A+B thesis analytically untenable, but it also completely fails to explain the facts. If it were true, there would have prevailed since the beginnings of the development of capitalism permanent and steadily increasing depression and unemployment rapidly declining into starvation and catastrophe. In fact, however, as has been observed,

[1] See *Purchasing Power and Trade Depression*, appendix, by E. F. M. Durbin; and 'Four Monetary Heretics' (ch. viii of *What Everybody Wants to Know about Money*) by Hugh Gaitskell, for a full analysis and criticism of Major Douglas's theories.
[2] Cf. pp. 182 and 183.

capitalist history has been a succession of rhythmical upward and downward movements. It is natural, therefore, that in periods of depression Major Douglas's theories become popular, and that in periods of recovery they lose their appeal. For what we have in fact to explain is not a permanent but a periodic deficiency of Total Effective Demand. In 1937 prices are rising; a world inflationary situation is developing; Total Effective Demand is in most countries in excess of Total Costs; and much less is being heard of Major Douglas's theories.

It would be a mistake, however, to conclude that Major Douglas's confused A+B thesis has nothing of value at all to contribute to the whole inquiry. For there is a very intricate time-problem involved. True, Major Douglas might say, the bakers' B payments represent the farm-labourers' wages of six months ago; but what use are they in getting to-day's loaves of bread sold? Now the answer to this, and so far as it goes the right answer, is that if the farm-labourer received six months ago the wages corresponding to to-day's loaf of bread, he is nevertheless to-day receiving the wages corresponding to the loaf of six months hence. To-day's loaf of bread no more has to be bought with the actual wages to which it has given rise, than it has to be bought with the wages of the actual labourers concerned. The whole process should normally be a continuous one; and if the flow of Total Effective Demand continues steadily to be equal to that of Total Costs, all will be well, however long the lag of a single item of demand or costs behind another.

But this is not a completely convincing answer. It certainly establishes that demand *may* keep pace with costs, but not that it *must*. For it may be that all, or a large proportion, of the items of effective demand and cost will tend to lag together. It is clear that the profit element in costs is paid to consumers at a very much later date than the wages corresponding to the same commodity. The wages, for instance, paid to a steel-worker for making steel that afterwards becomes a motor-car are paid perhaps a year, perhaps two years, earlier than the profits earned in the sale of the motor-car are paid out in dividends. Suppose, therefore, that there is a tendency all over the system for a rise in profits relatively to wages (as is happening all over the world in 1937), it is possible that Total Effective Demand might fall below Total Costs simply because costs would be incurred at once and the profits expected to be earned might never be earned. Suppose the economic system consisted exclusively of firms producing a type of commodity whose complete production took six months. And suppose that on January 1 all firms cut wages in the hope of increasing profits. Now Total Effective Demand between January and June would consist of the profits earned over the previous period (July to December), which would be at their normal level, and the wages of the January to June period, which had been reduced. Total Effective Demand in the January to June period would therefore be below the previous level. The goods on sale in the January to June period, however, would have been produced in the previous July to December period. But the costs of producing *them* had not been reduced. If, therefore, Total Effective Demand and Total Costs were in equilibrium in the previous (July to December) period, there *must* be a deficiency of effective demand in the January to June period. In this situation a depression might start before the expected increased profits of the second July to December period ever began to accrue.[1] It is perhaps not absurd to suggest that this may have been what happened in some of those countries that made extensive wage cuts between 1929 and 1932, e.g. Germany and the United States. The essential point is that in an economy where production takes time, the effective demand of to-day has to cover the costs of yesterday.

The time element is also crucial in determining the validity of another of Major Douglas's contentions. Depreciation charges, Major Douglas says, are not made even indirectly to consumers. They are simply put to reserve: and it may be several years before a firm expends the reserve on buying new plant. The answer usually given to this is that when one firm is putting money to reserve against depreciation, others are buying new plant. Here again, as Mr. Gaitskell points out,[2] if there was a sudden increase in one year in the amount charged to deprecia-

---

[1] May not this illustration throw some light on the controversy between Mr. Keynes and Mr. R. H. Brand contained in an addendum by Mr. Brand to the Macmillan Report. Mr. Keynes said wage reductions would reduce total demand. Mr. Brand replied that they would merely be a transfer from wages to profits. Mr. Brand does not seem to take the time element into account. 'The first impact', he says, 'of a restriction of costs is felt in an increase of profits or a substitution of profits for losses.'

[2] *What Everybody Wants to Know about Money*, ch. viii.

tion all over the system, Total Effective Demand might tend to become deficient. This really, however, is only one case of a sudden increase in saving, which must be considered later.

It appears, therefore, that various possible sources of a deficiency of Total Effective Demand may be at least gleaned from Major Douglas's contention. But these are all things that *may* happen, not things that *must* happen. They should be included as one among other possible deflationary factors. A deflationary factor may be defined as anything tending to reduce Total Effective Demand below Total Costs; and a reflationary factor as anything tending to raise Total Demand up to the level of Total Costs.[1] Now it cannot be denied that there are a great many possible deflationary factors and a great many possible reflationary factors. If this were realized, monetary discussions would be much elucidated; for such discussions often consist of a controversy in which one protagonist maintains that such and such is the one and only deflationary or reflationary factor, and someone else maintains that on the contrary it is something different.

Under sustained criticism of the A+B thesis most of Major Douglas's supporters have fallen back on their real Hindenburg Line, which may be called the 'technocrat thesis'. It is a view that ramifies very widely throughout current popular literature —or did in 1933-5—but it was most notably and noisily expressed by certain engineers and other persons calling themselves 'technocrats' in the United States in the spring of 1933. The central thesis is substantially this. As a result of technological progress, mechanization, and mass production, the output of all commodities is steadily increasing. But the flow of money is not increasing with corresponding rapidity: therefore the purchasing power available is insufficient to buy the goods produced, prices fall, and depression supervenes. Moreover, the effect of mechanization in throwing men out of work is to decrease the supply of purchasing power still further.

Now there may be some grain of truth in all this. But stated in this bald uncompromising form it rests on a single fallacy. For it asserts that an increase in the output of goods, in the absence of an increase in effective demand, must lead to depression. Sup-

[1] An inflationary factor would be anything tending to raise Total Effective Demand above Total Costs.

pose, however, that there were a community of 100 farmers, each of whose total costs (including profits) amounted to £100; and suppose that they normally sold 100,000 bushels of wheat a year. Total Effective Demand and Total Costs would be £100,000; and wheat would sell each year for £1 a bushel. Suppose then that as the result of the bounty of nature in some form or another, the wheat crop rose one year to 200,000 bushels. It is true that the price would fall to ten shillings a bushel. But the total money receipts (which we may call Total Revenue) of the farmers would still be £100,000, and it would consequently be equal to their Total Costs. Their profits would consequently be the same as before; and there would be no tendency towards unemployment or depression whatever.

The same must be normally true of the economic system as a whole. A fall in prices due to an increase in physical output is normally not a deflationary factor at all, because it does not start any tendency for Total Effective Demand to fall below Total Costs. In fact, the physical volume of output is completely irrelevant—though this is seldom realized—to the question of monetary equilibrium. *For it is the ratio of Total Effective Demand to Total Costs, not to Total Output, which determines whether entrepreneurs will make profits and consequently whether there will be unemployment or not.* Indeed, on reflection, this is obvious. For Total Effective Demand, which is a money flow, cannot in the nature of things be 'equal to' or 'keep pace with' or be 'equivalent to' Total Output, which is a flow of goods. £1 cannot be equal to one ton; still less can it equal to one ton+one gallon+two cows+three motor-cars. The only thing that the money flow of effective demand can be equal to is another money flow: and the flow that it must equal in fact is that of Total Costs. The 'general price-level'—the ratio of Total Effective Demand to Total Output—despite the great importance it has had in monetary theory, is really a conception of dubious relevance as well as dubious meaning. Indeed, a perfectly sound as well as thorough treatise could be written on monetary equilibrium and the trade cycle without ever mentioning the general physical output of goods at all. For an increase in the total output of goods due to increased physical productivity will reduce costs per unit by as much as it reduces prices per unit. A Total Effective Demand of £100,000 will always cover Total Costs of £100,000, whether it buys 100 tons, 100,000 tons or 1,000,000 tons.[1]

Violently paradoxical as this may appear to technocratically minded people, it is really common sense; and it applies not merely to the economic system as a whole but to single industries. If the coal industry by rationalization manages to produce 20 per cent more coal with the same amount of labour and capital, prices, i.e. receipts per unit, may fall as a result of the increased output, but costs per unit will clearly fall as well. The adjustment necessitated by simultaneous technological progress at different rates in different industries are of course intricate and innumerable; and it cannot be denied that deflationary factors tend sometimes to emerge. One adjustment in particular may be considered. It is a part of the technocrat thesis that the effect of mechanization is to increase unemployment and so decrease purchasing power. But what happens in fact when a new machine enables an entrepreneur to produce the same number of units with less labour, or more units with the same labour? Which of these alternatives he chooses, will depend on how far he lowers the price, and how the public's demand responds to that lowering of the price. Whatever happens, however, the public will either spend, in the aggregate, the same amount or less (or conceivably more) on his total output. If less is spent on his products, the public will have more to spend elsewhere; and the products of other industries will gain what this industry loses. An increased demand for labour in other industries will then balance the decreased demand in the first industry. That this normally happens in practice is shown by the fact that the total number of insured persons in employment in Great Britain rose from almost 10,000,000 in 1923 to 12,000,000 in 1937.

Though this is what normally happens, however, it seems that in certain circumstances a sudden increase in productivity in a single industry *may* be a deflationary factor. Supposing there is a sudden reduction in costs and prices in an industry producing some staple product. Consumers may for a time spend less on

---

[1] There are of course some falls in price which are associated with depression. But these cannot be mainly due to an increase in the output of goods, because they must be due to a fall of Total Effective Demand below Total Costs. A deflationary fall in prices is quite different from a non-deflationary one.

that product without spending more on anything else.[1] They may in fact hoard: simply because they are already buying all they are in the habit of buying. In so far as this does happen, it is of course a case of hoarding: and is covered by what will be said about hoarding in the next chapter.

There is also one other possible deflationary effect of mechanization. If a new machine is installed, a new interest charge may be incurred. Now, though cost per unit may be thus reduced, Total Costs for the system as a whole have been increased. A new cost payment has been introduced into the system (just as if the working population had increased), and unless other cost payments are reduced, which we have assumed in the short period to be impossible, Total Effective Demand must somehow be increased. But the question of increases in Total Costs due to expansion of population and capital must also be considered as a whole later.

In general, as a statement of normal tendencies, the technocrats' thesis is radically fallacious. They forget that the ratio of demand to costs and not to output is what matters, and they forget that unemployment caused by a transfer of demand from one industry to another does not normally cause a deficiency of Total Effective Demand. Nowhere are these fallacies better illustrated than in Mr. Harold Macmillan's odd book *Reconstruction*. The whole argument of this book rests on the two contentions that an increase of physical output leads to depression and unemployment, and that the emergence of losses or unemployment in any single firm or industry causes a cumulative deflation.[2] The remedy proposed by Mr. Macmillan is, in effect, a general restriction of production! The whole of this type of argument which looked plausible in the deflationary years of 1929–33, has lost even its superficial appeal to-day.

Most technocrats at least advocate an increase in production. But their estimates of the extent to which production could be increased in a short time by the full employment of all resources are reckless to the point of fantasy. Possible increases of 1,000 per cent are often mentioned. Reliable estimates of the extent

[1] Mr. H. D. Henderson has suggested in an essay in the symposium 'The Burden of Plenty' that a slackening in population growth may have this effect: since it is less inevitable that the same people should buy more things than that more people should buy the same things.

[2] *Reconstruction*, ch. i–vi.

to which output could really be expanded are hard to make; and they raise the difficult theoretical problem of 'weighting' one commodity against another. Perhaps the only method that is even roughly correct is to assume that output would be increased in the same proportion as unemployed labour could be absorbed. Unemployment in the capitalist world does not average more than about 10 per cent over good and bad periods. It consequently seems that a 10 per cent to 25 per cent increase in output is the maximum that could be hoped from a full employment of resources.[1] This is important enough, but it is far indeed from the wild estimates of Major Douglas and the technocrats. The discrepancy is very important; for Major Douglas and his followers base their hostility to socialism largely on the contention that general production can be rapidly and indefinitely extended. The poor, Major Douglas, would like to think, can be made richer without making the rich poorer. This is untrue. The poor cannot be made rapidly and substantially richer unless the rich are made poorer.

Nevertheless, if the contentions of Major Douglas and the technocrats are generally confused and misleading, they have at least done some service by calling attention to the fact that a problem of Total Effective Demand does exist, and that in a depression the remedy is somehow or other to increase Total Effective Demand. They have spoilt their good case by faulty analysis and by insisting overmuch—and grossly misrepresenting—spectacular but unimportant incidents such as the burning of coffee in Brazil.[2] But their heart is in the right place; and even their head is nearer to it than that of the cliché-ridden type of fanatic, who, in the face of depression and poverty, advises his less-favoured fellow men to tighten their belts and cut their coats according to their cloth.

[1] Mr. Harold G. Moulton, in *America's Capacity to Produce*, gives 25 per cent as the increase in output that America could have achieved in 1929. This is probably an outside estimate.

[2] Such incidents are, after all, only the effect of general deflation supervening on overproduction of particular commodities due to 'valorization' schemes. And it would be foolish to deny that overproduction of *particular* commodities can and does exist.

CHAPTER XVIII

SAVING AND INVESTMENT

From consideration of Major Douglas's thesis the conclusion emerges that in the normal course of events consumers receive as incomes enough to purchase the whole product of industry at remunerative prices, i.e. to cover Total Costs. But the fact that all *consumers' income* (which we may call Total Income) is equal to Total Costs does not necessarily prove that Total Effective Demand will be. For we do not yet know what consumers will do with their incomes. Now a great many socialists, including in particular the followers of Marx, hold, or appear to hold, that a great many consumers' incomes are never spent at all. This view is seldom very clearly expressed, and it takes various forms. In its less precise forms it underlies the argument of such persuasive works as Mr. H. N. Brailsford's *Property and Peace*.

1. 'Under-Consumption'

Most crudely expressed this view amounts to the assertion that only wage-earners spend their income. The entrepreneur, it is alleged, is perpetually engaged in 'cutting costs', i.e. wages, and attempting to increase profits. But this is a self-contradictory process, because the more wages are cut the more purchasing power falls, and the less profits are earned. The whole of this argument rests on the assumption that profits are never spent: for if profits are spent, an increase of profits at the expense of wages will mean no reduction of Total Effective Demand. But to found the case for socialism on the assertion that profits are never—or even seldom—spent is really to destroy that case. For the case for socialism really rests on the fact that profits *are* spent, and spent on luxuries on an enormous scale. And in any case there is no doubt about the facts. The total of property incomes (which is what the Marxists mean by 'profits') in Great Britain averages something like £1,250,000,000 a year; and the total net saving averages about £450,000,000 a year. Even then if nobody but the propertied classes saves at all, it is clear that the propertied classes spend not less than £600,000,000 a year (allowing for taxation), or about one-sixth of the whole national income. Indeed, those who think profits are never spent seem to be living in almost as narrow a world as the propertied classes themselves, who think only the rich pay taxes.

The chief grain of truth in this crudest version of the 'under-consumptionist' thesis seems to be the point that has already been made: that a sudden *reduction* of wages in the hope of increasing profits may start a deflationary process. Apart from this, convenient as the argument appears at first as a piece of socialist propaganda, it cannot honestly be accepted in its crude form. Much more sophisticated versions have consequently been put forward: and the more sophisticated they become, the larger seems to be the grain of truth they contain. One of the less sophisticated, and less convincing, is that advanced by Mr. John Strachey in his otherwise most illuminating book, *The Nature of Capitalist Crisis*. This view, which Mr. Strachey claims to be the only authentic message of Marx, is unfortunately made the logical foundation of his whole book. It runs like this. There exists, he assumes, a certain total of 'surplus value' which appears in the process of production, and which is proportionate to the total of wages paid in the relevant period. Suppose the total of wages is £5,000,000 a year, there is also a flow of 'surplus value', i.e. rent, interest, and profits, of say £1,000,000. The ratio of this flow of surplus value to the total of nominal capital[1] (say £20,000,000) is the 'rate of profit', in this instance 5 per cent. But as, with technological progress and mechanization, the total of capital increases, the ratio of 'surplus value' to total capital must fall. But this means that the *rate* of profit must fall: and in that case the only way in which the total of profit and surplus value can be kept from falling is to increase the total of capital. And since it is assumed that the whole system will collapse if the total of profit is not maintained, the capitalists and entrepreneurs must save and invest at an ever-increasing rate. But this after a

[1] This is supposed to consist of 'variable' plus 'constant' capital. But the distinction does not affect the essentials of the argument.

point becomes impossible: and therefore the system, after a series of sickening lurches, must finally capsize altogether.[1]

This is a strange argument. For if we grant Mr. Strachey all his Marxist assumptions about 'surplus value' being proportionate to wages, etc., it contains a logical and indeed arithmetical flaw. When the proportion of machinery to labour increases, Mr. Strachey says, the rate of profit falls and therefore to prevent the absolute amount of profit falling, capital itself must be increased. But the increase in the amount of machinery itself implies an increase in total nominal capital—for it is the money total of the nominal value of all capital that Mr. Strachey seems to have in mind. If it did not imply such an increase, the rate of profit would not have fallen. And the implied increase in total capital must be exactly sufficient to offset the fall in the rate: for it was nothing else but the increase that made the rate fall. Supposing, as was assumed above, that the total of wages is £5,000,000, the total of surplus value £1,000,000, and the nominal capital £20,000,000. If the nominal capital is increased to £25,000,000 by investment,[2] it is true that the rate of profit has fallen from 5 per cent to 4 per cent; but it is not necessary to raise the £25,000,000 still further in order to prevent the absolute amount of the £1,000,000 from falling. £1,000,000 after all remains £1,000,000, whether £20,000,000 is raised to £25,000,000 or £25,000,000,000,000. If, therefore, it is the preservation of the absolute amount of profit which is crucial, as Mr. Strachey appears on the whole to assume, there is no tendency whatever, even on his assumptions, for capitalism to collapse. It is true that in places Mr. Strachey appears to assume instead that the amount of profit has to be not merely maintained but increased if technical progress is to go on. This is a dubious assumption: for technical progress often comes through competition between entrepreneurs for a given amount of profit rather than through an increase in the total. But even if it were true, surely the effect would be, not that technical progress would be followed by collapse, but that it would not take place at all. For if surplus value were, as Mr. Strachey assumes, pro-

[1] *The Nature of Capitalist Crisis*, ch. xvi.
[2] The word 'investment' is used throughout in Mr. Keynes's sense of the purchase of capital goods, not in the popular sense of the purchase of a security.

portionate to the amount of wages paid, why should entrepreneurs expect to increase it by investing in more machinery? Mr. Strachey's argument, it is hoped, is not here misrepresented. If it is not, he would seem to have based his case against the possibility of gradual reform, and indeed his whole economic and political philosophy, on a faulty piece of arithmetic.

What we have now to do is to discover the real nature of the process of saving and investment. It has so far been assumed that all incomes received will either be spent on consumable goods direct or else saved and invested in, i.e. spent on, durable goods. But is this in fact true? May not people hoard? And may not even saving have a deflationary effect?

That consumers can hoard notes and coins, and that the effect must be deflationary, is not open to doubt. If a large proportion of the workers in the community, on receiving their weekly packets of notes and coins, proceeded to lock up 20 per cent of them in a drawer, Total Effective Demand must fall below Total Costs, and almost certainly a cumulative deflation must start. This is because those who have refrained from spending a part of their income have also deliberately prevented anyone else from spending it. If saving is defined as 'refraining from spending a part of one's income', we may thus define hoarding as saving and preventing anyone else from making use of the saving. Hoarding must clearly be deflationary. May, or must, saving be so?

A very influential school of thought, including many socialists, hold that it not only may but must.[1] The deflationary influence, it is argued, arises in two ways. First, when money is withdrawn from expenditure on consumers' goods there must be a tendency for effective demand for those goods to fall below the cost of producing them. Secondly, when the savings have been invested in new plant, the output of consumers' goods is increased and the deficiency of purchasing power becomes even greater. Each of these two arguments must be tested, as Mr. E. F. M. Durbin has pointed out, on two successive assumptions: first that a continuous process of saving and investment is going

---

[1] The most distinguished of these is of course Mr. J. A. Hobson, who expounds the thesis in his books, *The Industrial System* and *Economics of Unemployment*. Cf. also *Profits* by Foster and Cutchings. Mr. Cole and Mr. Brailsford often seem to be using the same argument.

on, and secondly that there is a sudden increase in saving.

Supposing a continuous process of saving is going on, there seems no reason why any deflationary influence should be created by the fact that a certain proportion of total income is being saved and spent on durable goods every year (and Mr. Hobson normally assumes that it is so spent). Supposing consumers save one-tenth of their income every year and the costs arising from the production of durable goods are equal to that one-tenth, there is no reason why Total Effective Demand should fall below Total Costs, simply in view of the regular withdrawal of one-tenth of total income from the market for consumers' goods. Nor does there seem to be any reason why the second factor, the increase in output due to the installation of more plant, should exert a deflationary influence. For this is really no more than an example of what we have already considered: an increase in physical productivity which involves no increase in Total Costs (apart from the new capital charges). Mr. Durbin,[1] looking at the problem from the point of view of costs per unit, points out that the whole purpose and effect of the installation of new plant is to reduce costs per unit by more than the rate of interest on the capital. Apart from the addition of new capital charges to Total Costs, which is discussed in chapter v, it does not appear that a continuous process of saving need have deflationary effects.

Suppose, however, that there is a sudden, or at least rapid, increase in the rate of saving, what will happen? The first effect will be to reduce the effective demand for non-durable goods below the costs of producing them, and so to provoke general depression throughout what are in effect the industries producing consumers' goods. Now according to traditional economic theory this is merely a case of a transfer of demand from one commodity to another. Just as demand may be transferred from the cotton to the rayon industry, so it may be transferred from the non-durable goods industries to the durable goods industries; and the increased prosperity of the one will balance the decreased prosperity of the other. This is the assumption made by Professor Hayek throughout his writings; savings constitute the 'demand' for durable goods, and if savings increase the demand for durable goods must increase. Mr. Durbin is

[1] *Purchasing Power and Trade Depression*, pp. 73–80.

surely right, however, in pointing out that there is an all-important difference, based on the fact that durable goods are in most cases producers' goods. The demand for rayon does not in any way depend on the existence of profits in the cotton industry, though the demand for plant and machinery does very emphatically depend on the existence of profits in the trades making consumers' goods. It is one of the most obvious facts of the business world that the demand for capital goods increases when high profits are being earned in the production of consumers' goods, and falls off when they are not. Since Mr. Durbin's book was published, his view on this point has been strikingly confirmed by Mr. Harold G. Moulton's work, *The Formation of Capital*. Mr. Moulton concludes, after an exhaustive statistical survey of American experience, that the demands for capital and consumable goods are not alternatives, but that the first depends on the second.

Neither on theoretical or empirical grounds, therefore, does it seem possible to doubt that a rapid increase[1] in savings will cause general losses in the consumers' goods trades and consequently a fall in the demand for capital goods. It is almost bound therefore, to start a cumulative deflation. Just, therefore, as a sudden drift from wages to profits may operate as a deflationary factor, so may a sudden increase in saving. This is a very important conclusion indeed, especially if we accept the view put forward as an axiom by Mr. Keynes in his *General Theory of Employment, Interest, and Money* that any general increase in a community's total production and consumption is likely to lead to an increase in the rate of saving.

If, however, an increase in saving is not followed by an increase, but rather by a decrease, in investment, it seems to follow that saving can take place without investment. Throughout all the theories considered so far it has been assumed that saving must automatically be followed by investment.

2. Must Investment be Equal to Saving?

Can there be saving without investment? It is at any rate clear that there can be individual acts of saving which do not have any direct causal effect on those responsible for individual acts of

[1] It is when the increase in the rate of saving is great enough to cause an absolute fall in expenditure on consumers' goods, that the trouble begins.

deliberate investment.[1] If people hoard coins in stockings, there is no discoverable reason why any deliberate investment should result: certainly there will be no fall in the rate of interest. Supposing, however, that savings are deposited in the banks or used to purchase securities, will any effect on investment be produced? Here again it seems best to distinguish between a continuous flow of saving and a sudden increase. If the whole system has for some time been in equilibrium at a given level of saving and investment, it seems reasonable to suppose that a continuance of that rate of saving will be accompanied by a continuance of that rate of investment. But will an increase in the rate of saving be accompanied by an increase in the rate of investment? We have already seen that an increase in saving will produce depression in the consumers' goods industries, and will consequently diminish entrepreneurs' demand for saving. But will it not cheapen the supply by forcing down the rate of interest? Even this does not seem certain. If the savings are used to buy a security, the price will of course tend to rise, and the long-term rate of interest will consequently tend to fall. And if these savings are put on 'deposit account' at the banks, the banks may find their ratio of deposit accounts to current accounts rising, may perhaps consequently lower their deposit rates, and simultaneously (perhaps) lower their advance rates. But suppose the savings are simply left on current account, it is hard to see why there should be any fall in any rate of interest or any chance of an increase in investment. For it is crucial to remember that an increase in saving does not increase the total of bank deposits. This total is determined by central banking policy in the way that has been explained. People do not create bank deposits in their own houses by the act of saving, and then put them in the bank. They leave on deposit what they have received in income by cheque, instead of spending it. And all that this does is to slow down the circulation of bank deposits. It does not in any way alter the structure or ratio of the banks' liabilities and assets. It merely means that Mr. A's £100 deposit in Barclays remains Mr. A's instead of becoming Mr. B's. This may become visible as a fall in bank clearings; but such a fall will most certainly not induce the banks to lower their interest rates.

It appears then that, as far as the mere mechanism of the

[1] i.e. purchase of durable or capital goods.

capital market is concerned, saving can take place only too easily without corresponding investment. Noting this, Mr. Keynes, in his *Treatise on Money*, made discrepancies between saving and investment the basis of his theory of the trade cycle. Broadly, the theory was this. There exists (as Wicksell believed) a 'natural' rate of interest, which is that which equates savings with investment. If the market rate of interest rises above this, investment will exceed saving: and if it falls below this, saving will exceed investment. If investment exceeds savings, the total income of the community will be more than sufficient to buy the total output of industry at current costs; for more will have been paid over to the producers of capital goods than has been withdrawn from the producers of consumers' goods. Abnormal profits will then appear, and production expand. If, on the other hand, saving exceeds investment, the income of the community will be insufficient to buy Total Output at current costs: for less will have been paid to the producers of capital goods than has been withdrawn from producers of consumers' goods. Therefore profits will be less than normal, and production will contract. Depression, in fact, consists of an excess of saving over investment, and recovery of an excess of investment over saving: and the first obvious remedy for depression is a lowering of the rate of interest.

Mr. Keynes's theory was of course not as simple as this. In particular, certain peculiarities in his definition of saving, investment, and profits complicated the issue.[1] But in substance he maintained, or at least was taken to maintain, that discrepancies between saving and investment, arising out of divergences between 'natural' and 'market' interest rates, were at the root of the trade cycle, and that the task of policy was to equate saving and investment. Now the most obvious flaw in this theory, illuminating as it was when put forward in 1930, is that saving and investment can be in perfect equilibrium, the natural and market rates of interest perfectly coincident, and yet half the

[1] He defined profits or losses as merely the windfall profits or losses (above or below normal profits) resulting from excesses or deficiencies of saving; and he excluded profits from 'income', so that 'if an entrepreneur spends part of his profits on current consumption, then this is equivalent to negative saving; and if he restricts his normal consumption because he is suffering windfall losses, this, on the other hand, is equivalent to positive saving'. (*A Treatise on Money*, vol. I, p. 124.)

labour and capital in the country be permanently unemployed. Many followers of Mr. Keynes have quite forgotten that when producers' resources are unemployed investment has to *exceed* savings, interest rates to fall *below* the natural rate, and prices to *rise*, for the whole period until full employment is restored. For, at the low level of production established there is of course a normal profit, a stable price level, an equation of savings and investment, and even of costs and expenditure, *corresponding to that level of output and employment*. In chapter xv Total Costs were deliberately defined as the total of payments which all producers of finished consumers' goods must receive *if full production and employment are to be maintained*. If Total Costs were instead defined as the cost payments actually being made to these producers, then an identity between these and Total Effective Demand would be just as compatible with 50 per cent unemployment as was Mr. Keynes's identity between saving and investment. The fact is that all sorts of different positions of monetary equilibrium are possible; but only one is compatible with full employment.[1]

This seems to have been one of the considerations which have led Mr. Keynes to re-state his analysis in a different form in his new book. For he now maintains that the problem is not to preserve equilibrium between saving and investment, but to preserve that one particular equilibrium between them which is alone compatible with full employment. He goes further than this, however. He maintains that in any case saving and investment must be equal. This *volte-face* of Mr. Keynes is not so perverse and paradoxical as it may appear; for much depends on the following two points: the time element on the one hand and the definition of investment and income on the other. Income Mr. Keynes defines so as to include the entrepreneur's actual realized profits[2] (which is the way Total Income was defined in the last chapter); and saving he defines normally as the excess of income over expenditure. Investment, however, he explicitly defines as including the 'increment of capital equipment' in any

[1] This follows directly and inevitably from the assumption made explicitly at the beginning of this argument that costs per head are in fact fixed. No other assumption is in the least realistic. The failure to make this assumption has led to a great deal of error both in theory and practice.

[2] Much complication springs from his attempt to decide whether a reduction in the value of capital equipment should or should not be deducted from entrepreneur's profits.

period, 'whether it consists of fixed capital, working capital, or liquid capital'.[1] He then argues as follows:[2]

Income=value of output=consumption +investment.

Saving=income—consumption.

Therefore saving=investment.

The significance of this can perhaps be illustrated by concrete examples. Supposing someone saves £100 and no corresponding decision is taken by an entrepreneur to spend £100 on capital goods, Mr. Keynes would have said, in the terminology of his *Treatise on Money*, that there was an excess of saving over investment of £100, that losses resulted, and that a deflationary movement consequently would start. He now says that income is reduced by £100, and that effective demand, investment, and employment all settle down at a lower level than they would have done if an additional £100 had been spent on capital goods. But at this lower level saving and investment (if investment is defined to include liquid and working capital) are in fact equal. Suppose—to take the example of money put on deposit—that a Mr. A saves £100 by simply leaving it on current account instead of spending it on a motor-car. There may be no additional act of deliberate investment by anybody, but deposits will not increase and interest rates will not fall. But Mr. B (a producer of cars), who would otherwise have sold the motor-car to Mr. A is compelled to go on holding it. Mr. B's decision, reluctant as it may be, to go on holding the motor-car is, on Mr. Keynes's definition, an act of 'investment'. It may be that it is financed by the extension of an overdraft, but in any case Mr. B is compelled to hold liquid capital instead of cash. Suppose, on the other hand, that Mr. A's decision to leave £100 on deposit had been accompanied by a decision on the part of Mr. C, an entrepreneur, to increase investment, i.e. to buy capital goods, then income, employment, and effective demand would all have been higher. But saving would still be equal to investment, because Mr. C's act of investment would balance Mr. A's saving; and though Mr. B, who in this case also had failed to sell his motor-car, had again performed an act of involuntary investment, this would be balanced by the 'saving' involved in Mr. D's selling capital

[1] 'Working capital' was defined in the *Treatise on Money*, vol. I, p. 28, as 'goods in process', and 'liquid capital' as 'goods in stock'.
[2] *The General Theory of Employment, Interest, and Money*, p. 63.

equipment to Mr. C and consequently holding cash instead of goods.

To put it briefly, if more is saved, and no more deliberate investment is undertaken, less is bought: but the shopkeepers are thereby forced to 'invest' in what they would otherwise have sold but now remains on their shelves.

It is, perhaps, more difficult to see why an increase in investment should automatically produce an increase in savings. But if the time element is kept in mind, and if Mr. Keynes's new definitions are accepted, it can be shown that this is true. Supposing the Government decide to spend an additional £100,000,000 of newly created money on roads over a period of two years. The amount will be spent gradually; and by the time, say £10,000,000 of it has been paid out in wages at least £5,000,000 will have been passed on by wage-earners to others, and incomes will altogether have been increased by perhaps £30,000,000 or £40,000,000. Some of the persons getting the new income, however, will save; and there is no reason why the total saving should not be as great as the £10,000,000 actually 'invested'. In fact, in Mr. Keynes's definition, this is what will happen. An increase in investment will generate an increase in incomes just great enough for the amount saved out of it to be equal to the increase in investment.

Is it possible, however, to re-define investment so as to preserve the idea, popularized by the *Treatise on Money*, of equating saving and investment? It might perhaps be defined as the purchase of fixed capital, rather than liquid or working capital, as Mr. Hawtrey has suggested, or alternatively as any *voluntary* increase in a man's holding of durable goods. The possibility of these definitions at least shows that there is really no dispute about substance; and that Mr. Hawtrey has in effect meant the same by his emphasis on changes in stocks as Mr. Keynes once meant by excesses and deficiencies of savings and now means by changes in the level of effective demand. The significant fact seems to be that there is a certain Total Effective Demand which is alone consonant with full employment; and that if this total is maintained saving and investment will both adjust themselves and will exceed or be equal to one another according to the definitions one chooses to adopt.

3. *The Rate of Interest*

Nevertheless, since Mr. Keynes thinks investment must be equal to saving, some may be surprised that he devotes most of his new book to considering how the volume of investment can be kept up when the volume of saving increases. But because investment cannot fall below saving, it does not follow that an increase in saving may not result in depression and unemployment. For it may lead to a situation in which effective demand, saving, and investment settle down at a lower level than that which is compatible with full employment. Mr. Keynes's analysis thus still confirms the conclusion already reached in this chapter that an increase in saving may start a cumulative deflation. How does he propose to prevent this happening? Mainly by increasing investment in order to maintain effective demand at the level compatible with full employment. He consequently considers the factors on which the volume of investment depends. These he regards as being on the one hand the 'marginal efficiency of capital', i.e. in effect the expected money yield of a given investment in real capital over a period of years, and on the other, the rate of interest. Next, in discussing what determines the rate of interest, Mr. Keynes propounds a rather extreme view. The rate of interest, he says, depends not on the volume of saving at all, but entirely on the quantity of money and the 'liquidity preference' of the public. 'Liquidity preference' means a desire to hold money rather than interest-bearing assets, or, in ordinary language, a desire to hoard. The lower the rate of interest, the less willing will the public be to hold securities, and the more willing to hold money. Therefore, given a certain liquidity preference, the rate of interest will depend on the volume of money alone. This means in practice that as the central bank creates more credit and buys securities more persons will sell the securities and hold bank deposits for each rise in the price of securities. The rate of interest thus falls. Similarly, if the liquidity preference of the public increases, and they start to sell securities for money, the price can be stopped from falling, and therefore the rate of interest from rising, if the banks buy securities.

There can be no doubt that, given a reasonably constant liquidity preference—i.e. assuming there is no panic buying or selling of securities by the public—the central bank can control the long-term as well as the short-term interest rate simply by the device of creating credit and buying securities, or destroying credit and selling them. But Mr. Keynes goes further than this. He denies that there is any truth in the ordinary theory, such as was expounded in chapter vi, that the rate of interest is the 'price' which brings the supply of and demand for saving into adjustment. The rate of interest, he says, is not the inducement to people not to consume—for they have already decided not to do that when they hoard—it is the inducement not to hoard, i.e. it induces people to hold interest-bearing assets rather than money. 'It should be obvious that the rate of interest cannot be a return to saving or waiting as such. For if a man hoards his savings in cash he earns no interest, though he saves just as much as before.' But to argue that interest cannot be a price of saving because some people save without receiving interest seems rather like arguing that wages cannot be a payment for work because some men work for nothing. It is true that if there were no rate of interest nobody would hold illiquid assets in preference to liquid assets: but does this prove that if there were no rate of interest the total of assets, liquid and illiquid, held in preference to consumption would be as great as it would have been if there had been a rate of interest? And although some people, as Mr. Keynes says, first decide not to consume, and then consider whether to hold money or interest-bearing assets, may not other people be influenced in deciding to refrain from consumption by the fact that there are interest-bearing assets to hold?

Mr. H. D. Henderson[1] has criticized this new contention of Mr. Keynes from another point of view. He points out that if the quantity of money really is a principal determinant of the rate of interest, one would expect to find a rate of interest indefinitely low in those countries, like Germany, Austria, France and Belgium, which have inflated their currencies more or less unrestrainedly after the war. Can one in fact *permanently* reduce the rate of interest to *any extent* by increasing the quantity of money? Mr. Keynes would probably answer that the quantity of money must not be measured in ordinary currency units but in 'wage-units'; i.e. if wages are £2 a week, it is the number of sums of £2 which matters, and if wages rise to £4 a doubling of

[1] In a review in the *Spectator*, 17th February 1936, of *The General Theory of Employment, Interest, and Money*.

the number of sums of £1 will bring no increase in the quantity of money. This gives at once one limit to the extent to which interest rates can be forced down by increasing the quantity of money. As soon as the resulting trade recovery begins to push wages up beyond a certain point, this method may no longer be efficacious. Mr. Henderson also points out that it is odd, on Mr. Keynes's view, that interest rates should rise in a boom when the quantity of money is usually increasing, and fall during a depression when it is often decreasing.

These factors taken together make Mr. Keynes's account of the determination of interest rates look at least a little improbable. Suppose it is admitted, however, that the supply of savings can exert some influence on interest rates, what in effect constitutes the supply of saving—the 'waiting' of the public or the volume of money? This question is certainly extremely puzzling. For though in the long run it seems fantastic to say that the quantity of money determines interest rates, it seems equally fantastic to say that in the short run the volume of savings determines it. Clearly, in the short run the main determinant is the volume of money created by the banking system. Can the volume of saving exert any effect in the short run? A mere leaving of money on current account in the banks, as has been pointed out already, need exert no effect on interest rates at all. If, however, these deposits were used by the public to buy securities, there would be such an effect. This is, of course, precisely the distinction between hoarding and holding interest-bearing assets on which Mr. Keynes insists: but surely the decision of the public not to consume but to buy securities instead must affect interest rates. Until this issue has been finally cleared up, therefore, it seems that one must be content with the usual view that both the quantity of money and the volume of saving affect interest rates.

There is at any rate no doubt that the quantity of money is in the short run the determining factor. And this is really all, or nearly all, one needs to know in determining monetary policy; for the quantity of money is in the hands of the authorities and the volume of saving is not. Within limits set by the danger of upsetting the public's liquidity preference, i.e. its 'confidence', and of stimulating a big rise in the wage unit, the quantity of bank money can of course determine interest rates in periods of the length which in fact have to be considered by monetary policy. This is a truth of the greatest importance: and it needs propagating in view of the widespread delusion that interest rates depend on the demand for and supply of saving alone, and that nothing can therefore be done to change them, however great the volume of unemployment.

And this is Mr. Keynes's main practical contention. As the national income increases, he thinks, the rate of saving increases; for as people get richer they save a larger part of their income. This increase in saving, however, Mr. Keynes believes, tends to reduce effective demand and so equates saving and investment at a level of employment below the maximum; and there is no tendency for the rate of interest to fall and bring about full employment in any foreseeable period. All this seems to be in accord with both the *a priori* and the empirical evidence. Mr. Keynes, therefore, proposes to maintain effective demand by stimulating investment through an increase in money and a fall in interest rates. Now unquestionably such stimulation of investment is *one* way of maintaining effective demand. But is it the only way? Surely a much more natural, direct, and beneficial way is to stimulate consumption. In the situation envisaged by Mr. Keynes a direct stimulation of consumption is not only an economically sound, but an economically necessary policy. The traditional belief that in a deflationary situation effective demand must always be stimulated by an increase in investment seems to be derived partly from the narrow banking view that a new loan must be 'productive' in the profit-making sense, partly from the mere fact that expansion has always occurred in this way in the past, and partly from the archaically confused idea that any other methods of expansion are 'inflationary'. There is no rational basis for this view whatever. It is consequently odd that Mr. Keynes does not advocate the direct expansion of consumption by new money more emphatically; for it is the logical conclusion of his argument. In a situation where effective demand has fallen below the level consonant with full employment a direct expansion of consumption will increase employment, saving, and investment—as a result of the increase in incomes—and it will not be inflationary unless it is pushed beyond the point of full employment. Of course, the expansions of investment and consumption are not incompatible policies.

They are both[1] ways of expanding effective demand: and both can be used in varying proportions at once.

4. 'Over-Investment'

Up to this point in the argument it has not been explained why Total Costs apply to the producers of finished *consumable* goods. It seems at first that Total Costs should mean the cost of producing all finished goods, producers' or consumers'; for a great number of workers are in the producers' goods or capital goods trades. There is, however, a conclusive objection to the inclusion of the incomes of the producers in the producers' goods trades in Total Costs. It has already been argued that the demand for producers' goods is a derived demand, i.e. that it is determined by the level of profits in the consumers' goods trades. If therefore there is full employment and normal profits in the consumers' goods trades but general unemployment in the producers' goods trades, it may mean, not that effective demand is insufficient, but that there is an excess of capacity in the producers' goods trades; in the sense that the ratio of capacity in the producers' trades to capacity in the consumers' trades is greater than the ratio of the community's saving to its spending. There is therefore labour and capital in the producers' trades which ought to be transferred to the consumers' trades. The remedy for this situation is not necessarily simply to increase expenditure on all finished consumers' goods; for this, by creating abnormal profits in the consumers' trades, would not merely, if at all, direct resources into these trades. It would also increase the demand for producers' goods, and so perhaps prevent the diversion of resources away from the producers' goods trades.

It is evident then that we must define Total Costs as the total of the incomes of *the producers of finished consumable goods when in full employment.* Total Effective Demand should therefore be conceived as the total demand for consumers' goods necessary

[1] Mr. Keynes of course admits this, though his emphasis is usually on investment. Cf. *The General Theory of Employment, Interest, and Money,* p. 325: 'Whilst aiming at a socially controlled rate of investment with a view to a progressive decline in the marginal efficiency of capital, I should support at the same time all sorts of policies for increasing the propensity to consume. For it is unlikely that full employment can be maintained, whatever we do about investment, with the existing propensity to consume. There is room, therefore, for both policies to operate together.'

to maintain full employment in the consumers' goods trades. Total Effective Demand and Total Costs do not then correspond to the national income; they correspond to total consumption. It consequently appears that the attainment of full monetary equilibrium entails another secondary objective besides the adjustment of Total Effective Demand to Total Costs. For if those are already adjusted, and there is surplus capacity in the producers' goods trades, a mere increase of Total Effective Demand above Total Costs may not be enough. For suppose the productive capacity in the producers' goods trades to be too large in proportion to the capacity in the consumers' trades than is warranted by the proportion in which the community works to save or spend its incomes. Then the necessary remedy is a transfer of resources from the producers' to the consumers' trades. But as has been pointed out, an increase of Total Effective Demand designed to generate abnormal profits in the consumers' trades may at once increase the demand for producers' goods and so do nothing to initiate the necessary transfer. We are again brought back to the paradox that an increase in demand in the consumers' trades may, and probably will, increase and not decrease demand in the producers' trades. This paradox may be one of the fundamental causes of the trade cycle. If an excess of capacity in the producers' trades ever comes into being contemporaneously with full employment in the consumers' trades, it is very difficult to see how it can be cured by any sort of orthodox methods. The real practical problem, therefore, may not merely be to maintain Total Effective Demand but also forcibly to divert resources away from the producers' trades.

The possibility of an excess of capacity in the producers' goods trades is the central idea in the comprehensive and acute theory of the trade cycle elaborated by Professor Hayek. His theory is based on the view that the upward movement normally consists of a process of 'overinvestment' or 'malinvestment'. In so far as Professor Hayek's theory can be expressed briefly in normal terminology, it is as follows.[1] Suppose the economic system is in equilibrium, and labour is fully employed. This, it will be

---

[1] Cf. F. A. Hayek, *Monetary Theory and the Trade Cycle*, for a description of the inception of the process; and F. A. Hayek, *Prices and Production*, for a description of its full working.

observed, introduces a note of unreality into the story from the first; and the extent to which it invalidates the conclusions will have to be considered later. Suppose, however, that in these hypothetical conditions the banks decide to lower the rate of interest below the 'natural' rate and to lend money in excess of the public's 'voluntary savings'.[1] The new loans are used by entrepreneurs to buy capital goods, and the producers of the capital goods are thus made to bid for labour and material against the producers of consumable goods, so bidding up the prices of those labour and materials and attracting them away from the consumers' goods industries. Here again the absence of unemployment is assumed. In the next stage the increased wages and profits in the capital goods industries are spent on consumable goods, and the prices of consumable goods consequently rise. This inference, of course, once more assumes productive capacity in the consumers' goods trades to be already so fully used that an increase in demand must mean a rise in prices. If we assume this, however, it follows that 'forced saving' has been inflicted on consumers as a result of the rise in prices.[2] For their unchanged money incomes do not go so far as they used to go. They will therefore tend to spend more money rather than less on consumers' goods. Since prices of consumers' goods are already moving upwards, profits in the trades making these goods will rise; and the producers of consumers' goods will in their turn be enabled to bid up the price of labour and raw materials against producers of capital goods.

If the banks continue issuing cheap credit, the process may go on for a time. In the end, however, it must either stop or develop into a 'high inflation', i.e. a process in which prices and wages pursue one another in a wild-goose chase such as was experienced in Germany, Austria, etc., after the war. If the banks do call off the credit expansion, however, the rate of interest will rise; and the producers of capital goods will find

---

[1] This again makes the rather naïve assumption that the banks 'usually' lend a sum exactly equal to the public's voluntary savings.

[2] Mr. Keynes and Mr. Harrod (see an article in *Economica*, November 1934) deny this. Making the more realistic assumption of unused resources, they hold that the increase in investment will increase incomes and therefore saving. They would presumably admit, however, that after the period of full employment had been reached 'forced savings' must result from a further expansion of expenditure.

their costs too high to carry on production at the expanded level of capacity elaborated under the influence of the previous fall in interest rates. At the same time the cessation of new loans diminishes the demand for capital goods; for the producers of consumers' goods can no longer borrow easily in order to buy new plant. Suddenly, therefore, production becomes wholly unprofitable in the capital goods trades, orders fall off, and heavy unemployment results. The consequent falling off of purchasing power now spreads a deflationary influence throughout the whole system. And since the producers of consumers' goods have indulged in extensions of plant when interest rates were low, they find it no longer profitable to maintain them when interest rates are high. The depression consequently becomes general. There has been 'overinvestment', and only when the excessive real capital has been liquidated can the machine start to function at full capacity again. In the early years of depression, it therefore seems, there is nothing to do but to sit and watch unemployment, poverty, and revolution spreading throughout the world.[1]

There are two main questions which may be asked about this theory. First, is it logically self-consistent? And secondly, has it anything to do with the trade cycle which appears in the real world? In considering the first question we must accept the assumption of full employment at the start; for its legitimacy is really only relevant to the second question. If we do accept this assumption, it seems that most of the events described by Professor Hayek would in fact follow such an expansion of credit as he specifies. The expenditure of the extra loans by the producers of capital goods would raise Total Effective Demand above Total Costs. Prices would rise throughout the whole system; there would be little, if any, increase in real production and consumption; and there would be a transfer of productive resources into the capital goods industries in excess of what was warranted by the community's preference for saving or spending. There would also be increased installations of plant in the consumers' goods trades. In what sense, however, would that be 'overinvestment'? And would it as a result be impossible to

---

[1] It is to be hoped that this is a fair, if summary, interpretation of Professor Hayek's argument in *Prices and Production*. It at least accords with that given by Professor Robbins in *The Great Depression*, pp. 36–44.

regain equilibrium without an intervening depression? These are the real crucial theoretical questions arising out of Professor Hayek's theory.

Words such as 'overinvestment', 'malinvestment', 'misdirection of capital', etc., are much too readily accepted. In the first place Professor Hayek is evidently not thinking of a mere direction of capital into the wrong consumers' goods industries. It is not that there is too much installation of plant in the gramophone industry and too little in the rayon industry. Nor of course can he mean that there is too much investment in plant in all the consumers' goods trades in relation to the possible demand for consumers' goods (though this is what many people seem to take him to mean). For of course it is no more possible to have more productive capacity[1] than there are people to want or need the goods produced than it is possible to have simple 'general overproduction', i.e. an excess of total output over total demand. This would be the crude fallacy underlying Mr. Harold Macmillan's book *Reconstruction*. There are two remaining things which Professor Hayek might mean. First, he might mean that the capital structure of the community as a whole had been so extended that there was not enough voluntary saving even to provide for depreciation and working and liquid capital.[2] There would then be not enough saving to keep the existing capital in existence, and the community would be in the position described on page 85, in which it is, in effect, using its fixed capital for firewood and scrap iron. If, for example, there had been a housing boom financed by credit inflation, and interest rates then rose, there would be—on this hypothesis —so little saving that nobody would be willing to invest in houses and bear the cost of repairing them. The houses would then fall down. Now if the volume of capital increased to such a point, and the volume of savings was so low despite full employment and incomes as to reach this position, the community would in fact be in the sad predicament described by Professor Hayek. The capital could not be maintained, more credit expansion would only make things worse, and the only

[1] There can only be an excess of capacity in relation to *money* demand— i.e. a deficiency of spending.
[2] This is the interpretation adopted by Mr. Erich Roll in his book *About Money*, pp. 180–3.

solution would be a long and painful process of liquidation.

There is, however, another possibility. Professor Hayek may mean not that capital is 'overdeveloped' everywhere, but simply that an excess of resources has been diverted into the trades producing capital goods.[1] This is the possibility which has just been mentioned in relation to the definition of Total Costs.[2] If, in this eventuality, there had been a constructional boom financed by credit inflation and forced saving, there would be an excess of labour in the constructional trades; and when the rate of interest fell, the unemployment in the constructional or producers' trades would cause a general shrinkage of purchasing power which might start a general deflation. This is what is widely expected to happen in Great Britain when the armaments boom is over.

Secondly, what reason is there to believe that either of the two situations envisaged above is likely to occur, or to have occurred, in the real business world? Professor Hayek himself admits with great frankness[3] that the whole of his theory was mainly designed as a logical structure calculated to elucidate underlying economic forces, and that it may very possibly have no counterpart in the real world. The existence of unused resources and fixed cost payments, Professor Hayek admits, removes some of the foundations of the logical structure. Professor Robbins,[4] however, has expressed the opinion that forces such as those imagined by Professor Hayek were the main cause of the Great Depression of 1929–32. It seems necessary, therefore, to compare the Hayek interpretation with the factual

[1] Mr. Durbin in *The Problem of Credit Policy*, p. 222, states categorically that this is the correct interpretation, and that that described in the previous paragraph involves a 'failure to understand' the position. In a sense the two interpretations may be said to come to the same thing, since the plant established in the capital goods industries is itself part of the capital structure. But there are two clear possibilities: one in which there is no unemployment in the capital goods industries, but insufficient saving to maintain the plant in the existing consumers' (and producers') goods industries, and another in which there is unemployment in the producers' goods industries. The former is, naturally, likely to lead in practice to the latter.

[2] Cf. pp. 193–4.

[3] *Prices and Production*, second edition, pp. 160 and 161.

[4] *The Great Depression*, p. 44. Here Professor Robbins contents himself with the cautious sentence: 'There is a considerable body of evidence which seems to afford a presumption that causes not dissimilar from the causes outlined above have actually been in operation.' The rest of the book, however, appears to assume that these were the main causes.

world. The possibility of an actual extension of capital beyond the point at which it could be maintained by voluntary saving may be considered first. Some adherents of Professor Hayek's theory forget that in order to keep a certain volume of capital in existence less saving is necessary than was required to bring it into existence. It is possible, therefore, for the 'forced' saving to cease, and for saving to shrink to its previous rate without it shrinking below the rate necessary to maintain the new capital in existence.[1] Suppose, for instance, that a community were saving, at the bottom of a depression, £400 out of a total national income of £4,000, and suppose that £300,000,000 was being used to maintain existing capital and £100,000,000 to finance new investment. If a process of forced saving extended the capital structure to a point at which £375,000,000 or even £400,000,000 was necessary to maintain it in existence, there would still be no lack of voluntary saving. It would have to be extended *beyond* this point for a lack of savings to appear. But when we remove the unreal assumption of fully used resources at the beginning of the process, this possibility becomes even more remote. For if there are unused resources in existence at the beginning of the credit expansion, the national income will increase as the credit expansion proceeds; and as it increases the aggregate of saving will increase. Moreover, it will increase fairly rapidly, since, as Mr. Keynes rightly points out, the richer people are the more proportionately do they save. Suppose during the period of credit expansion the national income rose from £3,000,000,000 to £4,000,000,000 (a quite realistic assumption, even if no sharp rise in prices is supposed), and savings rise from 10 per cent to 15 per cent of the national income. Then at the end of the process voluntary saving will have risen from £300,000,000 to £600,000,000. Supposing that £100,000,000 of the previously saved £300,000,000 was being used for new investment, then the sum available for maintaining existing capital in being has risen from £200,000,000 to £600,000,000 or 200 per cent. It would need a very large credit expansion indeed to extend a capital structure maintainable by £200,000,000 of savings to one not maintainable by £600,000,000 of savings!

It will be seen, therefore, from this brief quantitative compu-

[1] Professor Hayek, of course, recognizes this. Cf. *Prices and Production*, second edition, p. 138.

tation how unlikely on the face of it is Professor Hayek's logical structure, on this interpretation, to find a counterpart in the real world. For the proportions of total saving to total income, and of depreciation requirements to total investment, assumed above, are not far different from those obtaining in Great Britain in the last ten years. According to Mr. Colin Clark[1] the national income in Great Britain in 1925-9 averaged annually £4,250,000,000, the total investment about £700,000,000, and the total of depreciation requirements about £450,000,000. The figures given by Mr. Kuznets[2] for the United States suggest that new investment usually takes over 50 per cent of the total saving. If this is true it becomes almost inconceivable that the capital structure could be extended in a few years to a point at which more than 100 per cent of an increased total of voluntary saving should be required by depreciation and maintenance. That such extremes have actually occurred at any other time than, perhaps, in the great post-war inflation in Central Europe seems, on examination, most unlikely.

There are other inferences to be made, however, from the removal of Professor Hayek's unreal assumption that all productive resources are in use at the beginning of the expansion process. If this is not true (and Professor Hayek would admit that it is not), then the entrepreneurs producing capital and consumers' goods do not for a long time compete against one another for labour and materials, prices do not rise rapidly, and there are no immediate repercussions on costs. What actually happens, at any rate in the first two years of recovery, is that the rise in production takes up a great deal of slack in both capital and consumers' trades; output is increased without much rise in prices; and unit costs very likely fall as a result of the fuller utilization of plant. It is apparent therefore that the 'forced saving' (even if we believe in it at all) cannot begin till a very late stage in the expansion. For even if Professor Hayek would not accept Mr. Keynes's belief that investment generates incomes and therefore saving, he would admit that forced saving need not occur when prices are not rising and when credit expansion is generating new real as well as money incomes.

[1] *The National Income*, p. 117.
[2] Bulletin, No. 52, of the National Bureau of Economic Research.

And this is what would happen if unused resources existed. It therefore becomes improbable, almost to the point of incredibility, that the first version of Professor Hayek's theory can ever be realized in the actual world. And it was this version, it will be remembered, which justified the clear conclusion that steps ought not to be taken at the outset of depression to expand effective demand.[1]

The second version—that unusable excess capacity either always has been present or is created in the capital trades—is, as we have seen, much more plausible. If applied as an interpretation of the trade cycle, it amounts to this. After a period of intense investment—which may have started when there was already excess capacity in the producers' trades—there is bound to be a slackening in the rate of installation of plant in the consumers' goods trades, and there will be a sudden heavy fall in the demand for capital goods. Unemployment and losses will therefore appear in the capital trades more rapidly than demand can be transferred to other trades.[2] Now the mere fact that depressions always *have* been associated with a heavy fall in production in the producers' trades, and recoveries with intense activity in those trades, does not in the least prove either that there has been 'forced' saving during recovery or that the 'boom' made the depression inevitable, or that there is an excess of capacity in the producers' trades. It was pointed out long ago that fluctuations in prosperity in the consumers' trades must necessarily produce greater fluctuations in the producers' trades. For a slight addition to plant in the consumers' trades may mean a 50 per cent increase in production in the producers' trades. The

[1] Moreover, the removal of the assumption of fully employed resources reveals another defect in Professor Hayek's theory. Why is it, he has often been asked, that a bout of forced saving differs in its effect from an increase and then a relapse in voluntary saving. Because, he explains, in the former case consumption falls during the increased saving period while in the latter it does not; in that there is an inflation of prices in the former case. If, however, there are unused resources, this does not follow.

[2] Mr. R. F. Harrod's theory of the trade cycle (put forward in his book *The Trade Cycle*), attributes depression to the fact that the demand for capital goods must fall off after a point in recovery and that the consequent unemployment in the capital goods trades reduces total incomes. If this reduction in incomes could be somehow offset by an increase elsewhere, or if public works could in the first instance take the place of ordinary investment, the depression (on this interpretation) need not become general or cumulative.

whole known facts of the trade cycle, indeed, are perfectly consistent with the hypothesis that depression is simply an insufficiency of Total Effective Demand; and that, whether through an increase in consumers' expenditure or investment, Total Effective Demand is in the end raised above Total Costs, and that the cumulative process continues until some deflationary factor, or group of deflationary factors, again gets the upper hand. The truth is that a great many explanations of the trade cycle are consistent with the known statistical facts. A perfectly tenable explanation, indeed, why the boom came to an end in the pre-war cycle is simply that a point was always eventually reached when the banking system was compelled by its gold reserve and its conventional ratios to restrict its total liabilities, and so the total volume of credit, and thus to reduce Total Effective Demand, or at least to prevent it rising in proportion to Total Costs. It may be that many economists have after all a lot to learn from William Jennings Bryan's oft-derided remark: 'You shall not press down a crown of thorns upon the brow of labour; you shall not crucify mankind on a cross of gold.'

5. What Happened in 1929?

That the break of the traditional boom has been caused by credit restriction imposed by the banks, and that the return of cash to the banks during depression has stimulated credit relaxation and business recovery, is the view of Mr. R. G. Hawtrey who has given us perhaps the most brilliant combined theoretical and statistical analysis of the trade cycle that has yet appeared. Mr. Hawtrey's view cannot be shown to be inconsistent with the facts, any more than can that of Mr. Keynes (which it closely resembles), or of some versions of Professor Hayek's, or Professor Pigou's explanation in terms of the psychology of business men. Volumes have been written about the succession and causation of the events of 1929. Probably the two most penetrating statistical analyses are those of Mr. Hawtrey himself,[1] and that of Mr. H. G. Moulton.[2] These two accounts in the main agree. They show that production was increasing in *both* consumers' and capital trades throughout the 1925-9 period, that com-

[1] *The Art of Central Banking*, ch. ii, 'Speculation and Collapse in Wall Street', and ch. iv, 'The Art of Central Banking'.
[2] *The Formation of Capital.*

modity prices were, if anything, falling,[1] and that there was considerable unemployment even in 1927–9. Profits and savings[2] were on an enormous scale; and it was only the expansion of producers' credits which kept Total Effective Demand from becoming insufficient. Mr. Moulton and Mr. Hawtrey differ about the precise part played by the Stock Exchange boom and crash. Mr. Moulton thinks that towards the end of the pre-crash period effective demand was being held up only by the making and spending of Stock Exchange profits. If credit was being steadily created by the banks and lent to persons who bid up security prices, and later sold to other persons, who had borrowed more money; and if each successive group who had made profits spent them; then effective demand would have been maintained only by the highly unstable method of pumping money into the Stock Exchange. The psychologically inevitable Stock Exchange collapse would thus naturally have reduced Total Effective Demand unless really determined efforts were made by the Government to support it in other ways. Mr. Hawtrey, however, does not believe that Total Effective Demand was being supported to any important degree through Stock Exchange loans: he points out that the rise in brokers' loans was not mainly due to loans from banks. He thinks Total Effective Demand had already begun to fall off before the Stock Exchange crash, as a result of the efforts of the Federal Reserve authorities to restrict credit in order to damp down the 'boom'. At any rate both Mr. Hawtrey and Mr. Moulton agree that the proximate cause of the industrial depression was the falling off in consumers' expenditure[3] and the failure of the authorities to take any steps to maintain it. Mr. Hawtrey believes that a rapid

[1] This in itself is not necessarily a refutation of Professor Hayek, who would reply that unit costs were falling faster. Indeed, a great deal of scorn is customarily poured by Professor Hayek's more dogmatic followers on those who fail to notice, behind a veil of stable or falling prices, the inexorable forces discerned by Professor Hayek moving tragically to their climax.

[2] Here again Professor Hayek would point out that the statistics of money savings cannot distinguish between voluntary savings and newly created credit.

[3] Of all the statistical tangles which Professor Robbins gets into in his attempt to apply Professor Hayek's theory to the events of 1929 none is so surprising as the table on p. 70 of *The Great Depression*. Professor Robbins is here attempting to defend the thesis, forced on him by his theory, that consumers' buying actually *increased* for a year or so after 1929. The table shows nine commodities consumption of which increased after 1929. But on p. 46, where he is defending another thesis, Professor Robbins has a table which

and immediate lowering of interest rates after October could have saved the situation; and Mr. Moulton would agree that what was needed, whether or not at this point it was possible, was a stimulation of effective demand.

It is at any rate certain that throughout the years 1925–9 in America the increase in profits far exceeded the increase in wages, and that, partly as a result, saving was increasing rapidly. Total output increased between 1925 and 1929 by 23.4 per cent and total wages by only 6 per cent. The two factors, therefore, which we have agreed to be specially deflationary were acting forcefully: a drift from wages to profits and an increase in saving. For a time these deflationary tendencies were being offset by reflationary tendencies, among which, perhaps, was the stream of Stock Exchange profits. In the autumn of 1929 the deflationary factors, among which the Stock Exchange crash worked at any rate as a psychological influence, finally got the upper hand. Whether the initial recovery of January–April 1930 could have been maintained by an immediate lowering of the bank rate and by huge Government expenditure, nobody really can say. It may be that if consumption had been maintained by such measures no unmanageable surplus capacity would have appeared in the capital goods industries.

There are other more general grounds for thinking that the creation of surplus capacity in the producers' trades by credit inflation is not a determining cause of the trade cycle. If it were, one would expect to find everywhere that depression fairly immediately followed rapid credit inflations, and that it only ended when the process of liquidation came to its natural end. Actually, however, we do not find this. We find collapse and recovery to be correlated with specific monetary events or changes in monetary policy. There ought, for instance, to have been a calamitous slump, on Professor Hayek's theory, in Germany and Austria after the inflation of 1920–3. Actually there was a period of moderate prosperity. Professor Robbins argues

---

shows the production of consumers' goods turning down *in 1929* at exactly the same moment as that of producers' goods. These two tables can only be reconciled on two suppositions: either (*a*) that stocks of consumers' goods in general decreased after 1929, which is untrue; or (*b*) that out of a total of consumers' goods showing a fall in consumption after 1929, ten particular commodities have been selected, nine of which show a rise.

that the inevitable crash was held off till 1929 with the assistance of loans from America. But if an 'inevitable' crash can be held off as long as this, one cannot help thinking that it might have been held off indefinitely. Again, the depression which attacked almost every other country in the world after 1929 was admittedly due to the deflationary effects of the American crash, and the recall of loans and therefore gold to New York.[1] Are we therefore to attribute the whole world depression to 'overinvestment' in America alone?

Again, France and Belgium attached their currencies to gold in 1927–8, after a prolonged inflation. But there was no crisis or depression. On the contrary, there was great prosperity: and that prosperity only ended when the French and Belgian currencies became overvalued as late as in 1932. Again, in no country in the world has recovery come since 1932 as a result of 'natural liquidation'. In the sterling area it did not come till the depreciation of sterling permitted a credit expansion. In the United States, Japan, South America, South Africa, Belgium, Austria, Czechoslovakia, and elsewhere it did not come until effective demand was stimulated in the same way. In France, Germany, and Italy it did not come until effective demand was stimulated by Government expenditure on armaments.

6. *Consumers' Credits*

The real world does not present a picture of periods of 'overinvestment' followed by periods of natural liquidation. It presents a picture in which a whole multitude of deflationary and reflationary forces are perpetually fighting for the mastery of the situation, and in which the decisive step is often taken by the government. On the whole, then, the theory that excess capacity in the producers' trades is created by credit inflation must be regarded as a logical possibility whose descent to earth remains unproven. And any theory which advises inactivity in face of depression and increasing poverty cannot be accepted unless it is proved beyond all dispute. Moreover, it is the version of this

[1] It will hardly be suggested that 'overinvestment' was going on in Great Britain in 1925–9. At any rate, the volume of employment in the iron and steel industry was steadily falling in those years. This is hardly consistent with the theory that the industries producing durable goods were being over-developed.

theory which supposes the appearance of excess capacity in the capital trades that it is most likely to be realized; and it is in this form, as has been pointed out, that the theory least justifies the pessimistic view that depression cannot be prevented. Nevertheless, even if the theory cannot be regarded as relevant to the historical trade cycle, it at least furnishes us with the warning that the more an upward movement of trade is stimulated by investment, and the less by consumption, the less easy is it likely to be to prevent a recession.

Although, however, the historical facts do not prove that excess capacity in the producers' trades in relation to the consumers' trades is a reality, or even suggest that such excess capacity is habitually created by credit inflation, it *may*, nevertheless be true that excess capacity of this kind does in fact exist. This is a much more awkward disequilibrium than the others so far considered; for as has been pointed out, it cannot simply be cured by an increase in Total Effective Demand, since the resulting increase in profits in the consumers' trades would increase the demand for producers' goods, and so fail to lead to any diversion of resources away from the producers' trades. (Incidentally this is a dilemma which would not arise after a boom centred in house-building since houses are consumers' goods. In this case an increase of Total Effective Demand and an increase of profits in other consumers' trades would be the remedy.) It would seem that the only remedy in the case of a real proven surplus capacity in the producers' trades would be to combine an increase in Total Effective Demand with a prohibition of new investment or a tax on the producers' trades. This should result in a diversion of resources from the producers' to the consumers' trades; but it could scarcely be achieved by the orthodox policies of *laisser-faire* capitalism.

Apart from the possible case, however, of already existing surplus capacity in the producers' trades in relation to the consumers' trades—in which case no easy solution exists—there is a strong presumption in favour of normally re-employing surplus capacity by an increase of consumption rather than investment. This is the view taken by Mr. E. F. M. Durbin in his book *The Problem of Credit Policy*. In the course of an examination of the possibility of achieving equilibrium by the stabilization of the general price-level he comes to the conclusion that an expansion of credit designed to keep pace with the increased production of goods is more likely to succeed if it is effected by consumers' credits than by producers' credits. Producers' credits, he points out, will accelerate investment and consequent reductions of costs, and will therefore expand profits—as happened in the United States in 1925-9. But the expansion of profits will increase the demand for savings to invest: and profits will consequently grow at an increasing rate. When the resulting demand for credit begins to threaten an actual rise of the price of finished goods, the credit inflation should be stopped by a refusal on the part of the banks to issue more credit. Such a refusal, Mr. Durbin thinks, however, must start a recession: for the increase in profits must cease, and entrepreneurs who expected a continued increase will be disappointed and will contract production.

This assumption about the psychology of entrepreneurs may at least be questioned. It is not the purpose of this book to argue the case for the policy of stabilizing prices; rather it seeks to direct attention away from price levels altogether towards the much more relevant concepts of full employment and effective demand. Nevertheless arguments based on *a priori* assumptions about the psychology of entrepreneurs seem to be precarious. If entrepreneurs have been making increasing profits, and then profits suddenly cease increasing and become stabilized at a high level, will they necessarily—in disappointed rage—curtail production and start a depression? True those who have counted on merely holding goods for a rise in prices, and those who have instituted new processes on the basis of an assumed further rise in profits, may actually make losses. But it is a big assumption that these losses will necessarily be big enough and widespread enough to start a general depression.

It can, at any rate, be readily agreed that an expansion by consumers' credits is far less likely to start a recession. Such an expansion will not be stimulating a rapid fall of costs, and will consequently not promote the same degree of profit inflation. Whether, therefore, we are faced by the problem of climbing out of depression or of stabilizing an already attained position of full employment, there is a strong presumption in favour of operating the required credit expansion by consumers' rather than producers' credits. For consumers' credits will neither provoke the 'overinvestment' snags envisaged by Professor Hayek—however real they may be—nor produce an unnecessary degree of profit inflation. The inference drawn from an examination of Mr. Keynes's analysis is therefore considerably fortified; and we may conclude that there is a strong general presumption in favour of maintaining effective demand by increasing consumption rather than investment.

It thus appears that the central contention of Mr. J. A. Hobson, vaguely expressed but consistently felt by most socialists to be obviously correct, has a substantial measure of truth. An insufficiency of consumers' purchasing power, an excess of profits in relation to wages, and an excess of saving in relation to consumption, are often, though not always, the origin of monetary disequilibrium. We need not accept the view that profits are never spent; or that an increased output of goods always means deflation; or that saving must destroy purchasing power. But it is true nevertheless that an increase in saving, or an increase in the relative share of profits, may provoke deflation; that a rapid increase in output is likely to increase savings and profits even more rapidly; that the combination of a private banking system, the tradition of producers' credits, and the urge to make unlimited private profits is likely to lead to cumulative disequilibrium; and that a recovery stimulated by investment rather than consumption is at least liable, and perhaps likely, to be followed by another collapse. On these conclusions the consideration of monetary policy must be based.

CHAPTER XIX

MONETARY POLICY

Many people[1] find it difficult to understand why monetary policy is crucially important; and even some otherwise informed critics of social affairs still affirm that the influence of money cannot be great. How, they ask, can the mere manipulation of symbols or tickets affect the real production and consumption of goods? The answer is simple. The level of production, employment, and consumption in an economy organized for private profit depends on the ratio of costs to selling prices; costs are reckoned *in money* and largely fixed by law or convention; and prices are dependent on effective demand *in money*, which is itself partly dependent on the quantity of money created by the banking system. It is two quite simple and concrete facts in the modern world that have transmuted this peculiar phenomenon of money, which was once a puzzle for theorists, into a cause of poverty, war, and revolution. These two facts are the existence of legally fixed rent, interest, and even wage payments on the one hand, and the banks' unconsciously evolved power of creating money on the other. These two institutions grew spontaneously with the development of capitalism throughout the eighteenth and nineteenth centuries, and almost nobody thought of connecting the two. Between them, however, they explain the gradual appearance and intensification of most of the economic and many of the social upheavals of the last ten years.

The main problem of monetary policy is consequently the maintenance of equilibrium between the two quantities already discussed: the total of costs and the total of effective demand. For only in this way, as has been pointed out, can full employment be maintained. Since the level of wages, salaries, and interest payments per head[2] is practically fixed throughout the world,

[1] e.g. Lord Eustace Percy in a book called *Government in Transition*, ch. i.
[2] In the case of capital, it is of course fixed per unit of nominal capital.

and since the number of wage-earners, salary-earners, and entrepreneurs, and the total of nominal capital are also fixed at any
given moment, there is a certain stream of effective demand (per
year) which alone can produce full employment. It is vital to
realize that even the profit element in Total Costs is virtually
fixed in the sense in which Total Costs have been defined here;
for only if profits remain at about that level will full and steady
employment be maintained.

It seems that such an equilibrium between Total Costs and
Total Effective Demand is really what the advocates of most of
the traditional criteria of monetary policy have had in mind.
Even the first crude approximation to it, the idea that monetary
policy ought to be determined by equating the value of the currency with that of an ounce of gold, can be seen to have done
some service in its time. For where governments are corrupt and
incompetent, and central banks do not exist, it is probable that
even greater divergences between Total Effective Demand and
Total Costs would occur if unlimited credit and notes could be
issued than if the 'cross of gold' was always threatening to crucify an inflationist dictator. The survival of this idea, however,
in countries with highly developed parliamentary governments,
civil services, and banking systems is a mere confusion of thought;
and a central banker in a civilized country to-day who declares
his attachment to the unregulated gold standard is publicly,
though doubtless unconsciously, proclaiming himself unfit for
his job.

Similarly the policy of stabilizing the general price-level,
which was a great advance in its day over the crude gold standard, was really only an approximation to the idea of achieving
full employment by an adjustment of Total Effective Demand
to Total Costs. For the price stabilization movement originally
arose as a protest against the deflations and inflations imposed
on the economic machine by the gold standard. The best alternative to such clumsy upheavals seemed to be the maintenance
of constant price-levels. Such a policy has great social advantages: but it is an unfortunate confusion to base one's monetary
policy on its immediate social advantages rather than on its
conduciveness to monetary equilibrium. For monetary disequilibrium must in the end produce the greatest of social evils,
unemployment. The flaw in the price stabilization policy is the

possibility that stabilizing prices may mean a profit inflation, since unit costs are normally falling in proportion to the normal increase in productivity. Mr. Hawtrey, however, who has fought a long and honourable battle for stable prices against an unregulated gold standard, admits that by 'stable' prices he means prices falling in proportion to the increase in productivity. And in practice, Mr. Hawtrey would probably agree, the informed observer of the economic situation at any given moment in any given country watches primarily not the index of wholesale prices but the percentage of unemployment—unless the unemployment percentage has fallen below the normal. In Great Britain during the recovery successfully achieved by a variant of Mr. Hawtrey's own cheap money policy between 1932 and 1936, it was certainly the unemployment percentage rather than the price index that all economists came to watch. In Sweden[1] also in 1931–5 the central bank originally announced that it would pursue a policy of price stabilization; but it was very soon found that it was the percentage of unemployment that mattered: and the price index, like the exchange rate, was allowed to find whatever level was compatible with the attainment of full employment. In 1937, however, when abnormal unemployment has vanished in many countries, price movements are once again becoming important.

It was similarly in protest against the possible inflationary consequences of price stabilization that Professor Hayek began to advocate his policy of 'neutral money'. Much confusion has arisen over the meaning of this phrase. What Professor Hayek appears to mean by 'neutral money' is not a fixed quantity of money per head, nor a fixed expenditure on all finished goods, but a fixed expenditure on *all goods*. He wishes to stabilize the 'transaction velocity' of money, i.e. the quantity expended on all goods, finished and intermediate. The aggregate flow of money being exchanged against bread *and* flour *and* wheat would be added up and stabilized. Now such a policy means that if the number of transactions remains the same, i.e. if the number of stages in the economic process in which goods are exchanged against money remains the same, the total stream of money available to finance income payments, i.e. wages, salaries, profits, etc., must remain the same. But if this total remains the same, and the population

[1] Cf. Brinley Thomas, *Monetary Policy and Crises: Sweden's Experience.*

is increasing, not enough money will be available to provide full employment at existing wage rates. Since Total Costs have been defined here as the total necessary to provide full employment at existing wage rates, actual costs will have fallen below this level, and Total Effective Demand is bound therefore to fall below it too. Even if the population is not increasing, an increase in investment, and a consequent increase in the total interest bill, will raise Total Costs. And thirdly, as Mr. Durbin points out, the insertion of extra stages in the production process, as capital development proceeds, will introduce new transactions, and will therefore, in conditions corresponding to Professor Hayek's plan, lead to a further deflation of the sum available for financing income payments. To some extent of course financial amalgamations within industry reduce the number of transactions,[1] and the population in certain industrial countries is beginning to cease growing. But in general it can hardly be doubted that both the number of transactions and the stream of Total Costs is tending to expand in highly industrialized countries. It seems almost certain, therefore, that neutral money in this sense would in fact be persistently deflationary. Professor Hayek himself admits that, in its pure theoretical form, it must probably break in the real world on the rock of fixed costs.[2]

For these reasons Mr. Durbin proposes the stabilization of money incomes per head. The total stream of incomes per head of the population would in this case be kept constant. This would mean that if the number of transactions increased, the total quantity of money would be increased in order to maintain the aggregate required for cost or income payments. Similarly, as the population increased, the quantity available for such payments would be correspondingly increased.[3] An increase per head of the population would not of course provide extra money for the increase in the interest bill resulting from capital development. Indeed the unit in this case is really not the 'head' of the population but the pound or dollar of nominal capital. It must not be supposed that this is necessarily a negligible item; Mr. Hawtrey has estimated that the total increase in the

[1] Some think this is the cause of the decline in British industry's demand for bank advances in recent years.
[2] *Prices and Production*, second edition, p. 161.
[3] The complications of this policy are analysed in detail in part II of Mr. Durbin's book, *The Problem of Credit Policy*.

interest bill in the United States between 1925 and 1929 was £3,000,000,000; and a recent analysis in *The Economist* has shown that even in periods of very cheap money conversions of industrial debentures to lower rates of interest are a minute proportion of total industrial capital. It is evident that the total wages+salaries+interest+rent+profits stream may be growing more rapidly than 'income per head', strictly interpreted, would be. For this reason the simple conception of Total Costs as the total stream of money necessary to keep all factors fully employed may perhaps be more serviceable than income per head. Similarly, this may be advantageous in conceiving the aim of policy to be not to stabilize money income per head, but to stabilize the relation of Total Effective Demand to Total Costs. For, as Mr. Durbin recognizes, a mere stabilization of income will not stabilize expenditure. People may hoard, and the deflationary effect of this hoarding will be great. If Total Effective Demand were so far as possible kept adjusted to Total Costs, this difficulty would be avoided.

It must not be supposed, however, that this is a simple rule of thumb for monetary policy. Discussions of monetary policy in the past have often suffered from two illusions: first the belief that if one simple economic quantity was stabilized, all else would follow; secondly the belief that if one simple instrument of policy were used, all else could be neglected. It was supposed that the gold parity of the currency had to be stabilized, or savings kept equal to investment, or the market rate of interest adjusted to the 'natural' rate, or money kept 'neutral', or wholesale prices stable; and that everything could be achieved by the bank rate, or by increasing the quantity of money, or by varying the gold value of the currency, or balancing the budget, or by unbalancing the budget, or by public works. Many of the criteria of policy, however, suffered from the fact that they were unknowable: it could only be inferred, for instance, that saving exceeded investment, or the market rate the natural rate, by observing that employment was increasing or decreasing. And many of the instruments of policy, such as the bank rate, were not necessarily sufficient in themselves to achieve the desired result in all circumstances.

It may be, then, that the most practical plan at our existing stage of knowledge and technique is to regard full employment (properly defined) as the simplest criterion of policy, to realize that abnormal unemployment in the consumers' goods trades means a deficiency of effective demand, and to group all possible measures of monetary policy as reflationary or deflationary, i.e. as calculated to expand or contract Total Effective Demand. The index of prices will have to be used to supplement that of full employment; for if Total Effective Demand is inflated above Total Costs, it will be apparent from the fact that prices continue to rise beyond the point at which full employment is reached. This has become important in the boom conditions of 1937. The general aim of policy will then be to reflate when there is abnormal unemployment; and when full employment is reached, to attempt to avoid unemployment on the one hand and rising prices on the other. It is doubtful whether at present one can get much further than this.

'Full employment' must not be taken to mean the absence of all unemployment. Unemployment, as it exists or may exist in a modern industrial country, may be divided into three main kinds. First there is, at any given moment, the irreducible minimum of persons who are moving from one job to another, who are ill, or who are actually unemployable. This may be called normal minimum unemployment; it has been estimated that it would amount to about 6 per cent of the total insured population in Great Britain to-day (or about 750,000 persons). Sweden and South Africa in 1937 had succeeded in reducing their unemployment to this normal minimum. Secondly there is the general unemployment, extending throughout all trades—though more heavy in the durable goods trades—which may be called 'cyclical' or 'monetary' unemployment. This is the unemployment which is due to an excess of Total Costs over Total Effective Demand. It was this type of unemployment which dominated the world in 1932, and embraced almost the whole of the unemployment in Germany and America. Thirdly, there is the unemployment due to the exceptional necessity to make unmanageably large transfers from industry to industry. This may be caused by a drift of world demand away from an industry which is of dominating importance in a country's economy. The unemployment existing in the British distressed areas is mainly of this kind; and it was estimated as high as 800,000 persons in 1936.[1] It therefore

[1] Cf. *The Economist*, 17th June 1936, 'Britain's Economic Prospects'.

appears that full employment, as the aim of monetary policy, means the absence of cyclical unemployment. Normal minimum unemployment cannot be removed; and special unemployment cannot be removed rapidly by monetary policy, i.e. by the increase of effective demand. For, even when other industries are prosperous, it is very difficult to transfer 800,000 men rapidly from one industry to another. Nevertheless, the existence of special unemployment is an added reason for maintaining Total Effective Demand slightly in excess of Total Costs in order that profits may be high in the expanding industries, and the transfer of labour may be made as rapid as possible.

There is one more way in which the criterion of full employment must be satisfied. The assumption underlying its acceptance is of course that the money incomes of those employed shall be allowed to have their natural effect in increasing the consumption of goods and services. For the ultimate object of monetary, as of all economic, policy is to increase consumption. If, however, as Total Effective Demand is increased, measures are taken to restrict the supply of goods, whether imported or home-produced, the whole aim of the expansion of money is defeated. In these circumstances an expanded stream of money encounters a constant stream of goods, and there is no increase in consumption, but merely a rise in prices. This is what has happened in Nazi Germany, where the expansion of incomes resulting from the rearmament expenditure has been accompanied by a restriction of the supply of consumers' goods; and the mass of the people have consequently in no way benefited from 'recovery'. Such a manœuvre gives a bad name to the policy of maintaining 'full employment'. For in these circumstances the old-fashioned argument that a monetary expansion cannot increase consumption becomes valid. Normally, when there are unused resources, this argument is not valid. For the increase in effective demand then stimulates production of consumable goods, and the incomes of those formerly unemployed are spent on the increased supply of goods which their newly absorbed labour has made possible. The indispensable corollary of a full employment policy must consequently be the absence of measures restricting consumption.

Two further qualifications on the policy of adjusting Total Effective Demand to Total Costs have been mentioned in previous chapters and must not be forgotten. For that criterion of policy, though illuminating, is no more an absolute rule of thumb than the various old criteria. In the first place it is no good equating Total Effective Demand and Total Costs if the ratio between profits and other costs is allowed to become distorted; and for this reason it is better to supplement a deficiency of Total Effective Demand by increasing social services rather than raising wages.[1] Secondly, it is Total Costs in the *consumers'* goods trades which have to be covered by Total Effective Demand, and consequently it is full employment in the consumers' trades that must be taken as the criterion of policy.

This, as has been indicated already, raises the most difficult problem of monetary policy. Supposing there is full employment and normal profits in the consumers' goods trades as a whole, but widespread unemployment in the producers' goods trades, there is good reason to believe that the ratio of capacity in the latter trades to capacity in the former is greater than the ratio of the part of the community's income which it wishes to save to the part which it wishes to spend. There is thus in that sense an excess of capacity in the producers' trades. It is no doubt true, or has been argued, that the demand for producers' goods depends on the level of profits being made in the consumers' trades, rather than on the volume of saving; and it is also true that the volume of saving depends largely on the volume of incomes. But despite all this, if there is full employment in the consumers' trades, it must be impossible to expand investment by additional loans without raising prices and so inflicting 'forced saving' on all consumers. The existence of excess capacity in the producers' trades in relation to the volume of saving is really not different in principle from the existence of surplus capacity in, say, the cotton industry in relation to consumers' demand for cotton as opposed to, say, rayon. The remedy in this latter case is to maintain Total Effective Demand equal to Total Costs: so that the losses in the cotton industry are balanced by abnormal profits in the rayon industry, and labour and capital are drawn from the former into the latter. This simple policy will not work, however, if there is surplus capacity in the producers' trades in relation to consumers' trades as a whole; because the maintenance of Total Effective Demand equal to Total Costs (in all trades) while

[1] Cf. pp. 150 and 312–13.

creating high profits in the consumers' trades, would, as a result, produce even higher profits in the producers' trades, and resources would consequently not be drawn away from the producers' trades. Nor could the situation be saved by additional loans for public works designed to employ the labour in the producers' trades. For this would cause rising prices and forced saving, which could not be continued indefinitely, in the consumers' trades.

It has already been suggested that the only escape from this dilemma of monetary policy will be a combined maintenance of effective demand and prohibition of, and taxes on, investment. This should effect a transfer of resources into the consumers' trades. Alternatively, the surplus labour and capital in the producers' trades might be taken on directly by the Government and used for the production of consumers' necessities. These are policies, however, which could only be employed by a socialist government since they involve extensive interference with industry in the interests of the consumer and worker. Such a policy would of course only become necessary in the particular circumstances supposed, i.e. simultaneous full employment in the consumers' trades and general unemployment in the producers' trades. It may be that these circumstances are rare; but at any rate the obvious way to prevent them arising is to finance recovery by stimulating consumption rather than investment, and so averting so far as possible the appearance of surplus capacity in the producers' trades. Moreover, it will never be very easy in practice to demonstrate past all reasonable doubt the surplus capacity in the producers' trades, as well as full employment in the consumers' trades, does actually exist. And if it does not, the right policy is to maintain Total Effective Demand equal to Total Costs as it has been here defined, i.e. Total Costs of the trades producing finished consumers' goods; and the main criterion of policy, subject to the qualification mentioned, should be the maintenance of full employment in the consumers' trades.

If full employment in this sense is the aim of monetary policy, what are the main instruments for carrying it out? The assumption of the following argument is that the problem of preventing a recession after recovery is not fundamentally different from that of stimulating recovery after depression. It is recognized, of course, that if recovery has been mainly due to increased investment it will be more difficult to prevent recession than if it has been due to increased consumption. But, subject to the above qualification, a maintenance of effective demand is taken to be the essential aim in either case.

There are a whole series of reflationary measures (and their opposite deflationary ones) some of which are familiar and some are not. The first essential step in monetary policy in any country is to establish immediate and direct control over the central bank. This is perhaps the most urgent reform in a modern industrial country in the whole range of social and economic affairs. The retention of the sovereign power over the livelihood of the people in the hands of interested and irresponsible oligarchies is an anachronism and scandal for which no condemnation can be too strong. This is now coming to be generally recognized in most civilized countries: the United States, France, Belgium, Canada, New Zealand, Sweden, Denmark, Argentina, and many other countries have all established State control over their central banks in the last few years. The cry is, of course, usually raised that central banks should be 'independent of politics'. But bitter experience has shown that this seldom means anything more than allowing the banking oligarchy to pursue its own interests at the expense—and often to the ruin—of the rest of the community. Nor, when politicians refrain from 'interfering' with banking, do banks refrain from interfering with politics. A glance at the political affiliations of the directorates of the British 'big five' banks, or a survey of the record of the Bank of France in 1932-6, in which shabby political intrigue was added to incurable economic bigotry, will reveal how disinterested and pure is the bankers' doctrine that banking should be kept 'independent of politics'.

No sensible reformer would propose that central banks should be staffed by retired politicians.[1] It should be staffed by experts. But those experts should be responsible in matters of policy to the finance minister of the day, just as the military general staff is responsible to the defence ministers. It would be no more sane to put politicians in day-to-day control of a bank than in day-

[1] The Labour Party should not take as a precedent in this respect the National Government's appointment of a Conservative Minister of Labour to the Chairmanship of the Unemployment Assistance Board.

to-day control of an army. But we have surely passed the day when free and independent barons are allowed full liberty to make war on king, parliament, and people.

The reflationary measures which a nationalized central bank, in co-operation with the Government, would adopt, may be divided into two classes: investment measures and consumption measures. The most orthodox investment measure is the reduction of bank rate, which normally reduces interest rates throughout the system and so stimulates investment. To supplement this the basis of credit may be expanded by the purchase of securities by the central bank, by the relaxation of reserve ratios, the expansion of fiduciary issues, and, if necessary, by the reduction of the gold value of the currency. The Government may also guarantee private industrial loans, or even subsidize the rate of interest. How far such reductions in interest rates actually stimulate investment, is much disputed; and just as economists have come to estimate its effect as of rather less importance, experience seems to suggest that it is more important than ever. If all these measures fail, however, there remains the possibility that the Government should step in and undertake capital development itself. This method—the policy of public works—has perhaps been the most decisive factor, after currency depreciation and low interest rates, in stimulating recovery from the 1932 depression all over the world. In particular the experience of Sweden[1] and Belgium[2] should be studied as examples of how a reflationary investment policy can abolish cyclical unemployment in not more than two years. In both these cases the public control of the banking system was a crucial condition of success.

The argument of the last chapter suggested, however, that the main emphasis in a reflationary policy should be laid on stimulating consumption rather than investment. But it is essential to realize that consumption must first be stimulated by some method other than raising wages. For, as has been observed, the ratio between profits and other costs must be preserved. Failure to realize this seems to have been the main mistake made by President Roosevelt in the earlier stages of his reflationary campaign. Rightly trying to expand consumption, the president hit

[1] Cf. Brinley Thomas, *Monetary Policy and Crises.*
[2] Cf. Fernand Baudhuin, *La Dévaluation du franc belge.*

on the unfortunate method of raising wages by more or less coercive measures. As a result the restoration of the profit margin begun by the president's other monetary measures was retarded, and recovery held up for six months or more. Recovery in France was retarded for the same reason during the first year of M. Blum's 'New Deal'.

Measures to expand working-class purchasing power must thus be taken by some other instrument than the raising of wages alone. The obvious instruments are of course the budget and municipal finance;[1] and a vast mass of amelioratory measures are here available, only crying to be accepted. In Great Britain the easiest method of all would of course be to remit indirect taxation on necessities such as tea or sugar, or to grant a subsidy to local authorities to enable them to remit working-class rates. And behind this is the whole range of possible social expenditure. The first essential feature of such a policy—during a depression—is that it should be financed by a budget deficit. If the money to be spent on social services is raised by taxation or the rich there will be a mere transference of purchasing power and no reflationary effect.[2] It is therefore necessary that the public in all countries should come to realize, as it has already in some countries, e.g. Sweden, that a budget deficit may be a constructive reflationary measure.[3] In Sweden it was used as such; and the loans were repaid out of taxation in the 1936-7 budget as a restrictive measure after equilibrium had been attained. A budget deficit may not, of course, be reflationary, if it is financed by savings. But if it is financed by newly created

[1] Private consumers' credits are salutary, but cannot yet achieve very much.

[2] This only applies, of course, to the financing of social services as a part of *monetary* policy. When full employment is restored, social services must be financed by taxation of the rich. Taxation as a redistributive measure is discussed in part IV of this book.

[3] In the present state of economic education in Great Britain such a policy might be regarded as a blow to 'confidence'. And 'confidence' must not be ignored as a factor in the monetary situation. It is particularly relevant to a policy of lowering interest rates and to Mr. Keynes's 'liquidity preference'. For if investors sell out of panic, interest rates will rise. It is often salutary to ask, however, *whose* confidence is being invoked, and to remember that the 'confidence' of this or that vested interest can be bought at too high a price. The creation of investors' and entrepreneurs' confidence is one factor of which account must be taken in any situation. It is not a universal criterion of policy.

credit it will almost certainly expand Total Effective Demand by the aggregate amount of the deficit.

With our existing financial institutions such newly created credit could only take the form of interest-bearing loans from the banks. It is absurd, however, that when an expansion of money is necessary in the national interest, it should have to take the form of interest-bearing debt, and still more absurd that the interest payments should accrue to private institutions. The proper way to finance such a necessary credit expansion would be by the issue to the central bank of non-interest bearing bonds. No private bank would of course accept such bonds, since they would not rank as assets in the ordinary sense. This is one of the most important reasons for nationalizing the central bank. The issue of such bonds to a nationalized central bank would enable the authorities to keep a tight control not merely of the quantity of money but of the actual volume of effective demand. And it has been the problem of translating the one into the other that has so often baffled central banks and governments working separately. An increase in the issue of these bonds would reduce the ratio of the central bank's gold reserve to its total liabilities; but unless we are to allow the unemployed to be permanently crucified on the gold standard, this is an urgent political necessity, and its execution merely a matter of administrative arrangement. It need hardly be said that a credit expansion of this kind would not be inflationary unless it was continued after the point of full employment, as defined above, had been reached. To regard the financing of a deficit by new money, before this point is reached, as inflationary, is to misunderstand the fundamentals of the monetary problem. Moreover, if it is necessary to exert a deflationary pressure on the national economy, a budget surplus could be created by larger taxes on profits—a surplus would indeed appear, as a boom would *ex hypothesi* be in progress—and it could be used to repay the Government's debt to the bank and cancel the reflationary bonds.[1]

The financing of budget deficits in this way is only one instrument of reflationary policy; and it is unlikely to become a normal

[1] Cf. E. F. M. Durbin, *The Problem of Credit Policy*, ch. viii, for a detached discussion of reflationary policy, including budget deficits. In 1937 in Great Britain the Government ought to be paying off debt out of a surplus; for we have reached boom conditions. Actually, it is borrowing for rearmament!

one for many years to come. It should, however, be regarded as an ideal towards which to work. Meanwhile, the most urgent task is to attempt some co-ordination of all the different instruments of monetary policy; all the different measures, that is to say, of influencing the level of Total Effective Demand. We have to co-ordinate interest-rate policy, open-market policy, investment policy, public works policy, budget policy, and foreign trade policy; and not to let them all influence the system in different and often contradictory directions, as has tended to occur in the past. If such a co-ordination can be achieved, if full employment is specifically adopted as the criterion of policy and the control of effective demand as the aim, the cure of the trade cycle and of unemployment may be brought within our reach. Nor is the plea for such an attempt so very Utopian to-day. Already, in effect, at least in the sterling area, full employment has, almost unconsciously, come to be regarded as the criterion of success, and the stimulation or maintenance of effective demand as the real practical aim. The Social-Democratic Government of Sweden has shown that, when the central bank has been nationalized, all the measures of monetary policy here discussed can be co-ordinated with far-reaching success. President Roosevelt has blundered forward uncertainly on the right track; and even the British Treasury and the Bank of England have learnt something and perhaps forgotten much. There is every reason to believe that if full social control of banking was established in all the major countries, and if governments showed themselves willing to finance consumption, cyclical unemployment could in the end be cured and the productive resources of the world be ever more fully utilized.

PART IV
PRINCIPLES OF SOCIALIST POLICY

CHAPTER XX

POSSIBILITIES OF REDISTRIBUTION

The foregoing argument suggests that it is in the nature of an uncontrolled price system to ensure a production and distribution of wealth which ignore real needs and sacrifices, and that it is equally in the nature of an uncontrolled monetary system to ensure an almost perpetual under-employment of resources. But the cure for under-employment, it has been argued, lies in the adoption of the sort of rationalized monetary policy discussed in the preceding chapter. Such a policy is not necessarily socialist; though it could scarcely be adopted by a non-socialist government, and it would certainly be a most important part of any socialist government's programme, since everything else would probably be impossible without it—as the British Labour Government of 1929-31 discovered. The redistribution of resources and incomes, however, which is necessary to effect a better adjustment of resources to needs, must always be the central aim of socialist policy. Before discussing the methods of redistribution, however, we have to meet the objection that any substantial 'real' redistribution is not possible. Not only, it is argued, is any substantial raising of the standard of living of the masses by a redistribution of productive resources in practice impossible; but even the purely monetary effect of a redistribution of money incomes can be statistically shown to be negligible. The statistical argument derives from a notorious calculation made by Sir Josiah Stamp about the possibilities of statistical distribution in Great Britain in 1919.[1] Sir Josiah calculated that if in 1919 all incomes in excess of £250 a year had been pooled, the spendable surplus so obtained could have added little more than five shillings a week to the budget of families whose members' incomes were below the £250 level. Now even if this cal-

[1] *Wealth and Taxable Capacity*, pp. 98-9.

culation were impeccably sound, it would not prove the effects of redistribution to be negligible; for an addition of five shillings a week to every working-class budget would mean a colossal mitigation of inequality. To suppose that five shillings a week means little to a working-class family because it means little to a middle-class family is precisely to misconceive the nature of inequality and the purpose of redistribution.

But the calculation is also open to a great many statistical objections. Sir Josiah Stamp found that the net incomes of the persons with incomes over £250 a year was, after deducting direct taxes, £910,000,000. If all of these persons were left £250 a year each, they would receive in all £310,000,000; and a surplus of £600,000,000 would remain. From this, however, before ascertaining the distributable surplus, Sir Josiah deducted £450,000,000 as representing the yearly saving of the richer classes. There consequently only remained £150,000,000 to be distributed among 10,000,000 families with incomes of less than £250 a year. The whole of this calculation, as Mr. Josiah Wedgwood has pointed out,[1] depends on the dubious procedure of deducting £450,000,000 for the savings of the richer classes.[2] This figure is in itself an estimate and one which probably errs largely on the high side. And quite apart from this it is inadmissible to assume that a figure equal to the total savings made in a capitalist world need necessarily be made in a socialist world. A substantial rate of saving must of course be achieved under socialism: but at least some transfer from saving to consumption is a necessary and desirable accompaniment of redistribution, as the whole of the preceding argument on monetary policy has shown. Yet if Sir Josiah Stamp, allowing for this, had placed the amount to be deducted for saving by the rich at say £300,000,000 instead of £450,000,000, the amount to be distributed among the working classes would have been doubled: and each family would have got ten shillings instead of five shillings.

Even this, however, is probably an understatement. Mr. Colin Clark, in a much more up-to-date calculation published in 1932, estimated that 'even at the present time the equal distribution

---

[1] *The Economics of Inheritance*, pp. 6–7.
[2] It also does not allow sufficiently for 'institutional' saving. Cf. pp. 268–9.

of the national income, not excluding income from overseas, and with maintenance of the existing rate of investment, would give an average family income of £270 per annum to all, including the unemployed'.[1] Such an income would certainly represent an increase of more than ten shillings, and perhaps as much as £1 to the average working-class family. The discrepancy between Sir Josiah Stamp's figures and those of Mr. Clark arises from the fact that Mr. Clark is simply giving a figure for 'income per family' and making no allowance for saving and tax payments. His £270 per family must not therefore be taken as income available for consumption. In any case both calculations are very approximate statistically: and no certain positive inference can be based on them. We may safely conclude, however, that Sir Josiah Stamp has not 'statistically proved' the possibilities of redistribution to be negligible.

In a still more recent calculation Mr. Colin Clark (*National Income and Outlay*) has estimated the 'spendable incomes' (after allowing for taxation and savings) of those with incomes over £250 a year as £1,000,000,000 in Great Britain to-day. This leaves an enormous sum available for redistribution.

But there are serious objections to the procedure of dividing a total money figure of the national income equally between the total number of families. In the first place no absolutely equal distribution could be effected in practice without completely dislocating the productive mechanism. Secondly, Sir Josiah Stamp's and Mr. Clark's calculations made no allowance for the distinction between earned and unearned incomes. Thirdly, it is of course a fallacy to divide up a money figure of the national income between the total of families and imagine that the money income per family resulting from the calculations represents in any sense what the families in question would be able to buy in actual goods. For the poor families which received a larger income as a result of the redistribution will not wish to spend it on the same goods as those no longer bought by the rich families which now receive a smaller income. In the extreme case, where the rich, after buying necessities, spent the whole of their surplus income on rare works of art, redistribution could affect practically nothing. For the high price of the work of art is simply due to the competition of the rich men to buy

[1] Colin Clark, *The National Income.*

it; and if their money was given to the necessitous poor, the price of works of art would fall, and that of food and clothes would rise. But if there were no substantial number of artists and art-dealers who could be turned into producers of food and clothing, very little more food and clothing would be produced than before. And even if the incomes of the rich were spent mainly on jewels, the possibilities of redistribution would not be

Group 1	Income per head per week	Estimated average expenditure on food	Estimated Population	
			Numbers	Percentage
1	1s.–10s.	4s.	4,500,000	10 per cent
2	10s.–15s.	6s.	9,000,000	20 ,,
3	15s.–20s.	8s.	9,000,000	20 ,,
4	20s.–30s.	10s.	9,000,000	20 ,,
5	30s.–45s.	12s.	9,000,000	20 ,,
6	over 45s.	14s.	4,500,000	10 ,,
average	30s.	9s.		

great. For the poor would not want to buy jewels: and the number of persons engaged in the production and transfer of jewels might not be very substantial. In the real world, however, the incomes of the rich are not spent on these rarities. They are spent mainly on large houses, staffs of servants, motor-cars, travel, and a great many other things whose production demands the use of a large volume of capital and labour. Professor Robbins has remarked that it is only necessary to stay in the country houses of the rich to realize that most of their alleged servants are really engaged in looking after one another; and he implies that this is true over the whole economic system. Surely, however, it is a matter of common observation that this is not so. The building of large houses, the maintenance of gardens and golf courses, the transfer of peculiar foods and drinks from the ends of the earth, the production of motor-cars, etc., clearly absorb an enormous amount of productive labour and capital. If all this labour and capital were directed to the production of necessities, there can really be no doubt that the real incomes of the poor could be very substantially raised.

How far could they be raised? It is difficult to answer this question without falling into the theoretical fallacies involved in merely dividing out the money figure of the total national income. But in the case of Great Britain we may perhaps reach a reasonably reliable estimate in the following way. Sir John Orr, assisted by various eminent scientists and statisticians, has published an elaborate survey[1] of the food consumption of the different strata of society in Great Britain. He classifies the population by income groups and gives the average food expenditure per head of each group, as shown by the table on the previous page.

It is not very clear to what period these figures refer. This is important, at least in theory, since much depends on the price of food at the date of the calculation. It appears that the figures are an average for the period 1929-35, during the latter part of which the retail price of food did not alter greatly.

Sir John Orr found that the diets of those in classes, 1, 2, and 3 were all in some respects deficient in the substances necessary for the promotion of ordinary health and strength; while the diets of those in classes 4, 5, and 6 were adequate. All those, that is to say, who were able to spend ten shillings or more per week per head on food had an adequate diet, while those who were unable to spend as much had an inadequate one. If, then, we neglect for the moment the effect of a redistribution of incomes in altering food prices, we may approximately compute the total addition which would have to be made to the food expenditure of each group to raise it to a level compatible with proper nutrition.[2] Group 1 would require £70,000,000 a year, group 2 about £94,000,000, and group 3 about £47,000,000; and the total would be rather over £200,000,000. If we assume, therefore, that an additional expenditure of rather over £200,000,000[3] on

---

[1] *Food, Health and Income*, by J. B. Orr.

[2] This is to assume that the redistribution would take the form of a direct grant of food rather than money, since if it was given in money it would not, as the figures show, all be spent on food. The resulting figure is therefore a bare statistical minimum, and should not be taken to imply a preference for redistribution in kind.

[3] A figure about two-thirds of Great Britain's annual expenditure on armaments, and less than a third of Germany's in the years 1936-7. This does not necessarily mean that the money could have been spent on food: but it is an interesting sidelight on the comparative magnitudes involved in the problem of transferring productive resources.

foodstuffs would not raise prices at all, a mere transfer of that amount would secure an adequate food consumption for the whole population. Actually, of course, prices would be raised. How much they would be raised, is naturally impossible to say with anything approaching statistical accuracy. For it depends on the extent to which production of these foodstuffs could be increased without a rise in costs. It is worth noticing, however, that there was in the period in question an enormous surplus capacity in world production of wheat and meat and dairy products, Great Britain's chief food imports; and that fruit, milk, and vegetables, the chief form of home-produced foods, could undoubtedly be produced in very much larger quantities if this demand existed. In all these trades there is at present a problem of chronic over-production; if *additional* resources of land, labour, and capital were absorbed by them, their potential productive capacity would be very great. And since the total expenditure of the community on food in these years was about £1,000,000,000, an increase of the order of £200,000,000 would not proportionately be overwhelming. Bearing in mind these considerations, we still cannot estimate the exact additional expenditure on food by Sir John Orr's three lower groups which would allow for the resulting rise in prices; but we may perhaps reasonably infer that in normal times an addition of £250,000,000 to the income of the poorest, as they stood in the period in question, would go far to provide an adequate supply of food and drink for the whole community.

Some addition to these incomes would in fact naturally accrue through trade recovery resulting from an intelligent monetary policy and lower unemployment. For the purpose, however, of estimating the possibility of redistribution it is relevant to compare the figure of £250,000,000 with the total of unearned and of inherited incomes. Mr. Colin Clark, as has been observed, has estimated the 'spendable incomes' of the rich in Great Britain at £1,000,000,000, or four times the amount necessary. But how large is the flow of unearned income at present in private hands from which the £250,000,000 should be mainly drawn? In making such a comparison it is not of course possible to reach any sort of exact statistical accuracy; nor is it for the moment assumed that wholesale redistribution is economically possible.[1]

1 This is considered in the next chapter.

The purpose of the comparison is merely to show the rough order of magnitude of the two figures, so that *a priori* denials of the possibility of redistribution may be refuted. The total of 'rent, profit, and interest' in the national income is given by Mr. Colin Clark[1] as averaging about £1,200,000,000 between 1929 and 1935. But this is of course far from being the total of un-earned incomes, either in the income-tax sense or in the sense of inherited incomes. For the figures of 'profits from businesses, professions, etc.' in schedule D of the income-tax returns, on which Mr. Clark's figures are based, include many earned incomes. The Inland Revenue Acts do not give specifically the total of earned and unearned incomes. But Mr. Josiah Wedg-wood, on the basis of some percentages given to the Colwyn Committee, has calculated[2] the total of earned and unearned incomes for the years 1919–20. He gives the total of unearned incomes as £988,000,000, out of a total national income of £3,847,000,000, or almost exactly 25 per cent. Bowley and Stamp[3] show unearned income in the income-tax sense both in 1911 and 1924 to have varied between 20 per cent and 30 per cent of the national income according to the definition of national income.[4] Earned income as a percentage of 'social income' (the nearest to the sense in which we are here using the term 'national income') was 22 per cent, and as a percentage of aggregate in-come, 29 per cent. We shall therefore not be far wrong if we take unearned income in the income-tax sense as normally about 25 per cent of the national income, though it would probably be smaller in depression years.

If this proportion were maintained in the years 1926–31, the total of unearned income in those years must have averaged about £900,000,000 a year. This is most unlikely to be an over-estimate, since Bowley and Stamp give an aggregate figure for 1924 of £1,200,000,000. Earned income, as defined by the Inland Revenue Authorities, is income 'immediately derived by an individual from the carrying on or exercising by him of his

[1] *National Income and Outlay*, p. 94.
[2] *The Economics of Inheritance*, p. 44.
[3] This is based on income-tax statistics and represents personal incomes plus undistributed profits. It consequently represents no double counting in the case of securities held by dividend-paying companies: and it excludes the incomes of charitable institutions.
[4] *The National Income, 1924*, pp. 48–52.

trade, profession, vocation, or employment'. It therefore includes the 'profits' of small business men, professional men, and so forth; and it consequently accords fairly closely with the economic distinction between income for work (including entrepreneurs' salaries) on the one hand and incomes from property on the other.[1] There are several important deductions, however, that have to be made before we can approximate to an estimate of the total unearned income which is even theoretically available for redistribution. Allowance must be made for tax payments—since to this extent the incomes are being redistributed already, or at least are not henceforth available for redistribution—for savings, and for the fact that a small part of the unearned income already accrues to the poorer groups. In the years 1925–31 the total yield of direct taxation (less death duties, which are not a tax on income) was about £300,000,000, and the total yield of indirect taxes averaged about £250,000,000. If, therefore, the percentage of total taxation paid by recipients of unearned income was the same percentage of total receipts as those incomes of total incomes, i.e. 25 per cent, the total tax payments of recipients of unearned incomes would have averaged about £125,000,000. It is also usually assumed that the rich, i.e. those with incomes over £250 a year, pay about one-fifth of the indirect taxes and almost the whole of direct taxes, i.e. at least £350,000,000. And since about half of the incomes over £250 a year are unearned, it would seem that the recipients of unearned incomes pay at least £150,000,000, and more probably £175,000,000 a year in taxation. This is probably nearer to the truth than the figure mentioned above of £125,000,000. Deducting this £175,000,000 then from the total of £900,000,000 we are left with £725,000,000 of unearned incomes.

How much of this should we deduct for saving, allowing for the fact that redistribution is designed to effect some diminution of saving? A comparison of the figures of Bowley and Stamp and Mr. Colin Clark suggests that in the years 1924–31 the total national new saving averaged about £400,000,000. How much of this is saved out of unearned incomes? It would not be fair to assume that because 75 per cent of total incomes are

---

[1] Probably some income for risk-bearing falls into one income-tax group and some into another. But this income is so difficult to identify, both in theory and practice, that it does not affect the main argument.

earned, 75 per cent of savings are made out of earned incomes. For savings are mostly made by the rich, whose incomes are mostly unearned. On the other hand considerable sums must be saved out of earned income, as the figures of the Post Office, National Savings Certificates, and the insurance companies show. And savings out of unearned incomes cannot well be more than three-quarters of total savings, since it would then amount to £300,000,000: and that would mean that a third of unearned incomes were saved. Moreover, Mr. Colin Clark has estimated that net private saving by the rich has fallen to nil in recent years.[1] If we adopt a maximum estimate as being that most unfavourable to the argument of this chapter,[2] we need not, therefore, deduct more than £150,000,000 at the very outside from the total of £725,000,000 so far remaining; and we shall be left with £575,000,000 theoretically available for redistribution. From this again we must deduct the small total of unearned incomes already accruing to persons in Sir John Orr's three lower groups. Professor Bowley and Sir Josiah Stamp have calculated that the income from property accruing to persons whose total incomes were below £150 a year was £77,000,000 in 1924. This figure of £150 a year represents, of course, income per income receiver; while the figure of £1 per week (or £50 a year) which divides Sir John Orr's lower three classes from his upper three classes, represents income per head, i.e. per every member of the family. Since, however, the ratio of the total population to the total of income receivers is about 2½ to 1, it would appear that families with an income of £50 a year per head would in fact have total family incomes not much above £150 a year. To be on the safe side, however, the £77,000,000 may be increased to £100,000,000 to represent the total unearned incomes of persons in Sir John Orr's three lower groups. If we therefore make a further deduction of £100,000,000 from the £575,000,000, there remains say £475,000,000 theoretically available for redistribution.

---

[1] *National Income and Outlay*, ch. viii.

[2] And even this is to neglect for the moment the conclusion that redistribution ought to lead to some fall in savings. It is true that attribution of an individual to one of Sir John Orr's groups depends to a greater extent on the number of persons in the family as well as on the total family income. Over the whole community, however, this should not upset the calculation.

Now this represents the available residue of unearned incomes in the sense of property incomes as such, not inherited incomes only. It would include, that is to say, interest on savings made by the recipient out of his own earned income. If, however, the general socialist strategy is to redistribute merely inherited incomes, we wish to know what proportion of the section of £475,000,000 of propertied incomes are inherited incomes. To say what proportion inherited incomes are of all property incomes is not easy. Nobody would probably estimate this at less than half and few at more than three-quarters; and Mr. Josiah Wedgwood's calculations[1] suggest that it is between two-thirds and three-quarters. If, therefore, we estimate the available residue of genuinely unearned incomes at somewhere around £300,000,000 to £350,000,000 we shall perhaps be as near to the facts as it is possible to get.

This figure of £300,000,000 to £350,000,000 compares with the £250,000,000 which, according to Sir John Orr's calculation, would be sufficient to give half the population of Great Britain a sufficiency instead of an insufficiency of food. In so far then as the above calculations are reasonable approximations to the truth, it appears that a redistribution merely of large inherited incomes, after allowing for savings and taxation, would be sufficient to supply adequate food to the 20,000,000 people now hungry in Great Britain. And if this is true of Great Britain, where some attempt at least has been made to correct inequality by redistributive taxation, it is even more clearly true of the other great capitalist states. For in France taxation on unearned incomes and inheritance is far less developed than in Great Britain; in Italy, Japan, and—as yet—the United States there are no effective social services: and in Germany the Nazi Government has deliberately adopted the policy of taxing the poor and starving the social services, which under the Social-Democrats had begun to be really effective. In Scandinavia, Australia, and New Zealand, on the other hand, more redistri-

[1] Cf. *The Economics of Inheritance*, ch. v. Mr. Wedgwood decides after a detailed investigation that in the nineteenth century from three-fifths to two-thirds of the national capital was inherited at any given moment. The proportion must be certainly higher to-day, since saving must now be smaller in relation to the total capital. This incidentally implies that at the present time there is a total inherited income in Great Britain of at least £600,000,000.

bution has probably been carried out than in Great Britain, and with very great success.

The above figures, as has been explained, are of necessity approximations and not exact estimates. They are subject to many qualifications, such as the difficulty of applying them to exactly the same years, and there is an additional penumbra of uncertainty at each step in the argument. Those who are disposed to be sceptical about statistics may, therefore, if they choose, discount the whole calculation as valueless. If they do this, however, they must admit that no statistical light at all can be thrown on the possibilities of redistribution; and in that case the only reasonable attitude is to attempt to discover empirically whether redistribution is practicable. Either we must be completely sceptical about the statistics of this question and consequently admit that there is no case against attempting redistribution, or else we must place some cautious reliance on such statistics as we do possess. If we do the latter, we can but conclude that the abolition of inherited incomes in a modern industrial State would go a very long way towards abolishing hunger altogether.

CHAPTER XXI

PRINCIPLES OF REDISTRIBUTION

The principles of redistribution—the modifications, that is to say, which it is proposed to introduce into the system of private capitalism and free prices—must be dependent on the flaws inherent in the system. Some of these flaws are inherent in the legal framework and some in the price system itself; and there must consequently be two main types of reform: alteration of the framework and interference with the system.[1] It was argued in chapters ix, x, and xi that almost all the major distortions and injustices of the price system spring from the inequality of incomes, and that the worst *and* most unjustifiable inequalities spring from the institution of inheritance. It follows, therefore, that inheritance, and its consequence, inherited income, ought so far as possible to be abolished. And on the possibility of thus altering the legal framework of the price system without destroying the system itself, even Professor Hayek is with us: 'There is no reason to assume that the historically given legal institutions are necessarily the most 'natural' in any sense. The recognition of the principle of private property does not by any means necessarily imply that the particular delimitation of the contexts of this right as determined by the existing laws are necessarily the most appropriate.'[2] Socialists should therefore change

1 The distinction is not as absolute as it appears. Inheritance-taxation and other direct taxation would usually be considered an alteration in the social framework and the application of taxes and bounties to particular commodities an interference in the price system. Yet one is only direct taxation and the other indirect; one acts directly on the income structure and the other on the price structure. The unreality of the distinction is a pointed illustration of the impossibility of restricting reform to the institutional framework alone.

2 Cf. *Collectivist Economic Planning*, by Professor Hayek and others, p. 22, Professor W. H. Hutt, another uncompromising defender of free prices and competition, is in favour of taxing inheritance. Cf. *Economists and the Public*, by W. H. Hutt. Cf. Mill's opinion quoted on page 352.

the laws so as substantially to abolish inheritance.[1] On the substance of this there should be no compromise whatever. For inheritance is at once the chief cause of inequality and of the resulting poverty, and the most indefensible of all the trappings of modern capitalism. The payment of inherited incomes is not morally justifiable, because the recipients make no real effort or sacrifice in return; and it is not economically justifiable, because the passive service of merely refraining from consuming one's capital is one that can be performed with equal efficiency by the State. Moreover, just because inheritance is associated with the family, it inevitably produces a propertied class, with all its attendant evils. The abolition of unearned incomes and the consequent social ownership of property must be the centre and heart of socialism. The traditional socialist belief that unearned incomes are the main removable cause of poverty and inequality is true and of dominating importance. The tendency of socialists lately to think less of the dispossession of property and more of organization, 'planning', efficiency, and so on, is in many ways unfortunate. What society fundamentally needs is not so much planning as socialism.

The central aim, at any rate, of socialists must be the abolition of all inherited incomes rather than all large incomes or all incomes that can be called 'profit'. For, as was pointed out in chapter xi, the large earned incomes do not add up to a significant percentage of the national income; they are usually paid in return for highly important services; and they are often necessarily saved and not consumed. There must be a gradual levelling of all earned incomes; but this is an aim essentially secondary to the abolition of unearned incomes. Similarly, it is not 'profit' as such that socialism should seek to remove. The 'profit' of the taxi-driver or the hawker, or even the tenant farmer, is not unearned and is consequently not an abuse. And the profit of the non-salaried entrepreneur is in fact an earned income just as much as a salary. In general, therefore, at any rate in the first place, the State should take over the 'waiting' rather than the risk-bearing function. It is an attractive suggestion that the State should take over the risk-bearing function also, and by pooling non-insurable risk thereby destroy it as

[1] There must, of course, be qualifications and exceptions, which are discussed in the next chapter.

effectively as an insurance company destroys insurable risk. This would mean in fact that, by averaging out the profits and losses of speculative ventures, no loss would be sustained by any individual at all. In so far as property comes into the hands of the State in the form of ordinary shares, risk-bearing will become a social activity. But, as is argued in the later chapters (on planning) of this book, the profit to be made from undertaking to bear the risk involved in new ventures must for a long time be left to private entrepreneurs—though not to their children. For the imagination and initiative required to start a new venture are essentially the qualities which private enterprise is best fitted to show. Here is private enterprise at its best: and if it is allowed to operate at its best, it must be allowed in this sphere to make profits as well as losses.

Nor, of course, does the abolition of inherited incomes imply the abolition of private property as such. It would not prevent a man holding as much private property in his lifetime as he can continue to buy by saving out of his own earned income. And such property might take the form of land, a house, or even securities. How far private persons would save in the absence of inheritance, must be considered when the economic consequences of abolishing inheritance are considered; but it is clearly socially desirable that private saving should not be made legally impossible. For not only will savings be needed for national development, but individuals will always desire to save for old age, marriage, and a thousand other reasons—as they do in Russia. No doubt State pensions, insurance, and so forth, will diminish this need; but they will not destroy it. We may suppose that in the initial stages of socialism at any rate in a country like Great Britain, outlets for savings like the Post Office, Government loans, and even such industrial securities as remain will be available to the man who has saved out of his own earned income. Socialists have been mistaken in making ownership of the means of production instead of ownership of inherited property the test of socialization. For there is no abuse in a man saving £100 out of his earned income and investing it for a few years in the Post Office or in London Transport Stock; but there is a very great abuse in a man owning a vast country mansion and a park of a thousand acres, or a vast tract of slum property, inherited from his father, and handing it on to his children. It is not the ownership of the means of production as such, but owner-ship of large inherited incomes, which ought to be eliminated.

Indeed, the official Marxist definition of socialism, as propa-gated by Mr. John Strachey for instance, denotes a state of affairs which would be perfectly compatible with all the most unbridled abuses of private capitalism. Socialism, by this defi-nition means the abolition of private ownership of the means of production. But supposing, as might happen in Russia, that the State owned all the means of production, but that at the same time there was a class of rich rentiers living entirely on the inter-est on Government securities, and handing them on freely up to 100 per cent to their children. It would be possible, on Mr. Strachey's definition, to build up an entirely idle class of million-aire rentiers, and to say that 'socialism' had nevertheless been achieved. If we are to have the substance and not the shadow, therefore, we must define socialism as the abolition of private unearned or inherited incomes rather than of the private owner-ship of the means of production.

CHAPTER XXII

CONFISCATION AND TAXATION

The possible methods of redistributing incomes in a modern industrial State may be distinguished into several general types. The most obvious choice is between violent and non-violent methods. No more need be said on this issue here than that if the same results can be achieved in a reasonable period by peaceful as by violent methods, violence is presumably to be avoided. For violence is not only an evil in itself; it is also bound to result in injustice on the one hand and prolonged economic dislocation on the other. The economic dislocation will naturally be longer the more complex the economic system concerned; and we know that even in Russia, whose economy in 1917 was comparatively primitive, it took five or ten years to restore the standard of living of the masses to the pre-revolutionary level. To appeal to violence in a highly complex industrial community, quite apart from its moral justifiability, would be like burning a house down in order to achieve a more equitable distribution of the occupants between the different rooms. The question is one which everyone must decide for himself in every given case: but it seems most unlikely that in any community but the most primitive agricultural economy, violent revolution could raise the standard of living of the workers in much less than a generation.

What are the possible methods of peaceful redistribution? In the circumstances of to-day they would seem to be, in the main, three: trade-union pressure; legal confiscation; and taxation, supplemented by social services. The last two, legal confiscation and taxation, are of course not really distinguishable by any hard and fast line. The first, trade-union pressure, is undoubtedly of very great importance. Trade unions have been called the most beneficial institutions in the world: and rightly, since they exert the maximum of social pressure at the point of maximum social need. Indeed, the easiest way to tell a bad from a good government in the existing world is to inquire whether it supports or attacks the trade-union movement.

The object of trade-union pressure, however, is to secure the proper share due to labour under competitive conditions and to offset monopoly influences on the employers' side. For this reason trade unions are an urgent necessity: since without them, owing to the manifestly inferior bargaining position of the solitary worker, and the prevalence of imperfect competition among employers, labour will not often even secure its fair competitive wage. But trade-union pressure cannot in the nature of things directly alter the legal context of the price system: nor can it alter the distribution within that system, beyond a certain point, without dislocating its working. For the effect of trade-union pressure is to increase the income of labour at the expense not so much of unearned incomes as of profits. It encroaches, that is to say, not normally on rent and interest, but on the remuneration for work and risk-bearing of the active entrepreneur, big and small alike. As was pointed out in the preceding chapter on money and the trade cycle, the maintenance of a certain ratio between entrepreneur's profits and other costs is one of the conditions of equilibrium. If trade-union pressure, therefore, is carried beyond this point, it may lead to disequilibrium and depression. It is consequently essential to conceive trade-union pressure as a means of securing to labour its full competitive income in existing economic and social circumstances. For as a means of abolishing unearned incomes it has two radical flaws: first it normally encroaches on entrepreneurs' profits initially and on rent and fixed-interest payments, if at all, afterwards; and secondly it is likely to reduce the entrepreneurs' incomes below the level necessary to equilibrium before there has been any substantial encroachment on unearned incomes proper at all. It is true that in the case of public companies trade-union pressure would reduce ordinary dividends, which contain a large 'interest' element, before touching directors' fees or managers' salaries. But over the national economy as a whole the entrepreneurs' wages and payment for risk-bearing would be bound to be reduced before the bulk of rent and fixed-interest payments had been touched. Trade-union pressure, in fact, cannot discriminate between entrepreneurs' profit and unearned income. It cannot, therefore, serve as the main instrument for the abolition of unearned incomes.

There remain the expedients of legal confiscation and taxation. For it must not be supposed that nationalization or 'socialization' is itself any solution to the problem.[1] Public control of an industry is one thing and public ownership another: and without public ownership unearned income cannot be diverted into the hands of the State. Moreover, if public ownership is secured by the purchase of the shares of a firm or industry at market value, no transfer of income from rich to poor will take place at all. For if new stock or cash equal to the market value of the shares is given to the shareholders in the industry to be nationalized, they will still hold, or be able to buy, claims to unearned income approximately equal to what they previously received. In the case of London Transport, for instance, new stock was created and given in exchange for old: and private rentiers continue as before to draw an unearned income from the business. If, on the other hand, the stockholders are given new stock or cash of less than the market value of the shares, the difference has simply been confiscated; and the action of the State is exactly the same as if it had decided to confiscate, say, £1,000 from each one of an arbitrarily selected group of individuals. Similarly if a terminable annuity is granted in exchange for existing stock, either the capital value of the annuity must be equal to that of the stock, in which case there is no transfer of income and the recipient of the annuity can easily sell it for some permanent stock: or else if the capital value is less, the difference has once again been confiscated. An annuity of £50 a year for thirty years cannot without confiscation be given to someone previously holding a claim to £50 a year for ever; for the value of a claim to £50 a year for ever is greater than the value of a claim to £50 a year for thirty years. Again, the difficulty cannot be evaded by arranging for the amortization of the new stock over a period of time: for the extra amortization payments will, if confiscation is to be avoided, have to be great enough to enable the capitalist to re-invest in other claims sufficient to secure him a correspondingly large income.

[1] As Mr. Herbert Morrison says (*Socialization and Transport*, p. 247), a socialist government 'cannot solve the general problem of rent, interest and profit at the point of socialization of individual industries'. 'It must deal with it by means of death duties . . . or inheritance taxes.'

Socialists have long tended, and are still tending, to evade this crucial dilemma. Yet though certain considerations may be advanced which somewhat soften its rigour, the substance of the dilemma remains. It is true, for instance, that if the State were always to grant Government-guaranteed fixed-interest securities in exchange for ordinary shares, it would be able to pay a lower rate of interest. For it would itself be taking on a part of the risk-bearing function: and this would in such cases be a perfectly proper thing for it to do. Moreover, in so far as the increase in general productivity over long periods tends to enhance the capital value of productive capital, the State would gain a certain unearned increment in the long run; though if it was to do this it would have to grant only fixed-interest Government securities and not new variable-dividend shares also, as in the case of London Transport, in exchange for industrial stocks. Again, it has been argued by Mrs. Wootton[1] that the objection to terminable annuities already mentioned does not necessarily hold. It is true, she says, that the capital value of the annuity will have to be as great as that of the shares expropriated 'so long as an organized market exists for the purchase and sale of privately owned capital values'. If, however, she suggests, governments and municipalities only issue terminable annuities, and if the shares of all industrial enterprises are coming into the hands of the State, then there will not be sufficient claims to permanent unearned incomes for the would-be sellers of the terminable annuities to buy. In the circumstances which Mrs. Wootton conceives this would of course be so. But it would not help us much in the early stage of socialization in a country at the level of social development of say Great Britain, France, or the United States to-day. For in all these countries there exists an enormous volume of securities which could be bought in exchange for annuities. Mrs. Wootton's argument seems a sound reason for granting terminable annuities rather than permanent bonds in exchange for industrial stock. But it does not establish that such annuities will be an effective weapon in the early stages of the attack on unearned incomes.

May not legal confiscation be the better or perhaps the only way? The objection to confiscation is that it would be extremely

1 *Plan or no Plan*, pp. 286–7.

inequitable,[1] perhaps even more so than violence. For whereas violent revolution would dispossess the whole class of rentiers big and small alike, confiscation proceeding piecemeal industry by industry would select some and allow others to go scot-free in an exceedingly arbitrary fashion. The selection of industries for industrialization, if it is to be done according to a rational plan, must necessarily be decided on the kind of principles discussed in the succeeding chapters.[2] It ought not to be, even if it could be, decided by the necessity to dispossess the larger rentier first. Yet the shares of every industry and almost every firm are held by large and small rentiers at once. If, therefore, it is decided on adequate general grounds to nationalize say the electricity supply industry and the railways, and the method of 100 per cent confiscation is adopted, the small saver who has perhaps put his total life saving of £100 in one electricity company or railway will lose the lot, while the millionaire who happens to have no money in these concerns will be entirely unaffected. The bogy of dispossessing the penurious and thrifty widow, which is always called up against the socialist, would begin to assume some of the contours of reality if piecemeal confiscation were adopted. Confiscation allied to nationalization, in fact, must necessarily be extremely inequitable just because it cannot distinguish between large, small, and very small unearned incomes. Indeed, it must almost certainly be so patently inequitable as in most cases to provoke determined if not violent resistance.

Confiscation must consequently also be ruled out as a normal method of peaceful transition to socialism. There is no escaping the fact that when an industry is nationalized in a democratic community, either new Government stock or terminable annuities, equivalent in value to the market price of the existing shares —or of course cash—must be granted to the stockholder.[3] And this is the method proposed by most modern Social-Democratic parties. The report of the National Executive of the British Labour Party on 'Public Ownership and Compensation', officially adopted by the Southport Conference of 1934, laid down that

[1] Cf. *Practical Socialism for Britain*, by Hugh Dalton, ch. xviii, 'Terms of Transfer'.

[2] See ch. xxxii.

[3] Though these must not, of course, carry any rights of control; the other conditions of socialization are discussed in ch. xxxii.

property holders should be compensated on the basis of the 'reasonable net maintainable revenue of the undertaking concerned'. Mr. Herbert Morrison (*Socialization and Transport*, chapter xiv) analyses and defends the criterion of 'reasonable net maintainable revenue', which means in effect compensation at market values. The New Zealand[1] and Swedish labour parties, which have been most active in the execution of actual nationalization projects in the last few years, have also accepted the principle of full compensation based on market values. So has the French Popular Front Government in nationalizing the armament industry.

If confiscation is thus to be avoided, however, and if fixed-interest Government stock or annuities are to be given in exchange for industrial securities or land, how can any progress be made in abolishing unearned and inherited incomes? There remains in effect only one method, taxation, or (what amounts to the same thing) modification of the inheritance laws. For taxation is little more than confiscation so adjusted as to cause the minimum of inequity and the minimum of economic dislocation. Taxation is impartial as between persons: it falls on everyone according to their circumstances; it can be very carefully adjusted to ability to pay; it can be weighted against those incomes which have the least economic and moral justification; and it can take account of social and economic consequences. Taxation, in fact, is just as effective as violence or outright confiscation, and at the same time lacks all their disadvantages.

It has already been argued that the three chief aims of redistribution should be to reduce the highest earned incomes, to reduce by a much larger percentage all but the lowest unearned incomes, and to approach as near as possible to the abolition of inheritance. To achieve these aims by taxation is in fact to carry further the tentative reforms which have already been begun in the most progressive democratic countries. Such a policy means much higher direct taxation, particularly on unearned incomes, and very much higher death duties: and it consequently involves no violent or catastrophic innovation. It is often supposed, even by socialists, however, that redistributive taxation has proceeded as far, or almost as far, as is economically practicable in Great

[1] Cf. Mr. Walter Nash, 'Labour Rule in New Zealand', *New Fabian Quarterly*, December 1936.

Britain and other democratic countries. In the following chapters strong reasons are given for believing that this is a serious mistake, and that it is possible over a period of time to carry direct, and in particular inheritance, taxation very much farther than it has been carried yet.

CHAPTER XXIII

THE EFFECTS OF REDISTRIBUTIVE TAXATION

There are several general facts which should be borne in mind before the effects of redistributive taxation are examined in detail. In the first place one should remember that throughout the history of capitalism the damaging effects of taxation on work, savings, and enterprise have been continually exaggerated. The Minority Report of the Colwyn Committee recalled the following statements from pre-war parliamentary debates:[1]

In 1907 any income-tax 'as high as one shilling "reacted" directly upon the amount of employment for the people of this country' (Mr. Austen Chamberlain, *Hansard*, 22/4/07, 1440). The tax was also described as 'a very dangerous departure', only to be defended as an 'emergency tax' (Mr. Evelyn Cecil, *Hansard*, 22/4/07, 1479). In 1909 Mr. William Joynson-Hicks (later Lord Brentford) said that an income-tax of one shilling 'abolishes the reserve fund of the country' and 'affects both profits and wages' (*Hansard*, 17/5/09, 192). It was also said in the same year that to increase estate duty to a maximum charge of 15 per cent on unsettled estates would 'lead to a very considerable depletion of capital' which could only be accompanied by scarcity of employment growing greater from one year to the next' (Mr. J. F. Mason, *Hansard*, 20/5/09, 586).

The fact that conservative opinion exaggerated the deleterious effects of an income-tax of one shilling in the pound in 1907 and 1909 does not of course in itself prove that the same opinion exaggerates the effects of a tax of five shillings to-day. But it does show that we must be very sceptical of any argument simply based on the idea that the tax seems so high that it must be too high.

Much more important is the urgent necessity to think out the

[1] Colwyn Committee Report (p. 375). The Minority Report was signed by J. W. Bowen, H. B. Lees-Smith, and Barbara Wootton.

whole problem of the economic effects of taxation in terms of our knowledge of the phenomena of money and the trade cycle. The increased understanding of monetary phenomena in the last few years, and the experience of depression and recovery between 1929 and 1937, have set the whole problem of the influence of taxation on work, enterprise, and savings in an entirely new light.[1] In the brief discussion of money and the trade cycle contained in this book it has become apparent that the monetary forces determining the trade cycle are necessarily among the most powerful determinants of the volume of saving and the activity of enterprise. In particular it has been shown that the activity of enterprise over a whole economy varies mainly with variations between Total Effective Demand and Total Costs, since those determine the level of profits, and that the total of savings varies with the total of incomes. More important still, it appeared that at most stages of the trade cycle a reduction rather than a stimulation of savings was desirable. To illustrate further the new light thrown on the theoretical aspects of the problem by our increased understanding of the trade cycle one cannot do better than quote the following passage from the concluding portion of Mr. Keynes's *General Theory of Employment, Interest, and Money* (pp. 372–4), remembering that Mr. Keynes's book is not designed to examine the case for socialism at all but merely to study the phenomena of cyclical unemployment.

'Since the end of the nineteenth century', Mr. Keynes says, 'significant progress towards the removal of very great disparities of wealth and income has been achieved through the instrument of direct taxation—income-tax and sur-tax and death duties—especially in Great Britain. Many people would wish to see this process carried much further, but they are deterred by two considerations; partly by the fear of making skilful evasions too much worth while and also of diminishing unduly the motive towards risk-taking, but mainly I think, by the belief that the growth of capital depends on the strength of the motive towards individual saving, and that for a large proportion of

[1] It is interesting that the generally admirable and lucid section on the effect of taxation on saving and enterprise in the Majority Report of the Colwyn Committee (published 1927) almost entirely ignores the influence of cyclical and monetary factors; though it occasionally points out that 'trade depression' is more important than high taxation in causing unemployment.

this growth we are dependent on the savings of the rich out of their superfluity. Our argument does not affect the first of these considerations. But it may considerably modify our attitude towards the second. For we have seen that up to the point where full employment prevails the growth of capital depends not at all on a low propensity to consume, but is, on the contrary, held back by it; and only in conditions of full employment is a low propensity to consume conducive to the growth of capital. Moreover, experience suggests that in existing conditions saving by institutions and through sinking funds is more than adequate, and that measures for the redistribution of incomes in a way likely to raise the propensity to consume may prove positively favourable to the growth of capital.

'The existing confusion in the public mind on the matter is well illustrated by the very common belief that the death duties are responsible for a reduction in the capital wealth of the country. Assuming that the State applies the proceeds of these duties to its ordinary outgoings so that taxes on incomes and consumption are correspondingly reduced or avoided, it is of course true that a fiscal policy of heavy death duties has the effect of increasing the communities' propensity to consume. But in as much as an increase in the habitual propensity to consume will in general, i.e. except in conditions of full employment, serve to increase at the same time the inducement to invest, the inference thus drawn is the exact opposite of the truth.

'Thus our argument leads towards the conclusion that in contemporary conditions the growth of wealth, so far from being dependent on the abstinence of the rich, as is commonly supposed, is more likely to be impeded by it. But one of the chief social justifications of great inequality of wealth is therefore removed. I am not saying that there are no other reasons, unaffected by our theory, capable of justifying some measure of inequality in some circumstances. But it does dispose of the most important of the reasons why hitherto we have thought it prudent to move carefully. This particularly affects our attitude towards death duties; for there are certain justifications for inequalities of incomes which do not apply equally to inequality of inheritances.'

It will be seen therefore that the pure study of money and the trade cycle has led Mr. Keynes, independently of any social arguments for redistribution, to advocate taxation calculated to diminish savings.

There is also overwhelming evidence from the experience of the last four years which suggests that cyclical forces are far stronger influences than taxation in determining the extent of saving and enterprise. The Swedish Social-Democratic Government, which came to power in the depression year 1932, simultaneously introduced a monetary policy calculated to promote recovery, and an increase in direct taxation.[1] In particular there was a large increase in the death duties.[2] In the sequel the stimulating effect of the Swedish Government's monetary policy and of favourable cyclical factors far outweighed any depressing effects of increased taxation; production, incomes, and profits increased steadily; and the Government, while stimulating recovery and abolishing unemployment, was able to increase expenditure on social services out of the rising taxation revenues. Similarly, the New Zealand Labour Government, which came to power in the winter of 1935-6 in the full tide of cyclical recovery, was able to impose large increases in taxation on unearned income and inheritance (and incidentally to nationalize the Central Bank and reduce working hours as well) without arresting the progress of cyclical forces.[3] More significant still was the experience of Great Britain itself in the Great Depression, which, by a curious confused piece of thinking, has been thought to prove exactly the opposite of what it does prove. Even some socialists have been deluded into thinking that the crisis of 1931 was due to high taxation, and presumably that the recovery from 1932 onwards was due to reductions in taxation. They forget that far the heaviest taxation of recent times was imposed in Lord Snowden's Economy Budget of August and September 1931 and that this high level of taxation was maintained throughout the years 1932 and 1933, in which recovery began. The fact was that the increases in taxation of the autumn of 1931 almost exactly coincided with the departure from the gold standard, and that the cyclical recovery resulting

[1] For the details of Sweden's record cf. Brinley Thomas, *Monetary Policy and Crises: A Study of Sweden's Experience*, ch. vi.

[2] Ibid., p. 208. The increased yield of death duties was used to provide for the amortization of the public works loan.

[3] Cf. *The Economist*, 9 May and 4 July, 1936. Also Mr. Walter Nash, 'Labour Rule in New Zealand', *New Fabian Quarterly*, December 1936.

from that change in monetary policy once more far outweighed the effects of the sharp increases in taxation. Just as cyclical forces, supervening on the overvaluation of the pound, had caused the depression and crises of 1929–31, so cyclical forces resulting from a change in monetary policy mainly determined the recovery; and changes in taxation made no perceptible difference one way or the other.

One further example of an opposite kind may be taken to illustrate the same point: an example of reductions in taxation made during a depression which entirely failed to exert any stimulating effect. In March 1934 the French Government of M. Doumergue made substantial reductions in taxation on profits and unearned incomes on the ground that they would 'stimulate enterprise' and promote recovery. In fact deflation and depression continued uninterruptedly for fifteen months until Government spending on armaments, financed by loans, at last initiated recovery in the autumn of 1935. Here again, therefore, a change in taxation entirely failed to outbalance the influence of cyclical forces in stimulating or depressing enterprise. Practical experience thus confirms the conclusion of recent theoretical research that the volume of saving and enterprise is far more dependent on cyclical and monetary factors than on the level of direct taxation.[1] The detailed problem of redistributive taxation should accordingly be examined in the light of the general presumptions, first, that monetary policy will be the dominant influence on savings and enterprise, and, secondly, that an increase of consumption at the expense of savings is desirable if cyclical unemployment is to be permanently cured.

[1] The Colwyn Committee Minority Report contains a table showing that there was no discernible correlation in pre-war times between the level of taxation and the level of unemployment (Colwyn Report, p. 377).

CHAPTER XXIV

TAXATION AND EARNED INCOMES

The foregoing argument suggests that no very great increase in the tax on earned incomes, except the highest, is desirable beyond the point already reached, at any rate in Great Britain; for the discrimination against unearned incomes ought to be greatly increased, and there is naturally an upper limit to the tax possible even on unearned incomes. What then are likely to be the effects of a moderate increase in the tax on higher earned incomes? In considering the effects, it is necessary to decide what will be the incidence of the tax, i.e. who will ultimately pay it. For it may be that the person who apparently pays it actually passes it on to someone else. We may assume that the definition of earned income for this purpose is that employed by the British revenue authorities, or equivalent to it: for this definition, as has been pointed out, corresponds very closely to the real economic distinction. Earned income is officially defined by the British authorities as income 'immediately derived by an individual from the carrying on or exercise by him of his trade, profession, vocation, or employment'. It thus includes all wages, salaries, and also the 'profits' of professional men and private business men. In the case of a private company, dividends would be 'unearned' and directors' fees and managers' salaries 'earned'. In the case of public companies also, dividends are naturally unearned, and directors' fees and managers' salaries earned. There is little dispute about the incidence of an income-tax on wages, salaries, and the 'profits' of professional men, e.g. doctors' and lawyers' fees. This may safely be assumed to be paid to all intents and purposes ultimately as well as immediately by the person taxed. It is much more disputable whether the private business man (who is represented by a large class of small traders, farmers, shopkeepers, etc.) may not be able to pass on some part of the tax by raising the price of his product. This question can most conveniently be discussed, however, when we come to consider taxation on enterprise. For the moment it will be assumed that normally the great proportion of the incidence of a tax on earned income falls on the nominal payer.

What will be the effects of an increase of the tax on earned incomes? The effects on work, enterprise, and savings may be considered separately. It is usually said that the effect of a change in income-tax on the quantity of work done depends on the 'elasticity of a man's demand for income in terms of work'. This, however, simply means the extent to which he will work more or less in response to a change, due to altered tax rates, in the income he can earn by a given amount of work; and the question is how great the extent is in the case of the different classes of tax-payers. In the case of the great bulk of workers earning a fixed wage or salary, and of professional men earning a not very greatly varying total of fees, it would appear that an increase within reasonable limits, of the rate of tax will have no very great effect on the total output of work. For two contradictory tendencies will be operating. On the one hand some people may tend to work less on the ground that they can now earn less by a given volume of work. On the other hand others may tend to work more because they wish to maintain a given money income on which their standard of living is based.[1] It is probable that among the professional classes the latter will be the prevailing response: it is very unlikely that a professional man would allow the standard of living of himself and his family to be lowered rather than take such steps as are in his power to increase his income. In the case of the great majority of wages, salaries, and professional incomes, however, the 'elasticity of the demand for income' of any but the very long period is likely to be zero, i.e. the tax-payer will neither work more nor less, in response to a change because it is not in his power to do so. For he simply goes to his office and earns his fixed salary: and if the income-tax is increased, it is in the vast majority of cases not open to him to do anything but pay the increase and curtail his expenditure.

[1] The reduction of income by taxation automatically increases the importance to the now poorer tax-payer of earning another £1. Cf. A. C. Pigou, *Economics of Welfare*, second edition, p. 667.

There is a further psychological point, not always appreciated, that seems to confirm the conclusion that modest changes in the tax on earned income are likely to have little effect on the volume of work. It is usually assumed in theoretical discussions that the tax-payer conceives of the tax as a reduction of his income. In the case of government employees it must of course appear so, and very large tax-payers probably so regard it. But a great many small and medium tax-payers almost certainly regard their periodical income-tax payment as an expense, like paying the rent or the doctor's bill. It is consequently all the more unlikely that they will respond to an increase in income-tax by working less. Those who can earn more by additional effort will tend to do so: while those who cannot will just pay the tax. It might of course be argued that a rise in tax will make people less willing to work harder for a rise in salary. But here again two countervailing tendencies will be at work; and the Majority Report of the Colwyn Committee seems justified in concluding that 'on balance we doubt whether there can be any adverse effect on (the tax-payer's) work and enterprise'.[1]

If the tax on earned income were raised indefinitely, there would doubtless come a point at which the willingness to work would fall off. This point, however, might not come nearly as soon as is often supposed. For it must be remembered that though in the new situation created by the rise in the tax a man cannot earn as much for a given amount of work as he could before, nevertheless, he still can always earn more by working[2] more (in so far as it is in his power to increase his earnings at all). For the tax will of course still be so graded that more *absolutely* remains, after taxation, from a higher income than from a lower. Similarly it must be remembered that the amount of income for which a man is willing to work varies from generation to generation. It is very largely a conventional figure based on the existing scales of remuneration. If a man is getting at least *more* than those doing less skilled or arduous work, and if he is getting at least as much as those whom he considers to be doing equally skilled or arduous work, he will not within limits worry very much how much he is getting. A man's demand for income depends, that is to say, partly on the income other people are receiving. A

[1] Cf. Colwyn Report, p. 129.
[2] Cf. A. C. Pigou, *The Economics of Welfare*, second edition, p. 609.

highly responsible business manager now earning £20,000 a year would probably be as willing to work for £10,000 if he knew that no other entrepreneur were earning more than £10,000; though he almost certainly would not be willing to work so efficiently if his income (and everyone else's) were reduced to the level of the unskilled labourer.[1] It seems, therefore, that if the principle of differential earned-income taxation is preserved, and if a tax is imposed on earned incomes so that all of a given level suffer alike, the willingness to work of those with the higher incomes is not likely to slacken.[2,3] On balance, therefore, since such a tax will almost certainly stimulate effort among the classes earning the lower salaries, the net effect will probably be an increase of the output of work until a very high level of taxation has been reached.

Secondly, what would be the effect on *enterprise* of an increase in the rate of tax on earned income? An earned income-tax like the British falls not only on business managers' salaries and directors' fees, but also on the 'profits' of private traders, private companies, and so forth. These incomes and profits, though properly classed as earned, are the reward of risk-bearing and managerial work undertaken by the business men and traders concerned. Economically speaking, therefore, the earned-income tax is partly a tax on enterprise. But in the case of the salaried manager or director, who in effect bears no risk, the influence of changes in the tax is likely to be the same as it is on the work of the salaried classes; for the distinction is, in practice, a very unsubstantial one. No great fear need, therefore, be entertained of a strike by salaried entrepreneurs in res-

---

[1] This is in accord with the experience of Soviet Russia. The attempt to pay completely equal wages did not succeed. But the extra payments made to skilled managers, etc., did not have to be on anything like the scale of the highest earned incomes in capitalist countries.

[2] Cf. the Majority Report, i.e. the conservative section, of the Colwyn Committee, p. 130: 'Over the whole field of income we consider that the income-tax borne by employees and professional men has had no important effect on their work and enterprise.'

[3] There may of course be a tendency for highly paid persons to migrate to other countries, under the influence of heavy income taxation. This is not a very pressing danger in most cases, because the powers of habit and association, not to mention immigration laws, language, etc., are so strong. In any case, it is not relevant to the argument of this book, which is concerned with the world as a closed system and not with individual countries. In practice it would have to be met as particular circumstances determined.

ponse to moderate increases in the tax on earned incomes.

What is likely to be the effect in the case of one-man businesses, partnerships, and private companies in which the bulk of profits is received in the form of personal remuneration (whether salaries, fees, or dividends), and the earned-income tax is consequently also a genuine tax on enterprise?[1]

Since the profits of the small trader and partnership are in the commercial sense 'profits'—i.e. calculated as a surplus of revenue over costs—it becomes necessary to ask at this point whether an income-tax on profits can be passed on by an entrepreneur to his customers. If an income-tax is imposed on profits, can the business man raise the price of the commodity as he would if a turnover or excise tax had been imposed? The Colwyn Committee Majority Report decided that he could not;[2] but they rested their case on a theoretical argument which does not seem to be tenable. Since, the Report argues, income-tax is a tax on profits, and since profits are the 'surplus' remaining over after 'costs' have been paid, and since prices are determined by the level of costs in the 'marginal case', income-tax cannot 'enter into' prices. Prices, that is to say, are determined by costs; profits are a surplus remaining over; and income-tax simply chops a piece out of profits. Therefore income-tax cannot affect costs and prices: and the profit-earner simply has to pay the tax himself.

This argument, it will be noted, rests on the assumption that the traditional popular distinction between costs and profits is a true economic one. It implies that profits, i.e. entrepreneurs' remuneration, are not a payment for any service and therefore a true cost in the sense of a payment without which the commodity would not have been produced. It regards them simply as a surplus. This view, which is no longer held by economists, was rejected in chapter vi; and it was there argued that profits are in the real economic sense as truly costs as wages or interest. A tax on the entrepreneurs' profit is not, therefore, in principle

[1] The Colwyn Report (p. 154) defines the term 'private business' as covering the 'individual trading on his own account, the partnership and the joint stock company'. 'The last named', the Committee add, 'is virtually a partnership with limited liability, the great bulk of the profits going whether in the form of salary or dividend to the few persons who, in effect, own and control the business.'

[2] Colwyn Report, pp. 108–19.

different from a tax on wages: and we cannot on theoretical grounds deny the possibility of entrepreneurs passing the tax on to the consumers.[1] Here in fact it must be freely admitted that the argument is less favourable to the socialist case than the conservative members of the Colwyn Committee themselves believed. Indeed, the acceptance by the Colwyn Report of the view that income-tax *cannot* enter into prices seems to be a remarkable example of the governing classes accepting a view contrary to their own interests as a result of a traditional intellectual mistake.[2]

If the Colwyn Committee's argument is rejected and the theoretical possibility of income-tax being 'passed on' is accepted, need we suppose that this often happens in practice? On the whole it would seem that it can only happen to a very limited extent either in the short or the long run. For the success of the entrepreneurs' effort to pass on the tax will depend partly on the elasticity of the demand for his product, i.e. the extent to which consumers respond adversely to a rise in price; and partly on what might be called his own 'elasticity of supply of enterprise', i.e. the extent to which in the long run he is willing to pay the tax and go on being as enterprising as before. The response of consumers to a rise in prices is likely in most cases to be considerable. If, of course, enterprise was both equally taxed and entered equally into the cost of production in the case of all commodities, there might be a tendency for all prices to rise and the consumer, though naturally redistributing his expenditure to some extent, would be compelled to pay higher prices in many instances. In fact, however, enterprise will be a much more important element in costs in some cases than others: and it may be that in some cases, where it is important, no income-tax is paid. In small one-man businesses for instance, profits will be often too small to pay income-tax. The competition of these businesses, and of those in which enterprise is so small a factor in costs as to have no appreciable effect on prices,[3] —and incidentally of foreign imports, if the assumption of a closed system may for the moment be dropped—will prevent

[1] As Mr. D. H. Robertson pointed out in reviewing the Colwyn Committee's Report in the *Economic Journal*.
[2] Marxists should perhaps note it as the exception that proves the rule.
[3] Though here, it must be admitted, income-tax will be easily passed on.

prices being raised by other firms. Income-tax may thus discriminate to some extent against large firms, and against industries in which enterprise is a large element in costs; but it is unlikely that more than a small part of it will be added to prices over the whole system. If the attempt is made to do so, consumers will tend to buy from those firms and industries which are little if at all affected by the tax. Moreover, it is reasonably certain that monopolies will not pass on the tax. For 'monopoly revenue' is in the true sense a surplus and not a cost. A monopoly may be assumed to have fixed its prices at the point at which its monopoly revenue is greatest: and a tax on its revenue will not alter that point. In general, therefore, we may accept the conclusion, if not the arguments, of the Colwyn Committee, and presume that the great bulk though not perhaps 100 per cent, of income-tax is in fact paid by the entrepreneur himself. This conclusion accords with the general belief of the business world and in particular with the evidence of business men before the Colwyn Committee, most of whom stated that the average trader was 'disposed or inclined' to add the income-tax on to prices, though they doubted if he succeeded in doing so. Moreover, for the purpose both of achieving redistribution by taxation and of estimating the effects of taxation, it is not necessary that 100 per cent of income-tax should be borne by the taxpayer: it is only necessary that the great bulk of it should be. And of this there is no reasonable doubt.

If then the incidence of the income-tax in the case of the entrepreneur may be assumed to be mainly on the nominal taxpayer, what may we assume the effects to be of an increase in the rate of earned-income tax on the small or private entrepreneur? On the one hand it may be supposed that if a man hopes to make a profit of £50,000 from a certain venture he will not be deterred by a raising of the tax payable from £5,000 to £10,000. For he will still prefer making £40,000 to making nothing. It may be replied to this, however, that the degree of risk or effort an entrepreneur is prepared to incur depends on the scale of reward: and that he will not take the same risk for £40,000 that he might have taken for £45,000. Indeed, the ratio of the size of the reward to the degree of risk is the essence of the risk-bearing function.[1] Undoubtedly there is much sub-

[1] Cf. Colwyn Report, pp. 158–62.

stance in this argument. The risk-bearing entrepreneur is in a different position from the salary-earner who must go on with his work if he is to live; for the entrepreneur can in most cases abandon his more speculative plans and carry on his businesses —or one of them—comparatively safely on more conservative lines. He has many alternatives before him, whereas the salary-earner normally has not. It cannot be denied, therefore, that a rapid and heavy increase in the earned-income tax would, other things being equal, tend to modify the willingness to take risks of the smaller entrepreneur.

This conclusion must, however, be qualified in various ways. In the first place it should be observed that the British earned-income tax is hardly at all a tax on enterprise in the case of the large public joint-stock companies. For in this case the earned-income rate[1] is paid by the salaried managers and directors, who perform little or no risk-bearing functions (except in so far as they are also shareholders); while the ordinary and preference share-holders, who bear the whole of the risk, pay the 'unearned' tax rate. It is clear therefore, that a widening of discrimination in tax rates against unearned incomes will discriminate in favour of the enterprise of small, i.e. personal and private, rather than large businesses.

For the 'enterprise' of the small entrepreneurs will normally be taxed at the low 'earned' rate and the enterprise' of the public company at the high 'unearned' rate. If then, as is here proposed, the increase in the earned rate is slight and the increase in the unearned rate very considerable, the deterrent effect of the increase in the earned rate on the small entrepreneur should not be very great.

Secondly, though a fall in the reward of enterprise may in the first instance make the entrepreneur less willing to take risks, here again entrepreneurs as a class may over a period of time revise their estimates of what is the proper reward for a given degree of risk.[2] The speculative instinct of man may be such that

---

[1] No actual 'earned-income rate' as such is now in existence in Great Britain. But the various exemptions for the lower earned incomes work out as such.

[2] Cf. Colwyn Committee Majority Report, p. 162: 'The post-war rates of tax may appear formidable, but the fact that they can be and are borne is in itself sufficient proof that the effect of income taxation has been exaggerated in the past.'

the risk-taking entrepreneur will always embark on those ventures which offer the greatest reward in the circumstances, whatever the absolute amount of the reward may be. Even if a venture which would have meant a personal profit of £200,000 now means a personal profit of only £100,000, nevertheless, if that is the highest stake available, it may be that the speculator will risk it. It is unlikely, however, that the entrepreneur will readjust his ideas to changes in taxation nearly to the same extent that the salary-earner will; for, as has been pointed out, the undertaking of the more speculative risks is normally not the individual entrepreneur's only means of livelihood.

Thirdly, and most important, the rate of tax on earned income is only one of the lesser among many important influences upon enterprise, even in the case of the small entrepreneur. The predominant influence upon enterprise of all kinds, as has been pointed out, is general monetary policy. The question whether a business is going to make a profit of £100,000 or a loss of £100,000 is likely to be more effective in determining the business man's action than the question whether 15 per cent or 20 per cent is taken from him in taxation. If business as a whole is made profitable by a sound monetary policy, then a very high rate of tax on earned profits will be paid gladly by entrepreneurs; as the Swedish and New Zealand governments found in the conditions already described. If, on the other hand, business is made unprofitable by an unsound monetary policy, a very low rate of taxation on profits will not stimulate it; as the Doumergue and Laval governments in France discovered in the course of 1934–5. Monetary policy, in fact, will always remain a far more important determinant of the level of enterprise than taxes on income.

An increase in the tax on earned income, therefore, would have some slight deterrent effect on enterprise in the case of small entrepreneurs. But if it was accompanied by an increased discrimination against unearned incomes, and by a successful monetary policy, the deterrent effect would be normally insignificant.[1]

[1] Cf. the Colwyn Committee Majority Report, p. 169, discussing the effect of taxation on enterprise as a whole: 'We conclude with regard to enterprise, that the effects of high income taxation have been almost negligible in the field of employments and the professions: over a great part of the industrial field, while appreciable, they have not been of serious moment,

Thirdly what will be the effect on *saving* of an increase in the earned-income tax? The effect of income taxation on saving is, as the Colwyn Committee points out, of two kinds; physical and psychological. Physically taxation affects a man's capacity to save, and psychologically it affects his disposition to save.[1] The tax on earned income will affect the capacity to save in so far as it reduces the income which men have available after taxation. On the other hand it may affect the disposition to save in so far as a man is determined to save a certain fixed sum in any case and the reduction of his income consequently forces him to save a larger proportion of it and spend less. The desire to build up a certain fixed unearned income for old age may make the second effect very important among the less highly paid professional and salaried classes. On the other hand a steeply graded tax on earned incomes, as is here proposed, will certainly diminish the capacity of some of the earners of the larger earned incomes; a high proportion of saving out of earned income must be made by them. And since it is difficult to see why an increase in earned-income tax should induce even small salary-earners to save absolutely more than before, it therefore appears that on balance (other things being equal) such an increase will lead to some fall in net saving. The fall resulting from this cause, however, will not be large; for the bulk of savings comes out of unearned incomes, particularly company profits, and the taxes on unearned incomes and on inheritance are much more important influences than the earned-income tax on the rate of saving.

In general, therefore (agreeing with the Colwyn Committee Majority and Minority Report) we may accept the conclusion that the income-tax on earned incomes at the level customary in Great Britain has had practically no deterrent effect on work, and very little on saving and enterprise. We may also conclude that further increases within reasonable limits would not have great deterrent effects either. Much, however, depends on the meaning of the phrase 'reasonable limits'; for clearly a tax of

[1] Cf. Colwyn Report, p. 119. The Committee make the same distinction for enterprise. But this seems hardly accurate. A man's physical capacity for enterprise is only affected by the tax as the money available for speculative ventures is reduced. But such money is in fact savings.

but it is clear that they must have often put a check on the more speculative kind of business. This holds good particularly of private business.'

100 per cent or even 90 per cent on work and enterprise would have calamitous effects. There comes a point, admittedly, after which the increases cannot be continued. It is the contention of this book that that point has not been nearly reached in any of the great industrial countries, even in our time, and that if profitable conditions in industry were more or less permanently safeguarded by a sound monetary and general economic policy, the limit could be pushed even higher. Remembering that only a slight increase on any but the *highest* earned incomes is here proposed, we may for illustration examine the present scales of British income taxation. The effective rates of income-tax and sur-tax combined on a married couple with three children, were as follows in the financial year 1936–7:

Total Actual Income	Earned Income			Unearned Income		
£	£	s.	d.	£	s.	d.
300		nil			nil	
400		nil		3	3	4
500	3	3	4	11	17	6
1,000	83	2	6	130	12	6
2,000	296	17	6	368	2	6
5,000	1,346	5	0	1,417	10	0
10,000	3,716	5	0	3,787	10	0
50,000	27,654	0	0	27,725	0	0

The unearned scale may for the moment be ignored. In the earned scale the tax looks at first sight enormous: and doubtless if this table had been placed before a pre-war property owner, big entrepreneur, or conservative statesman, he would forthwith have declared in all good faith that such a scale of taxation would shatter the capitalist system to its foundations and spread bankruptcy and ruin throughout the world. Yet in fact in 1936–7 in Great Britain these rates were being paid, and the capitalist system was flourishing vigorously under the influence of favourable cyclical conditions and an expansionist monetary policy. There is nothing very revolutionary, therefore, in suggesting that the rates should be further increased. Moreover, it follows from the argument of this book that the tax on earned incomes should only be very high in the case of the largest incomes, and that the discrimination against unearned incomes should be sharply increased. Simply as an illustration of the kind of new scale here contemplated, the following changes in the British 'earned' scale may be suggested as a rough objective for a socialist government in normal conditions:

Tax on Earned Income

(Income-tax and Sur-tax combined on married couple with three children)

Total Actual Incomes	1936–7 Rate			Suggested New Rate		
£ 300	£	s. nil	d.	£	s. nil	d.
400	nil			nil		
500	3	3	4	2	0	0[1]
1,000	83	2	6	90	0	0
2,000	296	17	6	320	0	0
5,000	1,346	5	0	1,500	0	0
10,000	3,716	5	0	4,500	0	0
50,000	27,654	0	0	35,000	0	0

Such a scale represents practically no change in the tax on earned incomes of under £5,000 a year; and it still leaves a man earning £50,000 a year with an available income of £15,000. Naturally, the economic effects of any given scale must depend on the history and economic circumstances of any given country. But in the light of the preceding discussion it does not appear likely that the gradual introduction of the above scale in Great Britain in a time of expanding trade would have any effect on the volume of work done, or any substantial effect on the activities of saving and enterprise.

1 This reduction is in conformity with the suggestion that a socialist government should actually reduce the tax on low earned incomes in order to emphasize the point that the whole scheme is designed to reward workers of every kind (see p. 273, note). It is assumed that the change is brought about by an alteration of the graduation rather than of the standard rate. This would be mainly effected by raising, and re-grading, sur-tax.

CHAPTER XXV

TAXATION AND UNEARNED INCOMES

It might appear at first sight that increases in the rate of tax on unearned income would not affect the volume of work done. This, however, is not so. For a drastic increase in the tax on unearned income, accompanied by an only mild increase in the tax on earned income, would intensify the discrimination against unearned incomes, and so greatly strengthen the incentive to work. It may be that there are now few able-bodied men living wholly on unearned income in most democratic countries (though there are certainly a good many women). But unquestionably an appreciable number of men in the propertied classes depend preponderantly on unearned income, and only work part time, or part of their lives, as a result. The idle rich are not by any means a myth, and the 'gentleman' is still to be met both in town and country. In any case, since a sharper discrimination against unearned incomes could not possibly make anyone less ready to work, there is bound to be some positive, if small, increase in the total output of work as a result of it.[1]

The effect on *enterprise* of a great increase in the tax on unearned incomes is a much more important question. It must be considered from two points of view: that of the business man considering whether to undertake a risky venture, and that of the saver considering whether to buy gilt-edged or more speculative securities. In the main, two classes of business men will be affected, the managers of private companies who receive the bulk of their income in the form of dividends, and the managers

---

[1] It is of course a fallacy to suppose that the driving of rentiers to accept jobs would increase unemployment. An increase in the number of persons seeking work only increases unemployment if the demand for labour, i.e. the money available to be spent on all wages and salaries, is not increased. But in this case it will be increased by the Government's expenditure of what it takes away from the rentier. The State, in fact, will pay the rentier to do something useful instead of nothing, or almost nothing.

264

of public companies. The dividends of both sorts of companies will pay income-tax at the 'unearned rate'. But in a system of direct taxation like the British, in which income-tax on dividends is paid at source, but the gradation of income-tax and super-tax is adjusted to the size of personal incomes, the rate of tax does not increase with the size of the profit made by the company. From the point of view of the managers of the company the same *rate* of tax has to be paid on a profit of £500,000 as on one of £5,000.

In these circumstances what effect will an increase in the tax have on the managers of a private company, who draw most of their remuneration in the form of dividends, when they are considering whether to take a decision involving the possibility of a profit smaller than previously but at the same risk of loss? The increased tax will fall on their own dividends and it will vary in amount according to the size of their incomes, but for unearned incomes of a given size it will not vary according to the proportion of it which is derived from their own business. If a large proportion of their unearned income is derived from other sources, it might be argued that they would be more willing to take risks in their own businesses in order to make a larger profit in order to compensate for the loss on other unearned receipts. But if a large proportion of total income comes from their own businesses, it would seem that an increase in the tax would probably make them more cautious, since they would in any case be more exposed to the danger of losing a large proportion of their income. In either case the response of the entrepreneurs would probably vary largely from one man to another; and the Colwyn Committee[1] seems wise in refraining from concluding very definitely what the net effect would be. There is, perhaps, a presumption that in the case of private companies an increase in the tax would fairly soon lead to a falling off in the willingness of entrepreneurs to take any speculative risks. Here again, however, an entrepreneur's estimate of what is the proper reward for risk may very likely alter with time.

What, in turn, will be the behaviour of the manager of the public limited company? Their position is markedly different. An increase in the rate of tax on unearned incomes will only affect their incomes from the company in so far as they may hold

[1] Colwyn Report, pp. 168–9.

265

shares in it; and if they do hold its shares, the proportion of their total income coming from those shares is not likely to be a large one. The rise in the tax will not affect the declared profits of the company. It will on the one hand reduce the actual incomes of the shareholders according to their individual wealth or poverty, and it will reduce the total of undistributed profits available for reserves (for we are assuming that the standard rate of tax is raised). Now it is arguable that the chairman and directors of a public company are more interested in the size of their declared profit than in the actual incomes left to shareholders after payment of dividends. The success of the company, on which the reputation of the chairman and directors depends, is measured by the declared profit rather than by the amount actually available to shareholders after the payment of taxation. To some extent, therefore, the same money figures twice: first as a feather in the directors' cap and secondly as an item of revenue in the Treasury's hands. The amount of undistributed profits which are actually available for reserve will of course partly depend on the rate of tax. But though the directors may be influenced by the tax in deciding how much to put to reserve (and this must be considered under the head of saving), it is most unlikely that the prospect of an increased tax on undistributed profits will induce the directors to abandon a venture which they considered to have a certain chance of earning a certain extra revenue. Such a consideration would probably not be present in their minds at all. Compared with the general trade outlook, and the disposition of cyclical and monetary factors, its influence would be insignificant. There accordingly seems no need in the crucial case of public company policy to modify the Colwyn Committee's conclusion that the rate of tax is not a powerful influence on enterprise one way or the other. Undoubtedly monetary and cyclical factors are at any given moment overwhelmingly more important.

The investor is perhaps likely to be more affected. An increase in the unearned-income tax rate would diminish by a corresponding proportion the yield of a given sum invested in all securities, gilt-edged or speculative. It may be argued, therefore, that since the increase affects investment of every different degree of risk, it will not alter the *risk margin*, i.e. the excess of the yield of speculative over gilt-edged stock, and therefore will not affect the distribution of the investor's capital between the different sorts of stock. It might even be added that at least in the case of the high unearned incomes the unearned tax will make the capitalist seek higher yields and therefore a larger proportion of speculative shares.[1] It is assumed, here, however, that very high unearned incomes are to be virtually taxed out of existence: and this possibility must consequently be discounted. The recipient of a small unearned income, and the small saver, will probably be inclined on balance to play for greater safety if his income from saving is more heavily taxed. Even this, however, is not certain, and the Colwyn Committee seem justified in inferring that no sure conclusion can be drawn about the effect of high taxation on the willingness to take risk of either the small or the large investor in the mass. It would not be safe to assume, therefore, that there would be a substantial effect either way: though for safety's sake a slightly greater disinclination to bear risks should perhaps be foreseen.

Thirdly, what is the effect on *saving* of increases in the unearned-income tax rate?[2] Both the 'psychological' and the 'physical' effects have to be considered. The 'physical' effect, i.e. the actual absorption by taxation of sums that would otherwise have been saved, will certainly be appreciable if a steeply graduated tax is imposed on unearned incomes. The bulk of high incomes are unearned;[3] and a very considerable proportion of private saving certainly comes from the higher incomes. A heavy tax on high unearned incomes will certainly therefore diminish private saving, since it will leave the rich rentier with nothing left over after his conventional level of consumption has been provided for.

The physical effect of the tax on the savings made by institutions, i.e. companies, trade unions, building societies, and insurance companies, is likely to be much less. The sums available to companies in the form of undistributed profits which may be put to reserve will of course be reduced by the amount

[1] Cf. the Colwyn Report, p. 141.
[2] The total effect of the tax on national savings naturally depends on whether the Government saves or spends the money raised. Later it is argued that all money raised in death duties should be saved. Here we are simply concerned with the effect of the tax on private, i.e. personal and institutional, saving.
[3] Cf. Josiah Wedgwood, *The Economics of Inheritance*, p. 44.

of the tax on the companies' profits. But the tax will be paid at the standard rate, and will not be steeply graduated as in the case of the rich individual. In the case of the insurance company there should be little, if any, reduction in saving in the form of premiums, since these are paid by persons of all incomes and do not mainly depend on the maintenance of the incomes of the very rich. The resources available to the insurance companies for reinvestment will be reduced in so far as their own interest incomes on the one hand and their own undistributed profits on the other are subject to tax. But these again will only pay tax at the standard rate. The same will apply to the reinvestment of interest income by trade unions, building societies, and so forth.

In so far as the physical effects of a high unearned-income tax are concerned, it thus appears that there will be a considerable diminution of private saving but no great diminution of institutional saving. To reach a fair estimate of the net effect we must consequently inquire what proportion of the total national saving in a modern industrial country is done by private persons and institutions respectively. The Colwyn Report[1] adopted an estimate of the national saving which put the undistributed profits of companies alone at £194,000,000 out of a total new national saving of £500,000,000. It should be clearly understood that this figure represents new saving only, and therefore omits the saving that has been done out of income to cover depreciation and maintain existing capital intact.

Mr. Colin Clark[2] estimates that between 1932 and 1936 investment in fixed and working capital varied between £500,000,000 and £700,000,000. About £400,000,000 of this, however, was for depreciation and maintenance, leaving a provision for new or net investment which rose from £29,000,000 in 1932 to £305,000,000 in 1935. Since depreciation is covered by depreciation charges which are not subject to taxation, the only saving effected by taxation is that which has to cover new investment.

Mr. Clark shows that ever since 1924 institutional saving, i.e. undistributed profits of companies: working-class, and middle-class saving through the Post Office, building societies, insurance companies; and State and municipal saving, have

---

1 Colwyn Report, p. 17.
2 *National Income and Outlay*, pp. 180–92.

been *more than enough* to cover the total of new investment. For 1934, Mr. Clark estimates new investment at £274,000,000 and institutional saving at £461,000,000. In so far as these estimates are correct therefore, it follows that no private savings have been necessary at all to cover the investment that has been taking place in recent years. 'Large private incomes', Mr. Clark says, 'have ceased to count as a source of saving.'[1] To some extent of course taxation may affect 'institutional' savings, since a rich man may be dissuaded from incurring a life insurance policy if he has to pay more in taxes. But an increase in taxation on the *higher* income levels will leave practically unaffected the bulk of saving through building societies, savings banks, and undistributed company profits.

We may infer, therefore, that a tax whose main restrictive influence is on private saving will not produce any very great effect on the national total of saving. The physical effect of an increase in the tax may accordingly be taken as likely to be small.

The psychological effect will almost certainly be smaller. The private saver may be considered first. A tax on unearned incomes will reduce the rate of interest from the lender's point of view while leaving it the same from the borrower's point of view. If the lender is receiving £5 a year on his £100, and has to pay four shillings in the pound tax on it, his interest is reduced to £4 a year; but the lender still pays £5. In the first instance, therefore, there is no psychological effect on the borrower. What will be the effect on the lender? He may so desire to maintain his income at £5 that he will save and lend more in order to do so; and his attempt to do so may actually lower the rate of interest the borrower is willing to pay, in which case the lender will have to save even more to secure his £5. For instance, if the rate of interest (apart from the tax) remained at 5 per cent, the lender would have to secure another £25 in order to earn a nominal rate of interest of 6.25 per cent and so actual interest after paying tax of £4. His attempt to do so might push the rate of interest down; and he might have to add more than £25 to his original £100. It is thus clear that those savers who wish to secure a fixed unearned money income may be induced to increase their savings considerably by an increase in the tax.

[1] Mr. A. E. Feaveryear (*Economic Journal*, June 1936) confirms this.

TAXATION AND UNEARNED INCOMES

There will be others who will argue that it is not worth saving so much if the return is lowered. They will prefer to spend. If the return is lowered beyond a certain point it may not seem worth saving at all, and in the extreme case it may actually appear preferable to consume one's capital. If a man with an unearned income of £25,000 a year, a capital of £500,000, and an expectation of life of twenty years, were suddenly asked to pay £20,000 a year in taxation instead of say £10,000, he might well decide that it was worth his while to consume his capital at the rate of say £10,000 a year. Suppose he did this: then even if on the income of £15,000 a year that remained after twenty years he still paid a tax of £12,000, he would have an actual income of £3,000 compared with the £5,000 he would have had if he had not consumed his capital at all. And by consuming his capital he would have trebled his consumption during the interval. If, on the other hand, the steepening of the tax is not so great as to reach the figure of over ten shillings in the pound until it touches the highest incomes, and if the increase is gradual and not sudden, it is unlikely that an actual consumption of capital will result, though it is true that a tax as steep as that proposed on page 272 would disincline anyone with unearned incomes of £10,000 a year or over to save further out of their incomes. To some extent the individual capitalist's response will depend on what is likely to happen to his capital, and this in turn will depend on the death duties (to be discussed in the next chapter). But in general it seems that a gradual increase in the steepness of the tax will not induce actual consumption of capital on a very wide scale.

There will in fact be two tendencies offsetting one another: the increased savings of those anxious to build up or maintain a fixed income, and the decreased savings of those who think the return is no longer worth while. Which of these is likely to preponderate? We need not accept Mr. Keynes's extreme view that the rate of interest is independent of the volume of saving in order to endorse the conclusion of most economists that the volume of saving is, within limits, largely independent of the rate of interest. Recently, economists[1] have increasingly tended to accept the view that the volume of saving is very little influenced by the effective rate of interest offered. In the first place

[1] Cf. for instance J. H. Jones, *The Economics of Saving*.

a great deal of private saving is done in order to maintain a certain capital sum intact over a period of years as a reserve against marriage, illness, and other partially foreseeable circumstances. This would be quite unaffected by a tax on unearned income. Saving through insurance premiums would also be entirely unaffected, and the huge volume of savings owned by depositors in building societies, national savings certificates, etc., is largely owned by persons whose incomes are too small to be affected by a tax on high unearned incomes at all. Lastly, and perhaps most important, a very great many savers in the professional and middle classes are saving in order to build up a certain fixed unearned income for old age: and they will be impelled to increase their savings by a rise in the tax. On the whole, therefore, it seems that if the graduation of the tax is such as to be increased only moderately on medium-sized incomes and if the increase is not too sudden, the total *psychological* effect on private savers may not be on balance to reduce saving at all.

The general effect then of a sharp steepening of the tax on unearned income will be, in so far as the preceding argument is correct, some increase in the output of work, some slight slackening in the more speculative forms of enterprise, and some considerable slackening in private saving by the rich. Here again, however, much depends on circumstances on the one hand, and the precise extent of the increase in taxation on the other. The British system of direct taxation, which is in other respects sound, was greatly impaired by the abolition in 1921–2 of the separate scales of taxation for earned and unearned incomes. Since that date discrimination in favour of earned incomes has been given entirely by the exemption provisions, which are much more liberal in the case of earned incomes. The effect of this, however, as the table on page 262 shows, is that on incomes of £3,000 and over the earned tax is virtually as high as the unearned. This is a gross anomaly which seriously distorts our whole fiscal and social system. It could easily be remedied by preserving the present separate income-tax and sur-tax, as well as the standard rate of income-tax, and devising two entirely separate scales of taxation for earned and unearned incomes. Such a reform would have the necessary effect of reducing the large individual unearned incomes without penalizing actual productive units as such. There should be no hesitation in making the progressiveness of the unearned tax extremely steep, though much bigger proportionate exemption should be given for children and dependents than at present. The following table roughly illustrates the extent of change in the effective rate of income-tax and sur-tax on unearned incomes which a socialist government might take as the objective of, say, a five-year budget plan.

Tax on Unearned Income
(Income-tax and Sur-tax combined on income of married couple with three children)

Total Actual Income	1936–7 rate			Suggested New Rate		
£	£	s.	d.	£	s.	d.
300		nil		2	10	0
400	3	3	4	6	0	0
500	11	17	6	50	0	0
1,000	130	12	6	300	0	0
2,000	368	2	6	1,000	0	0
5,000	1,417	0	0	3,000	0	0
10,000	3,787	10	0	7,500	0	0
50,000	27,725	0	0	45,000	0	0

This represents an effective rate of 30 per cent on unearned incomes of £1,000, 50 per cent on £2,000, 60 per cent on £5,000, 75 per cent on £10,000, and 90 per cent on £50,000. To a man with an unearned income of £50,000 it leaves £5,000; to one with an income of £10,000 it leaves £2,500; and to one with an income of £2,000 it leaves £1,000. These remainders are, if anything, excessive; for the above rates are not intended as methods of raising revenue but as instruments for the abolition of unearned incomes in an equitable and peaceful manner.

Such a scale of tax on unearned incomes is likely to increase the disposition to work in the middle and lower range of incomes. It is unlikely to diminish enterprise appreciably; for it is assumed that the standard rate of tax will remain unaltered.[1] It will have some psychological effect on saving, since the disposition of the rich to save less will probably not be entirely offset by the disposition of the middle classes to save more. Clearly, a man with £10,000 a year unearned, paying a tax of £7,500 will not be very disposed to add to his capital if he would have to pay £45,000 out of an income of £50,000 a year. Such a scale will also have an indubitable physical effect in reducing saving. Those with incomes of £20,000 to £50,000 a year who previously saved £10,000 a year will almost certainly cease to do so. This physical effect is likely to be the only effect on the very rich. The late Sir John Ellerman, for instance, had a fortune of over £30,000,000 and an income of over £2,000,000 a year. It is probably impossible for a man to spend more than perhaps £200,000 a year at the outside. A very high tax will not therefore make him spend more or consume his capital; it will simply absorb into the Exchequer some part of what he otherwise might have saved.

If the above scale of tax is combined with that given on page 263, the following complete scale of direct taxation may be taken as a rough indication of the kind of scale toward which to work in present circumstances in Great Britain.

Tax on Earned and Unearned Income
(Income-tax and sur-tax combined on income of married couple with three children)

Total Actual Income	On Earned Income			On Unearned Income		
£	£	s.	d.	£	s.	d.
300		nil		2	10	0
400		nil		6	0	0
500	5	0	0	50	0	0
1,000	90	0	0	300	0	0
2,000	320	0	0	1,000	0	0
5,000	1,500	0	0	3,000	0	0
10,000	4,500	0	0	7,500	0	0
50,000	35,000	0	0	45,000	0	0

[1] For psychological reasons it might be best for a socialist government to

The result is a really sharp discrimination against unearned incomes.[1] The active business man, barrister, etc., earning £50,000 a year retains £15,000; but the rentier receiving an inherited £50,000 retains only £5,000. At the £10,000 level the earned remainder is £5,500 and the unearned £2,500. Such a discriminatory scale would be far more justifiable from every point of view than the present British system. And the effects of the gradual introduction of such a combined scale in a prosperous period might be expected to be some increase in the disposition to work, little change in the impulse of enterprise, and a moderate but not overwhelming fall in the total of private saving. Meanwhile, it would enormously increase the resources available for supplementing the incomes of all those workers and their families who lack the necessities of life.

[1] It will of course be argued that the discrimination would be avoided, that private companies would simply pay salaries instead of dividends, and that rich rentiers would form themselves into private companies. The whole question of evasion demands very cautious treatment. It is sometimes described by advocates of high taxation as a mere 'administrative problem'. This is too sweeping a reply: for administrative problems *may* be insoluble. On the other hand it is also too sweeping to argue, as do opponents of high taxation, that it obviously *is* insoluble. In fact the opinion of nobody but the Inland Revenue authorities is worth much on these points. The possibility of evasion must vary enormously according to circumstances. In the end the problem can only be solved by experiment, and experience has already shown that much higher taxation can be imposed than was once thought possible. The most sensible attitude to the evasion problem is to determine what kind of taxation is desirable, and then to discover in practice how far evasion can be combated. A great deal has already been done in Great Britain to prevent the particular forms of evasion here discussed, i.e. the fraudulent conversion of unearned income into earned income or capital appreciation by bonus shares, etc. It has been provided, for instance, that where a reasonable proportion of a company's income is not distributed in taxable form, sur-tax may be levied on the company's profits as such.

reduce the standard rate of income-tax. This would emphasize the point that the whole scheme was intended to reward work and penalize idleness, and it would discriminate in favour of company profits placed to reserve, as opposed to dividend payments. Company profits as such, it is assumed, would pay the standard rate. The 'earned' and 'unearned rates' would affect only individual incomes like the present exemptions and sur-tax rates.

CHAPTER XXVI

TAXATION AND INHERITANCE

Important as is the taxation of unearned income, taxation of inheritance must remain the crux of socialist policy, just as the case against inheritance is the core of the case for socialism.[1] For the tax on unearned income cannot distinguish much between the two types of income which are, as we have seen, fundamentally distinct: inherited income and interest on savings actually made by the recipient. Moreover, inheritance-taxation, as an instrument of socialist policy, must, to an even greater degree than the unearned tax, be conceived not as a method of raising revenue at all but as an instrument, and the most equitable and humane instrument, for the transfer of propertied incomes to social ownership.

1. *Forms of Tax*

There are, of course, all sorts of ways in which the transfer of private property to the State at death could be effected. A man's right to bequeath property, or in other words to control after his death the distribution of unearned income, is a man-made legal right which can be maintained, modified, or abolished in accordance with social policy. Moreover, the law of inheritance

[1] It is curious how inheritance-taxation has been neglected in recent socialist literature, even of the less dogmatic and less Marxist kind. Mrs. Wootton relegates the subject to a footnote in her book *Plan or No Plan*, p. 289. It is true that her book is mainly concerned with planning rather than socialism. But the need for inheritance-taxation is nevertheless in a sense the logical conclusion of her argument. Mr. Herbert Morrison in *Socialization and Transport*, which is also mainly concerned with organization problems, merely dismisses the issue as one of the wider problems of socialist finance 'not relevant to his book', p. 247. The fullest discussions are still in Mr. Hugh Dalton's *Inequality of Incomes*, Mr. Josiah Wedgwood's *Economics of Inheritance*, and on the practical side in Mr. Hugh Dalton's *Practical Socialism for Britain*. A more recent discussion is in Mr. J. E. Meade's *Introduction to Economic Analysis and Policy*, part III.

varies very greatly from one country to another.[1] The freedom of bequest allowed by English law, for instance, is exceptional. In most countries of Europe the law reserves a certain proportion of a man's property for his family, or one or another members of it; and all sorts of different systems are clearly conceivable. It would consequently be possible to effect the gradual abolition of inheritance by simply altering the law. In the extreme case a law could be passed[2] providing that all property whatsoever should revert to the hands of the State at death. Nobody, however, could seriously advocate such a procedure. But there are various small reforms, apart from taxation, which might with advantage be adopted. Mr. Dalton[3] suggests the abolition of primogeniture in the English law of intestacy, a limitation[4] of the range of relatives with a claim to benefit from intestacy, a limitation of intestate benefits to life interests, and the reduction of the power of a testator to bequeath the legal, as opposed to the equitable or beneficial, ownership of property.

Far the most important instrument for the socialization of property at death, however, is certainly inheritance-taxation. Every developed country has already adopted some measure of inheritance-taxation, and the easiest and most peaceful advance towards socialism is consequently the progressive increase of inheritance-taxes towards the 100 per cent level. What is the best method of inheritance-taxation? And what are likely to be its effects?

In the first place it should be clearly laid down that a testator should be permitted to leave a certain income to his wife, and perhaps to all near relatives, and certainly to children under twenty-one and to relatives who are old or invalid. In such cases,

[1] Cf. Hugh Dalton, *The Inequality of Incomes*, ch. vi–ix; and Josiah Wedgwood, *The Economics of Inheritance*, ch. iv.

[2] The Soviet Government by decree of 27 April 1918 declared simply 'that inheritance whether by law or will is illegal', though property below a certain maximum is allowed to revert to poorer relatives (cf. Hugh Dalton, *The Inequality of Incomes*, p. 292). This is the fundamental fact which is ignored by those who profess to see no difference between the Soviet and Fascist social systems. By the abolition of the inheritance of private property, Lenin established a social system potentially superior to any the world has yet seen. One can only hope that it will not be re-introduced by Stalin.

[3] *The Inequality of Incomes*, ch. x.

[4] A moderate limitation suggested by Bentham has not yet been adopted.

however, it would be best, as Mr. Dalton has suggested, for the legal ownership of the property to be vested in the Public Trustee, and for the income only to be paid to the beneficiary owner during his or her lifetime. After this it would wholly accrue to the State, and there would in any case be a not very high maximum, irrespective of class.

2. *Payment in Kind*

Secondly, a complete abandonment of the attitude towards inheritance-taxation prevailing among the financial authorities in capitalist countries to-day is essential. The yield of inheritance-taxation to-day is used as revenue, and in most cases the tax has to be paid in cash. The British Treasury, for instance, under the influence of the old idea of the revenue-producing inheritance-tax, is extremely suspicious of any plan which involves the payment of the duties in land or securities. In a reformed system the tax ought to be payable in securities or real property, and it ought to be placed to capital account. It naturally would not be possible to place the whole yield to capital account immediately, but a progressive change could easily be devised. At present, for instance, the British death duties yield about £90,000,000 a year out of a total of all estates 'passing' in a year of £450,000,000 or £500,000,000. A five-year budget plan could thus be devised by which the yield of death duties was raised to £100,000,000 in the first year, and to say £150,000,000 in the fifth year. The yield on any given year over and above £80,000,000 could be placed to capital account, and a huge fund of State capital would thus gradually accumulate. The growing interest on this fund could then be used as revenue, or saved, according to the necessities of monetary policy. After a short time a very high proportion of it would probably normally be saved and invested by the State.

It would be essential for the State to accept in payment practically any form of security or real property. A refusal to accept ordinary or speculative shares would defeat the aim of gradually absorbing all unearned income into the hands of the State. Moreover, there is little risk involved in holding ordinary shares if the State's holding is spread, as it ordinarily would be, over a large and growing variety of securities. Indeed, the State would at once obtain the high yield associated with ordinary shares, and avoid serious long-term risk; and it would thus secure the practical advantages contained in the idea that the State should take over the risk-bearing function. At the same time the owner of an estate (or his executors) would naturally not be allowed to foist worthless shares or property on the State. In Great Britain, in the case of securities, it could easily be enacted that any securities quoted on the Stock Exchange should be eligible for payment of the tax,[1] and that the proportion of trustee securities to be handed over to the State should bear the same relation to the total payments as the total of trustee securities bequeathed bore to the total estate. If a man left £100,000, for instance, half of which was in trustee securities, and the death duty was 50 per cent; then £25,000 out of £50,000 would have to be paid in trustee securities. This would prevent the State being loaded with nothing but highly speculative shares, while at the same time ensuring that a steady flow of industrial capital came into its hands.

There is no form of socialism more desirable than the ownership of land and houses, and therefore of rent, by the State. And the enforcement of really effective inheritance-taxation, payable in land and real property,[2] as well as securities and cash, as the most practical and equitable way to achieve it.[3] It must therefore be made permissible to pay the duties on land or real property of any ascertainable value; and the State must naturally undertake the responsibilities involved in the ownership of land and houses. This in itself will be an enormous advantage, as the municipal ownership of houses has already shown. It will be possible for the State to provide for maintenance and repairs in the case of houses, and capital development in the case of agricultural land, as well as to tax or subsidize rents when either is socially desirable.[4] A subsidy to agricultural rents, for instance, made conditional on the payment of something above the legal

[1] It is assumed that the Stock Exchange Committee, which admits shares to quotation, would be appointed by the Government.

[2] As has been pointed out, the original justification of the private ownership of land was that there was no other practical way of keeping order. The public ownership of land should therefore be one of the first duties of a socialist State.

[3] It will of course be open to a socialist government, if it wishes, on 'planning' grounds, to nationalize the land, give securities in return, and receive back the securities in the ordinary way on the taxpayer's death.

[4] Cf. ch. xxx.

minimum wage, would be one of the fairest and most effective ways of helping the farmer, agricultural labourer, and consumer at once. Whether or not the State should actually farm land, would probably depend on circumstances varying from country to country. But in Great Britain the gradual growth of State ownership of land need not produce a greater revolution than the gradual extension of the scope of such bodies as the Commissioner for Crown Lands and the State Forestry Commissions. Some technical difficulty might initially be caused by the fact that odd pieces of land and property of all kinds in different places would accrue to the State. But it would be open to the State to buy or sell property as it pleased; and it would in any case have available for investment that portion of the yield of the inheritance taxes which was still paid in cash. This could be used to make purchases which would fill up 'gaps': so that the actual assets in land and real property would fall systematically as well as steadily into national hands.

Such a policy need not involve separation of a family from a house, farm, or piece of land where a genuine personal tie existed. For in the first place a small house and even small farm would normally not have to be sold to pay inheritance-taxes, since the tax on estates of this size would be very low. And even where a sale was necessary, a man's family could continue to rent the house or farm in question from the State. It would probably be administratively possible, if the tax due were say half the value of the farm, for the right to half the rent to accrue to the State; so that the family in future paid an annual sum of that amount. By some schemes of this kind, at any rate, it would be possible to preserve the element of value in the ownership of small property without impairing the yield of the inheritance taxes.

Such would be the general strategy by which the mass of propertied incomes would gradually be absorbed into the hands of the State. The property so received would not be sold and spent as revenue, but would be held as a growing fund of capital; and a large and growing proportion of the interest income could itself be saved. What detailed tactics, however, should be pursued in devising a system of inheritance-taxation calculated to have as little disturbing effect as possible on work and savings? There are, of course, many conceivable methods of inheritance-taxation. In the first place it is possible to graduate the tax according to the size of the estate bequeathed, or of the legacy actually received by any single individual. The British Estates Duties are of the first kind; and the Legacy and Succession Duties —which are quantitatively unimportant—are of the second kind, since the graduation of the tax varies according to the nearness in consanguinity of those receiving the legacy. For this particular plan there seems little or nothing to be said: for as legacies to near relatives are normally larger, the tax falls on the larger legacies at a smaller rate. The objection to the pure Estates Duty is that it is possible for a single individual to receive an enormous bequest and therefore an enormous inherited income for life: while the pure Succession Duty on the other hand would enable the millionaire to evade inheritance-taxation altogether by dividing up his bequest into items small enough to fall below or nearly below the exemption level. The pure Estates Duty in fact tends to permit continued inequality: and the pure Succession Duty to retard the process by which capital should be falling into the hands of the State. Probably the best system is a combination, founded on the Estates Duty, but also devised to prevent the receipt of enormous bequests by single individuals. The Estates Duty might simply be supplemented by an absolute limit on the amount a single individual could inherit, such as was suggested by Mill but has not yet been embodied in British social policy.

3. *The Rignano Plan*

Much the most important suggestion, however, for the reform of the inheritance-tax is the so-called Rignano plan. This plan, devised by the Italian Professor Rignano, has been fully discussed and very widely approved by British economists.[1] But it is still curiously little known to the public. The plan is based on the economically sound and socially necessary aim of differentiating between property inherited and property acquired by

---

[1] Cf. J. C. Stamp and Rignano, *The Social Significance of the Death Duties.* Hugh Dalton, *The Inequality of Incomes*, ch. ix. Josiah Wedgwood, *The Economics of Inheritance*, ch. ix–xi. The Colwyn Report, pp. 313–16. A. C. Pigou, *The Economics of Welfare*, second edition, pp. 675–6. H. D. Henderson, *Inheritance and Inequality.* 'Administrative Difficulties of the Rignano Scheme,' paper by Mr. W. H. Coates and Discussion, in the *Journal of Royal Statistical Society*, March 1936.

saving. It is also designed at once to encourage rather than deter work and saving, and to enable a 100 per cent duty to be placed in the last instance on inheritance. The plan in its full form consists in the institution of three separate rates of tax varying according to the number of times an estate has been inherited. That is to say, on the part of an estate which a man has saved himself he pays, say, 50 per cent; on the part inherited from his father say, 75 per cent; and on the part inherited from his grandfather, 100 per cent. There would, of course, in the normal way be an exemption minimum below which an estate would escape taxation, as well as special exemptions for widows, young children, charities, etc. At the same time the rates of 50 per cent and 75 per cent could be made into scales, i.e. there would be two sets of graduations, each itself varying according to the size of the estate. Secondly, if this plan was thought too drastic for immediate introduction, a modified Rignano plan could be introduced by the grafting on to the existing estates duties of a single supplementary rate applicable to the part of an estate which had already been once inherited.

Before the effects of the Rignano plan are estimated, the practical difficulties have to be considered. The initial difficulty is to distinguish between the different 'parts' of the estate. There are two possible solutions to this difficulty. First the solution might be made purely quantitative. If we assume the three rates to be 50 per cent, 75 per cent, and 100 per cent respectively, the principle of the plan would be as follows. Supposing A, who had inherited nothing, died worth £200,000, and left it all to B, B would receive £100,000. He would then pay when he died a tax of 75 per cent on the first £100,000 of his estate, and 50 per cent on the rest of it. If he let it fall below £100,000 he would pay 75 per cent on the whole; while the further he raised it above £100,000 the greater would be the amount on which he only paid 50 per cent. Supposing he died worth £200,000, he would pay £125,000 (75 per cent of £100,000 plus 50 per cent of £100,000). His heir would thus receive £75,000, and of this 50 per cent, i.e. the proportion of the £200,000 left by B which counted as inherited, would on C's death be taxed at 100 per cent, the remaining 50 per cent at 75 per cent, and anything remaining over and above this at 50 per cent. If, of course, B accumulated nothing and left £100,000, then C would receive only £25,000 and would be liable to pay the 100 per cent duty on the whole of this. For every £1 which he left above this, however, he would only pay at the 50 per cent rate.[1]

Such an application of the Rignano plan would be mathematically watertight: it would never make an estate liable to pay a sum greater than its total value; and it would always leave it open to a man to increase by saving the amount he could leave to his descendants. The objection to this application is that owing to changes in capital values outside the individual's control, numerous hard cases (and as Mr. Dalton has observed, 'numerous soft cases of which less will be heard') might arise. If, for instance, in B's lifetime there was a marked rise in the rate of interest the gilt-edged securities which a man had inherited worth £100,000 might depreciate to £50,000, though he had never consumed his capital or indulged in speculation. Yet if he saved another £50,000 out of his income, he would still pay 75 per cent on the whole £100,000. A fall in the rate of interest would conversely present a man with an unearned increment, in capital values. Similarly, long-term changes in the price-level and cost of living might cause a certain amount of hardship. Mr. Dalton, however, has proposed a variation of the scheme which seems effectively to solve these difficulties. He suggests that inherited property should pass into the legal ownership of the Public Trustee (or whoever the appropriate public authority might be), and that a fixed income should accrue to the inheritor during his lifetime. The scheme would thus be revised as follows. If A died leaving £200,000 B would receive £100,000 on which the effective yield at the relevant date was £5,000. The capital would be held by the public authority, and B would receive a fixed income of £5,000 for life: and on his death 75 per cent of the £5,000 held by the public authority would automatically be extinguished. He would have, however, the right to decide the distribution of the remaining £1,250; but on the eventual death of the inheritor of this it would cease altogether. Meanwhile, on any property which B managed to accumulate

---

[1] Presumably if B let his fortune fall to £50,000 and C therefore received £12,500, he would on his death pay 100 per cent only on £12,500. Nobody in fact would be asked to pay 100 per cent on more than he actually received, even if he himself left more. If C had to pay 100 per cent on anything up to £50,000 he would be most unlikely, having inherited £12,500, to make the heroic effort necessary to save over £37,000.

by work or saving the 50 per cent tax would be payable, and the remaining capital sum would again revert to the legal ownership of the Public Trustee. Further variations of this plan have been suggested by Mr. Dalton himself in evidence before the Colwyn Committee,[1] by Mr. H. D. Henderson,[2] and Mr. Josiah Wedgwood.[3] The exact form which the plan should take must no doubt be determined by circumstances; but Mr. Dalton's application of it seems much the best method yet suggested for devising a system of inheritance-taxation that is at once effective, equitable, and economically sound.

The chief difficulties are administrative; and some of them are undoubtedly formidable. The first alleged administrative difficulty, however, is not really a difficulty at all but a decided advantage. 'The proposal', Mr. Wedgwood says, 'is clearly undesirable and impracticable unless it is part of some carefully planned scheme for the partial or complete nationalization of industry, and the Public Trustee's office is transposed into something quite different from what it is to-day.'[4] But this, of course, is exactly what is proposed: and it is precisely the ease (as Mr. Wedgwood would agree) with which this scheme fits into a general scheme of socialism and planning which makes it desirable and practicable. The Colwyn Committee, for instance, in implicitly rejecting the scheme, could think of no other objection to it than that it would be embarrassing for the Treasury as at present constituted to have the custody of an assortment of land and securities.[5] This is of course its purpose.

There are other administrative difficulties,[6] however, which are important. They are mainly of two kinds. First the feasibility of the scheme depends on the power of the taxing authority to keep a record of all substantial inheritances and gifts, whether of cash, securities, or real property. Dr. Dalton expresses the opinion that 'there seems no reason to suppose that the fiscal

---

[1] Colwyn Report, p. 316.

[2] H. D. Henderson, *Inheritance and Inequality*.

[3] Josiah Wedgwood, *The Economics of Inheritance*, pp. 250-5.

[4] *The Economics of Inheritance*, p. 259.

[5] Colwyn Report, p. 317. Sir. O. Niemeyer thought the scheme might 'land the State in the end in a loss'!

[6] In general, as has been observed, administrative problems can only be solved by experience. As this book is mainly concerned with the case for socialism, administrative questions cannot be fully discussed. But they are so important in the case of the Rignano scheme that they must be mentioned.

book-keeping necessary to carry out the scheme would, at the worst, be one-tenth part as elaborate and expensive as that involved in the administration of the National Health Insurance Act'. The Inland Revenue authorities informed the Colwyn Committee that apart from the question of gifts *inter vivos* and of life interests 'there would be no difficulty'. Apart from the question of gifts *inter vivos*, it is difficult to believe that an administrative system which has already evolved Somerset House, the income-tax machinery, and National Health Insurance would be unequal to the task.

The question of gifts is the crux of the practical problem. In a discussion of the 'Administrative Difficulties of the Rignano Plan' at the Royal Statistical Society in 1926[1] most speakers mentioned it; it was emphasized by the Colwyn Committee; and it has been admitted by the advocates of the plan. The main danger is this. Suppose a man has inherited £50,000 (on the interest from which he is already paying a heavy tax) and supposing he will have to pay a 100 per cent on half of it, and 75 per cent tax on the remaining half. Then, if in fact as he grows old he has not succeeded in accumulating more than he inherited, there may be a strong temptation to give it away. And if his estate has actually depreciated for one reason or another towards the point at which the 100 per cent rate will apply to the whole, the temptation to give it away, if it can be done, will be irresistible. But if gifts on a large scale begin to be made, the whole purpose of the plan will be frustrated; for there will tend to be no estates to tax, and the State will receive nothing. How far can this danger be met?

No doubt *some* evasions and giving away of capital is inevitable. The question is whether they will be so prevalent as in fact to frustrate the scheme. There are many reasons for believing they will not. For one thing, as experience of the death duties has shown, there are powerful motives impelling a rich man, even in old age, not to give away more than a small part of his fortune. A man does not know when he is going to die:[2] and he likes to keep his income and his control over his capital. This

---

[1] Cf. *Journal of Royal Statistical Society*, March 1926.
[2] Nor when his heirs are going to die. There have been cases where a man has given away millions to his son, and his son has died first—leaving him to pay the duties, as it were, twice.

motive may in many cases substantially outweigh his desire to cheat the Exchequer. Secondly under the Rignano plan very few persons will be in the position of having to pay 100 per cent on the whole of their estates at death. This will only be true of those who have dissipated their fortunes, or had exceptionally bad luck; and the prospect in itself would naturally enjoin caution. Moreover, it is very unlikely that owners of any of the very large estates will get into this position. For the larger the estate, and therefore the income, the less likelihood will there be of a man consuming his capital. The normal capitalist will expect to pay 100 per cent on a small proportion of his estate, 75 per cent on the remainder, and only 50 per cent on anything he may earn (or whatever the second two rates may be).

There is thus a general presumption that gifts *inter vivos* will not be on a colossal scale. But there are two particular devices which should prove effective in meeting them in so far as they are attempted. First, they can be taxed. The law making gifts within three years of death liable to death duties has shown that gifts can in the majority of cases be traced, and the existing stamp duties are the nucleus from which a really drastic progressive tax on gifts might be developed.[1] Much more important, however, is the fact that if Mr. Dalton's Public Trustee plan were adopted, a man could no more give away his inherited capital than he could consume it. His capital would be in public hands; he could if he liked save out of income, and subsequently dissipate his savings. But there would be a very great inducement not to dissipate these, since the minimum rate of tax would fall on them. Meanwhile he could not dissipate his inherited capital. And on this *ex hypothesi* the 100 per cent and 75 per cent tax would fall. This is a most important additional reason for adopting Mr. Dalton's emendation of the Rignano plan. It removes the main practical difficulty of the plan as well as a great many minor ones.[2]

[1] Mr. Wedgwood (*The Economics of Inheritance*, ch. x.) discusses various methods of preventing evasion of a gift tax.

[2] Moreover, in a system which combines high Rignano rates with Mr. Dalton's plan it will not be practical for a rich man to evade the purpose of the tax by insuring against it and so receiving a lump sum from an insurance company which can be handed on to the inheritor. For a man could only insure against the tax by paying an annual premium out of his income; and if the tax was likely to be something like 75 per cent of the nominal capital on which that income was paid the premium would be impossibly high.

There are thus strong reasons for believing that the Rignano plan,[1] modified in this way, would be the most equitable and effective instrument of inheritance-taxation. It could be drafted on to the British death duties; and could be introduced over a period of years. The progressiveness of the various rates could be made steeper gradually; the proportion of the estate accruing to the Public Trustee could also grow gradually, and naturally the 100 per cent would not become effective for a long time, since all existing estates could conveniently be treated as saved at the first time of passing after the introduction of the tax. Without elaborating exact details,[2] however, we may ask what would be the exact economic effects of the introduction of such a scheme.

4. Effects of Inheritance-Taxation

First it is necessary to decide the incidence of an inheritance tax. Does the estates duty fall on the man whose estate is taxed at his death, or on his successor, who otherwise would have inherited more? The answer depends mainly on whether the testator makes provision for the tax or not. If he works harder and saves more during his life in order to nullify the effect of the tax, the incidence is so far upon him. If on the other hand he entirely ignores the prospect of the tax, it is clearly the inheritor who pays. Unfortunately, it is extremely hard to say how far provision is made against the Estates Duty, except in the case of insurance against the tax, where a major part of the incidence is clearly on the testator. The Colwyn Committee did not think that 'the prospect of the Estates Duty has as much influence on work and saving as the annually recurring income-tax'. On the other hand the income-tax on the testator's income is just as

[1] The Colwyn Committee Majority Report, p. 316, concluded that 'some of us find the principle [of the Rignano plan] in itself attractive and think it possible from such consideration as we have been able to give to the idea, that it may in course of time have useful developments and enable some improvements to be effected in the death duty system'. The Committee was inclined, however, to reject Mr. Dalton's emendation for reasons which are most unconvincing. It doubted 'whether the plan would be commendable to the taxpayer'. Here one gets the impression that the Committee, usually careful, fair, and conscientious, felt it could not bother to 'give consideration' to an embarrassing and unfamiliar idea.

[2] Mr. Colin Clark has discussed statistically an imaginary socialist budget involving a Rignano tax superimposed on the death duties. Cf. Colin Clark, 'A Socialist Budget', New Fabian Reserve Bureau.

effective as the Estates Duty in diminishing what the inheritor receives; and nobody could say that the incidence of the income-tax in this case is on the latter. On those grounds the Colwyn Committee concluded by 'giving primary but not exclusive place to the notion that the incidence of the duty is on the predecessor'. The Legacy and Succession Duties, on the other hand, they thought, should generally be regarded as falling on the inheritor. There is something rather unreal about the whole question of the 'incidence' of inheritance-taxation; for the imposition of the tax makes so many other things other than they would have been that it is difficult to say where the 'incidence' stops. But if we remember that much depends on the reaction of the testator, we may accept the Colwyn Committee's general verdict.[1] At the same time it would appear that the incidence of the Rignano tax would be more heavily on the testator, since it would certainly promote a stronger incentive to him to work and save in order to offset the tax than would the ordinary estates duty.

Finally, what will be the effect of the inheritance tax on work, saving, and enterprise? First, it is necessary to be clear exactly what happens when death duties are paid. The popular idea is that they are a 'tax on capital' because they reduce the capital of the individual or family and because they are paid by the sale of capital or land. This, it has often been replied, is a fallacy. The securities and land sold to pay death duties are bought by somebody else's savings: all the death duty does is to prevent new saving coming into existence; and the income-tax does the same. This view, however, which seems to be currently accepted in expert literature,[2] surely takes us a little beyond the truth. To give the anti-socialist case its full due, it should be admitted here that the death duties (if the revenue raised by them is spent) are more likely to prevent new saving than the income-tax. For income-tax partly reduces savings and partly reduces expenditure: while the whole of the money which buys the land and securities sold to pay death duties is certainly saving. Inheritance-taxation, therefore (if the yield is spent), prevents savings coming into existence; and the question whether it reduces the national capital depends not on the form of the tax but on the

1 Cf. Colwyn Report, pp. 169–72.
2 Ibid., p. 197.

quantitative relation of the amount raised in tax to the volume of 'old' and 'new' saving. For instance, if a country is saving £400,000,000 a year for depreciation and £400,000,000 extra in new saving, the inheritance tax raises £80,000,000 and the whole £80,000,000 is spent, then the tax is merely reducing the amount of new capital accumulated from £400,000,000 to £320,000,000. Only if the yield of the tax rose above £400,000,000 could the nation be 'consuming its capital'.

It is proposed in this book, however, that inheritance-taxation should not be used for raising revenue at all but for transferring capital to the account of the State. The nearer,[1] therefore, the State budget approximated to the point at which the whole annual yield of the inheritance tax was held as capital, the nearer would it be to the point at which no direct diminution of new saving even resulted from the actual transfer.

What then would be the effects of the transfer on work, enterprise, and saving? The ordinary British death duties may be considered first and the Rignano plan second; and work and enterprise may for this purpose be classed together.

The effect of an inheritance tax on work and enterprise depends in the first instance on how far men are influenced, in determining the scale of their exertions, by a desire to provide their successors after their death with an income. On the whole it seems that this influence is very greatly exaggerated. Men certainly have a strong desire to provide their children with a comfortable upbringing, an expensive education, and a privileged career. But parents do not usually pay death duties until these aims have already been accomplished: and it is very doubtful if the desire to bestow further privileges after death remains very strong. It is an interesting fact that Carnegie and Leverhulme were strong advocates of the death duties, and that Lord Nuffield has no children. For in none of these cases do the incentives to work and enterprise appear to have been lacking. No doubt men are pleased by the idea of leaving money to their children: but it seems most unlikely that the fact of being able to leave a little less will positively deter active and ambitious

---

[1] It would not be possible owing to the loss of revenue immediately to devote the whole yield of death duties to capital account. But the amount used for expenditure need not even, at first, be much larger than the annual sum devoted to the repayment of the debt.

men from enterprise on a large scale.[1] And in so far as they are not deterred, the effect on work and enterprise will be negligible. The salary-earner and the entrepreneur will exert themselves just as if the tax did not exist.

Some influence, however, even if small, is bound to be exerted, though it is not at all certain in which direction the influence will work. For whereas some men may make less effort on the ground that less of the proceeds will accrue to their heirs, others will make more effort in order that as much may accrue after all. Moreover, in so far as the death duties prevent the heirs from finding themselves endowed with a ready-made unearned income, it is bound to spur them to greater work and enterprise. Whether on balance the effect will be to increase or decrease work and enterprise cannot be said with certainty.[2] But it is at least clear that the Rignano system will have a much more favourable effect than ordinary death duties in relation to the raising of a given revenue. For under the Rignano system a man will pay the minimum rate on bequests out of his own work and saving: so that the incentive to him, in so far as it exists, will be at the maximum. Meanwhile, the inheritor will receive, in general, less, owing to the incidence of the higher rates on the other parts of the estates: so that he will be less likely to be left an unearned income large enough to secure him from the necessity of working. There is consequently a strong presumption that a full Rignano system, even with very high rates of taxation, would be more favourable to work and enterprise than, for instance, the existing British system.

Most important, however, is the effect of inheritance-taxation on saving. It is evident that the physical effect, in a thoroughly reformed tax system would be much less important than the psychological effect. The physical effect consists in the actual transfer of a part of the estate to the State. There is no physical effect on the testator's ability to save up to this point: for both his income and capital remain intact. And as has been pointed

[1] The private business and partnership has often been thought to be a hard case, in which the death duties bear severely upon enterprise. But figures given by the Colwyn Committee show that this effect is in fact negligible. (Colwyn Report, p. 183.)

[2] The Colwyn Committee concluded: 'We doubt whether the estates duty is more damaging than the income-tax to enterprise. On the whole we are inclined to think it less so.'

out, no physical 'dissaving', or consumption of capital, takes place at all if the whole of the estate is either treated as capital or used for the extinction of debt, and if as great a proportion of the subsequent interest income is saved by the State as would have been saved by the private inheritor. If more is saved, the net effect of the transaction will have been to increase saving. There consequently need be no physically unfavourable effect on saving at all, either in the case of the death duties or the Rignano system, but merely a transfer of the function of saving from the private individual to the State.

Some psychological effect, however, there is likely to be. Under the ordinary death duties if a man were threatened by rates of 50 per cent and 75 per cent he would clearly be most unlikely to save towards the end of his life unless his unearned income was already so large that it was physically impossible to spend it. And if there was also a heavy tax on unearned income there might be a tendency for the recipients of most of the fairly large incomes actually to consume their capital or give it away. Even so it would be a mistake to suppose that this effect would be overwhelming unless the tax was very high indeed.[1] The Colwyn Committee thought that the 'psychological effect of the estates duty is comparatively slight. It does not either stimulate or discourage work and saving so much as the income-tax.'[2] And it has to be remembered that in certain cases a man may be actually stimulated to increased saving by the death duties, since he may work to leave a certain minimum income to his wife and children. Undoubtedly the habit of ensuring against death duties, which is equivalent to an increase in saving, is very prevalent. Probably on balance, however, the psychological effect is to reduce saving.

But just as the physically injurious effects of inheritance-taxation can be completely nullified by the policy of treating the yield of the tax as capital (which the Colwyn Committee did not contemplate), so also the psychological effects can be largely nullified by the combination of the Rignano system with Mr.

[1] The experience of the British death duties shows that even rates of 50 per cent do not stimulate mass consumption of capital, as was once predicted. In general rich men like to keep their capital till they die, and then leave it to be taxed. In New York State combined Federal and State taxation reaches 80 per cent on some fortunes. But it is paid.

[2] Colwyn Report, p. 194.

Dalton's plan. The danger is that the prospect of an ordinary inheritance tax will deter saving and even lead to a consumption of capital. But the Rignano principle provides a most powerful additional motive for saving, since the tax on savings actually made by the testator will be at the lowest rate; and Mr. Dalton's emendation provides that the whole of a man's inherited capital will be in the hands of the Public Trustee, so that it will be physically impossible for him to consume it. The average rich rentier, therefore, will be unable to consume his capital. He will have the alternatives of simply living on it and forfeiting the whole or nearly the whole of it on death, or else of saving and working, or both, and handing on a substantial proportion of the remainder to his children. Moreover, the very powerful desire of a rich man to have control of his capital will impel him to save out of his unearned (and perhaps earned) income. In these circumstances he will, at worst, since he must, refrain from consuming his capital, and at best be impelled to fresh efforts of work and saving. The most reasonable conclusion seems to be, therefore, that an inheritance tax on the Rignano principle, supplemented by Mr. Dalton's plan, will have very little effect either way on work or enterprise, and some considerable but not overwhelming deterrent effect on private saving. Since, however, private saving will become a steadily less important part of total saving, the net diminution in saving, though probably appreciable, will not be very drastic.

CHAPTER XXVII

REDISTRIBUTION AND MONETARY POLICY

It appears from the preceding argument that the total effect of increased taxation on earned incomes, a much steeper discrimination against unearned incomes, and a progressive inheritance tax will leave the volume of work and the activity of enterprise little changed but will exert some restrictive influence on saving. For the reward of work and enterprise will still remain high, and comparatively higher, owing to the low rate of tax on earned incomes; and the Rignano graduation will afford an additional incentive. The effect on saving of the coincidence of the 'unearned' and the Rignano taxes will probably be rather greater than separate consideration of the effect of the two individual taxes would suggest. For if a man is both taxed heavily on the interest he earns and taxed again, even at a comparatively low rate, on what he leaves his heirs out of his savings, he may in certain cases give up the struggle. Experience, however, of the income-tax and death duties, as well as the foregoing argument, suggest that this effect will not be overwhelming. And since private saving will be *ex hypothesi* of diminishing importance, one seems justified in inferring that even the 'unearned' and Rignano taxes together will only result in a moderate decline in the rate of saving. Meanwhile the volume of enterprise will always be mainly determined by monetary policy and cyclical forces.

Now the conclusion, it will be recalled, of the earlier discussion in this book on monetary policy and the trade cycle was that some restriction must normally be placed on saving if general equilibrium and full employment are to be maintained. For as incomes increase, and savings tend to increase with them, a gap will tend to appear between Total Effective Demand and Total Costs; and if Total Demand is to be maintained this gap must be covered by an increase in either consumption or investment. It was shown, however, that there are various dangers latent in the encouragement of investment beyond a certain point, and that an increase in consumption is at once the most effective and safest method of achieving a durable equilibrium. It appears, therefore, that the policy of redistributive taxation, so far from endangering economic equilibrium, is above all things best calculated to promote it. For the chief economic effect of redistributive measures, as has just been indicated, is to exert some restrictive influence on saving. And this restriction of saving is naturally accompanied by a corresponding increase in consumption. It is of course a gross error to suppose that the taxation of the rich destroys purchasing power. It transfers it from the rich to the poor: and if it were as likely to be spent by either, the economic effects would be the same in either case. In fact, however, a transfer on the scale discussed in the last few chapters will normally result in some diminution of saving. For though the increased saving by the State will make up for some of the diminished saving of rich individuals, the balance of the transfer will normally be spent by the State in satisfying the consumption needs of the poor.

The exact proportion in which the money transferred is distributed between saving and spending must depend on the existing state of the trade cycle and the needs of monetary policy. If Total Demand has to be expanded, the emphasis will be on spending and investment, and if it has to be restricted, on saving. On occasions a budget surplus or a budget deficit may be necessary to redress the balance one way or the other. And the most favourable moment for actual increases in taxation will naturally have to be carefully chosen. But at all times the power given by redistributive taxation to the authorities to control the relation of saving and spending will be the most helpful of all weapons in the gradual conquest of the trade cycle. The volume of saving itself, as Mr. Keynes has pointed out, largely depends on cyclical conditions and the resulting volume of incomes; and the activity of enterprise will in turn largely depend on the success of monetary policy in maintaining Total Demand equal to Total Costs and thus preserving the normal profit margin throughout the whole system. It is consequently misleading to conceive of the problem of redistributive taxation as merely a problem of preventing deterrent effects on work, enterprise, and saving. The whole issue is far more complicated than this. For if the correct ratios between saving, spending, and investment are preserved, the volumes of work and enterprise will largely look after themselves; while the task of maintaining these ratios will necessitate sometimes an increase in saving, and sometimes a decrease. Normally, however, a reduction in saving will be desirable, and this will become increasingly true as the standard of living rises and the propensity to save intensifies. Redistributive taxation, therefore, by virtue both of its flexibility and of its normal tendency to restrict savings, must be regarded as a valuable instrument not merely of social but also of economic and monetary policy.

CHAPTER XXVIII

REDISTRIBUTIVE EXPENDITURE

There is no need to discuss redistributive expenditure in detail. When the money has been raised, there will not be much difficulty in spending it, nor much serious dispute among socialists on what it should be spent. The stream of unearned incomes gradually becoming available will be used in the interests of the poor, and it will at the same time employ the capital and labour made available by the reduction in the spending of the rich. To suppose that unemployment would be created is, as has been pointed out, a mistake. There will be a transfer; and as the whole process will be steady but gradual, the transfer will present no very serious difficulties. Nor will the expenditure of the transferred incomes on the poorer and more deserving section of the community be in any sense 'charitable' or 'eleemosynary'. It will be merely the restoration to them of what they have earned by their work, but which an arbitrary social organization and distorted price system have taken away from them.

As a general principle it will probably prove best to provide the elementary necessities of life in kind rather than money. For where elementary necessities are concerned, ignorance distorts the working of consumers' choice, and men in a very real sense do not know what they need, or at any rate what their families need. It should be remembered that perhaps two out of three members of the average family only exercise a limited consumers' choice anyway. And where primary necessities are concerned the State will normally be a better judge than the spender of the family's income. Houses, heating, and sanitation, health services, education, food, and clothes should be made available to all. When a family is too poor to buy them, that is to say, the State should supply them out of the unearned income at its command. To provide systematically for primary wants in this

295

way would do more than anything else conceivable to abolish poverty and remove the main removable obstacles to happiness.

Over and above the provision of primary necessities in kind, the available resources should probably be spent in money and the advantages of free consumers' choice retained. Such a distribution need not wholly take the form of an actual disbursement of money in pensions and family allowances, though that could certainly be carried out. In large part it might take the form of a remission of regressive and unfair taxation. In Great Britain, for instance, the remission of local rates on all those with incomes of less than £4 a week, and the abolition of the tax on tea and sugar, would have an incalculably beneficial effect. Family allowances calculated to check the fall in population will also before long have to be fitted carefully into the redistributive system. The details, however, of redistributive expenditure must vary with circumstances and countries, and must in any case be determined by the representatives of the persons concerned. The essential principle is to provide for the elementary wants of the necessitious by the expenditure of the growing stream of socialized unearned income.

Besides the abolition of inheritance, and mitigation of inequality by redistributive taxation and expenditure, there are many possible alterations in the legal context of the price system which would make that system more equitable. Perhaps the most important of these is the removal of discrimination in education. For it is on the institution of educational selection by wealth instead of ability that most of the gross inequalities of opportunity and consequent 'monopoly revenues', in Great Britain at any rate, are based. Important as this is, however, it would itself be so largely removed by the abolition of unearned incomes that it need not be discussed separately here.

CHAPTER XXIX

SHOULD WE INTERFERE WITH THE PRICE SYSTEM?

If these alterations in the legal framework of the price mechanism had been made, but there had been no actual interference with the price mechanism itself, what sort of economic and social system would emerge? We may suppose that there would be a world in which all unearned income would be gradually falling as a result of inheritance-taxation, into the hands of the State, in which many large industries would be operated by public corporations working mainly on the price and profit principle, in which a vast number of small entrepreneurs would be still working on that principle, in which inequalities of earned income would be slightly but not much less than now, and in which consumers' choice would be absolutely free. The large and growing flow of unearned income falling into the Government's hands would of course be used to supplement the resources of those with the lowest incomes. In such a world both inequality and poverty would be very materially reduced; for the absence of private unearned incomes would remove the bulk of inequality and the expenditure of the State's unearned income in the interests of wage-earners would enormously relieve poverty. At the same time the price system could be maintained almost intact in the consumers' market, in the raw-material market, and in the labour market. Entrepreneurs and managers could adjust their production according to the moving price index just as they do, or are supposed to do now; and they could estimate their labour and raw material costs in the same way. Consumers' real preferences would be far more closely reflected in the money demand for consumers' goods, since inequality would have been drastically reduced. A very much closer approximation to a real distribution of productive resources according to needs would

297

therefore seem to have been achieved without the emergence of any very serious problems.

Such an economic system, in which free prices, free consumers' choice, and free competition are retained unimpaired, but unearned income is being gradually distributed in social services, is a perfectly conceivable system. If we ignore for the moment an important argument advanced by Professor Mises, to be discussed presently, we may regard it as a half-way house towards socialism. Indeed, it is more than half way. For the utilization of unearned incomes to raise the standard of living of the poorer wage-earners must always remain the real heart of socialism. All those, therefore, who regard free competition and free prices as the supreme economic value should observe that they can support this essential instalment of socialism without abandoning their principles. Here, at least, is a first objective which all liberals and radicals as well as socialists should be prepared to pursue in all countries where there is no agreement on the desirability of going farther.

Is it in fact desirable to go farther, and if so for what reason? There are two main classes of argument against the adoption of this limited objective. The first contends that it is impossible to stop at this point on the ground that the abolition of the private ownership of land and capital makes the working of the price system impossible; and the second contends that, since the perversions resulting from the price system derive not merely from the legal framework but from the nature of the price system itself, we must necessarily alter the system as well as the framework. Now if, as is argued later, the system can work despite the abolition of private capital and land, it would be theoretically possible to proceed no farther. The second argument, however, seems to establish conclusively the case for positive interference with the price system. In chapters viii and ix it was argued that fundamental maladjustments of resources to real needs arise from the existence of unequal incomes within the price system. And this is equally true of earned as of unearned incomes. The needs represented by the rich man's shilling would still exert a disproportionate pull on the price system compared with needs represented by the poor man's shilling, and the poor man would still exert a disproportionate degree of effort, even if unearned incomes had been abolished, and the inequality of earned incomes somewhat curtailed. And not merely would inequality of unearned income remain; but the fact of technical progress and 'increasing returns' would still tend to the creation of monopolies and the emergence of monopoly incomes. The fundamental misdirection of resources resulting from a system of completely free exchange would therefore still prevail. It seems desirable, therefore, that we should proceed beyond the mere abolition of unearned incomes, and if practicable make at least some alteration in the working of the price system itself.

Now this extremely important second step raises some fundamental difficulties, which socialists, it must be admitted, have hitherto been inclined to ignore. It has been thought sufficient to declare that socialism would institute 'production for needs', instead of 'production for profit', or institute 'order' instead of 'chaos'; or that it would 'organize' or 'regulate' or 'co-ordinate' the production and distribution of goods. But it has seldom been explained what these words mean, or on what principle the 'regulation' would be conducted. Yet this is really the crux of the matter. For it is plain that the automatic price system, though it misrepresents real needs and therefore fails to bring about a really 'economic' arrangement of production and distribution, nevertheless does bring about *some* arrangement. Resources are directed in certain directions and certain amounts of different commodities are produced. It has been argued in earlier chapters that they are to a large extent the wrong ones. But since this is the indictment against the price system, the socialist has to show that socialism can produce the right things in the right quantities. For, as Professor Hayek remarks: 'The difference between an economic and an uneconomic distribution and combination of resources among the different industries is the difference between scarcity and plenty.'[1]

This is a real problem, clearly if rather aggressively stated by Professors Pierson, Mises, Halm, and Hayek in the symposium *Collectivist Economic Planning*, and it has to be met if socialists are to convince the open-minded that they have an intelligible system to offer. The weakness of the argument of *Collectivist Economic Planning* is that the authors assume throughout that an 'economic' distribution of resources means a distribution in accordance with money demand. All the facts of social inequality (inheri-

[1] *Collectivist Economic Planning*, p. 216.

tance, etc.) are taken for granted: and such phrases as 'satisfying demand', an 'economic or rational direction of resources', production that is 'worth the cost', etc., as used by the authors, consequently beg the whole question.

There is a certain sign as the book proceeds that the authors are becoming uneasy about this glaring vacuum underlying their argument. Professor Mises, in an essay originally written in 1920, speaks unequivocally of 'demand'. Professor Halm and Professor Hayek, writing more recently, speak more cautiously of 'effective demand'; and Professor Hayek adds the argument criticized in chapters ii and iii of this book, that nothing is known by anybody about real needs and desires. Similarly Professor Mises pronounces any defection from the price system to be 'impossible'. Professor Hayek, writing after the Russian experiment, explains that this means any 'rational' or 'successful' defection to be impossible. He thus jumps from one hot brick on to another.

It has been argued at length in part I of this book that the unregulated workings of the price index do not produce a 'rational' or 'economic' distribution of resources. But what is the criterion of such a distribution? Mrs. Wootton[1] defines an 'efficient economic system' as one 'which gives the maximum surplus of satisfaction over effort' or 'one in which the time and resources of the people are employed in such a way as to give the result most satisfying to them'. The difficulty here, however, as was argued in chapters ii and iii (and Mrs. Wootton admits it), is that as soon as one asks whose satisfaction is to exceed whose effort, and whose time is to be employed in such a way as to give satisfaction to whom, the whole analysis, in terms of the delusively simple 'economic' concepts of satisfaction and effort, breaks down. We have to say, and say rightly, that it is better that this group of persons' needs for this should be satisfied rather than that group of persons' needs for that.

We are left, if the argument of chapters ii and iii was correct, with one general moral criterion supplemented by particular criteria, which may perhaps be called 'economic'. In general, that is to say, we know that a society in which certain needs of certain people are satisfied, and not certain other needs of certain other people, is better than one in which the position is

[1] *Plan or no Plan*, p. 168.

reversed; and in particular we can say with reasonable certainty that in specific cases the wants of this man are actually greater than the wants of that man.

How are the criteria to work in practice? It may be admitted at once that they cannot be applied with the mathematical exactitude with which the price system works *in theory*. They cannot be written down in equations and elaborated with the help of the differential calculus. This, however, is simply because the moral and psychological facts lying at the root of 'demand' and 'cost' are not quantitative and cannot be correctly treated in this way. Some of the precision claimed for the orthodox analysis of the price system is merely the false precision that results from making a grossly fallacious simplifying assumption at the start and then erecting meticulous inferences on it—as though one were to assume that the aesthetic merit of a picture were represented by the square root of its area in square inches and then proceed to evaluate the merit of all the pictures in the National Gallery accordingly.

Even if it is admitted, however, that theoretical precision such as this is a loss rather than a gain, there is a very serious basic difficulty to be met. To abandon the price index as the determinant of how much of each commodity is to be produced is to introduce authoritarian human direction into the system.[1] It is a mistake to suppose that under the price system there is no authoritarian direction; for the index itself is authoritarian. But it does not reflect real needs; it works out a sort of blind and mystical amalgam of money demands which on analysis appears to be irrational. In arguing that this blind index is likely to be more just than a conscious human director, defenders of the price system are on very weak ground. But in arguing that the price index is the only practical method of getting economic decisions reached at all they are on much stronger ground. Imagine, as Professor Hayek quite legitimately imagines,[2] a central economic body which has abandoned the price system *entirely* and has to decide, in accordance with a criterion of real needs, desires, and sacrifices, how much of all commodities

[1] The substitution of such direction for the price system may perhaps be called 'planning'. This question-begging word will be used in the following pages in the strict sense here stated.
[2] *Collectivist Economic Planning*, ch. v.

should be produced, where and when they should be produced, how much land and labour should be devoted to the production of each, and how much everyone should receive in return for their services. Such a body would have to know months in advance the exact preference of every individual for so many chocolates rather than peppermints, apples rather than oranges, cinemas rather than football, at all times of the day on every day throughout the year. And that is only one tiny fraction of what it would have to know. The problem would be utterly and beyond dispute impossible; and socialists had better admit this quite unequivocally. Moreover, if an attempt were made to solve it in practice, this central body would simply have to make decisions which Professor Hayek and Professor Mises may quite fairly describe as arbitrary. Suppose such a body had to decide how many acres were to be sown with wheat, how many with oats, and how many with barley, and had no price index to guide it. It would not in fact try to compute the desires of 50,000,000 individuals. It would ascertain, we may be sure, how many acres were planted the year before, and proceed more or less accordingly. But this would be to neglect possible *changes* in tastes and preferences of which even the price system would have taken some blundering account.

To abandon the price system entirely, in fact, would certainly produce a worse misdirection of resources than to obey it entirely. It would result, as the Russians found in the period in which they attempted to dispense with money and prices,[1] in the production of almost all the wrong things in the wrong quantities— in other words, 'poverty in the midst of plenty'. For it must be repeated, first, that the problem which the price system is trying to solve is the production of the right quantity of the right things: and secondly that this is an extremely difficult problem. The appearance of unsaleable surpluses alongside great destitution is partly a sign that the price system is not entirely successful in this task; but we must not forget the possibility that 'planning' might, in Professor F. H. Knight's words, 'do vastly worse', simply because no authoritarian human director of production can *know* the data on which his myriad decisions must be based. The price system at least 'feels' the data in a clumsy way in each and every corner of the system. But a central

[1] Cf. Barbara Wootton, *Plan or No Plan*, ch. ii.

human director, if he tried to do this, would simply fail everywhere. Indeed, the complete 'planning' of consumption so as really successfully to satisfy needs and desires is probably impossible in any unit larger than the family. And it is only successful there because the planner—the spender—knows comparatively intimately the desires, and the changes in desires, of the three or four consumers in question.

The wiser course would thus seem to be not, like the Russians, to abolish the price system outright and then reintroduce it wherever its absence was obviously disastrous, but rather to preserve it and to modify it bit by bit in all those ways in which modification is indisputably justifiable. What will those modifications be?

CHAPTER XXX

COSTS AND PRICES IN A SOCIALIST COMMUNITY

Perhaps the best way to consider just how far the price and cost system ought to be modified in a socialist community is to consider the arguments of Professor Mises and Professor Hayek which purport to show that no modifications can be made at all without dislocating the system entirely.[1] For the answer to these arguments, and the answer to the question how the price system can be made more equalitarian, in fact converge into one. The first argument advanced by Professor Mises is believed by him to be fatal even to the plan of abolishing unearned incomes and leaving the price system otherwise intact. If unearned incomes are abolished, he points out, and ownership of the bulk of land and capital comes into the hands of the State, there will be virtually no market for capital goods. If this is so, he goes on to argue, there will be no price of capital goods, and entrepreneurs and managers will have no means of calculating their land and capital costs; so that the whole costs and price mechanism will break down after all. This unquestionably appears a serious theoretical difficulty, since the absence of a price of land and capital would throw a monkey-wrench into the whole delicately balanced price complex which the economist analyses. But how great will the distortions be in fact, and how far will they be socially desirable?

This will depend on the principles according to which land and labour are distributed between the different productive resources. The conclusion of chapter xiv was that since the inequality of incomes was the chief factor apart from the legal framework which perverts the free price system, departures from that system should normally be made with the express purpose of mitigating inequality. In meeting the present difficulty this

[1] *Collectivist Economic Planning*, ch. iii.

principle must be followed; for some departure from the price system is almost certainly necessary in determining the price of capital goods in a socialist community. To some extent, as we shall see, the State can 'play at competition' in the capital market. But it cannot do so sufficiently thoroughly, even if it wishes, to discover the prices that full pure competition would involve; since there is one decision which it must take collectively, the decision how much of the national income is to be saved annually.[1] For though there will be some private saving, the bulk of national savings, as was argued in chapter xviii will be undertaken by the State; and it is impossible for the Chancellor of the Exchequer or the National Planning Commission to decide how long every individual would be willing to save or 'wait' in return for how large a rate of interest. It must be decided collectively that private savings will be supplemented by say £200,000,000 this year out of the State's unearned income. This, however, seems to be just the type of decision which an intelligent and well-informed public authority is admirably fitted to take. It does not involve impossible guesses about whether a certain individual in Carlisle prefers raspberries to strawberries. It simply involves a general judgement how rapidly the community should save or invest; and as soon as we admit that there may be at least as good ways of making this judgement as allowing a million separate judgements to add themselves up, it becomes apparent that this decision at least can be made on intelligible principles. A modern industrial State, for instance, would almost certainly be saving too little if no new investment were going on at all. It would also clearly be saving too much if it reinvested at the pace of Russia during the Five Year Plan or Germany during the rearmament programme (it is notable that the danger of State 'planning' in this field seems to be too much, and not too little, investment). Between these two extremes a guess can be made; and the margin of indefiniteness can be narrowed down by a deliberate appeal to the principle of diminishing inequality. If, for instance, the urgent needs of the wage-earner can only be met by durable goods, e.g.

[1] This is, of course, the celebrated question of the rate of interest in a socialist community which has exercised Professor Cassel, Mr. H. D. Dickinson, and others. Cf. Gustav Cassel, *The Theory of Social Economy*, vol. I; H. D. Dickinson, *Institutional Revenue*; Barbara Wootton, *Plan or No Plan*, pp. 99–100.

houses, investment should be maintained at a high level; but as soon as their needs are preponderantly for consumers' goods it can be allowed to fall. At the same time monetary policy, and the need to reduce or increase effective demand, must play a dominant part in determining the scale of investment. If the determination of the volume of saving and investment is drawn up on these general principles, it will be neither impossible to make collectively, nor in any sense 'irrational', nor subversive of the price system in general.

It might, of course, be argued that if the central authority is thus a monopolist of savings, individuals' preferences for saving and spending in certain proportions will not be carried out, and that to this extent the individual's choice is frustrated. This is only true in a very academic sense. For if private persons are allowed to save out of their earned incomes and receive interest in their own lifetimes, the intention of each individual saver will be fulfilled. It is true that the effect of this saving on the general price-level and on investment will not be the same as it would have been if there had been no central authority. But, as we have seen, the relation between saving, investment, and the volume of output and incomes is so complex that it is only in the most academic sense that the individual's act of saving can be expected to produce some special movement in these quantities under the price system. In fact such a central control as that described above would not in substance frustrate the individual's desire to save. It is perfectly true that the rate of interest which the central authority offered to the private saver might induce him to save a different amount than he would have done if an uncontrolled rate of interest had settled down at some other level. But in any case the rate of interest would be determined by circumstances outside the individual's control; so that the situation would not be significantly different.

Having decided how much to save, the central authority has to determine which public enterprises are to be allowed to make use of the available savings. Here there is no reason why we should not employ the price system supplemented by the principle of mitigating inequality and by general social considerations. It must be assumed that there would be a National Investment Board directing long-term investment and a socially controlled banking system and money market directing short-term investment; and that in general it would not be possible for producers to obtain capital except through these sources. How far producers would lend to one another or form an unofficial money market, would depend on relative interest rates on the one hand and the legal position on the other. It is here assumed that no important unofficial capital market would be allowed to exist, apart from the Stock Exchange: and that the Stock Exchange would only survive in the transition period and would even then be no more than a market for the exchange of old securities among persons who had saved out of their earned incomes. All new issues would be made through the National Investment Board; and that Board's power to fix rates of interest would therefore partly determine the general level of Stock Exchange prices. Moreover, a great and increasing volume of Stock Exchange securities would in fact be held by the Government.

In determining the direction of investment the central authority would act on the following principles. In the first place it would take account of specifically social objectives such as town-planning, security of employment, the preservation of the countryside, the need to revive distressed areas, and of all other social values—'costs' which Professor Mises's 'rational' price system would ignore. Over and above this, however, the economic principles guiding the banks and the Investment Board might be these. It would be perfectly possible throughout the whole planning system to distinguish, in accordance with the basic conclusions of chapters ii and iii, three broad classes of consumers' goods; necessities, luxuries, and a residual class of neutral goods. In the class of necessities would be included all those goods and services which are indubitably necessary to the life, liberty, and happiness of any human being: milk, bread, meat, vegetables, fruit, clothes, houses, medical services, holidays, etc. In the class of luxuries could be included all those commodities which quite indubitably no normal man would buy until all his staple needs were satisfied: private motor-cars, expensive wines, whisky, cigars, and so forth. All other goods could be then classed as neutral. There is really little doubt that such lists could be drawn up and would command general agreement—the committee appointed to revise the composition of the Board of Trade's cost of living index might be given the task. And, when such lists had been compiled, the banks and the National Investment Board would first determine a standard rate of interest. This would be so fixed that the total supply of savings already determined should be just absorbed by public utility boards and private entrepreneurs. The rate could, of course, vary with the length and riskiness of loans; for the Board and the banks would presumably be as well able to judge the riskiness of a loan as the present ill-directed herd of private investors. The standard rate of interest would be a kind of bank rate: all other standard rates would vary with it. In general any entrepreneur or State corporation providing 'neutral goods' would be required to pay the standard rate, and this would of course count among his costs. Producers of necessities would pay a lower rate; and producers of luxuries would pay a higher rate. In particular the supply of the most important consumers' durable goods, houses, could be increased in this way. The central authority could, for instance, make capital available for building and repairing working-class houses at a rate much below the standard rate. If necessary, working-class rents could be subsidized as well.

The whole structure of interest rates would of course have to be so devised that the 'market was cleared', i.e. that the whole supply of savings was borrowed at the existing rates and that no borrowers remained in any of the three classes who were willing to borrow at the existing rate but were unable to be accommodated for lack of funds. A monopolist, in fact, is not absolved from the task of seeing that the price is within the limits at which supply and demand correspond. He must not put the price so high that the supply is not all taken up, nor so low that there is a queue of unsatisfied customers—in this case borrowers. The central investment authority, however, by its power to regulate the total flow of savings, to fix the standard rates, and to control the flow of savings into each section of the market, need not find it impossible to maintain its discriminatory rates, and at the same time to allow a competitive rationing according to ordinary pricing principles within each section.

In distributing the supply of capital on these principles the State could be acting as a discriminating monopolist. It would also be perfectly possible for it to act as a simple monopolist and charge the standard rate of interest to all borrowers.[1] This in

1 If the technical difficulties of discrimination proved too great, it could

itself would meet Professor Mises's argument; for capital would be rationed by the rate of interest charged, and each producer would pay a definite rate which he would reckon among his costs. Professor Mises would doubtless contend that even in acting thus the State would be bound to fix the rate at an 'arbitrary' monopoly rate and perhaps to draw a monopoly revenue. An arbitrary rate in this connection may either mean any rate other than that resulting from free competition; and the whole proceeding argument is designed to demonstrate that arbitrariness in this sense is not necessarily undesirable. Or it means a rate determined haphazard and on no intelligible principles. But in this case the standard rate would be determined on intelligible principles, since it would *ex hypothesi* be the rate necessary to maintain investment at the level compatible with full employment.

The justification for proceeding beyond the existing rates, and elaborating special rates for the producers of necessities and producers of luxuries, is of course the necessity to correct the dislocating effects of unequal incomes on the price system. If this general plan were adopted by the investment authorities, the distribution of savings would be determined by the ordinary price index in so far as the production of neutral goods was concerned; and the production of necessities would at the same time be subsidized at the expense of the production of luxuries. The scheme would then at once be perfectly practical and at the same time would supplement other measures designed to mitigate inequality. For each producer would still have to pay a specific price for capital which would appear among his costs; and that price would be a much more faithful reflection of real needs than the unregulated interest rate of private capitalism. The advantages of the price system in this particular sphere would then be maintained, while some of its main defects would be removed. There would be nothing either 'arbitrary' or 'impossible' about such a plan. For the truth is that an interference with the price system, such as a subsidy, does not, as Professor Mises is inclined to argue, upset the price system in such a way as to prevent it working. It 'upsets' it in the sense that it induces it to work in an intelligibly different way. And this is precisely what we want it to do.

---

fall back on this and allow the other methods of subsidizing discussed later to mitigate inequality.

The treatment of rent might be similar. The State, as universal landowner, would not of course be troubled here with determining the supply; for this would be given. On the other hand, it would not be so easy to fix a standard rent, except perhaps for a few broad categories of land, since the value of land of different categories and in different localities varies indefinitely. We may assume at once that some land will not be let at any rent; including national parks and sea-coasts and strips of land along main roads. We may also assume that land for working-class houses, schools, and probably agricultural land—which is used for the production of necessities—will be let at a low rent, and land for golf courses, expensive hotels, and factories producing luxuries, at a high rent. But how will it be decided what is high and what is low, even for given categories of land? The State cannot simply continue to charge what was charged before; for not only do the value of money and the rate of interest change over time, but the relative values of different sorts of land also change. It seems that the State should simply charge the highest rent that anybody is willing to pay in all cases where there is no special reason for a subsidy. But in cases of land to be used for socially valuable purposes, or for the production of necessities, it will charge a lower rent and by this means in effect pay a subsidy.

In any case, the central authority would vary the general structure of rents, and the amount of land available for the main categories of tenants, in such a way that the supply was adjusted to the demand at the existing level of rents in each category. This again would enable the demand for land to be rationed by ordinary pricing methods among tenants in the same category; and it would supply the necessary calculus by which land could be reckoned as a cost in the production of commodities and in its use for all other purposes. Meanwhile the provision of working-class houses and gardens, open spaces, and the provision of food would be automatically subsidized: and the total of rents would at the same time accrue to the State and be available for expenditure on social services. At the same time all rents could be adjusted by a cost of living index to avoid injustices arising out of changes in the value of money.

There will perhaps in these circumstances be a certain arbitrariness in the fixing of rents which will not be adjusted with the delicacy and certainty imagined by theoretical economists. Only those, however, who believe that those delicacies also exist in practice, and perfectly reflect the real efforts and needs of individuals, can seriously argue that this slight element of theoretical indeterminacy outweighs the colossal gain of diverting the whole income from land into social hands and enabling land where necessary to be preserved or developed for social purposes.

If rent and interest are determined in this way, the producers —private or State-controlled—throughout the system will have the cost of capital and land determined for them just as definitely as they have now; and they will consequently be able to take these costs into account in the normal way in determining the volume and character of production. The individual rent and interest items will in many cases be different from what they would have been under a system of unregulated private capitalism. But the change—again if the fundamental argument in chapters ii, iii, ix, and x is correct—will have brought this into closer conformity with real needs. At the same time actual capital goods—machines, factories, etc.—can be bought and sold between the productive units in the normal way.

The remainder of the entrepreneurs' 'factor costs', i.e. wages and salaries, do not present the same fundamental difficulty. They *can* be determined on competitive principles in a socialist community if it is thought desirable. For there will be competition both between entrepreneurs on the one hand and workers on the other. Is it desirable, however, that they should be so determined? The alternatives are simply these. Either the incomes of the wage-earners and salary-earners may be increased by raising money wages and salaries; or else they may be increased by leaving money wages and salaries alone and making available the whole range of social services and subsidized supplies to those with the lowest incomes. (Some of these methods of readjusting the existing price system's bias in favour of the rich have already been discussed. Others will be discussed in the next chapter.) The effect of these two alternative policies in raising the real incomes of the wage-earners will be the same. But, as has been pointed out in the course of the preceding discussion on monetary policy;[1] the policy of attempting to raise wage rates by semi-coercive measures has the additional effect

[1] Cf. pp. 150, 216–20.

311

of distorting the ratio of different kinds of costs to one another, i.e. of destroying the entrepreneurs' earned income. If in the transitional period, when part of the economic system is socialized, a wage-raising policy of this kind is adopted, entrepreneurs' earnings will tend to be wiped out in the non-socialist section of industry. Or, to put it another way, the total wage-bill would have been raised and the total stream of cost payments necessary to secure full employment would have risen. An increase would then be necessary in Total Effective Demand; but this, unaccompanied by a real increase in productivity, would result in a rise in prices, which would in turn be resisted by the workers. Such a policy would almost inevitably result in monetary disequilibrium and unemployment in the non-socialized section of industry, as Mr. Roosevelt found when he tried to raise wages forcibly by the N.R.A. codes and M. Blum when he introduced the forty-hour week. And it would not be equitable to raise wages in the socialized section of industry alone far above those obtaining in the non-socialized section. The error underlying the preference for the wage-raising rather than the income-raising policy consists in its failure to see that the wage-raising policy works at the expense of the essential element of entrepreneurs' reward for work and risk-bearing instead of at the expense of the rentier's inessential unearned income. The relation of wage rates to entrepreneurs' profits is an essential element in preserving equilibrium throughout the non-socialized part of the system; while the relation of the rentier's income to the social services is not. For wages and entrepreneurs' profits are both a consumers' income and an essential cost of production; whereas the social services, etc., financed out of taxation on inherited incomes, are not. It does not matter to the entrepreneur deciding production whether his debenture interest is paid to a private individual or to the State. But it does matter to him if his profit margin is destroyed. This is a vital distinction which both socialists and anti-socialists have been inclined to ignore.

Since, therefore, both alternative policies will accomplish the aim of raising the wage-earners' income, and since the wage-raising policy may produce other unsettling effects (including unemployment, which may actually reduce the total real income of the workers), the policy of supplementing rather than raising wages is undoubtedly to be preferred in the transition period.

It must also be remembered that on the one hand all the element of 'profit' which goes to dividends rather than to business men's earned income will be gradually falling into the hands of the State through the abolition of inheritance; and secondly that trade-union pressure will in any case be perpetually directed to the forcing up of wages by the ordinary methods of collective bargaining. Moreover, with the gradual suppression of unearned and grossly unequal incomes, the structure of competitive earned incomes worked out by the price system will be approximating much more closely to a real reflection of abilities and even needs. As has already been pointed out,[1] it must not, therefore, be thought that the expenditure of a huge sum in social services rather than wages is 'charitable' or 'eleemosynary'. To think this is to fall into the major hypocrisy of capitalist psychology and fundamentally to misconceive the whole economic problem. It is the recipient of unearned income who is at the moment living on charity at the expense of the community; and the diversion of his income into the hands of productive workers is a necessary and salutary abolition of an indefensible eleemosynary system. Indeed, it is just because these workers will be receiving huge benefits in social services, etc., that their wages, and still more their total incomes, will reflect abilities and needs more closely. For as inequality is diminished the money and price calculus itself will lose much of its falsity.

If, then, in at any rate the foreseeable stages of socialism, the general plan is to allow wages and salaries to be settled on competitive[2] principles and supplemented by State services, what is the practical answer to the question, raised earlier,[3] whether persons should be paid according to their exertions or according to the value of their services? To this question there can be no theoretical answer; for the value of a man's services do not correspond either to his exertions or to his needs. A wealthy surgeon may in ten minutes without much effort save a man's life that nobody else could have saved. The best practical solution seems therefore to be, not to ignore exertions and needs altogether as the free price system does, but first to lay down the principle

[1] Cf. p. 141.
[2] Imperfect competition will still prevent the theoretical 'competitive' wage being discovered. But this injustice can most easily be removed through trade-union pressure and the social services.
[3] Cf. pp. 126-7.

that nobody shall be paid anything who performs no genuine service at all; secondly that over and above this all remuneration shall be adjusted to the value (determined by a reformed price system) of a man's services; and thirdly that all unearned income shall be diverted to provide for the needs of those—and their dependants—whose earnings are insufficient. Such would be the effect of abolishing unearned incomes, paying competitive earned incomes, and supplementing them with comprehensive social services. This general social strategy would at the same time leave unimpaired the delicate economic relation between costs and profits.

Within a framework in which land, labour, and capital costs are fixed in this general way, how should a socialist community determine the production and consumption of goods? How should it determine the quantity to be produced of each commodity and the quantity to be consumed by each consumer? Is it to be left entirely to the free play of incomes and costs already described? In strict logic there are a number of plans which it might adopt. Either the quantities of each commodity to be produced might be determined by the central authority without relation to the costs of production; or they might be determined entirely in accordance with costs; or some commodities might be produced in accordance with costs and others subsidized or taxed. Similarly, the distribution of consumers' goods might be left to the free play of consumers' buying in the open market; or the central authority might retain the whole supply; or it might retain some commodities and not others. And any possible combination of these different methods of production and distribution might in theory be adopted.

In choosing between these possibilities the most crucial issue to be decided is the value of free consumers' choice. Socialists have been inclined to depreciate the value of free consumers' choice for no better reason than that it has been used as a hypocritical defence of the unregulated price system. Complacent defenders of capitalism have emphasized the great importance of allowing the individual to spend his income as he likes, and have omitted to notice that he may have no income to spend. And socialists have rightly retorted that consumers' choice is of no more use to a man who is penniless than liberty to a man who is starving. Gross inequality, in fact, turns consumers' choice into a mockery. But may not the solution be to mitigate inequality rather than to abandon consumers' choice?

No sane man would presumably advocate the entire abolition or the entire acceptance of consumers' choice. There are by general consent certain spheres in which the collective judgement of the community, working through the imperfect but practically effective instrument of Parliament and the Civil Service, are more to be trusted than the unfettered decisions of individuals. We are all agreed that our society would be a worse one if the State did not forcibly save money by taxation and spend it on education and health; or if there was no prohibitive tax on the sale of gin and no embargo on drugs; or if doctors charged all their patients an 'economic' price for their services.[1] If all these things did happen, the intellectual and physical health of the community would degenerate in the direction of savagery under the beneficent influence of the price index. The basis for the unanimous conviction that these things should not be left to the price index is really the kind of value judgement about society as a whole which was argued in chapter iii to be at the root of all such decisions. We all agree that England healthy is better than England sick, and—on the whole—that England free would be worse than England drugged. It is the main contention of this book that exactly the same value judgement can and must be made about comparative needs. If there is an obligation on society to see that poor children should have medicine before a rich man has a cigar, there is an equally binding obligation to see that they should have milk. The orthodox view that one is a moral question and the other merely an 'economic' one rests on a fallacious philosophical view about the quantitative comparability of needs. In fact, where inequality is in question, we are as bound to depart from free consumers' choice as we are in education or health.

Is there any other reason, however, apart from inequality and the social necessity for health, education, etc., to depart from the principle of free consumers' choice? As between two consumers of roughly equal incomes, considering the consumption of say oranges or apples, is there any reason why the central

[1] As Mrs. Joan Robinson has pointed out, it is only because doctors adjust their fees to incomes on the principle of a discriminating monopoly that most of the community get any medical service at all.

authority should intervene? Here the case against intervention is surely overwhelming. It is sometimes forgotten that the 'real income', which may make the difference between happiness and unhappiness, does not consist in just consuming commodities, or even services. It consists in consuming the ones that one likes. To be given white bread or cigarettes when one wants brown bread and chocolate may be quite as great a loss of 'real income' as being given nothing at all. Those who wish to 'plan' everybody's consumption should recall what their feelings are in a restaurant when they order green peas and the waitress brings them onions. For there is no reason to believe that, if *universal* planning of consumption were adopted, the Whitehall authority's idea of planning would approximate any closer to the individual's likes and dislikes than the idea of the waitress. To minimize the value of free consumers' choice is really to show a lack of common human observation. Why is it that workers prefer payment in money to payment in kind? Why is it that children want pocket-money rather than gifts? Why is it that wedding 'presents' usually have to be sold, and Christmas presents are generally no use unless selected by collusion? In neutral circumstances, i.e. when no question of inequality or other moral issue arises, the value of free consumers' choice is almost impossible to overestimate. To a large extent, in these circumstances, it *is* freedom and it *is* happiness. Just as in fact liberty is worthless to a starving man, but of incalculable value to one with just enough to eat; so consumers' choice is worthless to a penniless man, but of incalculable value to one with just enough to live on.

There is an even more fundamental reason for retaining consumers' choice in the case of 'neutral' commodities. For the whole preceding analysis of the nature of free exchange showed that whereas the satisfactions of different consumers are not compared by the price index, the satisfaction obtained by the same consumer from different amounts of different commodities are compared by it. In the case, therefore, of a single consumer choosing between one commodity or another, or of two consumers of similar incomes, the free price system and free consumers' choice remain the best solution.

Surely then the guiding principle on which to plan production and distribution should be to permit the price index to work in all 'neutral' cases, and adjust its working wherever inequality or some other social need makes such adjustment necessary. Many of the social needs other than inequality in the strict sense have already been recognized by the 'planning' of education, justice, and so on. The most pressing necessity at present is consequently for a modification of the price system directly designed to reduce inequality; and socialism, in urging this as the crux of its practical case, is here again right.

How is it to be done? It has already been suggested that all the commodities and services produced in the community can be divided into necessities, luxuries, and neutral goods. To elaborate such a clarification in practice would probably be impossible if any other method was adopted than that of selecting all such goods as are indubitably necessities and luxuries, and classing all the rest as neutral. To draw up an initial list of necessities would not in fact be difficult. A great deal is now known statistically about the distribution of family expenditure; and the invaluable work on food and incomes produced by Sir John Orr and other eminent scientists and statisticians, lays down a standard diet as the ideal necessary for adequate physical health. To the commodities contained in this diet we might add the necessities already mentioned: adequate housing, lighting and heating, water-supply, holidays, and improvements in education and health.

Having compiled such a list, how is the planning authority to proceed? It will still have various alternative strategies before it. It might, of course, simply redistribute money incomes in the form of family allowances, pensions, etc., and trust to luck that working-class housewives would spend the money on 'necessities'. This would be the logical way of diminishing inequality while preserving the maximum of consumers' choice. Unquestionably there must be some redistribution of this kind; but there are at least two powerful arguments against the exclusion of all other methods. First housewives as a whole cannot be trusted to buy all the right things, where nutrition and health are concerned. This is really no more than an extension of the principle according to which the housewife herself would not trust a child of four to select the week's purchases. For in the case of nutrition and health, just as in the case of education, the gentleman in Whitehall really does know better what is good for people than the people know themselves. Secondly, there are almost certainly psychological advantages in effecting redistribution by other methods than actual money transfers from one man's income to another. It has been found in Russia that the man of ability works much better if he is paid a high money income and quietly excluded from certain economic concessions made to the poorer, than if he is paid a salary corresponding to his comparative real income. For one has to admit that in a socialist society—which is not a Utopia but a collection of normally self-seeking human beings—the prestige of money incomes will with the mass of men be great. Let us therefore exploit their semi-sublimated worship of Mammon by ceremoniously paying high salaries with one hand and discreetly taking them away with the other.

The redistribution of money incomes should not, therefore, be the only method of mitigating the inequality of earned incomes. For there are a number of other practicable methods by which the price system can be adjusted in favour of the poorer. By some of these methods the poorer can be induced as well as enabled to consume necessities: and by others they can be compelled. It seems unquestionably best in almost all cases to leave both the production and sale of all neutral goods to the working of the price system. By this means we shall preserve consumers' choice where it is most valuable, and we shall still enjoy the great practical efficiency of the price system. Meanwhile, we can subsidize the production of necessities out of taxes on the production of luxuries. (The discriminating rates of interest and rent suggested in the early part of this chapter are of course a subsidy of this kind). Such subsidies make necessities cheaper and luxuries dearer and so encourage the production and consumption of the former and diminish that of the latter. They are logical and easy methods of adapting the price system; for they gradually transfer productive resources from the luxury to the necessity industries without involving the planners in any impossible decisions about the scale of production of every commodity in every year. This scheme has already been adopted on a very large scale by the Russian planners, and is surely certain to figure largely in the economic mechanism of future socialist states. The danger of the subsidy and tax method is that subsidies might be exploited by private monopolists who refused to reduce prices. It will be argued in the next chapter, however, that completely uncontrolled private monopolists must not be allowed to survive.

Although in these circumstances most producers would still be working for profit according to the price index, and although consumers would be buying in a free market, powerful economic forces under the control of the central authority would be operating to mitigate inequality. The cumulative effect of the abolition of inherited incomes, the taxation of high unearned incomes, and the subsidizing of the production of necessities through the imposition of the various charges already enumerated on the production of luxuries, would be a rapid redistribution of real incomes throughout the community. Land, labour, and capital would be smoothly but surely transferred, under the immediate influence of the now socially guided price system, from the trades producing luxuries into the trades producing necessities. For, as a result of the various redistributive measures affecting both costs and demand, production in the latter trades would become more profitable and in the former less profitable. A second great advance towards the removal of inequality and poverty would thus have been made.

CHAPTER XXXI

MONOPOLY AND COMPETITION

Is it possible or desirable to proceed to a third instalment of socialism? By the second instalment, just discussed, a system of discriminating rents and interest charges and of taxes and bounties would be introduced to supplement the suppression of unearned incomes contained in the first instalment. This system of discrimination and subsidy, like the suppression of unearned incomes, could proceed gradually and would not dislocate the price mechanism or lead to monetary disequilibrium. But it would once again powerfully and permanently reinforce the economic factors making for a mitigation of inequality. It would tend cumulatively to harness the forces of enterprise as well as work and saving for the benefit of the poorer rather than the richer sections of the community. And such a system can be conceived as working in an economy in which the actual productive units are managed by private entrepreneurs working for 'profit', though the bulk of the dividends would naturally accrue to the State. Here, then, is a second logical stopping-place in the road away from inequality; and those who are disposed to go no farther may at least perhaps be willing to come as far as this. They may encourage themselves with the thought that socialism, so far, means little interference with private enterprise, free consumers' choice, the structure of earned incomes, or the interest of the small saver.

Nevertheless, there is a strong case for going substantially farther. In the first place the measures so far introduced are measures of ownership rather than control, and they will consequently tend to diminish poverty and inequality but to leave insecurity comparatively untouched, except in so far as it is indirectly diminished by the diminution of poverty. The crucial form of insecurity is of course the threat of unemployment; and the whole preceding discussion of money and the trade cycle is designed to show that the cure of unemployment is in the long run a matter of monetary policy. Monetary control, therefore, has been already accepted as necessary; and it must be 'monetary control' interpreted in the widest sense. It must include, that is to say, not merely nationalization of the banks but direct public control of investment and of the whole range of public works. There should be, as has been suggested, a public authority, which should keep a permanent reserve of work schemes and should always be prepared to employ at trade-union rates any man ready and willing to work.

1. Security and Public Control

Should this control be extended to the actual producing units themselves, to the 'nationalization', that is to say, of industry, commerce, and trade? It will be observed that 'nationalization', which has commonly been regarded as the essence of socialism, really appears at a very late stage of the argument. First, it has not always been realized that, without confiscation, practically no redistribution of incomes can be achieved; and, secondly, control seems simply to have been confused with ownership.[1] Some socialist writers on 'planning' seem to forget that a series of State-instituted monopolies could easily be set up, and their whole profit and interest earnings allowed to accrue to private shareholders.[2]

The real case for at least some measure of nationalization or control rests on two main arguments: the need to provide security of employment and the already established existence of private capitalist monopolies. What, fundamentally, does 'control' of the producer mean? It means that the producer is to be induced to recognize other aims and conditions than the mere maximization of profit. For if it is simply desired that the entrepreneurs should maximize their profit without regard for any-

[1] Many socialists are quite properly influenced in their desire for nationalization by their desire to break the political power that the ownership of industry gives to capitalist interests. This argument, however, is relevant to the question of political strategy and not to the case for socialism itself, and is consequently outside the scope of this book.

[2] Indeed, such an economic system, supplemented by corruption, nepotism, and intimidation, is the substance of what is nowadays called the 'Corporative State'.

thing else whatever, and pay the highest dividend possible to the State as shareholder, there is clearly no reason for instituting any further 'control'. In fact, however, it is just the *unrestrained* search for profits by every entrepreneur all over the system which, though it works in a sense for 'economic progress', leads to the extreme uncertainty of employment which is one of the major curses of private capitalism. A mere empirical glance around the system is enough to show that not merely in the Civil Service itself, or in those industries which have attained the status of public utilities, but even in the great private monopolies and semi-monopolies there are far greater security and far better conditions of employment. The supervision of working conditions, the enforcement of union rates and regulations, the limitation of overtime, and the provision of paid holidays are always the more likely to be found the more highly is an industry 'integrated' and the more closely is it supervised by the State. Nobody doubts that in Great Britain, for instance, a railwayman, or even an employee of Imperial Chemical Industries, is far better off in all these ways than a dock labourer or even a South Wales miner. A British railwayman may be comparatively sure that if he does his job well he will retain it as long as he likes.[1] And it is just those conditions of employment, including above all security, which may make almost the whole difference between a tolerable and an intolerable life. There is thus a strong *prima facie* argument for public supervision of working conditions. To some extent, of course, this can be achieved by the traditional method of factory legislation; but circumstances vary so multifariously from industry to industry and evasions and equivocations are so common, that factory legislation is not nearly so effective as is sometimes supposed.[2] The case for direct supervision of working conditions, where possible industry by industry, conducted by employers, employees, and the State in collaboration is consequently overwhelming. Factory legislation and the social services alone are not felt by the worker to be enough. State supervision, however, if it goes beyond mere fac-

[1] The same cannot apparently be said of an employee of the B.B.C.

[2] How many people outside the working classes realize that there is no legal limit on the hours of work of the great bulk of adult male workers in Great Britain? It is true that this is due to a weakness in the law rather than to the method of legislation. But the difficulty of regulating working hours universally by law alone is very great in a system of private enterprise.

tory legislation, almost inevitably implies the grant of monopoly privileges. For not only will the entrepreneur who is requested voluntarily to sacrifice profits ask in the transition period for some privileges in return; but effective control will be very difficult to administer in industries divided into numbers of competing firms. It would be possible in theory for the State to set up legally enforcible codes of fair competition which otherwise uncontrolled employers would be expected to observe. This logical extension of the principle of factory legislation was tried by Mr. Roosevelt in his famous N.R.A. plan. It failed, however, in fact long before it was declared unconstitutional, because the sheer practical difficulty of drawing up and enforcing separate detailed codes for *thousands* of different industries proved to be well beyond the wit of administrative man.[1] Again, it would be theoretically possible for the State to assume control of a number of small competing firms in an industry, and to enforce decent working conditions, while continuing as it were to compete against itself. It is hard to believe, however, that such a plan could be carried very far in practice; though it need not be assumed that nothing useful can be done by these two methods.

The case that can be made for the establishment of public monopolies on the ground of security is, however, even stronger than this. It is derived not merely from the necessity for individual security against employment, but from the need for a general monetary policy designed to cure cyclical unemployment. For if the central economic authority has the power even temporarily to suspend the working of the profit motive over certain sections of industry, its ability to overcome the trade cycle will be enormously enhanced. Suppose, for instance, that for some sudden and unpredictable reason Total Effective Demand fell below Total Costs, and the deflationary spiral was threatening to get under way before the corrective forces of interest rates, public works, deficit financing, and so forth could be marshalled in resistance. In these circumstances, if the central authority could enforce a large section of industry not to dismiss men, but to continue working at a loss with the financial assistance of the State, the situation might quite conceivably be saved. For it is just the dismissal of men and the consequent destruction of incomes which converts the original emergence

[1] Cf. E. M. Hugh Jones and E. A. Radice, *An American Experiment*, ch. iv.

of losses in the capital trades into an overwhelming deflationary avalanche. If men were kept on, even in one section of industry, and their incomes were maintained by the financing of losses, the avalanche might never begin, the losses themselves might very soon disappear, and the State's advances to the industry in question might then be easily repaid. Such a plan, however, would be impossible in a world of completely uncontrolled competing producers. For the sudden grant of discriminating loans or subsidies might raise insoluble problems of personal influence and rivalry among jealous vested interests.[1] Here, therefore, is at least one important way—and there are many others—in which the existence of a State-controlled section of industry would assist the monetary authorities in their all-important campaign against unemployment.

2. *Monopoly Dangers*

Such is the argument from security in favour of monopoly. The second argument—superficially the argument from efficiency—proves on analysis to be really based on the already widespread existence of private capitalist monopolies. The significance of this argument perhaps emerges most clearly if it is allowed to develop out of a criticism of the orthodox case against monopoly. The orthodox case is extremely strong; and here again it would be best if socialists honestly admitted it. It is in the main a twofold case. First it makes the practical point that monopolists draw a monopoly revenue and consequently exploit the public. This point can easily be met by the reply that in the socialist community the State will be rapidly becoming the only shareholder, and the monopoly revenue will therefore be distributed in social services—and that public monopolies will only be allowed to make limited profits.

The second fundamental argument[2] against monopoly, however, needs far more detailed consideration. To begin with, what is a monopoly? Socialists are sometimes inclined to avoid the issue and the word, and to fall back upon some dangerous

[1] The case of the taxes and subsidies proposed in the last chapter would be quite different. For they would be permanent: and would be offered not to individual firms and trades, but to the producers of certain commodities as such. They would resemble the existing system of indirect taxation and turnover taxes.

[2] The argument is fairly stated in the last chapter, by Professor Hayek, of *Collectivist Economic Planning*.

euphemism such as 'co-ordination' or 'integration', thus paying a hypocritical if unconscious tribute to the virtues of competition. Mr. Herbert Morrison,[1] however, firmly grasps the nettle. 'Once we have decided', he says, 'upon single undivided consolidated ownership, we have also committed ourselves to the economic doctrine of monopoly.' Monopoly means the control of the whole supply of a commodity by a single producing unit; it implies the consequent possession by the monopolist of the power to decide output and price; and it may involve the forcible prevention of outside individuals from entering the trade. It will normally be in the interest of a private monopolist to restrict the supply, and raise the price, beyond the point that would be reached under free competition. For under competition, as long as it is possible to increase the supply without bringing the price below the point at which the entrepreneur can no longer earn what he considers a fair return, either the existing producers or a new producer will see that supply is increased. Production, in fact, will be increased up to the point at which the costs of producing one more unit are only just covered by price, after which it no longer pays to produce another unit. The monopolist, however, or any producer working in conditions of imperfect competition, will only push production to the point at which the additional revenue derived from producing one extra unit covers the additional cost; and this point, as has been pointed out in chapter x, will normally be at a lower level of production than that of competitive equilibrium. Moreover, at this point average costs will normally be below price; and the monopolist will consequently both restrict production and earn a monopoly revenue at the expense of the consumer. He will also, as we have seen, normally exploit the wage-earner. Of course, it may be that the economies due to unification and large-scale production are so great that even if the monopolist is earning his full monopoly revenue, output may still be greater, and prices lower than under competition. But this will not always be so; and even when it is so, prices will normally be higher and output lower under a private monopoly than they otherwise might be. If, therefore, a number of monopolies are introduced all over the economic system, there will almost certainly be a general restriction of production.

[1] *Socialization and Transport*, p. 77.

Nor is this possibility a mere figment of the theoretical economist's imagination. There is nothing so grimly real or universally attested by experience as the tendency of the producers of any commodity to get together, to restrict production, to raise prices, and to extract a monopoly profit from the public. To organize such a conspiracy has been almost the first instinct of all producers throughout history, from the days of the guild to those of the 'Corporative State'. If anybody doubts this, they should ask themselves what the word 'regulation' means when used by the organizers of economic combines. It means, of course, restriction;[1] though the use of the polite word 'regulation' again shows that the monopolists are slightly ashamed of what they are really doing. Nobody ever yet heard of the producers of a commodity collaborating to increase the total output. There are, of course, occasions when restriction of the output of a particular commodity is justifiable; but each occasion requires its specific justification. It also sometimes happens that a *de facto* monopoly, as in the British rayon industry, deliberately keeps the price very low in order to restrain new producers entering the trade; though this is really little more than a proof of the danger of converting a *de facto* monopoly into a *de jure* one. And in general it remains true that private bodies which combine to 'regulate' production are, whatever high-sounding names they give themselves, in fact monopolies; and their object is to restrict production.

Secondly, though potential large-scale economies may exist, a monopoly cannot be relied upon to reduce costs to the lowest possible point. In the absence of the spur of competition a producer may be able to earn a comfortable monopoly revenue while allowing his costs to remain a long way below the level of real efficiency. Indeed, he may be able to point to the excellent technical condition of his plant, to protest the narrow margin of his profits, and to claim that he has never raised prices. Yet there may be enormous potential economies to be made which would have permitted a substantial reduction of

1 A salutary example is the scandalous and tragic history of the Jarrow steel-works scheme. Here the newly instituted British Iron and Steel Federation used its monopoly powers in the interest of the Tees companies' shareholders to prevent the erection of a modern plant that might have brought work to a Tyneside town with 75 per cent unemployment. Cf. *The Economist*, 18 July 1936.

price and increase of output. Indeed, the monopolist may in all good faith believe that he is working at the lowest level of costs possible; because, as has already been pointed out, if there is no competition, it may be impossible to know what that level really is. In order to illustrate the reality of this problem, and at the same time to give the anti-socialist case its full weight, the example of the British railways may perhaps be quoted. Immediately after the war the railways were amalgamated into four groups, but were left, with certain limitations, in private hands. Until 1929 they continued to earn modest profits; they presented a general appearance of efficiency; and they did not raise their fares or rates. After 1929, however, under the combined influence of road competition and cyclical depression, the railways were threatened with the possibility of not being able to pay their fixed-interest costs. A drastic campaign of cost reduction was therefore undertaken; and after four years a total of £4,000,000 to £5,000,000 over the four main groups was saved in operating costs. Moreover, these reductions consisted in the main not of wage reductions but of improvements in technique and organization—in a word, in the elimination of waste.[1] As a result large reductions in fares were made which gave the benefit of cheap transport to a wider section of the public; and as the railwaymen were organized in a powerful union, almost the whole loss resulting from road competition fell in a most salutary way on the ordinary and preference shareholders.[2] Now it can very plausibly be argued that if the railways had been 'unified' and nationalized in 1921 the State would have had to bear a huge loss from 1929 onwards, drastic legislation would have been passed to restrict road transport, and fares would never have been reduced. At any rate this is what has happened in a great many other countries.

[1] The average time, for instance, spent by locomotive and rolling stock standing in idleness was reduced; and innumerable similar economies made. Some of these, but not all, were of course the delayed effect of the post-war amalgamation.

[2] This succession of events recalls and confirms the remark made by Marshall in discussing the comparative effects of railway monopoly and inter-railway competition: 'Human nature being what it is, experience has shown that the breaking of a monopoly by the opening out of a competing line accelerates rather than retards the discovery by the older line that it can afford to carry traffic at lower rates.' *Principles of Economics*, seventh edition, p. 485.

There is thus a very real danger that even State-controlled monopolies[1] may restrict production and fail to reduce costs. It is not so much that the State trust will actually reduce production below what it was before, or raise prices above, but that it will fail to expand production and reduce costs and prices to the new levels that are from time to time made possible by the progress of knowledge and technique. There will be a tendency for the various monopolies to settle down at existing levels of prices and costs, which will reflect differing but incalculable degrees of inefficiency and monopoly extortion. A serious element of arbitrariness and indeterminacy as well as inefficiency may thus be introduced into the whole economy.

3. *Large-Scale Economies*

The case against monopolies as such is accordingly strong. And against any proposal to monopolize the whole of industry it is perhaps conclusive. Indeed, it would be conclusive against the creation or toleration of almost any monopoly in a socialist State were it not for two vitally important and complementary facts: the already established existence of monopolies under capitalism and the economies of large-scale production. These two facts are complementary because in many cases the existence of large-scale economies causes, and indeed necessitates, the eventual development of monopoly. It is now a commonplace that in modern manufacturing industries the technical economies of large-scale output, 'rationalization', single management, centralized research, selling, etc., tend to produce very large business units. And if these economies, or 'decreasing costs', still continue with increases in output up to the point at which the whole supply can be provided by a single firm, there is naturally a tendency towards monopoly.

It must not be assumed, however, to be either likely or desirable that this tendency should embrace the whole of industry. Even in the great manufacturing industries there are undoubtedly very many cases where after a point the colossal unit becomes unwieldy and dis-economies of large-scale production

[1] It need hardly be said that uncontrolled private monopolies are, with rare exceptions, indefensible abuses. Socialists should be on their guard against such vicious proposals when advanced by well-meaning 'planners' such as Mr. Harold Macmillan under the guise of 'self-government for industry' and so forth.

begin to set in. The problem of organization becomes impossible; no entrepreneur can be found with sufficiently outstanding ability; and size actually becomes the cause of inefficiency and waste. There is the well-known story of the individual who made a living by buying a commodity from one branch of a great British combine and selling it to another branch at a profit. Indeed, there appear to be not very many examples in the actual business world of whole industries which have become monopolized by the fact of decreasing costs. The chemical industry in most of the large industrial countries seem certainly to approach monopoly; and the rayon industry in Great Britain has also come near to it. Other great manufacturing industries, however, such as iron and steel, engineering, cement, and motor-cars, seem inclined to develop into a group of a few large firms—as if the enormous economies of large-scale production began to evaporate or become negative just short of the monopoly point. For it is necessary to distinguish very clearly between those industries like cement, oil, and flour-milling in Great Britain which have reached more or less formal price agreements between separate firms, and genuinely unified productive units exploiting large-scale economies. In addition there are, of course, innumerable trades, such as book-publishing, farming, most forms of retail distribution, the clothing trades and so forth, where there is very little evidence that large-scale production would bring substantial economies.

Moreover, as Mrs. Robinson has shown,[1] even where economies of size are so far-reaching as to produce monopoly, this is only because, owing to imperfections in the market—custom, convention, lack of knowledge, etc.—monopoly is the only way of achieving in practice what perfect competition should produce in theory. In effect, since perfect competition does not exist in the real world, we are in these cases confronted with the alternatives of monopoly on the one hand or imperfect competition involving chronic waste and surplus capacity on the other. This introduces us to a second class of industry, which from a practical point of view is extremely important. There are certain industries suffering from chronic imperfect competition and surplus capacity; these industries would in theory be made efficient by the introduction of perfect competition, but in practice it can

---

[1] Cf. *Economics of Imperfect Competition*, ch. xiv.

only be done by monopolization. But at the same time they show no tendency to become monopolies of their own accord. It is probable that the British cotton and coal industries are of this kind. There is no question that concentration in larger units would reduce costs and eliminate surplus capacity; yet little if any progress towards such unification has occurred for a very long time as the result of ordinary business motives. Hence, therefore, there is perhaps a case for deliberate Government action to create a monopoly; though even here it should be observed that larger units, and not actual monopolies, might very likely be the most efficient. Moreover, it would again be extremely dangerous to argue from this special case to the whole of industry, as both socialists and non-socialists have tended to do.[1]

Far the commonest class of actually existing monopolies, however, are again of a different kind.[2] They are industries in which monopoly is inevitable, or practically inevitable, for technical or physical reasons. 'In some industries,' as Mrs. Robinson says,[3] 'of which railways and the distribution of gas and electricity are familiar examples, the smallest practicable plant has a very large capacity output, and if the market is not sufficiently large to use one plant up to capacity there is no possibility of competition.' In the gas and electricity industries, for instance, the producers' fixed plant is actually geographically extended to every consumer. In this case any attempt at competition is almost bound to be hopelessly uneconomic. The same is clearly true of various forms of transport; and Mr. Herbert Morrison's convincing chapters iv and v in his *Socialization and Transport*, demonstrating the necessity for unification of London's passenger services, are really ultimately based on an appeal to the fact that congestion and chaos in the streets would result from free competition in London transport.

Here, once again, however, it is misleading to argue from the special case to industry in general; and this at times Mr. Morrison seems inclined to do. It is true that he says (page 137): 'The organization I propose for transport, and which I might urge in principle for other undertakings of a predominantly business or

[1] Cf. again Harold Macmillan, *Reconstruction*.
[2] Though fundamentally they are a special case of industries with indefinitely 'decreasing costs'.
[3] *The Economics of Imperfect Competition*, p. 168.

commercial character, must not be regarded as a pattern to be applied universally to all industries and services.' But some incautious readers may get the impression that Mr. Morrison has proved 'co-ordination' to be more 'efficient' than 'competition' in the case of London Transport, and that it consequently is so in other cases—particularly when he goes on to discuss 'the management of socialized industries,' and the 'benefits of socialization' (pp. 284-5). In fact, if we propose to monopolize an industry we have to show good reasons for supposing that it will be more efficient in a monopoly form than in any other. The essential point is that the need for the nationalization of a given industry must not be based on the need for redistributing the national income—for this nationalization cannot in the main achieve—but on a reconciliation of the need for security with the need for establishing the most efficient productive units. According to this criterion there are perhaps three general classes of industry where a strong *prima facie* case for supposing this will exist. First there are the industries which have indubitably become, or are becoming, monopolies under the influence of a continued tendency for average costs to fall with increasing output. Secondly, there are the industries which for physical or technical reasons do not admit of competition. In both these cases monopoly is both practically inevitable, in that competition cannot permanently survive, and desirable, in that unified control is bound to lead to increased efficiency. Here the need is to recognize the existence of monopoly, and to ensure that it does not remain in private hands. But again the mere existence of a monopoly or cartel in an industry does not prove that it belongs to either of these classes; it may be a mere anti-social price-raising agreement, only to be justified if there is a special case for ensuring the security of labour in the industry. Thirdly, there are those industries in which imperfect competition maintains surplus capacity and waste, but in which no automatic movement towards monopoly is discernible. Here, in turn, the need may be for an actual creation of public monopoly.

4. *What Should We Nationalize?*

There are, of course, other than purely economic reasons for nationalizing certain industries. The armament industry, for instance, ought to be nationalized because it is a menace to peace; and the banking system ought to be nationalized because it has the power to create money and is an essential instrument of monetary policy. These industries, and others, are 'specially affected with the public interest'. But the three classes of industry just described seem to be those in which the specifically economic case for unification is most conclusive. And though the argument is not always expressed in this threefold form, the actual strategy of nationalization currently proposed, for instance, in Great Britain seems to be in harmony with it. The official Immediate Programme of the British Labour Party puts finance, transport, and power at the top of the list. Mr. Hugh Dalton in his book *Practical Socialism for Britain* discusses, in the following order, broadcasting, electricity, transport, coal and its products, iron and steel, shipbuilding, cotton, engineering, textiles, flour-milling, and some other industries.[1] Again the authors of the 'non-party' programme, *The Next Five Years*, propose four different forms of public supervision and control. In the first category they place 'that minority of industries where real and permanent over-capacity exists and where consequently some reduction of the capital equipment of the industry can be justified', including coal, cotton, iron and steel, and shipbuilding. In the second and third are placed 'industries which do not require reorganization as do the depressed industries, and which the State is not prepared to take over, but over which it wishes to exercise a close control'. The second category includes industries which are already virtual monopolies, and the third industries 'peculiarly affected with the public interest', such as banking and insurance. For the second category, or 'public concerns', 'the utmost publicity for accounts and operations is recommended', and for the third category of 'public utilities', including gas and electricity supply, 'conditions as to publicity of accounts, limitation of profits, fixation of charges by a public tribunal, etc.' The fourth category, including transport, electricity supply,[2] some forms of insurance, the manufacture of armaments, etc., is claimed as 'suitable for complete socialization'. It is not the purpose of this book to apply the fundamental case for socialism to the conditions of particular

---

[1] The banks are considered in a separate section.

[2] Perhaps as the result of an oversight, *The Next Five Years* places electricity supply in both the third and fourth categories.

countries; but a mere glance at the Stock Exchange columns of the newspapers will show that a proposal to nationalize all the industries which have achieved and are approaching monopoly would affect, in Great Britain the railways, road transport, banking, iron and steel, electricity and gas, chemicals, sugar-refining, milk distribution, a section of the heavy industries, oil distribution, tobacco, and perhaps cement, bricks, rayon, and many other industries.

If unification on economic grounds is to be confined in the first instance to the industries in the three classes specified above, what is to be the position of other industries in the socialized State? Are the workers in those industries to be denied the benefits of security of employment, better working conditions, etc., just because there is no economic case for unifying those industries? Or may it not be that the social case for nationalizing them is conclusive, on grounds of security, etc., though the economic case for unifying them is not?

First it must be admitted that there is a very large class of industries to which nationalization would only be appropriate at a very late stage, if ever. This class includes very small, very speculative, and completely new trades. It has always been recognized that nationalization would cause the maximum amount of difficulty and do the minimum amount of good in the case of one-man or other very small businesses. To nationalize every taxi-driver, every bookmaker, every hawker, every village shop, or every garage would on the one hand contribute nothing to the redistribution of the national income, and on the other raise formidable and probably insuperable problems of organization. Nor can the central authorities normally undertake the organization of speculative ventures or the exploitation of new ideas. The essential factor in the readiness to undertake such ventures is the desire to make very large profits and the willingness to risk large losses. And the central authority would almost certainly be very unwilling to risk large losses and not particularly anxious to make large profits. The State will bear some risk through its holding of the ordinary shares of old-established companies; but it cannot well undertake such highly speculative risks as these.

Yet one of the most real of all the dangers of socialism— much more real than the alleged discouraging effects of taxation—is the danger of discouraging the undertaking of speculative risks. For it is essential to the maintenance and advance of the standard of living that such projects should be undertaken. It is essential that there should be a speculative sector, as it were, of the national economy, where the riskier types of entrepreneurs are perpetually trying out new ideas, testing potential demands, and generally tapping all the unsuspected ways in which demand and supply can be brought together. For many of the greatest industries grow out of such beginnings. The sort of economy contemplated in the foregoing argument would permit the operation of such entrepreneurs. They would be able to raise capital, either by saving out of their own earned incomes, borrowing privately within the limits set by the State monopoly of the capital market, or borrowing from the banks, which would normally be guided by ordinary principles of 'credit worthiness'. They would then, within the framework of existing labour legislation, and of a structure of money incomes now much more faithfully representing real needs, be able to earn within their lifetime a high earned income, to pay a great deal of it to the State in direct taxation, and to forfeit almost the whole of the accrued capital, including the shares in the business, at death. There would be nothing, in fact, in such conditions to prevent the community from tapping those of the services of a Lord Nuffield which would indubitably be valuable to it; though he would not be permitted to found a dynasty of rentiers who would live on the services of their fellow men to the last syllable of recorded time.

Such new, small, and speculative ventures would accordingly be left un-nationalized unless and until they had proved their worth and the shares consequently began to pass in the ordinary way through inheritance-taxation into the hands of the State. For this is the extreme case where too little security could be bought for too great a loss of progress if rigid control in the interests of security of employment were imposed. Labour in these industries would accordingly have to be taken care of by the social services, the ordinary labour legislation, the general monetary campaign against unemployment, and by all the fundamental egalitarian measures described in the previous chapter.

There is still another and important class of industries, however: those which are neither monopolies nor potential monopolies on the one hand, nor small and speculative ventures on the other. This would include such established but not unified industries as the motor-car trade, branches of the textile and engineering trades, and certain distributive firms. Here we have well-established large-scale firms, likely to endure, but no evidence that further unification would promote real economies— though probably some of the evils of imperfect competition are inherent in them. Would it be possible in these instances to institute some form of public control? To set up actually competing public corporations seems, as has already been suggested, hardly practicable. Would new private firms be allowed to come into the industry and drive the public corporations out of business? And if they were not allowed, would not the industry be saddled with all the disadvantages of vested monopolies without any of the economies of unified control? And if, instead, the existing private firms were to be forced to undertake special responsibilities for labour conditions, accounts, etc., over and above those legally enjoined on all trades whatever, they could fairly ask to be given monopoly privileges in return. To grant such privileges, however, would be to incur still more of the disadvantages without the advantages of monopoly. This intermediate and very numerous class of industries seems to be a case where it is hard to say whether public control as well as public ownership is desirable. It may be that the problem will be solved along the lines of 'public concerns' and 'public utilities' proposed by the 'Next Five Years Group'.[1] But exactly how much control should be extended to exactly which of these industries, is not really a question of principle. In so far as it is possible to obtain greater security of employment, limitation of profits, financial publicity, etc., without ossifying an industry and creating vested interests, there will always be a strong case for doing so. And there will be two particular concessions besides monopoly in return for which a socialist State will be able to demand these safeguards. First it is one of the secondary benefits of the system of permanent subsidies and taxes already discussed that though their prime object is to readjust production to needs, the subsidies can be withheld from producers who do not conform to those standards of labour laid down by the State for

[1] Cf. chapter, 'The Organization of Industry'. Also Hugh Dalton, *Practical Socialism for Britain*, ch. x, 'Forms of Socialism'.

these particular circumstances. Subsidies normally granted to an industry, for instance, could be refused to individual firms who employed non-union labour. Secondly, in so far as tariff protection is granted to an industry, similar concessions should be demanded in return.

It is also probable that the co-operative movement may help to solve the problems of this intermediate class of industry which it is undesirable to monopolize. The co-operative movement is certain to be of growing importance—at any rate in the distributive trades. And though it provides reasonable conditions and security of labour and does not pay dividends to large shareholders, it is nevertheless well fitted, though itself monopolistic in organization, to compete with ordinary private firms. Its encouragement may consequently be the best method of developing social control in the intermediate trades without creating cast-iron monopolies.

If it is agreed that at least three classes of industries—those already monopolized by the fact of large-scale economies, those technically incapable of competition, and those suffering from chronic over-capacity—ought to become or remain monopolies, there are two crucial questions still to answer. What form are these monopolies to take? And how do we wish them to behave?

In answer to the first question little need be said here. It is clear that if there are to be monopolies they must be public monopolies. In return[1] for the granting of monopoly privileges we must see that the monopoly revenue is limited or accrues to the State, and that security of employment, shorter hours, trade-union recognition, publicity for accounts, and so forth are achieved. Marshall (*Principles of Economics*, book V, chapter iv) discussed the problem of monopoly largely in terms of a balancing of the advantages of large-scale economies against the disadvantage of monopoly profits. The public monopoly at least secures the best of both worlds here. Further, it is now agreed by practically all socialists and radicals that the best organization of a public monopoly is not the Government department but the public corporation or board; the Port of London Authority, the B.B.C., and London Transport are oft-quoted

---

[1] It may be recalled that the London Underground combine, although it already held something approaching a monopoly, was extremely glad to have it made legally watertight. The 'pirate buses' were few but exasperating.

examples. The arguments for the public board as against the Government department are conclusively stated by Mr. Herbert Morrison in chapters viii and ix ('The Management of Socialized Industries' and the 'Public Corporation') of his *Socialization and Transport*; and nothing of substance remains to be added.[1] The essence of the argument is that business ability is a specific quality, and business organization a specific form, which are appropriate and necessary to the satisfactory management of a business. By the public corporation is consequently meant a single productive unit, organized on business lines, and owned perhaps in some degrees by private shareholders, but managed by a board of business men appointed by a body responsible to the State. The details may of course be varied according to circumstances; but such is the essential pattern.

5. *How Should Public Boards Behave?*

More fundamental, however, in the long run, and more relevant to the basic case for socialism, is the question how we want our public monopolies to behave. On what principle are our public boards to decide the volume of output and the level of prices? This question is fairly asked by Professor Hayek,[2] and it is much more real and more difficult than is apparently sometimes supposed. First of all Professor Hayek asks if we can be sure that a public board will feel the same responsibility and personal interest in the concern as an entrepreneur who is himself a shareholder or responsible to private shareholders. It is true that the motive of personal responsibility and ownership has been one of the most powerful incentives to business efforts; as for instance in the case of the Lancashire cotton kings who worked sixteen hours a day and regarded their businesses with the fanatical egotism that springs from a combination of personal possession and creative pride. But this nevertheless does not seem to be a serious defect in the public corporations. It is not apparent why Lord Ashfield's concern for his business should be less now than when it was a private combine. Moreover, there is no reason why the public directors should not be paid

---

[1] Mr. Hugh Dalton, *Practical Socialism for Britain*, ch. x, and the 'Next Five Year Group' are in substantial agreement with him (*Next Five Years*, ch. iv).

[2] Cf. the last chapter of *Collectivist Economic Planning*.

partly a small percentage of the profits, nor why they should not hold a few of the ordinary shares not yet held by the State.

It is much more difficult, however, to say how the directors are actually to manage the concern. Superficially and in the short run, it seems that they can simply be instructed to conduct the business efficiently, to reduce costs and prices where possible without reducing wages, to pay not more than a 5 per cent dividend even to the Exchequer, and so forth. We may even instruct them to consult the 'public good' or to 'serve the public', or to seek 'social need' rather than 'private profit'. But when these phrases are more closely analysed, they can be seen to be little more than phrases. Would it be to the public good to reduce prices by so much, and therefore profits by so much, or to reduce them so far as to wipe out profits altogether, or to raise them in order to pay a higher monopoly revenue to the State as shareholder? The busmen's strike of 1937 against the London Transport Board showed that these are very real questions. Moreover, if a public board is making high profits, how is one to tell whether this is due to greater efficiency or to greater monopoly extortion or to the fact that the demand for its services is growing? And if it begins to make losses, how is one to tell whether this is because it has become inefficient, or because it is charging very low prices, or because the demand for its products is shrinking? What, in fact, is to prevent the monopoly being cautious, unenterprising, and inefficient, yet maintaining a modest level of profits by charging full monopoly prices? Might not the British railways, if nationalized in 1921, have maintained high fares, done little to reduce costs, complained after 1929 that they were being ruined by 'unfair' road competition, and that the State must reduce this competition or pay the losses? Is there any answer to these questions? And if there is not, will not the effect of the introduction of public monopolies be to distort the working of the price system, to interfere with the adjustment of resources to demand, to impede technical progress, and so to retard the natural increase in production all over the system?

It is the conclusion of the whole foregoing argument of this book that though the unregulated price index in present circumstances is a false guide to real wants and needs, nevertheless when the social and economic conditions of inequality have been altered, the price and profit index remains, at least where 'neutral'[1] goods are concerned, the best practical guide in any given circumstances. The price index must therefore be taken into account in drawing up the general principles according to which the directors of public boards are to act. Remembering, accordingly, that the profits are being paid increasingly to the State and that incomes have become far less unequal, would it be correct to instruct the public monopolies in general so to plan their production and prices, within the framework of the labour standards and so forth enjoined on them, as to make the largest possible profits? Whether or not this is the best theoretical policy, it is certainly not the best practical one. For it would perpetuate monopoly revenues and monopoly restrictions over a large part of the system. Theoretically, these monopolistic abuses could be prevented, and the ideal output indicated, by one of several policies. It would be theoretically possible to instruct the monopolists to seek the maximum profits and to devise a system of taxes and bounties which would ensure that the output would be the correct one. But the devising of the taxes and subsidies would only be possible, as Mr. J. E. Meade points out,[2] if the various entrepreneurs' estimates of the 'marginal productivity' of their workers and plant were known to the public authority. These estimates, however, depend on technical and local knowledge, and they are continually changing. It would consequently be quite impossible, as Mr. Meade argues, for a system of taxes and bounties of this kind to be devised in practice.

Secondly, it would be theoretically possible for the central authority to prevent monopolistic abuses by enforcing minimum prices and maximum wages on the monopolists, and enjoining them within these limits to earn the maximum profits. The fact of monopoly, or imperfect competition, enables the producer to charge higher prices and pay lower wages than he would in competitive conditions. In theory, therefore, if he was compelled by the authorities to pay the wages and charge the prices that would be established by competition, he could then be safely instructed to earn the maximum profit. Here again, however, it seems certainly impossible in practice that such wages and prices could be enforced simply because they could not be

---

[1] i.e. neither necessities nor luxuries.
[2] Cf. *An Introduction to Economic Analysis and Policy*, part II, ch. vii.

known. The correct wages and prices would be for ever changing, and it is inconceivable that any central authority could calculate them even in the case of a single industry.

Both the above methods, however, are really devised for application to *private* monopolies. On the assumption that monopolists must seek the aim of maximum profits, they are the only methods of securing the correct output. The advantage of socializing monopolies is precisely that if necessary other instructions can be given them. Mr. E. F. M. Durbin[1] argues that the correct instructions should be as follows. The various socialist trusts (and such private producers, if any, as survive) will be competing in the market for land, labour, and capital; so there will be a price for these factors of production and the trust will consequently be able to calculate its costs. Since it is a monopoly, however, as a seller of its product, the price of its product will depend on the amount that it sells. In these circumstances, Mr. Durbin argues, the correct procedure would be to estimate the average cost of producing different amounts of the commodity with various sizes of plant, to estimate the demand at various prices, and to choose the size and output at which the demand coincided with the output producible at the lowest average cost.[2] At this level of output the firm would be earning a normal profit, but not a monopoly revenue or therefore maximum profit.

Naturally, the exact method of determining the ideal output for a socialist monopoly is a technical question of economic theory. The essential point is that an intelligible answer can be given to the question, and a rational policy consequently enjoined upon the socialist producers. It is also evident that the calculations necessary to make the estimates required for this policy will not present very great practical difficulties. Estimates of the average costs involved in varying levels of output are naturally made by ordinary capitalist firms every day; and estimates of demand at varying prices can be made within certain limits of error. Of course, if the directors of the public board

[1] Economic Calculus in a Planned Economy, *Economic Journal*, December 1936; also J. E. Meade, *Economic Analysis and Policy*, part II, ch. viii. See also *The Economic System in a Socialist State*, by R. L. Hall, for a full discussion of the same problem.

[2] For the details of this argument see *Economic Journal*, December 1936, pp. 680–2.

were being paid a share of the profits, they might tend to draw up estimates of average costs which were deliberately framed up to justify a level of output which was really monopolistic. The only safeguard against this would be to appoint the right sort of managers or else, perhaps, to pay them a fixed salary only. Exactly how practicable it would be to enjoin instructions of this kind on socialist trusts must probably be decided by experience; but here we at least have a rational principle on which to work.

6. *Safeguards against Monopoly*

In so far, however, as such a policy proves impracticable there will remain a number of empirical restraints on the impulse of the monopolies to restrict production and raise prices. In the first place public opinion and the State's attitude to the monopoly would be such that any actual *reduction* of output or rise in prices would be considered unjustifiable, unless plain evidence of changes in demand were available; and the board in question would be regarded as having shown itself incompetent. It is plain, for instance, that if the London Passenger Transport Board raised fares substantially, or withdrew recognized services, public opinion would compel it to reverse its policy. This is at least some safeguard against actual increases in prices. But it does not help much in the long run; for in the long run costs and prices ought to fall with technical progress.[1] In the case of the British railways, for instance, a mere maintenance of existing fares after 1929 would have been a sign of substantial inefficiency. And in any case an economy which relied on the stabilization of the prices of particular commodities and services would be extremely clumsy and insensitive in adjusting itself to change; for it is implicit in the working of the price system that particular prices should be allowed to move up and down with shifts in demand and all sorts of other changes. A mere public disapproval of increases in prices, therefore, though it would set some limit to monopolistic exploitation, would be a very rudimentary safeguard.[2]

[1] This of course depends on the monetary policy followed; but the policy contemplated in ch. xix of this book implies a fall in the general price-level proportionate to the fall in costs per unit of output.

[2] An interesting example of public opinion actually inducing a public monopoly to put its prices too low was the recent introduction of the shilling trunk calls during night hours by the British Post Office. The reduction in

A second and much more powerful empirical safeguard would be the existence of competition between industries. For it must be remembered that even where an industry has an absolutely water-tight monopoly of a certain commodity, that commodity is almost always in more or less direct competition with other commodities. Indeed, it is practically impossible in this sense to distinguish between one commodity and another. A railway, for instance, usually has a monopoly of transport in its own area; but it is nowadays in direct competition with the roads to provide what may be the virtually identical commodity of transport from one place to another. For instance, if the British railways had been amalgamated into a public corporation after the war, but the roads had been allowed to compete freely with them, the public corporation would probably have made quite as great reductions as those actually made by the private companies. If the railways were to be nationalized, therefore, and if road transport were entrusted to a second corporation, and a measure of competition permitted between the two, there would be very little danger of inefficiency and high prices. Similarly a public coal corporation would have to compete with gas and electricity, and a cotton corporation with rayon and wool, and a gas corporation with electricity and coal; and even a broadcasting monopoly has to compete with cinemas and theatres. Perhaps the supply of electricity for lighting in a given area is one of the few examples of a practically cast-iron monopoly.

A third and equally important safeguard is foreign competition. In general the subject of foreign trade is ignored in this book. But it must be noticed here, since it is a crucial fact in the situation. In the first place a monopolized industry that has to compete directly with imports will in effect be in the position of an ordinary competitive firm. It will not be able to restrict total supply or raise prices; it will be impelled to reduce costs by the ordinary desire to undersell its foreign competitors. Here everything will depend on the tariff policy pursued by the Government. It must not allow itself to be persuaded by the unscrupulous

---

some instances led to so great a demand that the lines were inadequate, subscribers had to wait 'in a queue' for their calls: and those who would have liked to pay more for a quick call were unable to do so. The monopoly had put the price below the minimum point at which the supply and demand would balance. Such can be the influence of public opinion on a public monopoly.

exploitation, on the part of vested interests, of the cry that cheap foreign labour is undermining the domestic workers' standard of living. In some cases some measure of protection may perhaps be justifiable on these grounds; but the power to lower tariffs and reduce quotas will always be the most powerful weapon in the Government's hand in compelling public corporations which compete with imports to aim at efficiency rather than restriction of output. In Great Britain, where foreign trade is so large a proportion of total trade, this weapon will be particularly potent. If the iron and steel trades were converted into a public corporation, for instance, the power to reduce the tariff and cancel the import quota would be more than sufficient to cure the corporation of any tendency towards inefficiency or a holding up of prices.[1] To a great extent, in fact, the success, and the justification, of the policy of nationalization will depend on the pursuit of a liberal tariff policy.[2]

In the second place all those industries which export a substantial percentage of their output will be compelled to seek profits through greater efficiency rather than restriction. In export markets they will be unable to control the total supply or to raise prices. Here, then, all will depend on the Government's refusal to adopt any proposal from an exporting public corporation to raise a levy by charging a higher price for home production in order to subsidize the selling of exports at a lower price.[3] This the corporation will almost certainly want to do; and it will represent the proposal as a most beneficial and ingenious form of 'planning'. If this device were permitted in any form, however, the whole influence of the export market in stimulating the public corporations would be lost. For they would be able to restrict output, raise prices, and earn a monopoly revenue at home, and subsidize cheap sales abroad out of a part of their monopoly profits. Such price discrimination against the home consumer would of course be impossible if foreign pro-

[1] The National Government's policy, it may be observed, in the case of iron and steel, has been the exact opposite: to grant high protection and monopolistic privileges without securing any of the benefits of public control in return.
[2] Though in times of threatened depression tariffs might have to be temporarily raised as part of monetary policy.
[3] Again such powers might be granted in emergency periods as part of a monetary policy designed to stop a depression; but in general they should be refused. The power to grant them at appropriate times would be one of the advantages of nationalization.

ducers were able to compete in the monopolist's home market as well as abroad, and if protectionist devices were not adopted to prevent them. But if they were not able, nothing but a direct prohibition of the public monopoly from discriminating against the home consumer would be effective. If such a prohibition were enforced, however, a further limitation would be placed on the monopolists' powers to defeat the public interest, and the limitation would be the more powerful the more important was the monopoly's export trade. It is plain, for instance, that a British coal or cotton corporation could be forced to make the greatest possible reduction in costs and prices at home by a refusal, or drastic limitation, of the right to discriminate against the home consumer. The economies of a central (i.e. monopolistic) selling organization covering home and foreign sales could then be conceded to a coal or cotton board without any fear of unjustifiable price-raising; so keen would competition always remain in foreign coal and cotton markets.

There is one other class of public monopoly which is bound to be important in Great Britain in the future, and probably in many other countries as well: the agricultural marketing board. There are two good reasons for the existence of properly conducted agricultural marketing boards: in the first place, security of employment and the substantial volume of 'social' capital invested in rural communities are strong grounds for preserving agriculture or at least letting it contract slowly; and in the second place the products of agriculture are in most cases prime necessities. Wheat, milk, meat, butter, and vegetables are obvious cases for the grant of a subsidy financed out of luxury taxation. Such a subsidy would have the double effect of lowering food prices, rescuing the farmer and the agricultural community dependent upon him for existence, and ensuring fair labour conditions and efficiency in return, without any necessity for drastic restriction of imports. The aim of a public meat and milk board, in fact, ought to be to use its power of granting a subsidy or limiting imports as to force the farmer gradually to increase efficiency and lower prices. The board would keep as close to a policy of free imports as was possible without producing a sudden and far-reaching collapse in home agriculture; and its aim would be so to increase efficiency of home production as to allow absolutely free imports and a consequently more abundant and cheaper supply of food. If an agricultural marketing monopoly were conducted on these lines, it would almost certainly be as effective as free competition in ensuring efficiency and low prices, and it would in addition avoid the sudden and violent dislocations inherent in the maintenance of free prices for world agricultural products.

It thus appears that in Great Britain at any rate there would be very powerful sanctions, over and above the not negligible ones of public opinion, operating to restrain monopolistic exploitation in the case of almost all industries which it is normally proposed to nationalize here. Transport, coal, gas, electricity, iron and steel, cotton, and agriculture could all be exposed to a bracing competitive stimulus, if the Government's powers of control over foreign trade were intelligently and disinterestedly used as a supplement to existing domestic competition. The danger of monopolistic exploitation and inefficiency does not therefore seem to be quite so formidable, even if the theoretically perfect method of controlling monopolies suggested by Mr. Durbin proves difficult in practice.

Many of the empirical safeguards against monopoly enumerated above would not be available if we assumed a closed economic system, entirely organized in monopolies. And it is probable that the virtually universal adoption of monopolies in a closed system would tend to produce inefficiency and restriction. It is difficult to believe that these dangers are not in fact inherent in a practically water-tight system of monopoly like that of Soviet Russia. But if used against the proposal to introduce measures of nationalization gradually into an already highly developed capitalist economy, the argument loses most of its force. In the first place, as has been shown, the potential safeguards are in the relevant instances numerous and powerful. More important still, however, if it is proposed, as in the foregoing argument, only to monopolize those industries which already under capitalism are, or ought to be, monopolies for fundamental economic reasons, the argument falls entirely to the ground. It is not an argument against socialism at all, but against monopoly. And as soon as it is conceded that under capitalism monopolies do, and must, exist, it becomes irrelevant to the issue. It must also be remembered that in so far as the socialized industries are those where the economies of large-scale production are considerable, it is possible that even if the full monopoly revenue were charged, output might be still as high, or higher, and prices low or lower, than they would have been under imperfect competition. The actual question, in fact, is whether we prefer private monopolies or public ones. And the conclusive case for preferring public ones rests not merely on the fact that monopoly revenues will then accrue to the State, and that proper labour conditions can be assured, but also on the fact that the stimulus of competition between industries and competition with foreign products can be just as easily applied to public monopolies.

There is one further difficulty which, it is sometimes alleged, will prevent the directors of public monopolies from reaching rational decisions about prices and output. It was argued in the preceding chapter that the interest and rent costs, and the value of capital goods, affecting the producer in the socialist community will be precisely determined according to certain principles and that these will consequently enter into his reckoning of costs in the usual way. But how, it may be asked, will the public corporations be able to compute the costs of producing one particular commodity among the many produced by their all-embracing monopoly? Suppose a large number of chemical firms were amalgamated into a single trust, all raw materials were bought *en bloc*, and all products sold by a single selling organization. A firm previously producing one of the chemicals in question would necessarily know the exact cost of producing that chemical, and it could consequently regulate output so that the proceeds of selling it just covered the cost. But if the small firms were merged into a large one, how could it be calculated what proportion of, say, the expenses of management of the whole concern, or of the cost of the sales organization, or of advertisement, should be imputed to the cost of producing this particular commodity? And if it were not known, how could the management know if it were producing that commodity at a loss or a profit? And if it did not know, on what principle could it decide the relative amounts to be produced of the various commodities?

This is certainly one of the more serious problems facing any very large productive unit. But again it is a difficulty inherent not in socialism but in the existence of large-scale firms controlling different productive processes. Wherever capitalism develops into monopoly, a certain indeterminacy of this kind will appear. It is said that in the example just mentioned, the chemical industry, large combines have often been totally ignorant for years of the cost of producing particular commodities, and have been glad to discover the true figure from smaller firms. It is also said that the great British railway companies in the past have been ignorant of the cost of running particular branch lines, and consequently have not known whether these lines paid or not. One may also perhaps doubt whether the average small farmer has any but the haziest idea what is the cost per unit of producing each separate commodity.

Now it is clear that part of this uncertainty must be due to inefficient management. Rigorous costing methods could discover the cost of labour on the branch line, of permanent way, of rent and rates, of the maintenance of the stations, of engine mileage, and so forth: and it is understood that British railways to-day, partly under the stimulus of road competition, are making great advances in the purely technical side of the problem. Here a public corporation would probably be at its best. It would have every opportunity, by virtue of its ambitious organization, of carrying out elaborate investigations into costs; just as it would have every opportunity of conducting technical research. The undertaking of such investigations should be made one of the conditions of the grant of monopoly powers. The other part of the uncertainty about costs relates to the proportion of general expenses such as obsolescence, depreciation, directors' fees, advertisement, selling, etc., that is to be imputed to the production of separate commodities. Here there is no technically correct solution to be discovered by more accurate methods; and an empirical solution would have to be found by the fixing of arbitrary percentages. Such costs, however, would not normally be a large proportion of total costs; and though the theoretical problems involved are difficult, it is unlikely that any serious distortion of output or prices would accrue in this way. The problem is one which has to be decided by monopolies or large-scale units, whether they remain in public or private hands. And on the whole it seems likely that it will be more scientifically tackled by a public monopoly, if it is specifically required to do so.

In general, then, it does not seem that the rational management of a public board or socialist trust will be fundamentally an insoluble problem. If the theoretically best solution proves difficult, all those socialized industries which compete either with foreign goods, or more or less directly with rival commodities, can be safely instructed to maximize their profits within the framework of the conditions imposed on them. In this way efficiency and a lowering of costs will be ensured by competition; the benefits of large-scale production and organization will be attained; the greatest possible security of labour consistent with the preservation of free consumers' choice will be guaranteed; and the actual business managers can be encouraged by some small share in the 'profits'. But the bulk of those profits will nevertheless flow into the Exchequer through the fiscal channels already described.

CHAPTER XXXII

THE LIMITS OF PLANNING

The various kinds of planning, or interference with the price system, described in the last chapter are possible rather than necessary elements of socialism. Inherited incomes could be abolished, and inequality enormously diminished, without the adoption of any of these measures at all. But if it is desired to attack insecurity as well, and to diminish inequality still further, we can select such measures of planning as seem to be justifiable. It is a mistake to suppose that any interference with the price system as such is good or bad. Such interferences may be either progressive or regressive or neutral, i.e. they may either decrease inequality, or increase it, or leave it unaffected. It is even a mistake to suppose that all interferences with the price system that increase security are justifiable. For those interferences which involve control in most cases increase producers' security at the expense of consumers' freedom. And it may be in any given case that the cost is too great. Again, it is a mistake, though a plausible one, to suppose that we must either plan wholly or not at all. Planning has to be intelligent, not comprehensive. A single tax on the producers of a luxury, for instance, to finance a subsidy to the producers of a necessity, would be wholly beneficial in its effects on a given community; and it could be justified, or executed, without reference to other planning measures, as long as its own special effects were properly understood. Professor Hayek[1] and Professor Brutzkus[2] have attempted to infer from Russian experience that partial planning cannot work. In particular they point out that the Soviet Government could not induce the peasants to produce wheat unless they were forcibly collectivized or else paid what they considered a fair price for it.

[1] *Collectivist Economic Planning.*
[2] *Economic Planning in Soviet Russia.*

349

Now, it is of course true that if the Soviet Government would not pay the independent peasants what they considered a fair price, they would not produce wheat. But it was perfectly open to a planning government to pay them such a price; and if the Government wished to sell to the consumer at a lower price, the difference could have been made up by a subsidy. If it had been desired to leave the peasant outside the planning system, it would have been just as possible for the Soviet to buy wheat from them at the price demanded as to buy it from Australia or Canada. The experience of the Soviet Government with the peasants does not prove that you cannot leave a section of the national economy outside the planning system; it proves that you cannot leave it outside and treat it as if it were inside at the same time.

Since, then, partial interference with the price system is possible but wholesale destruction of it is not desirable,[1] the limits of interference have to be recognized. In general it has been argued in this book that, where inequality or insecurity can be diminished without too great a loss of consumers' freedom, and without the creation of uneconomic monopolies, there is a strong presumption that it is desirable. On these grounds a case has been made for discriminating rents and interest charges, for 'progressive' taxes and subsidies, and for the socialization of monopolies. It must not be thought that this is an exhaustive list, or that all the items in it would necessarily be practicable in any modern industrial State. In few countries, for instance, in existing social, political, and administrative conditions, would a really thorough system of taxes and subsidies for producers be practicable politics. Indeed, to some this proposal may seem impracticable and superficial; though for the reasons stated in chapter xxxi it would in the long run prove fundamental. The development of inheritance-taxation and social services, and the socialization of monopolies, would be a much more immediately realizable objective in most parts of the world. All the above measures of planning, in fact, are simply examples of the principal kinds of interference with the price system which would be desirable in those cases where circumstances favoured them.

This, it may be said, is a lame and impotent conclusion, which offers us nothing but a vague empirical criterion. How

[1] As was argued in ch. xxx.

arbitrary and confused, the advocates of universal competition will say, compared with the simple theorem that competition is always best! And there is a good deal of substance in the protest. For the appeal to an empirical criterion, the weighing of good against bad in each particular case, opens the way in practice for every sort of corruption, special pleading, and political pressure. 'We must have a larger and larger subsidy,' the wheat producers will say; 'for we alone produce the staff of life.' Since, however, competition does not produce a perfect distribution of resources, and since intelligent departure from it may in certain cases diminish inequality and insecurity without too great a loss of freedom, the criterion inevitably and logically must be empirical, or rather specific; and we must work by an intelligent judgement in each case. We should make that judgement, however, with the clearest perception that planning has its limits and its dangers. If carried too far, it may injure the community as consumer; and if inadequately controlled it may open the door to corruption. Planning, in fact, requires a measure of both integrity and intelligence. So, however, do the ordinary functions of democratic governments; for such governments find themselves already on innumerable occasions in conflict with the vested interests of monopolistic capitalism. The transformation of this conflict into a real régime of socialist planning will be justifiable exactly in so far as greater security and equality are purchased at the expense of existing monopoly interests and not at the expense of the freedom of the consuming masses.

CHAPTER XXXIII

THE CASE FOR SOCIALISM

The case for socialism is mainly economic, and it rests on fact. One need not be surprised, therefore, that those who have penetrated most deeply into economic realities should have expounded the truths that represent the genuine basis of socialism. Nothing could be more false than to suppose, as some socialists appear to do, that all non-Marxist economists have been wholly wrong and all Marxist economists wholly right. Such monopolies of truth and falsehood in any case seldom arise in the history of human thought. And in fact the greatest economists have always recognized the three fundamentals of the socialist case: the arbitrary effects of free exchange, the peculiar character of unearned incomes, and the profoundly anti-social consequences of the institution of inheritance.

The quotations already made in this book from economists in the English tradition are sufficient to illustrate this. Mill wrote as follows in his *Principles of Political Economy* more than seventy five years ago:[1]

'The laws of property have never yet conformed to the principles on which the justification of private property rests. They have made property of things which never ought to be property, and absolute property where only a qualified property should exist. They have not held the balance fairly between human beings, but have heaped impediments upon some, to give advantage to others; they have purposely fostered inequalities, and prevented all from starting fair in the race.'

Mill accordingly made the proposal that an absolute limit should be set to the amount that any private individual could inherit.

Marshall explicitly recognized the fact that free exchange

[1] Ashley's edition, pp. 208–9.

352

only promoted a 'maximum of satisfaction' in the sense that each individual obtained under it the greatest satisfaction that he could obtain in the circumstances, and not in the sense that the community as a whole must be better off than it could be under any system. And he explicitly inferred from this fact that it was desirable to modify property rights. Speaking of the doctrine that free exchange must produce a 'maximum satisfaction' Marshall wrote as follows:[1]

'There is indeed one interpretation of the doctrine according to which every position of equilibrium of demand and supply may fairly be regarded as a position of maximum satisfaction. . . . It is true that a position of equilibrium of demand and supply is a position of maximum satisfaction in this limited sense, that the aggregate satisfaction of the two parties concerned increases until that position is reached; and that any production beyond the equilibrium amount could not be permanently maintained so long as buyers and sellers acted freely as individuals, each in his own interest.

'But occasionally it is stated, and very often it is implied, that a position of equilibrium of demand and supply is one of maximum aggregate satisfaction in the full sense of the term: that is, that an increase of production beyond the equilibrium level would directly (i.e. independently of the difficulties of arranging for it, and of any indirect evils it might cause) diminish the aggregate satisfaction of both parties. The doctrine so interpreted is not universally true.

'In the first place it assumes that all differences in wealth between the different parties concerned may be neglected, and that the satisfaction which is rated at a shilling by any one of them, may be taken as equal to one that is rated at a shilling by any other. Now it is obvious that, if the producers were as a class very much poorer than the consumers, the aggregate satisfaction might be increased by a stinting of supply when it would cause a great rise in the demand price (i.e. when the demand is inelastic); and that if the consumers were as a class much poorer than the producers the aggregate satisfaction might be increased by extending the production beyond the equilibrium amount and selling the commodity at a loss. This point, however, may well be left for future consideration. It is in fact only a special

[1] *Principles of Economics*, seventh edition, pp. 470–2.

case of the broad proposition that the aggregate satisfaction can *prima facie* be increased by the distribution, whether voluntarily or compulsorily, of some of the property of the rich among the poor.'

Here in the form of Marshall's 'broad proposition' is the main essential of the socialist case plainly stated.

Wicksell—to quote a great Scandinavian economist—stated the same fundamental truth with equal plainness:[1]

'It is not difficult to imagine that an exchange between a rich man and a poor man may lead to a much greater total utility for both together—and therefore for society as a whole—if it is effected at a suitable price fixed by society than if everything is eft to the haphazard working of free competition.'

Professor Pigou has similarly written that 'in making distribution more even there is a wide field for State planning.'[2] Professor F. H. Knight, perhaps the greatest living American economist, declares that 'where the family is the social unit the inheritance of wealth, culture, educational advantage, and economic opportunity tends towards the progressive increase of inequality, with bad results for personality at both ends of the scale'.[3] And finally Mr. Keynes, in the passage already quoted,[4] reaches the conclusion that drastic redistribution among the poor of the incomes of the rich is economically as well as socially necessary. 'In contemporary conditions', he writes, 'the growth of wealth, so far from being dependent on the abstinence of the rich, as is commonly supposed, is more likely to be impeded by it. One of the chief justifications of great inequality of wealth is, therefore removed. . . . This particularly affects our attitude towards the death duties.'[5]

There were once, of course, a few economists, such as Bastiat, who attempted to prove that unrestricted competition must produce some mystical harmony of interests. But the great English economists, at any rate, have harboured no such illusions. The case against them, if any, is not that they shut their eyes to the truth, but that they left it to others to advocate those socialist policies which the truth plainly demands. Those, therefore, who

[1] *Lectures on Political Economy*, p. 77.
[2] *Economics in Practice*, p. 121.
[3] *The Ethics of Competition*, p. 50.
[4] Cf. pp. 248–9.
[5] *The General Theory of Employment, Interest, and Money*, p. 373.

profess socialist convictions need not feel under any obligation to depreciate the economists' intellectual achievement; nor need those who respect that achievement feel ashamed of their socialist convictions.

For the drastic application of a socialist policy does not necessarily involve, for economic reasons, a revolutionary break with the methods of social reform that have been followed in the last century in democratic countries. The progressive expansion of the social services, the steady extension of social ownership and control, and the even more drastic modification of property and inheritance rights—all these are policies which need not cause any violent upheaval in the machinery of the economic system. It may be that efforts to control the trade cycle will fail, and that the rocking of the system will be so violent as to provoke political catastrophe. In that case the hope of peaceful reform may well vanish in the general chaos. But only experience can show whether the control of the trade cycle is beyond the wit of man or not. And it would be inhumanly foolish to assume that it is before the attempt had ever been made.

It may be, again, that peaceful reform is impossible, not for economic, but for political reasons. It may be that the propertied classes will defend their unjust privileges not merely by force (which would not matter; since force is met by force whenever a man is threatened with imprisonment for not paying his income-tax), but by political force. And it may be that the appeal to revolution will in the end provoke international war. It is not the purpose of this book to discuss these political arguments; and only two things need consequently be said about them here. First there is no economic reason why a clash of this kind must be inevitable. There is no economic reason why a modern industrial State, under the kind of leadership which the Social-Democrats have given Sweden, M. Blum has given France, and Mr. Roosevelt has given the United States in the last five years, should not simultaneously overcome the forces of the trade cycle and redistribute the incomes of the rich. Those who proclaim the inevitability of violent revolution are always anxious to base their argument on economic grounds. But a disinterested examination of the economic facts reveals no such inevitability; and those who proclaim it often seem really to be inspired, not by any economic analysis at all, but by an irrational eagerness to believe in the imminence of calamity. It may be, or it may not be, that a failure to control the trade cycle will provoke general political violence. But apart from this unresolved question there are no demonstrable economic grounds for thus resigning ourselves to the worst.

Secondly, in so far as the argument rests on political foundations, it must again be proved right or wrong by experience and not by the writing of books and by *a priori* analysis. Will the propertied class defend its privileges by violence in every country? Nobody can say. In some countries it has; in others it almost certainly will. But in others again, where the political tradition, the political temper, the standard of living, and the general level of human sanity, are different, it very well may not. Experience may show that even in the democratically inclined countries the attempt to introduce socialism peacefully will meet with forcible resistance. In that case violence would become a necessity, and therefore an obligation. But those who recognize that the realities of personal and intellectual freedom are as precious as those of economic justice will probably be of the opinion that the attempt is at least worth making.

INDEX

INDEX

INDEX

Jarrow steel-works scheme, 326
Jones, E. M. Hugh, 323
Jones, J. H., 270
Joseph, H. W. B., 29
Journal of Royal Statistical Society, 280, 284
Joynson-Hicks, Mr. William (Lord Brentford), 247

Keynes, J. M., 71, 147, 150, 164, 168, 172, 180, 183, 185–93, 195, 199, 200, 202, 208, 220, 248–9, 270, 293, 354
Knight, F. H., 9, 15–17, 29, 31, 33, 36, 95, 109, 118, 126, 142, 302, 354
Kuznets, Mr., 200

Labour Government (1929–31), 225
Labour Party, 218, 244, 332
Land tax, 46
Lansbury, Mr., 41
Laval Government (France), 260
Layton, Sir Walter, 41–2, 151
Lectures on Political Economy, 15, 102, 354
Lees-Smith, H. B., 247
Legacy and Succession Duties, 280
Leven, Mr. Maurice, 52–3
'Liquidity preference' (Keynes), 220
London Transport, 330–1, 336, 338, 341

MacGregor, Professor D. H., 82, 152
McKenna, Mr. R., 164
Macmillan Committee (and Report), 162–5, 172
Macmillan, Mr. Harold, 176, 197, 328
Managers (business), 43, (salaried company), 265
'Marginal' (the principle), 11–13, (analysis), 14, 29, (net products), 22
Marshall, A., 2, 11, 14, 37, 110, 116, 168, 327, 336, 352-4
Martin, Mr. P. W., 168

Marx and Marxism, 36, 66, 109, 126, 130–1, 133, 145, 153, 178–80, 239, 257, 275, 352
Mason, Mr. J. F., 247
Meade, J. E., 103–4, 123, 275, 339–40
Mill, 116, 280, 352
Minimum wages, 279
Mises, Professor, 14–15, 108, 117, 299, 300, 302, 304, 307, 309
Monetary (failures in economic system), 60, (policy), 209–22, 260, (and redistribution) 292–4, (problem), 149
Monetary Policy and Crises, 211, 219, 250
Monetary Theory and the Trade Cycle, 149, 164, 168, 194
Money (in the economic system), 61, (and the trade cycle), 145–222, (and credit), 154–67
Monopoly (profits), 78, (and competition), 117–24, 137–9, (in socialism), 320–48, (dangers of), 324–8
Morrison, Mr. Herbert, 242, 245, 275, 325, 330, 337
Moulton, Mr. Harold G., 52–3, 177, 183, 202–4
Municipal finance, 47–8
Murry, John Middleton, 88

Nash, Mr. Walter, 245, 250
National capital, 44
National debt, 46–7
National expenditure, 46
National Government, the (and taxation), 49, 51, 218, 343
National income, 38–9, 200
National Income and Outlay, 39–41, 43, 48, 50, 52, 200, 227, 231, 233, 268
'National Investment Board', 306, 308
Nationalization (i.e. socialization), 242, 331–7
Nature and Significance of Economic Science, The, 15–16, 19, 21, 23

360

INDEX